PRAISE FOR *MANAGEMENT AND THE GOSPEL*

This book brings together the study of management, business ethics, and theology in a scholarly yet accessible way. It is an outstanding achievement that all of us involved in those fields need to take account of.

C.R. (Bob) Hinings
Professor Emeritus, University of Alberta

This well-documented work is a worthy addition to Lukan studies, and not least to management alternatives in the twenty-first century. Every member of an organization (*oikos*), from a small family unit to a large corporation, should read this book.

Dr. V. George Shillington
author "An Introduction to the Study of Luke-Acts"
Professor Emeritus, Canadian Mennonite University, Canada

Dr. Bruno Dyck has delivered a provocative and compelling alternative to traditional interpretations of Luke's relevance to work and business. Whether readers end up agreeing with Bruno's perspective or not, they will surely have benefitted from reading an engaging and well-supported critical evaluation of dominant perspectives that just might change their way of thinking and acting.

Dr. Mitchell Neubert
Chavanne Chair of Christian Ethics in Business
Baylor University, USA

In an increasingly technological and secular world, we may be tempted to think that sacred texts such as the Gospels are irrelevant to the complex world of managing organizations. Bruno Dyck's *Management and the Gospel* says otherwise. The book provides a compelling and convincing argument that the Gospels are central to an understanding of management that has at its core the growth and development of people. While modern management has become technically sophisticated, it has also become morally primitive. As JRR Tolkien put it "Ours is an age of improved means to deteriorated ends." *Management and the Gospel* marries spiritual and moral ends to sophisticated and technical organizational insights to give a vision of management that is desperately needed for today's organizations.

Dr. Michael J. Naughton
coauthor "Managing as if Faith Mattered"
Moss Chair in Catholic Social Thought, University of St. Thomas, USA

This book challenges us to reconsider the gospel with a view toward transforming relationships within and between organizations. Bruno Dyck applies careful attention to the biblical text and appreciation for historical context to interpret Jesus' teachings and apply them to contemporary management practice. His study signals the kingdom of God, salvation, and the Holy Spirit as central for a practical Christian theology of management.

Dr. Kent Miller
Professor of Management, Eli Broad Graduate School of Management
Michigan State University, USA

This book is a most welcome addition to growing scholarship on the theology and spirituality of management. Its ability to take account of both the first and the twenty-first centuries on their own terms makes it an especially valuable contribution. In spite of the rigour and depth with which Dyck covers such a diverse range of scholarly material—from New Testament theology, to leadership theories, to the philosophy of management—the writing throughout is accessible, clearly argued and highly engaging.

Dr. Sarah Drakopoulou-Dodd
Academic Director, AHEAD-ALBA Hub for Enterprise and Development, Greece

This fascinating interdisciplinary work contemplates and re-frames central themes of modern management theory through the wisdom and values of the ancient world, particularly through a critical inquiry into "management" in the New Testament Gospel of Luke. Here emerges a persuasive argument that Max Weber's "iron cage" view of modern rationalized society need not be so iron-clad as commonly assumed. Moreover, the book urges that a broader hermeneutic and dialog with important religious traditions can provide modern productive organizations with a reservoir of alternate values and institutional understandings.

Dr. Douglas E. Oakman
coauthor "Palestine in the Time of Jesus: Social Structures and Social Conflicts"
Pacific Lutheran University, USA

Anybody with a desire to live out God's call to them should read *Management and the Gospel: Luke's Radical Message for the First and Twenty-First Centuries*. Dr. Dyck takes an insightful and fresh look at Jesus' life and words. It engaged my head and challenged my heart.

Galen Lehman
President, Lehman's Old Time General Store, Kidron, Ohio, USA

I thank Bruno Dyck for this remarkable book. Just as theologian John H. Yoder proposed the Practices of the Christian community as paradigms for Christians in business and all other human organizations, so Bruno Dyck shows in a refreshing and challenging way how Jesus as presented in the Gospel of Luke offers God-given ways to incarnate God's character in business management. With this book, Dyck may well become known as one of those "new prophets" contributing to "the rebirth of old ideas and ideals" which Max Weber was talking about a century ago.

Dr. Werner Franz
Professor of Ethics and Bible, Dean of the Department of Theology
Universidad Evangélica del Paraguay, Paraguay

Previous Publications

Management: Current Practices and New Directions
Bruno Dyck and Mitchell J. Neubert

MANAGEMENT AND THE GOSPEL

LUKE'S RADICAL MESSAGE FOR THE FIRST AND TWENTY-FIRST CENTURIES

Bruno Dyck

MANAGEMENT AND THE GOSPEL
Copyright © Bruno Dyck, 2013.

All rights reserved.

First published in hardcover in 2013 by PALGRAVE MACMILLAN® in the
United States—a division of St. Martin's Press LLC, 175 Fifth Avenue,
New York, NY 10010.

Where this book is distributed in the UK, Europe and the rest of the world,
this is by Palgrave Macmillan, a division of Macmillan Publishers Limited,
registered in England, company number 785998, of Houndmills,
Basingstoke, Hampshire RG21 6XS.

Palgrave Macmillan is the global academic imprint of the above companies
and has companies and representatives throughout the world.

Palgrave® and Macmillan® are registered trademarks in the United States,
the United Kingdom, Europe and other countries.

ISBN: 978–1–137–37733–3

The Library of Congress has cataloged the hardcover edition as follows:

Dyck, Bruno, 1961–
    Management and the Gospel : Luke's radical message for the first and
twenty-first centuries / Bruno Dyck.
      p. cm.
    Includes bibliographical references.
    ISBN 978–1–137–28088–6 (alk. paper)
    1. Management--Religious aspects—Christianity.
    2. Organizational behavior—Religious aspects—Christianity.
    [1. Bible. N.T. Luke.] I. Title.

HD31.D924 2013
261.8′5—dc23   2012028680

A catalogue record of the book is available from the British Library.

Design by Newgen Knowledge Works (P) Ltd., Chennai, India.

First PALGRAVE MACMILLAN paperback edition: November 2013

10 9 8 7 6 5 4 3 2 1

To my family.

Contents

TABLES

Figures

PREFACE AND ACKNOWLEDGMENTS

The goal of this book seems simple: to examine what the Gospel of Luke says about management theory and practice. But, as will become apparent, to do this with scholarly rigor requires a great deal of interdisciplinary breadth. Thus I am very thankful to the Social Sciences and Humanities Research Council of Canada for providing the funding to enable me to complete this project at its current level, and to the team of scholars who have guided me along the way since my first formal proposal. John Kloppenborg early on advised me to focus my study on the Gospel of Luke, and has provided important counsel along the way. David Schroeder has been helping me to study and think about how biblical writings connect with management thinking and practice for well over a decade, and has always been gracious, patient, and supportive. Laurence Broadhurst, Dan Epp-Tiessen, and Gordon Zerbe are other biblical scholars who have always taken time to read different drafts and have provided superb feedback. In particular, Laurence was deeply involved in the analysis underpinning part five of the book, and he worked very closely with the students we had hired to look at the Journey Narrative literature and chiasms—thank you to Ian Brown, Katelyn Cove, and Buffy Cowtan for your diligent work. I also thank Matthew Penner for his comprehensive review of the organization and management theory literature on this topic, to Glenn Sawatzky for his research help on the topic of the kingdom of God, to Jade Weimer for her research help in understanding management in first-century Palestine, and to Cal Dueck for his contributions during the formative period of this project.

Of course, I am also thankful for the feedback and support of colleagues at my home institution, the University of Manitoba. In particular, Fred Starke has always provided a listening ear and excellent advice in many years of walks around our neighborhood talking about this project, and everything else under the sun. Other colleagues have also played important roles in various steps of the project with their support and counsel: thank you to Reg Litz, Nathan Greidanus, Norm Frohlich, Sue and Ed Bruning, and others.

I have especially appreciated the support and feedback from my colleagues at other institutions and conferences. I discussed a first draft of this book over the course of several presentations at Seattle Pacific University, and the pointed feedback was appreciated and I hope helped to make a strong book. Thanks especially to Randy Franz, Ross Stewart, Denise Daniels, Jeff van Duzer, and Kenman Wong (who first introduced me to my "second family" at SPU). Thanks as well to Geoff Bell and his colleagues and all the students at University of Minnesota-Duluth who hosted me as a "Distinguished Scholar" and provided helpful feedback on an earlier draft of the book. Also thanks for the feedback from Jim Lehman and his colleagues and students at Eastern Mennonite University, where I also made presentations based on this project. In addition I'm appreciative of feedback from Ben Teehankee and his colleagues at De La Salle University in Manila, where I presented material from this book at the inaugural Bro. Rafael Donato Professorial Lecture. Similarly I'm thankful for the feedback from other colleagues at different conferences where I've presented parts of this research, including the Academy of Management, the Christian Business Faculty Association, and a conference at Trinity Western University where I gave two keynote addresses on this topic. I'm thankful as well for the ongoing interest and encouragement from colleagues and others associated with my alma mater, University of Alberta, including my mentor Bob Hinings, Tom Lawrence, Elden Wiebe, Royston Greenwood, Michael Mauws, and many others. Finally, a special thanks to Sarah Drakopoulou-Dodd for her enthusiastic support and extensive feedback on an earlier draft of this manuscript.

Others whose interest and support I am thankful for include Rick Beaton, Cara Beed, Spencer Cowles, Aiden Enns, Dennis Felbel, John H. Elliott, Len Friesen, Sheila Klassen-Wiebe, Phil Kniss, Wally Kroeker, Monty Lynn, Will Messenger, Kent Miller, Janet Morrill, Mike Naughton, Doug Oakman, Bro. Bernie Oca, FSC, Elsa Peterson, George Shillington, Yvonne Smith, Andrea Soberg, Paul Stevens, Bro. Mike Valenzuela, FSC, Dorothy Jean Weaver, Lachlan Whatley, Walter Wright, Wayne Yerxa, and the staff and librarians at the University of Manitoba for the support in getting books from all over campus and around the world. I'm sure there are others I should have added to this list—thank you all!

Thanks also to practitioners and lay readers who read earlier drafts of the book, including Galen Lehman, Matt Penner, Dan Wiens, interested family members, and members of Charleswood Mennonite Church where I presented material related to this book. Your feedback helps me to be confident that the book is accessible and will appeal to a wide range of readers. I am especially thankful for the support of my family, particularly my wife Heather.

Finally, thanks also to Paul Loewen for his help with the artwork in the book and to all the people working with Palgrave Macmillan for their support in helping to bring this book into print, including Joel Breuklander, Leila Campoli, Samantha Hasey, Deepa John, and Charlotte Maiorana.

I

INTRODUCTION

This book lies at the intersection of two highly influential social institutions. The first is the institution of human organizations, and more specifically of organizations producing goods and services. In modern times this includes businesses, but it also includes nonprofit, governmental, and other organizations. Such organizations provide jobs and goods and services required for the overall economy. For most of the history of humankind, such organizations fell under the overarching umbrella of *oikos*, the Greek word referring to organizations producing goods and services from which we get the modern English word "economics" (literally, *oikonomia* means the management of *oikos*).

The second influential institution is religion, and this study will focus on sacred scriptures associated with Christianity, the largest religion in the world today. In particular, this book will examine what the life and teachings associated with the nominal founder of Christianity, Jesus of Nazareth,[1] say about organizations producing goods and services (*oikoi*) as interpreted in their original socioeconomic context, namely, first-century Palestine.

In some ways this book starts where Max Weber's most famous book, *The Protestant Ethic and the Spirit of Capitalism*, finishes. Max Weber is widely considered to be the father of organization theory and a leading moral philosopher of management. Even though his writings are a century old, he remains one of the most-frequently cited authors in organization and management theory. His analysis in *The Protestant Ethic and the Spirit of Capitalism* is so compelling that there continues to be widespread agreement that modern organization and management theory are based upon a Judeo-Christian ethic associated with the Reformation.[2]

Weber recognized that this Protestant ethic had already long been secularized even when he was writing. He also recognized the two key pillars of this secularized Protestant ethic were its emphasis on (1) individualism (e.g., consistent with an emphasis on personal salvation, versus salvation via the church community), and (2) materialism (consistent with seeing financial wealth as a sign of God's blessing, rather than as a sign of greed). With remarkable foresight Weber recognized that, although this materialistic-individualistic ethic would lead to unprecedented financial prosperity, it would inevitably fail. In what has become perhaps the most famous metaphor in the social sciences, he argued that this ethic imprisons people in an "iron cage": "Specialists without spirit, sensualists without heart: this nullity imagines that it has attained a level of civilization never before achieved."[3]

Although he was an agnostic, Weber concludes his book by arguing that escape from this materialistic-individualistic "iron cage" could best be accomplished via "entirely new prophets" or "the rebirth of old ideas and ideals." Moreover, one "entirely new prophet" could be Jesus of Nazareth as described in the biblical narrative interpreted in its first-century historical context: Weber speculates that the secularized Protestant ethic that underpins modern organization and management theory may not be consistent with the biblical Judeo-Christian ethic.[4]

Many contemporary practitioners and management scholars agree with Weber's speculation, and often refer to teachings ascribed to Jesus to critique contemporary management theory and practice.[5] Even so, little work has been done by way of a focused, comprehensive, historically grounded, rigorous, scholarly analysis of the meaning of management in any of the four biblical Gospels that present the life and teachings of Jesus. The lack of such a study is all the more surprising given the growing scholarly and popular interest in the topic.[6]

At its core then, this book responds to the implicit and explicit calls of Weber and many others to develop an understanding of management based on a rigorous analysis of the biblical narrative. Of course, as will become apparent in the following pages, this is no small task. The next three chapters provide an introduction and overview of this task. The first chapter provides a brief summary of the book, thereby highlighting the key steps taken to achieve this goal. The second chapter explains in some detail why this study focuses on the Gospel of Luke in particular, and briefly describes the place of the Gospel of Luke in the larger biblical narrative. The third chapter provides an introduction to the role of managers and of organizations producing goods and services in first-century Palestine.

1

OVERVIEW OF THIS BOOK

The goals of this book are to describe what management theory and practice looked like in the first century, to use this as a lens to examine what the Gospel of Luke says about management, and then to draw out implications for today. It turns out that management is a dominant theme in the Gospel, that its message is consistently countercultural, and that Luke contains a four-phase process model to help readers implement change. The book presents a new way to understand the Gospel and the moral foundations of modern management.

PART I: INTRODUCTION

This first chapter provides an overview of the book. The second chapter describes why, of the Bible's four different Gospels that describe the life and teachings of Jesus, the Gospel of Luke was chosen for this study—because it seems to contain the most material relevant to the topic of management. The second chapter also describes the role Luke has in the larger biblical narrative, marking the transition between humankind being saved from oppressive structures and systems, toward ushering in new salvific ways of living. The third chapter provides background information about the increasing importance of managers, and the nature of organizations producing goods and services, in first-century Palestine.

PART II: PROBLEM RECOGNITION: HOW INTERPRETING LUKE VIA A FIRST-CENTURY MANAGEMENT LENS CHALLENGES THE CONVENTIONAL INTERPRETATION OF TWO KEY MANAGEMENT PARABLES

The three chapters in part two describe how management was understood in the first century, and then demonstrate how using this first-century understanding as a lens to examine two key teachings about management in the Gospel of Luke leads to interpretations that differ significantly from common twenty-first-century interpretations. Taken together, part two suggests that failing to interpret Luke via a first-century lens may result in interpretations that are contrary to what was intended in the first century.

An important organizing framework used throughout the entire book is presented in chapter four, which reviews how the general idea of "management" in first-century Palestine encompassed three general elements. These three elements serve as the "lens" through which to interpret what the Gospel of Luke says about management. This lens is key for understanding how first-century listeners and readers would have understood the teachings presented in Luke. Two thousand years ago management was seen as having three basic dimensions: (1) managing relationships *within* organizations (*oikonomia*); (2) managing money (*chrematistics*); and (3) managing relationships *between* organizations (benefaction/patron-client relationships).

Managing Relationships *within* Organizations (*Oikonomia*)

The first main role played by managers in the first century was to administer the operations within the organizations producing goods and services of the day. In Greek such an organization was called an *oikos* (plural is *oikoi*), and the Greek word for management was *oikonomia*—which is where we get the modern word "economics." Luke mentions variations of the word *oikos* (or *oikia*)[1] over 50 times, and makes reference to another 50 *oikoi* without using that word. In short, *oikoi* play an important part in Luke, being referred or alluded to on average about four times per chapter.

Unfortunately, the word *oikos* is usually translated as "house" or "household" in contemporary translations, and thus *oikonomia* becomes "household management."[2] This misleading translation of *oikos* may be the single most important reason why modern interpreters of biblical writings generally overlook their implications for management. Understandably, twenty-first-century readers think of "house" in terms of their own biological families and homes. Unlike the first century, the modern idea of a "house" would seldom include a multinational organization that maximizes its profits with dealings in distant markets. Nor does the modern idea of a "house" include a business organization that produces goods and services, nor would it even include small-scale agricultural or fishing companies. In short, the word "house" makes virtually invisible the goods and services producing function of the first-century *oikos*, and as a result modern readers become "blind" to the organizations that produce goods and services in biblical times. More to the point, it makes readers blind to the fact that the Gospel of Luke says a lot about how to manage organizations producing goods and services.

Ever since Aristotle, it was common to think about three basic dimensions to managing relationships within an *oikos*. These were the relationships between husband-wife, parent-child, and master-slave. These relationships were fairly rigid, and especially the master-slave relationship was seen as quite hierarchical. In the first century most managers were slaves, and while being slaves was obviously not highly desirable, it often offered more security than being poor peasants who were unable to feed themselves.

Managing Money (Natural versus Unnatural *Chrematistics*)

Aristotle's second dimension of management focused on finances, what he called "*chrematistics*." Aristotle described two approaches to *chrematistics*. Aristotle used the term "natural *chrematistics*" to describe using money to facilitate trade in a way that maintains holistic ongoing relationships within and between *oikoi*. This is called "sustenance economics." And he used the term "unnatural *chrematistics*" to describe using money to make money, which he found to be morally repugnant. This is called "acquisitive economics." There was an ongoing debate since the time of Aristotle through to the first century about the relative merits of acquisitive economics, which by then had become widespread among the Romans and among the Jewish elite. As a result of this emphasis on acquisitive economics, there was a widening gap between the rich and the poor, and absentee landholders often appointed managers to administer (and grow) their vast estates. The idea of money is alluded to over one hundred times in Luke's Gospel.

Managing Relationships *between* Organizations (Patron-Client versus Classic Benefaction)

In addition to administering within an *oikos*, managers were also important in managing relationships with other *oikoi*. In the first century, this arena of management was regulated by the norms and customs associated with patron-client relationships. In simple terms this meant trying to develop long-term relationships so that other *oikoi* would become subservient to your *oikos*. For example, if a peasant *oikos* received a loan from an elite *oikos*, the peasant *oikos* would thereby become the long-term client of the richer patron.

Along with the increasing emphasis on acquisitive economics, first-century Palestine was also witnessing increasingly negative repercussions of the distinctly Roman understanding of patron-client relationships. Whereas a classic Greek understanding had more of an emphasis on the patron as benefactor (e.g., rich people who helped others without demanding anything in return), under Roman norms a rich person who helped a poorer person essentially had a moral duty to ensure the person being helped became a "client" obliged to the "patron" who had provided the help. This was not all negative for clients (because they had patrons who also had some obligations toward clients), but in the longer term it served to widen the gap between the rich and the poor. There are over two hundred allusions to benefaction and/or patron-client relationships in Luke.

Chapter five uses this three-dimensional first-century lens to interpret what the first of two key passages in Luke says about management. "The Parable of the Shrewd Manager" (Luke 16:1–8) is the only parable in the New Testament that has an *oikonomos* as a central character. While this might suggest the passage would be front-and-center in efforts to understand what the Bible says about management, it turns out this parable has been notoriously difficult to interpret for contemporary scholars. For example, it was never mentioned in the first ten years of articles published in the *Journal of Biblical Integration in Business* (over fifteen hundred other biblical passages were cited over that time frame).

In a nutshell, the parable describes a manager who is accused by others of scattering his master's wealth. When the master hears about the accusation, he asks the manager for an accounting and tells him he will no longer be able to serve as his manager. The manager, who has no financial resources of his own, continues to scatter the rich man's resources by way of reducing the debts others owe to the rich man. The manager is praised by the rich man (and implicitly by Jesus) for his actions.

From a twenty-first-century perspective it is very difficult to see why the manager was praised for his actions.[3] In contrast, from a first-century perspective it is easy to see why Jesus commended the manager—he was scattering the rich man's resources in a way that reduced the gap between the rich and the poor, and thus enhanced community. Similarly, there is a plausible first-century explanation for why the rich man commended the manager—his scattering of some of the rich man's wealth endeared the rich man to others in the community as a benefactor, and in the first century such benefaction would have brought honor to the rich man (and at that time "honor" among people was held to be more valuable than mere "financial wealth").

Chapter six uses the first-century lens to analyze a second key management passage, namely, "The Parable of the Ten Pounds" (Luke 19:12–27). This has become the "poster child" parable for contemporary scholars who integrate biblical teachings and management studies. This parable and its sister parable of the talents (Matt. 25:14–30) are cited often because their teaching seems to be very consistent with modern management theory and practice.

The parable describes a nobleman who travels to the emperor to get more power. Before he leaves he gathers ten managers and gives each one pound of money (the equivalent of about four months of wages for a day laborer) to "do business with" while he is away. When the nobleman returns, he finds the first manager has used his pound to make ten more pounds. The nobleman praises this manager and gives him ten cities to rule over. A second manager has made five pounds, and is given five cities to rule over. However, a third manager buried the pound, because he knew the nobleman was a harsh man who took what he did not deposit and reaped what he did not sow. The master took this third manager's pound and gave it the first manager, saying: "I tell you, to all those who have, more will be given; but from those who have nothing, even what they have will be taken away" (Luke 19:26).

From a twenty-first-century perspective the message of this parable is easy to interpret. Managers who do business with money and achieve five- and tenfold returns will be praised and rewarded by their master, and are to serve as an example for others.

An interpretation based on our first-century lens may be just as easy, but comes to a very different conclusion. This is a story of patron-client relations at their worst, where a ruler who admits to taking what did not belong to him gains power. Moreover, this ruler surrounds himself with people who are like him, who use money to make more money (acquisitive economics). For most people in the first century the real hero of the parable is the third manager, who refuses to use the money for exploitive acquisitive economic purposes.

In sum, a first-century lens leads to interpretations of these two parables that contrast starkly with their common interpretations via a twenty-first-century lens. This raises the possibility that interpreting other biblical texts without reference to their first-century contexts may lead to interpretations that are opposite to those of first-century listeners.

Part III: Action Response: Performing a Comprehensive Examination of Passages in Luke Related to Each of the Three Dimensions of the First-Century Management Lens

Part three builds on and expands the analysis from part two. In particular, the chapters in part three provide a comprehensive analysis of the other passages in Luke related to the three dimensions that characterize a first-century understanding of management. Do the relevant passages in the rest of Luke lend support to the unconventional first-century interpretations of the two key management parables described in the previous two chapters, or does the rest of Luke undermine such radical interpretations?

Chapter seven focuses on the three aspects of managing relationships *within* organizations, examining each passage in Luke that describes husband-wife, parent-child, and master-slave relationships. It is striking how consistently these passages present a countercultural understanding of management: women are empowered, children are called to extend and transcend the boundaries of their *oikos*, and slaves are treated with dignity and respect (and indeed become models of "servant leadership").

Chapter eight examines the eighteen passages in Luke that make some reference to money, finances, wealth, and possessions. In analyzing these passages, there is a striking difference between the nine passages where the word "rich" is mentioned, and the nine where it is not. In passages that mention "rich," there is a clear and consistent message to share wealth and to sell belongings and give to the poor ("woe to you who are rich"). In contrast, in passages that talk about money but do not refer to the rich, the management of money is not in any way seen as dishonorable or frowned upon. Put in first-century terms, the message in Luke is clearly and consistently opposed to "unnatural *chrematistics*" (i.e., acquisitive economics, using money to make more money in a way that widens the gap between the rich and the poor), but supportive of "natural *chrematistics*" (i.e., sustenance economics, using money to facilitate the exchange of goods in everyday life in a way that nurtures community).

Chapter nine, which focuses on managing relationships with other organizations, examines the six main passages where patron-client and/or benefaction relationships are most evident. Again, these passages have a clear and consistent countercultural message. These passages lament situations where one *oikos* is indebted to another *oikos*, and applaud managers who act as benefactors by sharing their *oikos* resources without making others become indebted clients to be lorded over. Notably this countercultural orientation is prominent in the Lord's Prayer: "for we ourselves forgive everyone [financially] indebted to us" (Luke 11:4).

In sum, these passages provide consistent and strong support to the first-century interpretations of the parable of the shrewd manager and the ten pounds offered in chapters five and six. Distributing the resources of the rich is praiseworthy (shrewd manager) whereas widening the gap between the rich and the poor is lamentable (ten pounds).

Taken together, the first three parts of the book provide support for calling Luke "the management Gospel." Passages about management, *oikos*, *chrematistics*, and patron-client relationships play a central role in the Gospel. More importantly, the messages in these passages are consistently and profoundly countercultural—they are not merely background passages that provide a setting for the Gospel. This begs the question: Are other key overarching themes in Luke also rife with implications for management? This is the focal point of part four.

PART IV: NEW WAY OF SEEING: MANAGEMENT, THE KINGDOM OF GOD, SALVATION, AND THE HOLY SPIRIT

In order to further test the idea that management issues really do play a central role in Luke, and are not merely some artifact of clever (or misguided) analyses, this part examines whether the first-century management lens is also helpful in providing new understanding to other dominant themes in Luke. In particular, part four focuses on three themes that Luke is known to place particular emphasis on—the kingdom of God, salvation, and the Holy Spirit—and examines whether they have anything to say about management, and vice versa. A typical twenty-first-century understanding of these themes would not place much emphasis on management issues. Perhaps it would even denigrate management insofar as management is seen as grounded in this world, and ideas like the kingdom of God and salvation are seen as more spiritual and other-worldly. If there were overlap between management and these larger theological themes, it would be of interest not only to management scholars, but also to the growing number of practitioners and scholars interested in integrating faith and the workplace.

Chapter ten looks at the 21 passages in Luke that refer to the kingdom of God (KOG), which is known as the topic Jesus taught about most often. Although a popular understanding of the KOG often equates it with a heavenly afterlife, Luke is actually quite clear that the KOG is something that is already evident on earth and which Jesus' followers are called to enact on earth. Note also that the term "kingdom" is somewhat misleading, because it is clear that the KOG is not a geographically bounded region, but rather a better translation might be the "reign" of God. Moreover, given that the language of the monarchy is somewhat dated, perhaps a better contemporary translation would be the "managerial character of God."

A content analysis of the KOG passages shows that they can be categorized into two basic groupings. Of the 21 passages, 9 describe the KOG being proclaimed and taught, but with little specific reference to what the KOG actually looks like in practice. The remaining 12 passages describe how the KOG is enacted or manifest. It is striking that an *oikos* setting plays a central role in 83 percent of the passages that describe what the KOG looks like. In particular, the KOG is evident when people who previously did not have an *oikos* to belong to (i.e., the poor, the dispossessed, the outcasts) are welcomed into countercultural alternative *oikoi*/communities. Managers of a KOG *oikos* focus on the bottom rung, not the bottom line. Put differently, a KOG *oikos* emphasizes sustenance economics, not acquisitive economics.

Chapter eleven examines another theme Luke is noted for, namely, salvation. In the first century there were two related meanings of salvation. Jews tended to emphasize being *saved from oppression*, and were waiting for a Messiah who would allow them to get out from under the tyranny of the Romans and again manage their own affairs. The Greco-Roman view tended to emphasize being *saved for transformation*, which might include receiving blessings associated with new structures and systems. The Roman emperor was often described as a Savior who had brought peace and stability to the people.

A variation of the word salvation is mentioned 25 times in Luke, appearing in 19 different passages. Taken together these passages suggest that salvation has a lot to do with societal structures and systems. A sign of this occurs when social outcasts, sick, and homeless people are healed and thus are allowed to become reintegrated into *oikoi*. Another hallmark is when people voluntarily create new alternative forms of *oikos* that are inclusive and welcoming of everyone, where boundaries separating people are porous. These themes are underscored in one passage in particular.

It is striking that the *only* time *Jesus* uses the noun form of "salvation" is when he talks about a rich man who has introduced new KOG-like structures and systems for managing his *oikos* (Luke 19:9). Can the rich be saved? Apparently they can if they transform the way they manage their organizations. Is there a relationship between salvation and how organizations are managed? In Luke this is undoubtedly true—it seems that salvation has a lot to do with how people manage organizational structures and systems.

Chapter twelve examines what Luke says about the Holy Spirit, whom Luke refers to more often than the other three Gospels combined. Luke is clear that the Holy

Spirit is an essential part of salvation and KOG-like organizational structures and systems. Of the 16 mentions of the Holy Spirit, 11 identify people who speak of salvation; everyone who is able to recognize or describe salvation in Luke has been filled with the Holy Spirit. The remaining 5 passages describe general teachings about the Holy Spirit. Taken together, the passages in Luke indicate that managers cannot sustain KOG organizations without the Holy Spirit.

From the perspective of managers and other first-century readers, the analysis thus far may be both encouraging and daunting. On the one hand, some may find it exciting to think that managers play such a central role in facilitating salvation and in developing the organizational structures and systems that enact and manifest the KOG. On the other hand, some managers who wish to put these teachings into practice may find them daunting, because it is challenging enough merely to keep up with conventional expectations for managers. To say that managers must now be concerned with sustenance economics, remove oppressive structures and systems, and focus on the bottom rung instead of only the bottom line may seem overwhelming. Indeed, it is difficult enough to manage religious organizations according to KOG principles: How can this ever be accomplished in the rough-and-tumble world of "regular" businesses in the marketplace? Part five provides a "how to guide" for implementing the kinds of institutional changes called for in Luke.

Part V: Institutional Change: A Four-Phase "How to" Process Model for Putting into Practice Management Principles Described in Luke

KOG structures and systems take time to develop and implement. Indeed, according to Luke the *process* of developing and implementing such structures and systems is more important than *imposing* them. This is better seen as a journey to a destination, rather than a goal to be achieved. The hallmarks of this journey are described in a section of Luke fittingly called the "Journey Narrative," which describes Jesus' journey to Jerusalem.

Chapter thirteen describes how the literary structure of Luke's Journey Narrative (Luke 9:51–19:40) draws attention to a four-phase process model that provides a helpful framework for managing the transition from conventional management to KOG management. The first phase—*problem recognition*—is to identify and name shortcomings associated with the status quo. The second phase—*action response*—is to take some actions that are designed to address the problem. This phase has an experimental and experiential learning element to it. Consistent with the processual nature of the model, these actions may not guarantee immediate success, but rather they are designed to be steps in the right direction. They are occasions for generating insight and learning. The third phase—*changed way of seeing*—has a reflective nature. Having experienced a new way of acting (phase two) often results in a new way of seeing the world. In particular, the experiential learning from participating in countercultural actions can inform an alternative worldview. The fourth phase— *institutional change*—draws attention to larger structures and systems, recognizing that institutions shape subsequent behavior. For example, Luke describes how the misinterpretation of Hebrew Scriptures by first-century religious leaders results in rules and customs that inhibit salvation. Implementing social structures and systems consistent with KOG values requires encouraging the elite to transform conventional norms and practices.

Chapter fourteen examines the passages in the first half of the Journey Narrative, and describes in some detail how they are sequentially ordered to move (in three cycles) from: problem recognition → action response → changed way of seeing → institutional change. For example, in the first cycle—dubbed the Samaritan cycle—the narrative moves from: Jesus rebuking two of his disciples for wanting to destroy a Samaritan village (problem recognition) → Jesus sending his disciples to Samaritan villages in order to live with them and serve them (action response) → Jesus noting how this experience allowed his disciples to "see things" that remained unseen by even the most elite of thinkers in the dominant conventional paradigm (changed way of seeing) → Jesus telling listeners to follow the example of a Samaritan who helped out his neighbor/enemy rather than follow dysfunctional conventional purity laws (institutional change).

Chapter fifteen points to the bidirectional nature of the four-phase process model, examining passages in the second half of the Journey Narrative and describing how they are sequentially ordered to move (in three cycles) in the reverse direction, namely, from: institutional change → changed way of seeing → action response → problem recognition. For example, in the first of this trio of cycles—dubbed the Benefaction cycle—the narrative moves from: instituting new norms where resources are deliberately shared with marginalized people who cannot possibly repay (institutional change) → exposing shortcomings of a worldview based on status and possessions (changed way of seeing) → acting in ways that help the lost and the lowly (action response) → resolving the ongoing tension between serving God versus serving money (problem recognition).

PART VI: IMPLICATIONS FOR TWENTY-FIRST-CENTURY MANAGEMENT THEORY AND PRACTICE

Whereas the first five parts of the book examine what the Gospel of Luke says about management through a first-century lens, this final section discusses some implications of applying these findings to contemporary management theory and practice. Part six is subdivided according to the three main elements of the first-century lens: (1) managing relationships *within* organizations; (2) managing money; and (3) managing relationships *between* organizations. In addition to providing a critique and alternative to key theories and concepts in the mainstream literature, each chapter also provides contemporary examples of organizations where glimpses of the sorts of management promoted in Luke are evident.

In terms of managing relationships *within* organizations, chapter sixteen looks at three key topics in the area of organizational theory and behavior. First, it describes a conventional and an alternative approach to the four fundamentals of organizational structure, and discusses how the organizational structure found at a business named Semco reflects practices consistent with Luke. At Semco members choose their own hours, their own bosses, and their own salaries. Second, it looks at motivation theory, in particular Maslow's hierarchy of needs, and speculates why it has been so popular despite not being supported by empirical research. The practitioner example here is the story of James Despain at Caterpillar Inc, and how he found that consistently treating people with dignity helped to create a profound sense of motivation in the workplace. Third, the chapter discusses perhaps the most popular leadership theory, situational leadership, identifies its shortcomings from a Lukan perspective, and introduces an alternative situational leadership model grounded in Luke. The exemplar here is Robert Greenleaf, noted champion of servant leadership, and the four-step friendly disentangling process he followed at AT&T to facilitate institutional change on behalf of socially marginalized groups.

In terms of managing money, chapter seventeen provides a brief discussion of the hallmarks of contemporary economics, finance, and accounting. First, it describes how the dominant theories in economics assume that people will act in their self-interest with guile, which serves as a self-fulfilling prophecy that undermines the likelihood that people will act with benefaction and to enhance mutual interests. The exemplar here is Aaron Feuerstein of Malden Mills, who famously voluntarily paid his employees while his burned down factory was being rebuilt. Second, the chapter looks at finance, and in particular at how an emphasis on trading ("using money to make money") differs from an emphasis on investing, and how financial activities that seek acquisitive economic gains are often separated from the actual amount of goods and services being produced, which can be especially detrimental to marginalized players. The exemplar here is Mohammed Yunus, and the four-step process he used to set up the Grameen Bank, which provides funding to poor microentrepreneurs unable to get funding from conventional banks. Third, the chapter looks at accounting theory, and describes differences between the four basic assumptions of Generally Accepted Accounting Principles from both a contemporary and a Luke-based perspective. The practitioner example here comes from the "Economy of Communion," a group of 750 organizations associated with the Focolare Movement (the largest lay movement within the Catholic Church).

With regard to managing relationships *between* organizations, chapter eighteen looks at marketing, supply chain management, and strategy. First, it contrasts a Luke-based versus a conventional approach to the well-known four P's of marketing. The exemplar here is Wiens Family Farm, a pioneer in the Shared Farming movement that values relationships between urban people, rural people, and the land: "It's not just about vegetables." Second, the chapter describes the difference between linear supply "chain" thinking with holistic supply "cycle" thinking, which emphasizes the importance of ensuring that any organizational "waste" become transformed into "inputs" for other organizations. The exemplar here is the global carpet manufacturing giant Interface, which, by a combination of reducing its own negative effects on the environment and by reducing the negative effects of other organizations, is poised to give back more to the planet than it takes. Third, the chapter reviews the highly influential "five forces" strategy framework developed by Michael Porter, which essentially describes how organizations can gain power over other organizations (e.g., buyers, suppliers, rivals), much like the patron-client relationships of the first century. A Luke-based variation of the five forces models shows how it can be used to identify opportunities to develop mutually beneficial relationships with others. The exemplar here is a community of organizations in Kalundborg, Denmark, who achieve mutually beneficial relationships that are also good for their larger social and ecological community.

By way of concluding thoughts, this study is of *scholarly importance*, addressing fundamental research questions posed by Max Weber, still one of the most cited and influential organizational scholars. The book is also timely and of *practical interest*, especially for anyone interested in what the world's best-selling book has to say about one of the world's most influential leaders. Indeed, an increasing number of people are looking to spiritual sources to escape the materialistic-individualistic iron cage that characterizes modern management theory and practice. This book is different than previous "best sellers" written in this area because of its emphasis on interpreting Luke through a first-century understanding of management.[4]

2

A SHORT INTRODUCTION TO THE
GOSPEL OF LUKE

An important question motivating this book is whether there is any new insight to be gained from using a first-century management lens to interpret the Christian scriptures about the life and teaching of Jesus. In particular, will such a lens lead to interpretations that are qualitatively different from conventional twenty-first-century interpretations? Or will they simply reinforce the ideas that Max Weber associated with the "Protestant ethic," which he argued provide the moral underpinning for modern-day capitalism and conventional management theory and practice? If a first-century understanding of these scriptures provides support for a different approach to management, then they may represent an important response to Weber's call to escape the "iron cage" via a "rebirth of old ideas and ideals."[1]

Early on in working on this book it became clear that any attempt to analyze the entire biblical text with these questions in mind would prove too ambitious, so the decision was made to choose a biblical book that was most appropriate for the task. This resulted in deciding to choose one of the four Gospels in the New Testament—Matthew, Mark, Luke, and John—because each of these describes the life and teaching of Jesus of Nazareth, the nominal leader of Christianity. Of these four Gospels a preliminary analysis quickly showed that the Gospel of Luke was the most relevant for this study.[2] First, the author of Luke is one of the most prolific writers in the Bible. The two biblical books attributed to him—The Gospel of Luke, and The Acts of the Apostles—together account for about 27.5 percent of all the words in the New Testament, more than any other author.[3] His second volume, the book of Acts, essentially describes how the early church grew after Jesus' life on earth, and thus provides a glimpse into management issues facing the early church that Luke may have been attuned to in writing his Gospel. Having access to Acts can also help to corroborate some of the themes and findings that become apparent in the study of Luke's Gospel.[4]

Second, Luke is considered to be one of the most educated biblical authors, and he is probably the most likely of the four Gospel authors to have seen the larger Greco-Roman world as his audience (rather than, e.g., writing mostly for Jews and Christians). This enlarged worldview may have made Luke more sensitive to the sorts of issues modern-day management scholars and practitioners face and think about, as is evident in the next point.

Third, compared to the other three Gospels, Luke seems to place much greater emphasis on issues related to management and material wealth.[5] This is illustrated by some very simple word counts, which, though unsophisticated, provide a rough measure of relative emphases in Luke versus the other three Gospels. Most notably, Luke contains 7 of the total of 8 mentions of the Greek words for "management" or "manager" (*oikonomia, oikonomos*) that appear in all four Gospels combined. More broadly, a word count was performed on a basic list of Greek words that could be related to managerial roles: *oikonomia/os* (manager, management), *oiko/despote/s* (owner of house), *epitropos* (steward), *epistates* (master), and *kurios* (lord/master; note that references to God or Jesus as *kurios* were not counted[6]). In total these words are mentioned 86 times in all four Gospels, and of these mentions 44 (51 percent) are found in Luke.[7] Along the same lines, Luke contains 57 (43 percent) of the four Gospels' total 134 mentions of *oikos/oikion*, which is the primary organization producing goods and services in the first century.[8] And finally Luke is more likely than the other Gospels to refer to material *oikoi* resources that need to be managed. In particular, of a simple list of fixed *oikos* assets—possessions, property, and goods—Luke accounts for 17 of 25 (68 percent) mentions in all four Gospels combined.[9] When adding more fluid *oikos* resources—money, rich/es, wealth, coin/s, *denarius/i*, pound/s, silver, gold, talent/s—then Luke accounts for 56 of the 126 (44 percent) mentions across all four Gospels.[10]

These figures—showing the high relative emphasis in Luke on words related to management, *oikos*, and money—are especially remarkable because only 42 percent of the content in Luke is unique to Luke (about 21 percent of Luke overlaps with Matthew, and an additional 35 percent overlaps with Mark and often Matthew).[11] Taken together, this suggests that Luke places special emphasis on what today would be considered to be management issues, and thus in this regard it may be said that Luke is "the management Gospel."

BACKGROUND INFORMATION ON THE GOSPEL OF LUKE

Biblical scholars are unsure of exactly when Luke-Acts were written. It could be as early and 60 C.E., but it is generally assumed to be about 80–90 C.E., or about 50 years after the death of Jesus. While the earliest copies of the manuscripts do not contain the author's name, the present book will follow convention and suggest that both Acts and the third Gospel were written by an author named Luke. Tradition suggests Luke was a medical physician, though the evidence supporting the speculation seems weaker now than it had been 50 years ago. What we do know is that Luke was highly educated, writing at least in part to an educated audience, and that he was probably a Gentile. Scholars generally agree that Luke "is a first-class historian" in terms of "his descriptions of settings, customs, and locales."[12] Even so, as appropriate for his time, this "does not mean that Luke cannot rearrange material for emphasis, summarize events in his own language, or bring out his own emphases as drawn from the tradition."[13] For example, often in Luke "[t]he sequence [of the passages within the Gospel] itself provides the larger meaning."[14] In sum, it is widely admitted among Luke's interpreters that his form of historical writing "fit into categories of ancient literary writing, and [thus] were never intended to live up to the standards of modern historiography."[15]

Luke writes in a language called *Koine*, halfway between modern Greek and the Attic prose of ancient antiquity.[16] He strives to find a middle path between the vernacular (found in Mark) and the "artificial Greek" that goes back to ancient antiquity. "What Luke *writes* is not, of course, what one *spoke* then." Luke's giftedness as a writer is evident in his ability to incorporate stylistic elements (e.g., sentence construction, vocabulary) consistent with the Hebrew Scriptures (i.e., essentially what Christians today would refer to as the Old Testament) in order to emphasize the continuity with the past, and yet also reflect a Hellenistic style and "classical biography" familiar to his Greco-Roman readers.

Numerous ways of subdividing the Gospel into various parts have been developed in order to provide an overview of it. There is no need here to review them all, but the following basic organizing structure is well accepted among scholars and suitable for present purposes. After a short prologue (Luke 1:1–4),[17] the Gospel of Luke is often subdivided into four basic sections, as follows.[18]

Jesus' Birth and Preparation for Ministry (Luke 1:5–4:13)

The first section of the Gospel basically describes the social, political, and religious context for the life of Jesus. Here we read about how Israel longs for a savior as it endures Roman rule.[19] Upon his birth Jesus is proclaimed to be the Christ (the Messiah) who will bring salvation to the people, and this is confirmed when the infant Jesus is presented at the Temple in Jerusalem.[20] John the Baptist, the last of the Old Testament style prophets, prepares the way by proclaiming that through Jesus all humankind will see God's salvation.[21] This first part of Luke ends with Jesus being baptized, and with the Holy Spirit sending him to the desert where he is tempted for 40 days.[22] Preparation for Jesus' public ministry is complete.

Jesus' Ministry in Galilee (Luke 4:14–9:50)

This second section presents the core ideas and ideals of Jesus' message, which are encapsulated at the very beginning when Jesus, in the synagogue of his hometown Nazareth in Galilee,[23] reads scripture from the prophet Isaiah: "The spirit of the Lord is upon me, because he has anointed me to preach good news to the poor. He has sent me to proclaim release to the captives and recovery of sight to the blind, to let the oppressed go free" (Luke 4:18–19). The section then goes on to describe how Jesus chooses his 12 apostles and how he brings many social outcasts back into community (via healing them). The longest passage at the heart of this section—sometimes called the "Sermon on the Plain" (Luke 6:20–49)—starts with four beatitudes that have been called "the Gospel in a nutshell"[24]: blessed are the poor, the hungry, those who weep, and those who are rejected by society. The section ends with additional miracles, further teachings, and Jesus foretelling his death and resurrection.

Jesus' Journey to Jerusalem (Luke 9:51–19:40)

This third section, which presents a series of teachings and events that describe how followers can put Jesus' teachings into practice, is presented in the form of Jesus' journey to Jerusalem. This section is of special interest to the present study because it contains most of the passages of particular relevance to management theory and practice. For example, even though this third section of Luke accounts for (only) 38 percent of the total number of words in Luke, it contains 73 percent of all the keyword mentions associated with management and financial wealth (in particular, this section contains *all* the mentions of "management," "wealth," and "possessions").[25] As will be described in part five, this section has embedded within it a recurring four-step process model that unfolds as follows: (i) problem recognition; (ii) action response; (iii) changed way of seeing; and (iv) institutional change.

Jesus' Death and Resurrection in Jerusalem (Luke 19:41–24:53)

The final section of Luke presents the last few weeks of Jesus' earthly life including his death, resurrection, and ascension. As this section proceeds, it describes the heightening tension between Jesus and religious and political leaders, provides additional teachings and prophecies, has Jesus instituting what has been called the Lord's Supper (Holy Eucharist or Communion), and ends by describing Jesus' arrest and trials, his death on the cross as an innocent man (which demoralizes his followers), his unexpected resurrection on the third day (despite Jesus having told his disciples earlier that it would happen), and his ascension.

THE GOSPEL OF LUKE IN THE LARGER CONTEXT OF THE BIBLE

It is also helpful to situate the role the Gospel of Luke plays within the larger context of the biblical story. Jesus saw himself in continuity with a much longer history of God at work on the earth, going right back to the creation story. In particular, Jesus was born a Jew, died a Jew, and was deeply steeped in the sacred Hebrew Scriptures, which provide the context for his life and teachings. The larger biblical story line is often presented as a "salvation history" that unfolds in four different phases—Creation, Fall, Salvation, and the kingdom of God—each of which will be looked at in turn. In this four-phase story line, the Gospel accounts of the life of Jesus play a key role in the third phase, Salvation (i.e., in the transition from the Fall to the kingdom of God).[26]

Creation

The first phase begins with the Creation story at the start of the Old Testament (Gen. 1), which describes how God works systematically to create a world that is "good" and then enlists humankind to col*labor*ate with God in working out its details. God creates humans "in the image of God" as God's representatives on earth to manage creation consistent with God's character. Genesis describes God giving humankind three "creation mandates" or management responsibilities[27]:

1. to "have dominion" over creation in Godlike ways[28];
2. to engage in meaningful work[29]; and
3. to live in and nurture community.[30]

As part of Creation, God places a "tree of the knowledge of good and evil" in the Garden of Eden. Even though God gives Adam and Eve the free will to eat its fruit, God specifically asks them not to do so.[31]

Fall

The second phase of the biblical salvation history starts with the so-called Fall, when Adam and Eve eat the forbidden fruit from the tree of the knowledge of good and evil (Gen. 3). As a result of God's response to this, fulfilling the following three creation mandates becomes considerably more challenging:

1. The ability to care for creation is made more challenging by the animosity between some creatures and humans.[32]
2. Work becomes more challenging and choresome because of weeds and thistles.[33]
3. Nurturing community becomes less egalitarian because men begin to "rule over" women.[34]

These new challenges—which are relevant for managing organizations producing goods and services—prompt a long period of waiting for a savior who will help to escape oppressive structures and systems and restore humankind to more Eden-like ways of living. The remainder of the Old Testament describes how God's chosen people—Israel—sometimes stay close to God and sometimes stray away. It is a story of liberation events (e.g., Moses redeeming God's people from the oppressive work conditions of Egypt) and successes (the wisdom of King Solomon), but also many failures (e.g., political maneuvers to steal birthrights and wives). This phase is sometimes called "the time of the law and the prophets" or the "Period of Israel." This second phase of the biblical salvation history comes to its final moments in the first section of Luke (i.e., Luke 1:5–4:13), where Luke explains how Jesus is born at a time when Israel was waiting for their Messiah to save it from the oppression of the Romans, and where we find John the Baptist representing the last of the Old Testament style prophets.

Salvation

The third phase of the biblical salvation history—which some scholars call the "Period of Jesus"—is associated with the public ministry of Jesus, and this is the focus of the rest of the Gospel of Luke (Luke 4:14 through Luke 24:53).[35] Hallmarks of this phase, which differ from traditional Jewish Messianic expectations, include an emphasis on salvation being available for everyone (not only for the Jews), salvation not involving a violent or military liberation from Roman oppression (salvation transcends politics), salvation being an ongoing process that involves peoples' active participation (it is not a one-time event), and salvation being countercultural (e.g., woe to people who are rich, well fed, and well spoken of). In short, Jesus is presented as a Messiah who enables the salvation of all humankind who accept his invitation to follow him. Salvation enables people to be saved *from* the temptations represented by the Fall, and to be saved *for* the kind of life that fulfills the creation mandates.

Kingdom of God

Phase four, sometimes called the "period of the Church," starts after Jesus' ascension and encompasses the rest of the New Testament—that is, all the books after the four Gospels, starting with Acts—through to the present time. This includes the formation of the early church, the missionary journeys and letters written by Paul, and all the subsequent activity in the Christian church in the ensuing two millennia. The present time also includes the idea of living in the kingdom of God on earth as it is in Heaven.

Expressed in terms of the original creation mandates, the question for contemporary management theory and practice becomes: How does the salvation that Jesus offers help humankind to

1. manage the created world in "the image of God";
2. engage in meaningful work; and
3. live in and nurture community?

This brings us to the core question of this book: What does the Gospel of Luke have to say about management theory and practice? Of course, this is relevant both for business and nonbusiness organizations, and this is also clearly relevant beyond issues of management narrowly defined.

SUMMARY

Of the four Gospels, Luke may be dubbed "the management gospel" because of its emphasis on concerns and issues that are relevant to management both in the first century and today. Of the four sections that Luke can be divided into, the third section called the Journey Narrative contains the most material relevant to management. In the context of the overall biblical story, Luke may be particularly helpful in understanding the role management plays in fulfilling the creation mandates going forward from the time of Jesus.

3

MANAGERS, GOODS AND SERVICES PRODUCING ORGANIZATIONS, AND FIRST-CENTURY PALESTINE

In order to interpret what the Gospel of Luke says about management via a first-century lens, it is necessary to understand the role of managers, and that of goods and services producing organizations, in their first-century socioeconomic context.[1] Failing to understand the historical context of Luke makes readers likely to interpret it with modern assumptions and expectations. Unfortunately, contemporary Western readers "are rarely attuned to the differences between a first century Mediterranean context" versus their modern societal context.[2] For example, the holistic nature of management in the first century is one of its key differences from a twenty-first-century understanding. In first-century Palestine, religion and management and economics and politics were seen as an integrated whole—to talk about one as though it did not have implications for the others would have been inconceivable. Whereas today some people may be keen to separate "business" from the holy affairs of the "church," such a separation was impossible in the first century. In the first century, one's understanding of God and religious faith pervaded all aspects of one's life.[3]

For an instructive example of the importance of understanding the local socioeconomic conditions when interpreting a biblical passage, consider the well-known passage where Jesus tells his listeners to "turn the other cheek" if someone strikes them on their right cheek (Luke 6:29; Matt. 5:39). On the face of it (pun intended), without knowledge of first-century social customs and laws, *this passage seems to teach listeners to passively accept abuse from others.* And indeed, this is how it has generally been interpreted by contemporary scholars who seek to draw management lessons from it. For example, as Charles Manz puts it in his book *The Leadership Wisdom of Jesus*:

> [Jesus] suggested that we should treat people well, as we would like to be treated, even when they don't deserve it, and even when they act in ways that are harmful to us. He went so far as to suggest that if they attack us (strike us on the cheek) we should not fight back but allow them to attack (turn the other cheek).[4]

A similar interpretation, invoking ideas from reverse psychology, is found in Bruce Winston's *Be a Manager for God's Sake*: "Many times evil people (*poneros*) mistreat those under them just to see those of lesser status react negatively. Consider the evil one who does not get a 'rise' out of the victim; he will soon seek another victim."[5]

However, the meaning of Jesus' lesson in this passage becomes very different when interpreted in light of first-century Palestine management practices. First, note that in order to hit someone's right cheek, it means that the person doing the hitting would use either (a) a left-handed fist, or (b) a right-handed back-of-hand slap. Jesus' listeners would have known that he would *not* have been referring to a left-handed punch (because at that time the left hand was used only for unclean tasks, like wiping one's behind).[6] Instead, Jesus was referring to a back-of-hand slap using one's right hand, which was the customary symbolically demeaning way for managers to discipline their subordinates at the time. Indeed, hitting a *peer* with such a humiliating back-of-right-hand slap exacted a monetary fine one hundred times greater than a full-fisted right-handed punch.

Thus in light of its first-century context, rather than encouraging a passive response to abusive managerial behavior, in this passage Jesus seems to be teaching his listeners to boldly *confront managers who abuse their power*! By turning their left cheek to face an abusive manager, a subordinate was in effect saying: "I will not accept being demeaned by you by such a back-handed slap. I demand to be treated as an equal!" In short, Jesus is telling listeners to use nonviolent resistance to challenge institutionalized inequality.[7]

Similar acts of nonviolent resistance would not have been unheard of to Jesus' listeners. In 26 C.E., shortly after he had become procurator in Judea, Pilate had busts of the emperor brought into the temple. When Jews complained, Pilate summoned them to a stadium on the pretext of giving them an answer. When the stadium was full, he had it surrounded by soldiers and threatened to kill the Jews if they refused to accept the emperor's image in the temple. When the soldiers drew their swords the Jews bared their necks, prepared to die for their beliefs (metaphorically, they turned the other cheek). Rather than massacre all these able-bodied men, Pilate ordered the busts to be removed from the temple.[8]

Lest the reader is unsure about whether the message of nonviolent resistance is the correct interpretation of this "turn the other cheek" teaching, it is immediately reinforced with a similar teaching when Jesus tells his listeners that if anyone sues them for their coat, they should also give their undergarments (Luke 6:29; Matt. 5:40). Again, if we read this verse without consideration for its socioeconomic context, it seems consistent with business scholars who suggest that Jesus was counseling his listeners to surrender to accusers and, more generally, to *go beyond the requirements of the law*.[9] However, Jesus' first-century listeners would have known that his teaching was about a person who was so poor that he had nothing other than a coat to give in collateral for a loan, and moreover that according to Hebrew Scriptures creditors should return by sunset any coat left to them in collateral by a debtor.

> If you lend money to my people, to the poor among you, you shall not deal with them as a creditor; you shall not exact interest from them. If you take your neighbor's cloak in pawn, you shall restore it before the sun goes down; for it may be your neighbor's only clothing to use as cover; in what else shall that person sleep? And if your neighbor cries out to me, I will listen, for I am compassionate. (Exod. 22:25–27; see also Deut. 24:10–13)

Thus Jesus' teaching was publicly exposing the creditor, who was suing for the coat, as being an illegitimate moneylender who participated in reducing "an entire social class to landlessness, destitution, and abasement."[10] If debtors were to put Jesus' counsel into practice in a courtroom, and removed their undergarments, they would be stark naked. Nakedness was taboo in Judaism, with greater shame falling on the person who viewed or caused the nakedness than on the naked person (Gen.

9:20–27). Thus, in its first-century context, the counsel to give your undergarments to someone suing you for your coat is not about cowering to those who have power. Rather, *it is about boldly exposing the moral nakedness of an oppressive economic system* that fails to follow the requirements of Hebrew Scriptures.[11]

BACKGROUND ON MANAGEMENT IN THE FIRST CENTURY

Although relatively little research has focused on the meaning of management in first-century Palestine,[12] there is general agreement that the role of management was increasing in importance. For example, consider the fact that the Roman Empire was becoming—in terms of its geographic size, its real national product (equivalent to about 1.7 tons of gold), and its population (approximately 55 million people)—larger than any Western nation would be until the mid-nineteenth century,[13] and that it has been suggested that its real genius was its management expertise.[14] Moreover, it has been argued that the Hebrews, though relatively small in number, have had a substantial influence on civilization partly because of their management skills. For example, the biblical account of Moses's approach to management "affords us one of the earliest and most commonly available records of a philosophy and plan for organization."[15]

The number and role of managers would have been increasing in first-century Palestine, as in the rest of the Roman Empire. A primary reason for this is related to the Roman approach to expansion, which has been summarized as: "Romanization by urbanization for commercialization."[16] In order to efficiently funnel resources from laboring producers throughout the empire to the more centrally located Romans in charge, Rome would often undertake commercialization projects in its territories, encouraging growth of urban centers that would serve as marketplaces to which people from surrounding towns and villages could bring their wares to be traded and taxed. This process represented the promise of stability and inclusion for subject peoples, but it also brought with it a political economic hierarchy[17] (e.g., including evermore managers who oversaw far-flung estates for absentee landowners), the social effects of which were playing out in first-century Palestine.

For example, a short three miles from Jesus' hometown of Nazareth (population of about two hundred), the Rome-appointed ruler in the region—Herod Antipas—was rebuilding the local capital city of Sepphoris (population around eight thousand). In the first century cities like Sepphoris were not manufacturing centers; rather, people living in the cities were relatively unproductive and relied on the goods and services producing activity of the *oikoi* in the surrounding region. The markets of Sepphoris would in turn become part of the distribution channel funneling resources to Rome. This also involved increased taxation rates of enterprises in surrounding areas, which are estimated to have been about 35–40 percent at that time.[18] All this pressure caused many *oikoi* to become bankrupt and their land to become increasingly owned by absentee landowners in Rome. Indeed, it has been suggested that "in the time of Jesus, most of Galilee was parceled out to foreign landlords."[19]

Absentee landowners could not be on site to manage their estates, and nor did they want to be involved in hands-on management. The increasing number and size of estates owned by absentee landowners created an increasing need for "professional" (i.e., nonowner) managers, who were sometimes call stewards, retainers, brokers, scribes, and accountants. The increase in professional managers often coincided with an increasing emphasis on acquisitive economic management practices, and a further widening gap between the rich and the poor. Moreover, these managers often had incentives to maximize financial returns for masters, and/or to take money for themselves. We also know that among the elite during this time there was an increasing emphasis on conspicuous consumption, though this may have been more pronounced in Jerusalem and Judea than in backwaters like Galilee.[20]

It can be estimated that perhaps 8 percent of the population in first-century Palestine could be seen as somewhat analogous to what we would today call professional managers. This includes not only the landholders who headed various enterprises, but also the managers who were appointed to help absentee landholders manage their properties, the scribes and religious leaders within Judaism, and the tax collectors and officers in the military.[21] Figure 3.1 provides a simple "organization chart" showing the relative status of different kinds of positions in first-century Palestine.

However, it is not sufficient to merely contrast and compare where different members of society are on an "organization chart."[22] To really understand what management means in that society requires becoming familiar with the underlying institutions, processes, and systems that give rise to, inform, and sustain power differences and how they are managed.

The remainder of this chapter will introduce readers to the idea of *oikos*—the primary organization producing goods and services in first-century Palestine—and how a reinvented understanding of *oikos* played a central role in the identity of the early church.

GOODS AND SERVICES PRODUCING ORGANIZATIONS IN FIRST-CENTURY PALESTINE: THE IMPORTANCE OF *OIKOS*

As it has been for most of the history of humankind, the *oikos* (usually translated as "household") represented the basic building block of social and economic life in first-century society in the Middle East.[23] The vast majority of people—including the emperor, the tenant farmer, the merchant, and the centurion—each belonged to an *oikos*. The *oikos* is widely accepted as "a basis of and model for Greek social, economic and political life from Homeric times through the advent of Roman rule . . . the household or estate was also the basic economic unit of production and self-support."[24] "Used throughout the New Testament, *oikos* meant much more than the idea of 'household' means today; in that time the household was truly the center of economic production, faith, and family life."[25]

There are at least two important differences in the ancient concept of an *oikos* (or *familia*) and the modern ideas of a household or home. First, whereas a modern idea of a household typically refers to a two-generational nuclear kinship family—that is, parent(s) with child(ren)—such a definition limited to biological kinship ties was not evident in the first-century understanding of household: "Neither in Greek nor in Latin is there a term for our word 'family' in the meaning of 'husband and wife with one or more children' (i.e. 'the nuclear family')."[26] Rather, the first-century idea of an *oikos* had a kinship family at its core (husband, wife, and children) but the prototypical *oikos* was comprised of many different kinship family groups, including slaves and servants and their kinship families.[27] Indeed, it was not unusual for an *oikos* to have one hundred or more members.[28] Moreover, not unlike today's large corporations, the first-century idea of an *oikos* could include tens or even hundreds of thousands of people. For example, the Roman emperor was sometimes depicted as the master of an *oikos* that encompassed the entire empire.[29] Along the same lines

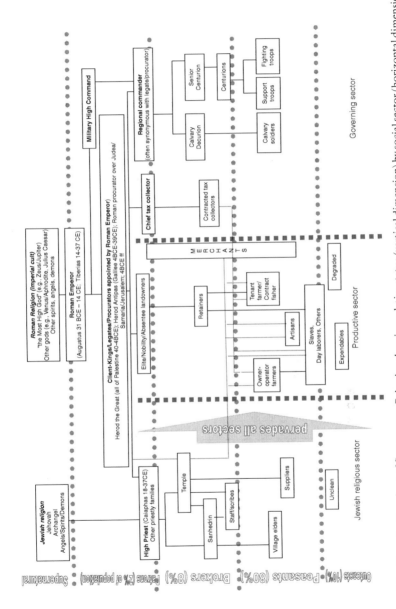

Figure 3.1 Organization chart of first-century Palestine showing relative status (vertical dimension) by social sector (horizontal dimension) (Dyck, Starke & Weimer [2012]).

Luke talks about Israel as the "house [*oikos*] of Jacob" (1:33), about the "house of David" (1:27, 1:69, 2:4), and about Jerusalem as a "house" (13:35).

Second, whereas the modern idea of a household considers it to be mainly a unit of *consumption* (i.e., members meet the needs of the household by being employed outside of it), in ancient times the *oikos* was both a consuming *and* a producing unit. In fact, *the oikos was the primary productive organization in ancient society.*[30] The great majority of *oikoi* were in the agricultural sector, but they were also prevalent in fishing, pottery, carpentry, and other industries. Today's households, because they are neither productive nor self-sustaining, would have been considered to be deficient by first-century standards.[31]

In light of this, rather than translate the biblical word *oikos* as "household," it would be much more helpful and accurate to translate it as a "goods and services producing organization," or as an "enterprise," or as a "company."[32] This would remind modern readers that, in the biblical times, the term *oikos* can be made up of many different kinship groups, and that it was the primary goods and services producing organization of the day. It might even be more helpful to translate *oikos* as a business rather than as "household," but that may be misleading if it prompts readers to assume that *oikoi* were seeking to maximize their financial wealth. While there likely were profit-maximizing *oikoi* in the first century, these would not have been living up to the classic understanding of *oikos* in the ancient world, which deemed an *oikos*'s physical outputs (e.g., its products and services) as secondary to its role in sustainably contributing to the moral fabric of the larger society. The *oikos*

> was much more than a business enterprise. The driving force of the *oikos* economy was not profit in the modern sense of the term. The *oikos* was a moral and religious entity in its own right whose purpose was not just the generation of legally recognizable citizens, but the proper formation of morally acceptable members of the particular *polis* community where it was located, and the passing on of the household's religious cults to future generations. Material resources were intended primarily to sustain this enterprise; they were to be held in trust for the next generation. In that sense, even the property of the *oikos* was not purely private.[33]

Given that the *oikos* is the most prevalent and important organizational unit in ancient times, it should come as no surprise that *oikos* plays a prominent role in the biblical text.[34] In particular, the term *oikos* is found 57 times in Luke.[35] In addition, Luke alludes to first-century *oikoi* on at least 64 other occasions[36] without specifically using the term *oikos* (e.g., a Samaritan brings a wounded traveler to an *innkeeper*, a *gardener* is planting mustard seeds in his vegetable garden, a baker is using yeast in her *bakery*, Jesus reveals himself in an *oikos* in Emmaus). In total, about 53 distinct first-century *oikoi* with identifiable goods and services are mentioned in Luke.[37]

Despite being so numerous in the text, there are several reasons why modern readers may be "blind" to the importance of *oikoi,* and to management more generally, in Luke. First, because the word *oikos* is typically translated as "house," contemporary readers are not likely to see that it refers to the dominant goods and services producing organizations of the day. Second, modern readers have been taught to read the scriptures as though there is a separation between the sacred versus the everyday, thus forgetting that in the first century the two were intertwined and could not be separated. And third, contemporary readers typically have little understanding of the scope, complexity and managerial challenges and competencies evident in first-century Palestine. For example, consider the skills required to manage the temple in Jerusalem, which was the largest sacred precinct in the whole Roman Empire and one of the wonders of the world. During festivals like Pentecost or Passover, Jerusalem's population of about thirty-two thousand (around 30 C.E.) would swell to one hundred and fifty thousand people or more. The temple was managed by the high priest and other high priestly families, who together controlled its ritualistic, administrative, and economic activities. Managing the *ritualistic* activities included overseeing the raising and sacrificing of thousands of animals each year, and up to fifteen hundred priests for weekly services. Managing the *administrative* activities included overseeing a police force that was basically like a private army. And managing the *economic* activities included collecting the temple tax and purchasing and storing temple provisions. The large staff that carried out these duties included two overseers, seven accountants, three treasurers plus additional staff responsible for special treasuries (e.g., bird offerings, libations, clothing for priests), and scribes and moneychangers.[38]

Understanding *oikos* in its first-century context, and putting it in the foreground rather than seeing it as background noise, provides a new lens for interpreting Luke. Perhaps the *oikos* serves as the primary setting for practicing and exemplifying the teachings of Jesus in Luke, just as Aristotle recognized the *oikos* as a primary unit of analysis for embodying the virtues.[39]

> The household [*oikos*] or family provided the early Jesus-group members with one of their basic images of social identity and cohesion. It is important, therefore, to understand what family meant to ancient people. In the Mediterranean world of the antiquity the extended family meant everything. It was the only sources of one's status in the community, but also functioned as the primary economic, religious, educational, and social network. Loss of connection to the family meant loss of these vital networks as well as any connection to the land. Loss of family was the most serious loss one could sustain. Yet a surrogate family, what anthropologists call a fictive kin group, could serve the same function as a family of biological origin. *Jesus groups, acting as surrogate families, are the locus of the good news for all the Gospel writers.*[40]

Of particular concern in Luke are people who do not belong to a conventional *oikos*; such people comprised 10 percent or more of the population.[41] This included strangers or foreigners (*paroikia* = homeless) and those who were considered impure or unwelcome and therefore "denied access to the *oikos*, to livelihood, to the family of Israel's God." These social outcasts could be divided into four main groupings:

> (1) the destitute poor, (2) the sick and crippled, and (3) tax collectors, sinners, and prostitutes [and (4) foreigners/strangers (*paroikos*)] . . . Jesus causes the greatest offense by offering home to the marginal people, the homeless and sinners, and by offering good news to the poor and exploited . . . *Early Christian movements radically transformed the Greco-Roman concept of* oikos. *Because the political and social reality of the Greco-Roman world was largely conceived and based upon the* oikos, *the Christian revision of the* oikos *had vast implications for the whole of social and personal life in antiquity.*[42]

The distinctly Christian *oikos* was an important part of the identity and expression of the Christian faith in the early church:

> Households thus constituted the focus, locus and nucleus of ministry and mission of the Christian movement . . . It is thus evident that the households are a dominant influence not only on the structure and internal conduct of the early Christian groups but also

upon their theological perspectives and socioreligious symbols . . . *For the Christian, in other words, the* oikos *constitutes not simply an additional form of social identity and religious adherence alongside others such as the temple, the synagogue or the city. The Christian* oikos *is rather a decisive alternative according to Luke.* Membership in the former involves constant conflict with and critique of the latter . . . All this makes it abundantly clear that the significance of the household and the family for the mission, growth, organization and self-understanding of the Christian movement can hardly be overestimated. In the focus upon the household and the community as *oikos* of God we have a striking example of the correlation of social reality and theological reflection, of theory and praxis.[43]

SUMMARY

In sum, the role of managers, who represented about 8 percent of the population, was growing and becoming increasingly important in first-century Palestine. The rich were getting richer, and they used managers to rule over their expanding *oikoi*. At the same time, the poor were getting poorer, and 10 percent or more of the population did not belong to an *oikos* and thus were living without the safety net it provided. The *oikos* was the primary goods and services producing organization in the first century, and it plays a prominent role in the Gospel of Luke, which refers or alludes to more than 50 distinct *oikos* organizations and the goods and services that they provide. The next chapter will describe the three main management roles in first-century Palestine's goods and services producing organizations.

II

Problem Recognition: How Interpreting Luke via a First-Century Management Lens Challenges the Conventional Interpretation of Two Key Management Parables

Part one described how, ever since Max Weber wrote his book *The Protestant Ethic and the Spirit of Capitalism*, there has been wide agreement among scholars and philosophers that modern management theory and practice is based on a Protestant ethic. Even so, there is also increasing agreement among many scholars that modern management is not based on a first-century Judeo-Christian ethic. The previous chapter demonstrated that managers were becoming increasingly numerous and prominent in the first century, and that the *oikos* was the primary goods and services producing organization of the day.

Part two introduces a first-century understanding of management, and then uses this as a lens to interpret two key management parables in the Gospel of Luke. It turns out that both these interpretations challenge first-century (as well as twenty-first-century) conventional management theory and practice.[1] Part two has three chapters. The first chapter describes the three main elements of management as understood in first-century Palestine. These are related to

1. managing relationships *within* organizations (radical versus conventional *oikonomia*);
2. managing money (natural versus unnatural *chrematistics*); and
3. managing relationships *between* organizations (benefaction versus patron-client relations).

The chapter will review some of the history of these ideas, and also describe the "state of the art" management in the first century.

The second and third chapters in part two use this first-century understanding of management to interpret what are perhaps the two most important *parables* on management attributed to Jesus. Parables are short stories with an underlying theological message. In general Jesus' parables, because of their emphasis on applying values to everyday life, have proven especially useful for understanding implications of biblical teachings to the practice of management.[2] Parables help to put flesh and bones on teachings. As metaphors of what Godly living looks like on the ground, parables can "become the vehicle through which paradigms become actualized in the mind of the theorist."[3] The collection of parables found in Luke are known as the most vivid and memorable in the Bible "because they present us with realistic and often conflicted characters of questionable moral fiber and display unusual attention to detail in a genre elsewhere known for its economy of description and stock characters, setting, and motifs."[4] As we shall see throughout the book, it seems that the further one gets from the first century, the less likely it is that the parables are interpreted in the same way they would have been by their initial audiences.[5]

The first parable, examined in chapter five, has been called "The Parable of the Shrewd Manager" (Luke 16:1–15). This is a key passage because it contains five of the total of eight mentions of the word "manager" or "management" in all four Gospels. Yet despite the obvious importance of this passage to the topic at hand, scholars and popular writers alike have been hesitant to refer to it for reasons that will become self-evident when we look at the passage more closely. The second parable, examined in chapter six, has been called "The Parable of the Ten Pounds" (Luke 19:11–27). This parable, together with its more popular variation "The Parable of the Talents" (found in Matt. 25:14–30), is considered to be the "poster child" of Gospel teachings on management.

Consistent with scholars who suggest that a first-century Judeo-Christian ethic is very different from the moral point of view that underpins modern management theory and practice, our preliminary analysis will show that a first-century interpretation of these two exemplary management parables is quite different from conventional twenty-first-century interpretations. Moreover, the first-century interpretations seem to challenge rather than to support contemporary management theory and practice. These preliminary findings point to the need for a much more rigorous and comprehensive analysis of the Gospel of Luke, in order to examine whether this countercultural first-century interpretation of the parables is consistent with the rest of the Gospel. This will be the focus of part three.

Before we can interpret any passage in Luke through a first-century understanding of management, we need to first develop a first-century understanding of management. That is the focus of chapter four.

4

A THREE-DIMENSIONAL FIRST-CENTURY
LENS FOR UNDERSTANDING MANAGEMENT

While it is helpful to know that managers were becoming increasingly important and prevalent in the first century, and that the *oikos* represents the primary goods and services producing organization of the day, this does not yet tell us what management theory and practice looked like in the first century. For that we need to look at what was being written about management in that day, and what were the main debates about management.

At that time management was seen to have three basic dimensions, and writing (and debating) about these dimensions dates back at least as far as Aristotle. This chapter will review key issues related to each of these three dimensions, in the following order:

1. Managing relationships *within* organizations (radical versus conventional *oikonomia*);
2. Managing money (natural versus unnatural *chrematistics*); and
3. Managing relationships *between* organizations (benefaction versus patron-client relations).

MANAGING RELATIONSHIPS *WITHIN* ORGANIZATIONS (*OIKONOMIA*)

Initially the role of *oikonomia* ("management") was played by the head of the *oikos*. For a smaller *oikos*, the householder would still be its only manager, but already by the second century BCE it was quite commonplace for the landed elite to delegate the management of their *oikos* to others.[1] Usually these appointed managers were slaves in the *oikos*. Such managers had a lot of power, and the actions of the manager were often treated as if they were the actions of the householder. For example, managers who were irresponsible or incompetent with the possessions of their *oikos* were not only embarrassing themselves, they were also embarrassing the head of their *oikos* and all its other members.[2]

Aristotle (384–322 BCE) wrote what arguably remains the most profound analysis of *oikonomia* among ancient writers.[3] Regardless of who the manager was, attention needed to be paid to three basic relationships within an *oikos*. The three relationships Aristotle identified were husband-wife, parent-children, and master-slaves (and/or freemen).[4] We will look at each in turn.

Husband-Wife Relationships

According to Aristotle, the relationship between a husband and wife was "constitutional" in nature. In principle this meant the two were equal. However, usually the husband ruled the wife: "For although there may be exceptions to the order of nature, the male is by nature fitter for command than the female, just as the elder and full-grown is superior to the younger and more immature."[5]

In practice, wives were usually in charge of within-*oikos* religious life and the children's early education, with husbands taking responsibility for socializing sons at about six or seven years of age.[6] The wives' supervisory roles in this regard never stopped, and they performed their socializing/educative function without much assistance from a formal public school system. "Males were socialized to procreate, to be courageous, obedient, protective, and eager to increase the family's reputation or wealth. Females, on the other hand, were virtuous if they remained sexually exclusive, submissive to their fathers and then their husbands, defensive of their own and their families reputation."[7]

The husbands' role was to manage most of the other aspects of the *oikos*, including its slaves/servants and financial affairs. The male head of the *oikos* is its master (*kurios*) and as such ultimately responsible for everything within it, including the behavior of his wife. "Socrates suggests that a husband will be judged by the behavior of his wife, in the same way that 'when a sheep is ailing, we generally blame the shepherd.'"[8]

Parent-Child Relationships

Second, there was a "royal" relationship between parents and children, with parents ruling "by virtue both of love and of the respect due to age."[9] In this model, children are viewed as sort of "junior parents" or as "*oikos*-masters-in-waiting."

The Romans invested a great deal of time and effort in schooling children to understand, value, and honor their *oikos*.[10] In part this is because a person's identity was directly linked to the *oikos* to which they belonged, not to any personal traits of the person. In first-century Palestine the "most elementary unit of social analysis is not the individual person" but rather it is "a person in relation with and connected to at least one other social unit, in particular, the family. People in this cultural area might be said to share 'an undifferentiated family ego mass.'"[11] In short, the parents were raising their children to become honorable members of the *oikos*. And for the Romans being honorable meant protecting and seeking to improve the interests of their *oikos*.

Master-Slave Relationships

According to Aristotle, the relationship between master and slave was in part like the relationship between a master and his possessions. Aristotle's description of a slave as being *a possession with a soul* is the closest thing there is to a legal definition of slaves in Greek sources.[12] He suggests that slaves have virtually no deliberative capacity, and that it is best if slaves are under the rule of a master.[13] Aristotle says that slaves have the capacity to reason and to form moral concepts, but slaves can only *perceive* reason (i.e., "to follow directions that originate in reason") and cannot initiate a line of reasoning themselves.[14] He also argues that slaves are by nature lazy, and if treated harshly they will seek to undermine their masters.[15]

Aristotle describes how the *oikos* is explicitly managed to serve the interests of the wife and children, but adds that this also usually happens to serve the interests of the slave. On the whole, Aristotle argues that being and keeping slaves is part of the moral order, in particular where "nature intended" one to be a master and the other a slave (e.g., some people simply do not have the nature to lead an *oikos*). Aristotle also suggests that a slave is more than merely a possession and that a slave should also be seen as "part of the master," which means that abuse of authority by the master over the slave "is injurious to both." He concludes that "where the relation of master and slave between them is natural they are friends and have a common interest, but where it rests merely on law and force the reverse is true."[16]

From a twenty-first-century perspective it is almost incomprehensible that in the first century slavery per se was not considered morally repugnant—instead, slavery was simply considered to be part of everyday life, just as being married and having children were. A partial explanation is that, because a slave was the permanent property of the householder, slaves could enjoy a more secure lifestyle than their "free" compatriots: "The freer the peasant, in the political sense, the more precarious his position."[17] Thus, societal members who did not belong to an *oikos*, for whatever reason, lacked a social and financial "security net" in difficult times.

MANAGING MONEY (NATURAL VERSUS UNNATURAL *CHREMATISTICS*)

Aristotle recognized that money management (*chrematistics*) was an important *sub*-role in *oikos* management. *Chrematistics* "ensures a supply of objects, necessary for life and useful to the association of the *polis* or the household."[18]

To begin, note that Aristotle welcomed the advent of money insofar as it provided a more convenient way to trade goods compared to its forerunner, bartering. This proper use of money he called "natural *chrematistics*." For example, imagine Person A brings potatoes to the market hoping to trade them for some shoes, and Person B at the market has shoes but does not need potatoes (but does want an oxen). Aristotle noted that money could facilitate this kind of exchange because money provides a universal yardstick to measure and evaluate diverse goods and services. Money meant that Person A could sell potatoes to Person C, and use the proceeds from that sale to purchase shoes from Person B, who in turn could save money to buy an oxen from Person D.

Although Aristotle recognized how money provided a valuable *means* to facilitate *oikos* management ("natural *chrematistics*"), he was also careful to point to the danger if financial management became the *ends* of *oikos* management ("unnatural *chrematistics*"). In particular, he was the first to draw the distinction between "use value" and the "exchange value" of money. The term "use value" refers to money when it is used as a *means* to meet the more holistic goals of the *oikos*, which thereby facilitates creating "true wealth." In contrast, the term "exchange value" describes situations where money itself is treated as a useful commodity to make more money.

The "use value" of money—natural *chrematistics*—is sometimes depicted as C-M-C (commodity-money-commodity), which means that someone sells a commodity to get money, which they then use to purchase a different commodity. This was illustrated when Person A sold potatoes for money, and then used that money to buy shoes. This process has a natural "end" when everyone has finished trading their good or services. In contrast, the "exchange value" of money—unnatural *chrematistics*—is depicted as M-C-M (money-commodity-money), which means that someone uses money to buy a commodity with the hopes that they can sell it for more money to make a profit. For example, M-C-M is illustrated by Person E who buys potatoes for $X with the hopes of selling them for $X+2 and thereby make a profit. While the action of buying and selling may appear to be identical in C-M-C as in M-C-M (e.g., potatoes are sold), the purposes of the transaction are very different. Within the "exchange value" view money becomes an end in itself—while this may in fact increase monetary profits at an abstract level ("spurious wealth"), it does not do anything to increase the amount of tangible goods and services being produced (and it has no terminus, or sense of having enough).[19]

Aristotle argued "natural *chrematistics*" to be a "necessary and honorable" component of *oikos* management in order to truly "live well." However, for Aristotle "unnatural *chrematistics*" undermined the holistic values of *oikos* management and the larger society:

> Hence some persons are led to believe that getting wealth is the object of household management, and the whole idea of their lives is that they ought either to increase their money without limit, or at any rate not to lose it. The origin of this disposition in men [*sic?*] is that they are intent upon *living only*, and not upon *living well*; and, as their desires are unlimited they also desire that the means of gratifying them should be without limit.[20]

Thus, Aristotle states that there are "two sorts of wealth-getting." The first is the natural, "necessary and honorable" use of money as one dimension of *oikos* management (C-M-C; natural *chrematistics*). The second is the unnatural use of money to make more money ("which makes a gain out of money itself"; M-C-M; unnatural *chrematistics*): "For money was intended to be used in exchange, but not to increase at interest."[21] "Aristotle argued that it was possible to have too little money ('a penurious standard of living') or too much ('luxurious one'), and thought that the ideal distribution of wealth was one 'in which every citizen has enough for virtue and happiness, and none have more.'"[22]

Karl Polanyi suggests that Aristotle's distinction with regards to the different ways to manage money "was probably the most prophetic pointer ever made in the realm of the social sciences" and "certainly still the best analysis of the subject we possess."[23] Taken together, these two approaches to *chrematistics* point to two distinct approaches to economics or *oikonomia*.

1. *Acquisitive economics,* associated with an emphasis on "unnatural *chrematistics*," "refers to managing property and wealth in such a way as to maximize the short-term monetary value for owners. Modern economic theory has refined this basic notion and explicitly adds the assumption that all economic entities are self-interested and are prone to lie, steal, cheat and give out bad information in a calculated effort to mislead or confuse partners in an exchange."[24]
2. *Sustenance economics,* associated with an emphasis on "natural *chrematistics*," "refers to managing property and wealth to increase the long-term overall well-being for owners, members and other stakeholders. Sustenance economics emphasizes community-oriented values, long-term multi-generational concerns, and stewardship. It speaks to issues of quality of life that cannot be meaningfully expressed or reduced to quantifiable measures like financial wealth, income or goods consumed."[25]

To be clear, acquisitive economics were already very apparent in Aristotle's day. For example, Xenophon (430–354 BCE) argued that "making large profits" was the "chief objective" of *oikonomia*.[26] Moreover, Aristotle was fully aware of how acquisitive economics could be used to generate wealth. He opposed acquisitive economics and lived according to sustenance economic principles because he believed this was the right thing to do. Even so, sometimes people like Aristotle felt pressure to demonstrate that they could achieve acquisitive economic success if they wanted to. Aristotle provides several examples, including the following anecdote of Thales the Milesian, which describes what he did when his critics said that his financial poverty proved that his sustenance economic philosophy was useless. Thales, because of his skills forecasting the weather, knew while it was still winter that there would be a great harvest of olives that year. He thus made a deposit to use all of the olive presses in that region during the harvest, which he could do at a low price because no one bid against him. Of course, when harvest time came the demand for olive presses was very high, and having a monopoly he could charge a high price for their use. As Aristotle notes, the method Thale used "for getting wealth is of universal application, and is nothing but the creation of a monopoly." Thales was more interested in truly "living well" than in using his abilities toward the acquisitive economic generation of wealth, thus pointing to a higher ambition.[27]

Aristotle's concepts provided the foundation for subsequent thinking about money-management and had been elaborated upon by the first century. By then his counsel against managers participating in acquisitive economics held little sway, and acquisitive economics had become the norm among the rich.[28] Other thinkers and writers increasingly considered moneymaking (acquisitive economics) to be the "most important" part of *oikonomia*.[29] The elite were becoming evermore interested in increasing their wealth and in conspicuous consumption. Moreover, the management practices associated with acquisitive economic principles were clearly taking a toll on the relatively poor in first-century Palestine. At that time, the economy was basically understood to be a "zero-sum proposition." In other words, for some people to get richer, others would have to get poorer.[30] The only ways for the rich elite to acquire more wealth was via

1. expanding the size of their landholdings (whether that be the size of the territory ruled by the empire as a whole, or the size of estates of absentee landholders within the empire);
2. increasing the amount of goods taken from the poor (e.g., higher taxes); and/or
3. manipulating supply and demand.

All three of these mechanisms had a negative effective on the livelihoods of most people.[31]

Managing Relationships *between* Organizations (Benefaction versus Patron-Client)

In the first century, patron-client relationships were the dominant way to manage relationships between organizations.[32] In a nutshell, patron-client relationships helped to establish and sustain the "pecking order" between organizations in first-century Palestine. Patron-client practices were the means by which relatively elite *oikoi* (i.e., patrons) gained power over the relatively weak (i.e., clients). A patron-client relationship could be established by something as simple as borrowing money, where the party providing the money would become a patron and the party receiving it would become the client.[33] A patron could offer a client a wide variety of benefits, such as a loan, protection against enemies, support in legal cases, food, and political appointments.[34] Clients responded by giving honor (which was often considered to be more valuable than financial wealth), information, political support, loyalty, and tributes to their patrons.

Four characteristics of patron-client relationships are especially noteworthy. First, managers were duty-bound to create and maintain clients for their *oikos* whenever possible, to bring honor to their *oikos* by "seeking endlessly to take it away from others."[35] Under the Roman idea of patronage, if anyone of a higher social status provided a benefit to a party of a lower social status, the party of higher status had a duty to ensure that the party of lower status would become an indebted client. This duty to look after the interests of their *oikos* was deeply engrained, and was often expressed in terms of bringing "honor" to the *oikos*.

> Classicists consider "honor" to be the most important value in the ancient world...All ancient people were socialized to depend on what others thought of them as their source of worth and identity. Children were taught that family and friends were always evaluating them and expecting them to do what they could to bring honor to their families [i.e., to their *oikos*].[36]

By the first century it was not unusual for honor to be closely related to wealth, and shame to be closely related to loss of wealth. "Wealth and honor are not individual possessions, but rather are the property of the family or kinship group [i.e., *oikos*]."[37] To honor one's *oikos* included maintaining, and when possible enhancing, its wealth.

Second, patron-client relationships were long term. These were not one-time interactions, and thus defy easy explanation for modern Western ideas of contracts and transactional economics. In ancient societies patron-client reciprocal exchanges signaled voluntary, ongoing relationships (versus single transactions) between two parties of unequal status.[38] Moreover, patron-client relationships often became hereditary across generations among *oikoi*, and clients who defrauded their patron faced severe punishment.

Third, although in theory patron-client relationships were supposed to be mutually beneficial for both clients and patrons, in practice the unequal status of the parties often led to exploitation of the poor by the rich.[39] Patrons lorded it over clients, and clients were indebted to patrons. It is also true that patrons had responsibilities to look out for and protect clients, but for the most part the relationship was of greater benefit to the patron than to the client. "Patronage was a ubiquitous social framework in the ancient Mediterranean basin. Patrons were people with power who could provide goods and services to their clients. In return, clients provided loyalty and honor to the patrons. Social inequality characterized these patronal relationships, and exploitation was a common feature of such relationships."[40]

Fourth, patron-client relationships were evident at all societal levels. The relationship between an emperor (i.e., the patron) and the kings in various provinces (i.e., the clients) is often used to illustrate the key elements of the patron-client relationship. The emperor was the most powerful patron in the Roman Empire, controlling all political and military appointments in the empire. Regional "client-kings" appointed by the emperor played an important role in managing the empire's military and its financial and religious bureaucracies. These client-kings, who governed specific geographical areas, pledged allegiance and paid tribute to the emperor. The client-king position was often hereditary (i.e., based on *oikos*, but subject to Roman approval), and typically included substantial military and financial resources.[41] Client-kings were responsible to build and to maintain the infrastructure in their domain, and often paid homage to the emperors by constructing various public works and temples to honor Roman gods.

Of special relevance for the present study is the idea of "brokerage" inherent in patron-client relationship, especially once the patron-client relationship goes beyond two hierarchical levels. In this way, for example, King Herod could be seen as a client of the emperor *and* as a patron to municipal appointees, or he could be seen as a *broker* between the emperor and municipal leaders in Palestine. Such "brokers" can in some ways be seen as forerunners to modern middle-managers, as sort of a go-between between people of higher status and lower status. Brokers had responsibilities to manage resources to serve the interests of their patrons, while at the same time keeping their clients motivated and not rebellious.[42]

Patron-client dynamics were not limited to the upper societal echelons; they were also evident in relationships in lower parts of the social hierarchy, such as in villages.[43] Here patrons provided first-order resources like land and jobs, and their managers dispensed second-order resources like access to patrons and other strategic contacts. For example, absentee landowners (patrons) provided the managers of their far-flung estates with a good salary, a residence, political connections, and military protection. The landowners trusted their managers to make important decisions on behalf of their *oikos*. Managers reciprocated by running the estates and by making financial decisions that were in the best interest of the landowners while trying to keep slaves and peasants satisfied.[44]

A classic Greek understanding benefaction stood in stark contrast to the Roman norm of patron-client relationships. Even though the language of "patron" and "benefactor" are often used interchangeably in the first century—for example, the Greeks called the Roman emperor their "benefactor"[45]—there are significant differences between how Aristotle understood benefactors versus how patrons were understood in the first century. Unlike patrons, benefactors are not largely motivated by financial self-interests, nor are they seeking to create clients who are subservient to them. Rather, benefactors provide resources to others because it is good for the larger community.[46] According to an Aristotelian understanding, a benefactor is someone who provides benefits without expecting to receive honor in return (though, according to Aristotle, the benefactor should gladly receive honor if it comes, and the value of this honor outweighs the loss of financial wealth[47]). Classic benefaction places high value on fostering social (versus merely instrumental) relationships within society. Benefactors "who have done a service to others feel friendship and love for those they have served even if these are not of any [instrumental or financial] use to them and never will be"; in contrast patrons who create clients "have no friendly feeling to their debtors, but only a wish that they may be kept safe with a view to what is to be got from them."[48] Seneca (4 BCE–65 C.E.) adds that the true benefactor gives without concern for repayment, just as the ideal beneficiary both receives and returns benefits willingly.[49]

The four key characteristics associated with patron-client relationships are useful for highlighting important differences between a patron-client approach versus classic benefaction (elaborating on Aristotle's ideas).

1. In a patron-client approach managers have a duty to enhance the status of their *oikos*; in contrast, with classic benefaction managers have a duty to enhance the well-being of society (*polis*).

2. In a patron-client approach transactions outside of one's *oikos* are expected to create and sustain ongoing patron-client relationships; in contrast, with classic benefaction transactions foster friendships and mutuality across society.

3. In a patron-client approach relationships tend to benefit patrons more than clients in the long term (though in theory they are of equal benefit to clients); in contrast, with classic benefaction relationships work primarily to benefit the recipients of benefaction (though they can also provide honor and status for the benefactor).

4. Both patron-client and classic benefaction relationships can be found at all levels in society.

SUMMARY

First-century management theory placed attention on three dimensions of managing, and within each dimension there was some debate about the "best way to manage." Table 4.1 illustrates the debates between two different approaches to each dimension: the conventional approach that served as the dominant paradigm in the first century versus a radical approach. In the first century, this debate was developed more clearly for the dimensions of managing money (sustenance versus acquisitive economics) and for managing relationships between organizations (classic benefaction versus patron-client relations) than for the dimension of managing relationships within organizations. Even so, as highlighted in table 4.1, a radical alternative for managing relationships *within* organizations can also be easily conceived: wives could be treated as equals, adult children could be encouraged to start their own *oikos*, and slaves could be seen as full persons worthy of being treated with dignity.

The next two chapters will use this three-dimensional first-century understanding of management to interpret two key passages in the Gospel of Luke where managers play a dominant role, namely, the Parable of the Shrewd Manager (chapter five) and the Parable of the Ten Pounds (chapter six). As we will see, these interpretations

Table 4.1 Conventional and radical approaches to first-century management theory and practice

Three dimensions of management	Conventional first-century approach	Radical alternative approach
1. Managing relationships *within* organizations —husband/wife —parent/child —master/slave	—Husbands rule over wives —Adult children duty-bound to honor parental *oikos* —Slaves as possessions incapable of moral reasoning	—Husband and wife equals —Adult children encouraged to create new/alternative *oikoi* —Slaves as role models, full persons and worthy of being treated with dignity
2. Managing money	Acquisitive economics (use money to make money; maximize financial gain)	Sustenance economics (use money as medium to facilitate the transfer of everyday goods and services)
3. Managing relationships *between* organizations	Patron-client relationships (honorable managers are duty-bound to gain power over other *oikoi* whenever possible)	Benefaction (honorable managers seek community-nurturing ways to reduce the gap between the rich and the poor whenever practical)

suggest that Luke is more supportive of a radical than a conventional approach to management.

Reflection Point: Comparing Contemporary Research and the Three-Dimensional First-Century Understanding of Management

Are first-century ideas and debates about management still relevant today? It turns out that the academic disciplines and departmental structures found in most modern business schools are surprisingly consistent with the three main first-century dimensions of management. To be sure these three dimensions have been elaborated and fine-tuned. First, in terms of managing relationships *within* organizations, contemporary business schools focus on human resource management, organizational behavior and leadership, and production and operations. Second, in terms of managing money, today's business schools focus on accounting, finance, and economics. And third, in terms of managing relationships *between* organizations, business schools focus on strategy, marketing, and supply chain management. It also turns out that although today's dominant paradigm is clearly grounded in acquisitive economics, there is ongoing and growing interest in management theory and practice grounded in sustenance economics, glimpses of which can be found in areas such as corporate social responsibility, stakeholder theory, and the triple-bottom line.[50]

5

Interpreting Luke's Parable
of the Shrewd Manager via a
First-Century Lens

The parable of the shrewd manager and the parable of the ten pounds examined in the next chapter are of particular interest for this study because each has a manager at the center of the action, and also because each contains aspects of the three dimensions of management: (1) managing relationships within an *oikos*[1]; (2) managing money; and (3) managing relationships between *oikoi*. In sum, these two parables seem to provide a particularly relevant opportunity to see whether a first-century lens provides new interpretive insights not evident via conventional twenty-first-century interpretations.

On the face of it, the parable of the shrewd manager (Luke 16:1–15) should be the most well-known parable for developing a biblical understanding of management. It is the only parable in the New Testament that has an explicit *oikonomos* ("*oikos* manager") as a central character. Nevertheless, this parable is rarely discussed by scholars who attempt to apply biblical passages to management theory and practice. For example, this parable is not among the more than fifteen hundred biblical passages cited in the first ten years of *The Journal of Biblical Integration in Business*. This oversight may be because this has been described as one of the "most difficult," and "puzzling," of Jesus' parables to understand via a modern lens.[2]

The parable seems to affirm unethical and unprofessional management conduct. The parable describes how a manager goes behind the back of his master and lowers the amount of money that clients owe his master. And yet this same manager is then praised by his master and, so it seems, by Jesus. The parable and its elaboration are presented in table 5.1, which also provides an overview of a twenty-first- and a first-century interpretation of this passage.

A Brief Twenty-First-Century Interpretation
of the Parable of the Shrewd Manager

This parable is challenging to interpret from a twenty-first-century perspective because the manager in it violates fundamental assumptions about what is generally deemed to be responsible management behavior. We moderns assume that managers have a duty to enhance—or, at worst, to maintain—the financial well-being of their enterprise.[3] Thus, any actions by a manager that deliberately undermine the financial wealth of their employer are considered to be criminal, wasteful, dishonest, and unrighteous. So when the manager in the parable acts in such a way, we would expect the moral at the end of parable to be along the lines of: "White collar criminals get sent to prison." Instead, in the parable the manager is commended because he acted shrewdly.

Table 5.1 Two interpretations of the parable of the shrewd manager

I. Body of parable (Luke 16: 1–8a)	A common twenty-first-century interpretation.	An interpretation via a first-century lens.
1. *Manager is accused*: Then Jesus said to the disciples, "There was a rich man who had a manager [*oikonomos*], and charges were brought to him [*diaballo*] that this man was squandering [*diaskorpizon*] his property."	A manager is accused of negligence, of wasting his master's money.	A manager purposefully disperses some of his master's resources.
2. *Master's first response*: So he summoned him and said to him, "What is this that I hear about you? Give me an accounting of your management [*oikonomis*], because you cannot be my manager [*oikonomein*] any longer."	The outraged master fires the manager and holds him accountable.	The master strips the manager of his title and asks for an accounting.
3. *Manager's response*: Then the manager [*oikonomos*] said to himself, "What will I do, now that my master is taking the position away from me? I am not strong enough to dig, and I am ashamed to beg. I have decided what to do so that, when I am dismissed as manager [*oikonomos*], people may welcome me into their homes [*oikous*]." So, summoning his master's debtors one by one, he asked the first, "How much do you owe my master?" He answered, "A hundred jugs of olive oil." He said to him, "Take your bill, sit down quickly, and make it fifty." Then he asked another, "And how much do you owe?" He replied, "A hundred containers of wheat." He said to him, "Take your bill and make it eighty."	After performing an instrumental cost-benefit analysis of his options, the manager decides that it is in his financial self-interest to reduce the debt that clients owe to his master (in doing so, the manager hopes to ingratiate himself with the clients).	After engaging in some soul-searching, the manager notes his personal financial poverty, and decides to continue to purposefully scatter the master's resources (thereby the manager cements his radical reputation and brings honor to the master).
4. *Master's second response*: And his master commended the dishonest manager [*oikonomos tes adikia*] because he had acted shrewdly.	The master admires the manager for outwitting him.	The master admires the manager for bringing him honor.

II. Meaning of parable explained (Luke 16: 8b-15)

1. *Jesus' lesson*: For the children of this age are more shrewd in dealing with their own generation than are the children of light. And I tell you, make friends for yourselves by means of dishonest wealth [*mamona tes adikias*] so that when it is gone, they may welcome you into the eternal homes [literally, Tabernacle]. "Whoever is faithful in a very little is faithful also in much; and whoever is dishonest [*adikos*] in a very little is dishonest [*adikos*] also in much. If then you have not been faithful with the dishonest wealth [*adikos mamona*], who will entrust to you the true riches? And if you have not been faithful with what belongs to another, who will give you what is your own? No slave can serve two masters; for a slave will either hate the one and love the other, or be devoted to the one and despise the other. You cannot serve God and wealth."	Jesus' followers should be just as shrewd in managing God's *true* riches as the manager was in maximizing his financial self-interests. In part, this requires *not* wasting the property they are managing for others; it is by their prudent (conventional) financial management that they demonstrate that they are serving God rather than money.	If you can't be trusted to purposefully "scatter" to those who need the worldly wealth of a rich *oikos*, then who will trust you to properly manage God's true riches? It is in their "scattering" of resources that managers reveal who their *true* master is.
2. *Listeners' response*: The Pharisees, who were lovers of money, heard all this, and they ridiculed him.	Lovers of money confuse money with *true* riches.	This parable warns lovers of money.
3. *Jesus' response*: So he said to them, "You are those who justify yourselves in the sight of others; but God knows your hearts; for what is prized by human beings is an abomination in the sight of God."	Don't love money more than God (but it goes without saying, don't waste money).	Whereas society may prize acquisitive economics, God prefers benefaction.

From a conventional twenty-first-century perspective, the manager is clearly a villain. When he gets caught wasting the financial resources of his *oikos* he gets fired. But before he leaves his employer the manager adds insult to injury by committing a final illegal and selfish act: he lowers the amount that clients owe to the *oikos*.[4] Although this seems to reinforce his reputation as a dishonest manager, and hamper his ability to find future employment as a manager, he is hoping that his actions will allow him to sponge off the debtors whose loans he has reduced. In a sense, the manager can be seen as trying to position himself as sort of a patron to the master's clients.

What is difficult to understand at first is why this dishonest manager is commended by the master (and by Jesus). That puzzle is solved when the reader realizes that Jesus was obviously not commending the manager's *practice* of squandering his employer's wealth; rather, Jesus was simply approving the *idea* of the manager being shrewd for God.[5] The master's admiration can be explained because he realized that the crafty manager had bested him at his own game: by finding a loophole in the accounting system, the manager had maximized his financial self-interest.

The passage goes on to explain that Jesus' disciples should be trustworthy in how they manage money. It goes without saying that this will be unlike the manager in the parable. Anyone who is untrustworthy in managing someone else's money—even if that money is gained by dishonest means—will not be trusted to handle true riches. And people who aren't trustworthy in managing property belonging to others surely won't get property of their own. This is also consistent with the idea that it is impossible to serve both God and money. The inference is that people who serve God will not act selfishly with others' money. The passage ends with the observation that God knows people's hearts, and by implication whether people will be good managers of others' money.

In sum, a modern interpretation gets around what appears to be the most problematic part of the passage—namely, that the manager is praised for reducing the amounts of money that clients owed to the rich master—by arguing that it was not the act of wasting the master's resources that was admirable, but rather how the manager had been shrewd in playing the worldly economic game by its own rules. "Jesus used this story to suggest that Christians should be just as creative and clever in working in the world for kingdom values as this manager was in taking care of his own needs."[6]

AN INTERPRETATION OF THE PARABLE VIA
A FIRST-CENTURY MANAGEMENT LENS

The first key difference between a twenty-first-century versus a first-century interpretation of this passage revolves around how to translate the word *diaskorpizon* (literally, "to scatter in all directions") found in the very first verse of the parable (Luke 16:1). Most modern English Bibles translate the word as "wasting" or as "squandering."[7] This paints the picture of a meaningless throwing away of resources. In contrast, in other biblical passages the same word *diaskorpizon* is usually translated as meaningful and positive "scattering" (e.g., farmers scatter seeds in their garden).[8] In any case, there is no direct evidence in the parable that the manager was "misappropriating funds for selfish of immoral activities."[9] The interpretation of this parable changes a great deal if the accusation against the manager is translated as him "scattering"—instead of as "wasting"—his master's resources. The manager's behavior thus becomes more purposeful since the word *diaskorpizon* has the connotation of deliberate action (e.g., scattering seeds, benefaction) as opposed to wastefulness. Instead of careless wasting, the image is one of careful scattering.

If *diaskorpizon* is translated as "scattering," then the opening verses of the parable could be interpreted to say that the manager was accused of deliberately dispersing his master's money in a way that accusers found objectionable, hence their complaint to the master. The parable does not specify who the accusers are, but if we assume that they are accusing the manager of deliberately sharing resources to the benefit of the larger community, then perhaps the only people who would find this objectionable are acquisitive economic-minded rich landlords. If so, then the verse suggests that they were applying a form of peer pressure in order to have the sustenance-economics minded manager removed from the marketplace.

After being told that he will lose his job, the manager makes a plan to ensure that he will find employment in another *oikos*, because he can't see himself doing blue-collar work or depending on handouts or doing any other kind of job. So he wants to do something that will make it more likely that he will get to work as a manager in a different *oikos*. He decides to cement his reputation as a sustenance economics manager who brings honor to his employer, thus making it more likely to be hired as such a manager to work in another *oikos*. The manager's reduction of the clients' debts represents a continuation of his thoughtful scattering of his master's wealth, in a beneficent way that enhances community and thereby brings honor to his master.[10] Recall that such bringing of honor would have been valuable for the master because "in both Jewish and Greco-Roman societies of New Testament times, honor was just as important as wealth—if not more so—to a man's social status."[11] The master had priorities other than maximizing the financial return on his possessions. One of those priorities, to gain honor, could be met by deemphasizing conventional patron-client relationships and instead practicing benefaction:

> While some modern people see it as unbelievable that a rich man would praise an employee for giving away his money, almost every scholar who employs the [ancient] honor-shame paradigm would dispute this. Many sociologically oriented critics have pointed to the frequency with which the rich engaged in benefactions and the spectacular amounts often involved as proof of their claim that honor is more important than money.[12]

Thus, from a first-century perspective it is entirely reasonable that the rich owner would commend the manager for his shrewd handling of the *oikos* resources. The rich man recognized that the manager had marched to the beat of a nonconventional drum, and had used his surplus financial wealth to create honor for him.[13]

A first-century lens also helps to clarify what exactly it is that is being called "dishonest" (*adikias* = unrighteousness; *adiko/s* = unjust). Rather than see the manager as dishonest, the awkward phrasing—*oikonomon tes adikis* (Luke 16:8)—may suggest that it is the resources themselves that are being called dishonest, perhaps because they were accumulated via patron-client relationships and acquisitive economics.[14] This possibility is strengthened in light of another unusual phrasing—*mamona tes adikias* (literally, money of unrighteousness; Luke 16:9)—and together they may be pointing to some larger "unrighteousness" that both the manager and the money are part of. In particular, perhaps it is the conventional socioeconomic system itself that is being called unrighteous, a system based on acquisitive economics and patron-client relationships, a system that results in widening gaps between the rich and the poor, and a system that slanders managers who scatter resources for honorable goals such as friendship and the common good. Jesus goes on to ask, if managers can't be trusted to honorably share dishonest wealth (*adikos mamona*; Luke 16:11)—that is, if managers refuse to scatter "unjust wealth" that was acquired via patron-client relationships and acquisitive economics—then how can they be trusted to manage *true* riches?[15]

Additional support for this interpretation is evident when Jesus tells his listeners to follow the example of the shrewd manager—to challenge conventional *oikos* norms, to challenge acquisitive economics, and to practice benefaction—so that they may be welcomed into "eternal" homes by their newfound friends and fellow members of a sustainable economy (Luke 16:9). It is important to note that the phrase "eternal" homes refers neither to everlasting nor to endless dwellings, but rather it would be more accurate to think of them as a new "era" of socioeconomic structures and systems that are managed according to radical principles.[16]

This brings us to a crucial observation. A first-century interpretation suggests that Jesus was literally encouraging his listeners to follow the example of the shrewd manager and to redistribute worldly wealth in a sustenance economic beneficent way, that is, in a way that seems "unjust" (*adikos*) based on patron-client acquisitive assumptions.[17] This stands in stark contrast to a conventional twenty-first-century interpretation. Although we don't have access to first-century "commentaries" to help us understand how Luke 16 was actually interpreted in that time, we do have some writings from early leaders of the church. On this important point there is support for a literal interpretation of the parable from several sources. For example, Cyril of Alexandra (376–444) seemed to interpreted Jesus' teachings literally with regard to the manager scattering his master's wealth:

> Anyone may readily learn the meaning and view of the Savior's words from what follows. He said, "If you have not been faithful in what is another's, who will give you what is your own?" [Luke 16:12] We again say that what is another's is the wealth we possess. We were not born with riches, but on the contrary, naked. We can truly affirm the words of Scripture that "we neither brought anything into the world, nor can carry anything out." . . . *Let those of us who possess earthly wealth open our hearts to those who are in need.* Let us show ourselves faithful and obedient to the laws of God. Let us be followers of our Lord's will in those things that are from the outside and not our own. Let us do this so that we may receive what is our own, that holy and admirable beauty that God forms in people's souls, making them like himself, according to what we originally were.[18]

Additional support for the contention that Jesus literally wanted listeners to follow the example of the shrewd manager is also evident in the writing of John Chrysostom (394–407), another early leader in the church:

> What excuse will we have if we heedlessly lock our money behind closed doors and barricades, and we prefer to leave it lying idle? Instead, *we should make it available to the needy now,* so that in the future we may count on support from them. Remember that Scripture says, "Make friends with ill-gotten gains so that, when you go down in the world, they may welcome you into their eternal dwellings" [Luke 16:9].[19]

Finally, support for a literal interpretation of the parable can also be inferred from the writings of Augustine (354–430), which suggest that, rather than consider the actions of the shrewd manager to be fraudulent, it would have been fraudulent not to share the resources.[20]

In its conclusion, the passage suggests that no person can serve two masters. Either he will hate the first and love the second, or he will be devoted to the second and despise the first (Luke 16:13). You cannot serve both God and money. You either serve God by acting according to ways that nurture community and sharing of resources with those in need, or you serve money by reinforcing acquisitive economic principles and patron-client relationships. The Pharisees, who were lovers of money (acquisitive economics), ridiculed Jesus, perhaps for what they considered to be his naïve views. Jesus responds by essentially saying: "Woe to you who give into peer pressure and justify yourself in the sight of other members of the social elite: what is highly valued by conventional social norms is an abomination in the sight of God" (paraphrase of Luke 16:15).

Summary

Viewing the parable of the shrewd manager through a first-century management lens results in an interpretation that may seem foreign to twenty-first-century readers. From a first-century perspective the parable affirms the actions of the shrewd manager, who challenges both the acquisitive economic and the patron-client norms of the day. In terms of the three dimensions of management, this first-century interpretation clearly lends support to a radical approach to management.

First, with regard to managing relationships *within* the organization, the parable affirms the countercultural moral reasoning of the shrewd manager and elevates the role of slaves in an *oikos*, thereby countering the norms of the day that saw slaves as having no moral capacity and beholden to the narrow self-interests of their masters.

Second, in terms of managing money, the parable clearly promotes sustenance economics (i.e., reducing the gap between the rich and the poor), again countering the dominant norms of the day that favored acquisitive economics.

Third, in terms of managing relationships *between* organizations, the parable represents a move toward benefaction and away from conventional patron-client relations.

In sum, a first-century interpretation of this parable challenges conventional first-century norms, and is also very different from a conventional twenty-first-century interpretation. The next chapter will examine whether the same countercultural findings are true for the second exemplary parable, the parable of the ten pounds.

Reflection Point: Connecting Contemporary Research and Luke's Parable of the Shrewd Manager

How realistic is this first-century interpretation of the parable of the shrewd manager? Perhaps conventional interpreters find it difficult to accept such an interpretation because they cannot imagine: (1) a manager who cares more about the well-being of the larger community than about focusing first on his own self-interests; (2) a manager who intentionally chooses not to maximize the financial wealth of the firm he is managing for his employer; and (3) that such a manager would be praised or commended or deemed competent by their employer. And yet, this unexpected finding is entirely consistent with a landmark study published in the *Academy of Management Journal*.[21] John Senger examined how much emphasis each among a group of 244 US managers placed on "religion" (a factor based on items measuring "worship, church and religion"), and compared this with a series of other measures. First, as with the shrewd manager who seems to favor the well-being of others in his community over his own financial wealth, the religious managers in Senger's study placed relatively high emphasis on "To be a constructive force in the community" and placed relatively low emphasis on maximizing their own personal satisfaction. Second, just like the shrewd manager in Luke, the religious managers in Senger's study placed relatively low emphasis on items related to financial well-being (e.g., "To make the largest possible, long-run profit," "To make a lot of money"). Third, and perhaps most surprisingly, just as the shrewd manager was praised by his boss, so also the religious managers in Senger's study received the highest competency rating from their superiors. As far as I know, no one has ever attempted to replicate Senger's study. Moreover, his counterintuitive findings are rarely cited or acknowledged in the literature. Perhaps, just like the first-century interpretation of the parable of the shrewd manager, the findings are ignored because they seem too countercultural and thus difficult to believe.

6

INTERPRETING LUKE'S PARABLE OF THE TEN POUNDS VIA A FIRST-CENTURY LENS

As has been noted, the parable of the ten pounds (Luke 19:12–27) has become a "poster child" parable in regards to Jesus' teaching about management. Together with its sister parable of the talents from Matthew, these are perhaps the most-cited of all parables among contemporary scholars seeking to apply biblical scriptures to management theory and practice. Thus, if an interpretation of this parable using a first-century lens differs significantly from a conventional twenty-first-century interpretation, implications will be considerable.

As shown in table 6.1, this parable essentially describes the story of a master who was born into a wealthy *oikos* and goes to a distant land (e.g., Rome) to see if he can gain royal power (e.g., become a client-king for the Roman emperor). This master has many managers, ten of whom he gives money "to do business with" while he is away. In other words, the master wants his managers to engage in acquisitive economics.[1] The master's regal aspirations are opposed by some of the people whom he wants to rule, and they send a delegation to ask the emperor not to empower him further. When the master returns having received royal power, he asks his managers to give an account of their work. One manager achieved a tenfold return, and the master rewards his trustworthiness by giving the manager ten cities to rule. A second manager achieved a fivefold return, and is given five cities to rule. A third manager explains that he hid away the money because he knew that the master was harsh and exploitive.[2] The master calls this manager wicked and takes the money from him and gives it to the first, saying: "I tell you, to all those who have, more will be given; but from those who have nothing, even what they have will be taken away. But as for these enemies of mine who did not want me to be king over them—bring them here and slaughter them in my presence" (Luke 19:26–27).[3]

A BRIEF TWENTY-FIRST-CENTURY INTERPRETATION OF THE PARABLE OF THE TEN POUNDS

Perhaps it is no surprise that the parable of the ten pounds (and its more popular "sister" parable of the talents) has become a favorite among management scholars applying biblical principles to business, because this is the *only* passage in the New Testament where the purpose of money is designated to increase profit ("to do business with").[4] Five different functions of money have been identified in the New Testament, and here

Table 6.1 Two interpretations of the parable of the ten pounds

Parable of ten pounds (Luke 19:12–27)	A common twenty-first-century interpretation	An interpretation via a first-century lens
[Jesus] said, "A nobleman [*eugenes*] went to a distant country to get royal power for himself and then return. He summoned ten of his slaves, and gave them ten pounds, and said to them, 'Do business with these until I come back.'	Assumes that the nobleman represents Jesus (Lord), who entrusts to his servants valuable gifts to "do business" with while he is gone.	Assumes that the nobleman is a harsh/exploitive householder despised by his subjects, who takes what he did not deposit and reaps what he did not sow.
But the citizens of his country hated him and sent a delegation after him, saying, 'We do not want this man to rule over us.'	Sometimes people hate Jesus and don't want him to rule over them.	People do not want this hated man to rule over them.
When he returned, having received royal power, he ordered these slaves, to whom he had given the money, to be summoned so that he might find out what they had gained by trading.	Jesus holds people accountable for what they have been given to be used for acquisitive economic gain.	The exploitive master holds his managers accountable to him, to find out how much profit they made for him.
The first came forward and said, 'Lord [*kurios*], your pound has made ten more pounds.' He said to him, 'Well done, good slave! Because you have been trustworthy in a very small thing, take charge of ten cities.' Then the second came, saying, 'Lord [*kurios*], your pound has made five pounds.' He said to him, 'And you, rule over five cities.'"	The first two managers are admired because they obediently used the money they were given to make more money. Jesus is pleased when managers multiply God-given resources, and Jesus celebrates and rewards such people with greater power and responsibility.	The first two managers make impressive financial gains for the master, and thus show that they are cut of the same cloth as the exploitive master. It is disturbing when the rich get richer on the backs of the poor, and when acquisitive economically oriented people are given further power and responsibility.
Then the other came, saying, "Lord [*kurios*], here is your pound. I wrapped it up in a piece of cloth, for I was afraid of you, because you are a harsh man; you take what you did not deposit, and reap what you did not sow."	The third manager fails to act responsibly with the gift Jesus had given him, and instead hid it far away from others.	The third manager recognizes the exploitive nature of his master, and opts to remove the money from circulation rather than use it to widen the gap between the rich and the poor.
He said to him, "I will judge you by your own words, you wicked slave! You knew, did you, that I was a harsh man, taking what I did not deposit and reaping what I did not sow? Why then did you not put my money into the bank [literally, the table used by money-changers]? Then when I returned, I could have collected it with interest."	Jesus judges the third manager, condemning him for his lack of actions, and for failing to at least collect interest from a bank (i.e., to use the money to make money).	The exploitive master blows his lid, angered that his reputation as a harsh man did not bully the third manager into action. Lest there be any doubt, the exploitive nature of the master is further demonstrated by his desire to collect interest on his money.
He said to the bystanders, "Take the pound from him and give it to the one who has ten pounds." (And they said to him, "Lord [*kurios*] he has ten pounds!") "I tell you, to all those who have, more will be given; but from those who have nothing, even what they have will be taken away. But as for these enemies of mine who did not want me to be king over them—bring them here and slaughter them in my presence."	Jesus abundantly rewards those who do his bidding, and severely punishes those who refuse to accept Jesus as ruler over their lives.	The exploitive master rewards his cronies (who widen the gap between the rich and the poor), and kills people who refuse to bow down to his profit-maximizing (community-disrupting) style of kingship (just as Jesus is crucified by the kings of his day).

they are in order from most to least frequently occurring in the Gospels:

1. The most common function of money is as a standard of payment usually provided to patrons, such as political rulers (e.g., taxation to Caesar, Luke 20:25), religious institutions (e.g., donations to temple, Luke 21:1–2), and to service debt (Luke 7:41).
2. The second most frequently described function of money is to store wealth, as it was for the third manager who wrapped the rich man's money in a cloth for safe-keeping (Luke 19:2) and for the woman who had lost her coin (Luke 15: 8–9).
3. The third most-described use of money is to purchase goods (e.g., to purchase oxen or land, Luke 14:18–19) or services (e.g., when the Good Samaritan pays the innkeeper to take care of the robbery victim, Luke 10:35).
4. Although there are no examples of it in Luke, the Gospels also describe how money can be used as a means to measure the value of something, as it was for the woman who poured 300 *denarii* of oil on Jesus head (Mark 14:5; money that could have been given to the poor) or for the 200 *denarii* it would have cost to feed the 5,000 people at Jesus' sermon (Mark 6:37).
5. Finally, money can be used to make more money (acquisitive economics, M-C-M exchange), where the sole example is the parable of the ten pounds (Luke 19:11–27; and the Matthean "twin" parable of the talents, Matt. 25:14–30).

In short, this is a parable about acquisitive economics, and thus of particular interest from a twenty-first-century understanding of management that is steeped in the ideas of profit-maximization and financial value-creation. Perhaps it is not surprising, then, that many modern commentators are quick to conclude that the parable seems to provide support for profit-maximization:

> It is interesting to note that Jesus had a parable set aside for the businessperson, and that parable was about making money. From this parable, I believe we can learn that Jesus wants us to make money.[5]

> [S]ervants of Jesus must occupy themselves in profitable service during the time of his absence, and that judgment and deprivation await the unprofitable servant.[6]

As summarized in table 6.1, according to a twenty-first-century interpretation, the meaning of this parable is quite straightforward: great managers increase their masters' assets tenfold, good managers increase them fivefold, and every manager should at the very least achieve the equivalent of collecting interest from a bank. This interpretation rests on the following three main assumptions:

1. The master in the parable represents Jesus.[7]
2. The managers who increase the financial assets entrusted to them by their master are commended by Jesus.
3. The manager who refuses to use his money to make money acted irresponsibly. Put differently, in most common twenty-first-century interpretations, the first two managers are heroes, while the third is vilified.[8]

INTERPRETATION OF THE PARABLE OF THE TEN POUNDS VIA A FIRST-CENTURY MANAGEMENT LENS

A first-century interpretation of the parable would question each of the three assumptions that characterize the common twenty-first-century interpretation.

Does the Master Represent Jesus?

It seems that a first-century reader would be hard-pressed to think that the master in the parable represents Jesus, when the description of the master so clearly points to a different direction.[9] The parable describes the master as a power-hungry, despised, and exploitive man who takes what he did not deposit, reaps what he did not sow, and promotes violating the biblical prohibition of charging interest. Moreover, the master explicitly agrees that this is an accurate description of himself, perhaps because for him (and among his peers) successfully exploiting opportunities to maximize one's profits is considered to be a badge of honor.[10]

And indeed, this sort of behavior and oppression was commonplace in first-century Palestine for many people who were living under the thumb of absentee landholders and foreign rule. This is why the Jews were longing for a savior. Moreover, the story of the parable would have sounded painfully familiar to them. Commentators note that elements of this parable are strikingly similar to the history of the ruling family in that region as described by the historian Josephus (writing in the first century). After Herod the Great died in 4 BCE his then 19-year-old son Archelaus (brother to Herod Antipas, ruler of Galilee) went to Rome to confirm his kingship of Judea (as specified in his father's will). Archelaus was followed by a delegation of 50 people protesting his appointment. He received the kingship, and went on to kill about 3,000 Pharisees who opposed his rule.[11]

Taken together, it seems unlikely that first-century listeners would assume that the nobleman in the parable represents Jesus.

Is it Truly Commendable to Increase Financial Wealth Five- and Tenfold?

First-century listeners would recognize the financial returns described in the parable as inherently dubious instances of acquisitive economic activity (i.e., using money to make money). Moreover, the usual rates of return at that time were 4–12 percent, and anything greater was considered to be oppressive.[12] Recall also that in the first century the economy was seen as a "fixed pie" meaning that in order for one person to gain ten pounds (equivalent of three years' labor), someone else would have to lose ten pounds. In other words, in order for the rich nobleman to get richer, someone else would have to get poorer.[13] And finally, note that collecting interest on money went against the usury laws of Hebrew Scriptures, and that elsewhere Jesus is clearly opposed to the exploitive practices of money-changers.[14]

In sum, although the social elite may have found it commendable to amass riches via five- and tenfold returns on money, it seems likely that the vast majority of people in the first century would have found this to be morally and ethically reprehensible.

Is it Responsible to Refuse to Engage in Acquisitive Economic Behavior?

It is not unreasonable to suggest most people living in first-century Palestine would have admired the third manager for taking this acquisitive economic (inherently "unjust"?) money out of circulation. They would not think that helping the rich get richer, on the backs of the poor, makes the world a better place. The punch line of the parable has the master saying: "I tell you, to all those who have, more will be given; but from those who have nothing, even what they have will be taken away" (Luke 19:26). This maxim widens the gap between the rich and the poor, and though it may be entirely consistent with an acquisitive economic orientation, it flies in the face of the passage appearing in Luke right before this one—a passage where salvation comes to the *oikos* of Zacchaeus thanks to his giving half his money to the poor—and it is exactly the opposite to the maxim associated with another master (*kurios*) described in Luke who serves and wants members of his *oikos* to be treated with dignity: "From everyone to whom much has been given, much will be required" (see Luke 12:35–48; this latter maxim reduces the gap between the rich and the poor). Thus, the exploitive manager in this parable serves as a counterexample to other managers who are commended by Jesus.

In sum, from a first-century perspective the third manager is the true hero of the parable, and the first two managers are the villains. Again, this first-century view is consistent with some of the earliest writings of church leaders. For example, Eusebius (269–333) suggests that the manager "who hid the talent . . . was accepted with joy," whereas the manager "who multiplied the gain . . . [was] rebuked."[15] A similar view may be seen in writings of Origen (185–254)[16] who also seems to suggest that the third servant is more exemplary than the first two:

> The *hidden good is greater for a faithful and wise man* [e.g., the third manager in the parable] than what was promised to the man who increased his *minas* [i.e., pounds] tenfold or fivefold [i.e., the first two managers]. And it is no surprise why the reward of those [the third manager] who differ from them [the first two managers] is greater. For, cities are to be given to those who increased their amount of their *minas*, and abundance for those who double the *talents*. For, *much more belongs to* those—not only to be set over an abundance, but "over all the master's substance," which is laid up by *the faithful and wise steward* [third manager].[17]

Finally, the idea that the third manager is the true hero of the parable is also evident in the very last scene of the parable, which has the master calling for his enemies to be brought to him in order to be slaughtered in his presence. This foreshadows what Jesus will be facing, and aligns Jesus with the enemies of the exploitive master. The very next verse of the Gospel (Luke 19:28) describes Jesus "going up to Jerusalem" where he too will soon be slaughtered by the political powers of that time.

SUMMARY

Analyses of both the parable of the ten pounds and the parable of the shrewd manager through a first-century management lens leads to interpretations that seem foreign from a common twenty-first-century perspective. Via a first-century lens, both parables affirm the countercultural moral reasoning of managers (the shrewd manager, the third manager) who challenge the acquisitive economic and the patron-client norms of the day. There is notable consistency and symmetry in the message of the two parables along each of the three first-century dimensions of management.

First, with regard to managing relationships within an *oikos*, both parables point to exemplary managers as independent moral agents, enacting values that challenge conventional *oikos* relationships. The parable of the shrewd manager affirms the manager who acts as a countercultural moral agent by unilaterally redistributing his master's wealth, and the parable of the ten pounds affirms the manager who counters his master's wishes by refusing to exploitatively use money to make more money.

Second, with regard to managing money, the parable of the shrewd manager affirms managerial behavior consistent with sustenance economics (implicitly challenges acquisitive economics), and the parable of the ten pounds affirms managerial behavior that undermines acquisitive economics (implicitly supports sustenance economics).

Third, with regard to managing relationships between *oikoi*, the parable of the shrewd manager affirms benefaction (moves away from conventional patron-client relationships), and the parable of the ten pounds rejects patron-client relationships (implicitly affirms benefaction).

Taken together, both parables hint that Luke calls for a new and different approach to management. This new approach challenges conventional views of: master-slave relationships, acquisitive economics, and patron-client relationships. But it is premature to base Luke's critique of conventional management on only two parables, regardless of how relevant or compelling they may appear to be. Thus, the next section of the book will provide a much more thorough analysis of what Luke says about management, that is, about the nature of *oikonomia*, *chrematistics*, and patron-client relations.

REFLECTION POINT: CONNECTING CONTEMPORARY RESEARCH AND LUKE'S PARABLE OF THE TEN POUNDS

Does research support the concerns evident in Luke about the gap between the rich and the poor? In the past 40 years we have seen a widening gap between the rich and the poor within organizations, within countries, and between countries.[18] Despite the condemnation in Luke, the maxim of the greedy and powerful nobleman seems alive and well today: "I tell you, to all those who have, more will be given; but from those who have nothing, even what they have will be taken away" (Luke 19:26). In contrast, consistent with some of the ideas associated with the "Occupy Wall Street" movement, contemporary research lends considerable support to the merit of Jesus' call for reducing the gap between the rich and the poor: "From everyone to whom much has been given, much will be required" (Luke 12:48). For example, research shows that reduced levels of income inequality in society are associated with improved life expectancy, social trust, mental health, social mobility, and many more desirable social features.[19] Moreover, this research also suggests that a reduction of income inequality provides benefits for both the relatively poor and the relatively rich (i.e., even the rich are better off when income inequality is lower).

III

Action Response: Performing a Comprehensive Examination of Passages in Luke Related to Each of the Three Dimensions of the First-Century Management Lens

The previous section identified three key dimensions for understanding management in first-century Palestine: (1) managing relationships *within* organizations (*oikonomia*); (2) managing money (*chrematistics*); and (3) managing relationships *between* organizations (benefaction versus patron-client relationships). This first-century understanding of management was then used a lens to interpret two key Lukan parables about management—the parable of the shrewd manager, and the parable of the ten pounds. These interpretations were very different from how the two parables are typically interpreted from a twenty-first-century point of view.

In order to determine whether these countercultural findings are unique to these two parables, or whether they are consistent with the rest of the Gospel of Luke, the goal in this section is to provide a more thorough analysis of these three dimensions by considering *all* the passages in Luke that make mention of them, and looking for common themes among these passages. While the analysis is designed to be thorough and exhaustive, it has been written with an eye to being fast-moving enough so that it is not exhausting to read.

In terms of a quick preview, the consistency of the findings in the next three chapters is truly remarkable. As described in chapter seven, in stark contrast to first-century norms, Luke's description of husbands and wives who manage households almost invariably draws attention to the power of women. Similarly, Luke's descriptions of parent-child relations almost invariably challenge status quo first-century norms, and in particular often encourage the adult children to leave their parents' *oikos*. Luke's description of master-slave relations almost all point to the need for masters to treat slaves with dignity, and on numerous occasions acting in the role of a slave is seen as noble and desirable. As described in chapter eight, Luke's descriptions of money consistently affirm sustenance economics and everyday use of money, but consistently condemn acquisitive economics and wide disparities between the rich and the poor. And as described in chapter nine, Luke's extended references to patron-client relations consistently invert the status quo of the first century, and promote acts of benefaction that deliberately refuse to create dependent clients. Taken together, these passages are entirely consistent with and supportive of the first-century interpretations of the parable of the ten pounds and the shrewd manager provided in the previous two chapters.

7

Passages about Managing Relationships *within* Organizations (*Oikonomia*)

Scholars have recognized that Luke makes more references to *oikos* than any other New Testament writer, that Luke generally promotes nonconventional forms of *oikos*, and that for Luke *oikos* becomes "the scene and symbol of divine action, salvation, and human community."[1] In order to examine what Luke says about *oikonomia*, we will examine Luke's descriptions of its three key dimensions: husband-wife relationships, parent-child relationships, and master-slave relationships. Taken together, these passages in Luke consistently critique traditional first-century organizational structures and systems, and point to alternative ways of doing *oikos*.

Husband-Wife Relationships

It turns out that there are not many mentions of married householders in Luke. While the most famous married couple may be Jesus' parents, Mary and Joseph,[2] the most frequently mentioned couple is Elizabeth and Zechariah, the parents of John the Baptist (Luke 1:5, 13, 18, 24). In addition, Luke mentions only two other named couples: Herodias and her husband Philip (half-brother of Herod Antipas, Luke 3:19), and Joanna[3] and her husband Chuza (chief steward of Herod Antipas, Luke 8:3).

Luke seems to have a special fondness for mentioning widows, which he does on at least seven occasions. This includes a widow named Anna who blesses the infant Jesus (Luke 2:36), and a series of unnamed widows including: widows living in the time of Elijah (Luke 4:25, 26); a widow whose son had died whom Jesus would raise (Luke 7:12); a widow who modeled persistent prayer by pestering a disrespectful judge to act justly (Luke 18:3, 5); a widow who had married seven brothers but was still childless (Luke 20:28ff); widows whose households are devoured by religious elite (Luke 20:47); and a widow who contributes more alms to the poor than very rich people (Luke 21:2, 3). In addition, Luke mentions an unnamed husband who refuses the invitation to a banquet because he has just married a wife (Luke 14:20), many unnamed couples who married prior to Noah entering the ark (Luke 17:27), to Lot's wife (Luke 17:32), and to a husband who left his wife for the sake of the kingdom (Luke 18:29).

In terms of issues related to management, one obvious overarching theme among these mentions is that, given the norms of first-century Palestine, it is striking how much voice is given to the women in Luke. Indeed, this happens literally when

Zechariah loses his voice, and his wife Elizabeth announces that their child's name will be "John" (Luke 1:60). At that time, women would not normally have had the power to name their children, and especially to *not* name the eldest son after his father. Similarly, among Joseph and Mary, Mary is the one who is given special attention as being Jesus' mother and it is her "song" of praise that is recorded in Luke. Along the same lines, Joanna is credited for providing financial resources for Jesus and, in a more sinister way, Herodias is blamed for Herod Antipas's fatal turn against John.

This tendency to draw attention to the power of women is also evident in the frequent mentions of widows, who invariably are cast in a positive light. This is evident, in a back-handed way, even in references such as the husband who is unable to compel his new wife to come to the banquet. Clearly, Luke seems intent on emphasizing that women are not generally subordinate, and indeed often presents even widows as more than equal to men.

The implication for *oikonomia* in the first century is clear: these passages consistently counter conventional first-century norms of wives being in some way second class or subservient to husbands.

Parent-Child Relationships

Luke makes 188 references to pronouns that designate some sort of parent-child relationship, however, many of these do not refer to a first-century *oikos* setting (e.g., God as father, son of Abraham).[4] The focus in this section will be on each of the eight passages in Luke that offers a relatively developed description of a parent-child relationship.[5] Seven of these eight passages directly challenge conventional views of *oikos*, and the passages consistently encourage adult children to leave their birth *oikos* in order to start a new kind of *oikos*. The one passage that does not challenge conventional norms is also the only passage where the child is not yet an adult (Luke 11:11–13).

Jesus is in His Father's *Oikos* (Luke 2:41–51)

This is the first of two passages that describe Jesus interacting with his parents (Mary and Joseph). In this passage we find the 12-year-old Jesus with his parents walking from his hometown of Nazareth to the city Jerusalem where they will celebrate the festival of the Passover. When the Passover is finished his parents start the walk home to Nazareth, assuming that Jesus was with the group of travelers from their region. However they discover that Jesus is not with the group. After three days of searching they find Jesus in the temple in Jerusalem among the teachers, listening to them and asking them questions. Upon finding Jesus his mother asks, "Child, why have you treated us like this? Look, your father and I have been searching for you in great anxiety." Jesus replies, "Why were you searching for me? Did you not know I must be in my Father's house [*oikos*]?" The first recorded words Jesus utters in Luke are, in a manner, talking back to his mother![6] In sum, as soon as Jesus became an adult in that society (symbolized by going to the Passover in Jerusalem as a 12 year-old), he begins to differentiate himself from his parental *oikos*.

Jesus' Earthly Family is Not Limited to His Biological Kin (Luke 8:19–21)

The second time we read about Jesus and his parents, we find his mother and brothers waiting outside of a crowded house where Jesus is teaching. When he is told that his (biological) family members want to see him, Jesus responds: "My mother and my brothers are those who hear the word of God and do it." Thus, the two passages where Jesus speaks about his parental *oikos*, he distances himself from it and points to a new kind of *oikos*.

God is Benevolent Like a Father (Luke 11:11–13)

Of the eight parent-child passages being examined here, this is the only one where the child is not yet an adult, and it is also the only one where the child's conventional membership in the parents' *oikos* is affirmed rather than challenged. Rather, the emphasis is on the benefaction of God, which transcends even the benefaction of parents toward their children:

> Is there anyone among you who, if your child asks for a fish, will give a snake instead of a fish? Or if the child asks for an egg, will give a scorpion? If you then, who are evil, know how to give good gifts to your children, how much more will the heavenly Father give the Holy Spirit to those who ask him!

Conventional Household Norms and Rules Can be Broken: Think Outside the Box (Luke 15:11–32)

Certainly the longest passage dealing with parent-child relationships is the well-known parable of the prodigal (i.e., wasteful) son. This multilayered parable has been interpreted in many different ways. For the present study, perhaps the most remarkable feature of this parable is to note how it repeatedly serves to undermine the conventional understandings of father-son *oikos* relationships, and thus opens the space for the development of a new form of *oikos*.[7] Conventional markers of *oikos* are subverted at almost every step of the story, such as when

- the youngest son asks for an early inheritance from his father;
- the father gives both his younger and older sons an early inheritance;
- after scattering his inheritance in a foreign country, the younger son wishes to return to his father's *oikos* and work as a hired hand;
- the father (benevolently) welcomes the younger son back, gives his son authority as a master in the *oikos*, and hosts a large banquet for the community;
- the older son fails to show deference to his father and refuses to attend the banquet, and claims that he has worked like a slave rather than as a master-in-waiting.

Thus, by subverting traditional parent-child norms this parable serves to subvert conventional *oikos* structures and systems, and promotes thinking about alternative forms of *oikos*.[8]

Invert Traditional Understandings of What it Means to Honor Your Parents (Luke 18:18–25)

This is another passage of particular interest because it is directed at how adult children should treat their parents, and again challenges conventional norms. In Luke 18:18–25 a certain ruler asks Jesus what he must do to inherit eternal life.[9] Jesus replies by listing a subset of the Ten Commandments that apply to managing an *oikos*. These are as follows:

- "You shall not commit adultery" (i.e., you should treat your partner with respect and loyalty);
- "You shall not murder" (e.g., don't use violence against others who may stand in your way);
- "You shall not steal" (e.g., don't take advantage of your suppliers and customers);
- "You shall not bear false witness" (e.g., no false advertising); and
- "Honor your father and mother" (respect your parents' *oikos*).

By drawing on the Ten Commandments, this passage seems to support the tested-and-true conventional teachings about the *oikos*, and specifically about the need to treat parents with honor. And recall that, in the first century, treating parents with honor often went hand in hand with enhancing the financial wealth of the *oikos*.[10] In this light the passage takes an unexpected, and clearly subversive, turn when, upon hearing the ruler say that he has followed these commandments, Jesus tells him: "Sell all that you own and distribute the money to the poor, and you will have treasure in heaven; then come, follow me" (Luke 18:22b).

To a first-century listener, Jesus' statement would go against the commandment to "Honor your mother and father." How can selling everything he owns possibly bring honor to his parents? Certainly not in any traditional understanding of honoring the *oikos*. It is reasonable to assume that this rich ruler would come from a long-standing wealthy *oikos*, and one that has been successful enough at the patron-client game to get their son to become a ruler. To traditional first-century eyes, to sell all of this would be to abandon the *oikos* and thus to greatly dishonor one's parents.

Children Should Forsake Their Traditional *Oikos* and Start Qualitatively Different Kinds of *Oikoi* (Luke 12:51–53; 14:26; 18:29b-30)

The final three passages should remove any doubt regarding the subversive theme underlying parent-child relationships in Luke. An emphasis on challenging the status quo *oikos* is very clear in the three statements by Jesus in the three final passages to be examined here:

> Do you think that I have come to bring peace to the earth? No, I tell you, but rather division! From now on five in one household will be divided, three against two and two against three; they will be divided: father against son and son against father, mother against daughter and daughter against mother, mother-in-law against her daughter-in-law and daughter-in-law against mother-in-law. (Luke 12:51–53)

> Whoever comes to me and does not hate [i.e., disavows their primary allegiances to their][11] father and mother, wife and children, brothers and sisters, yes, and even life itself, cannot be my disciple. (Luke 14:26)

> Truly I tell you, there is no one who has left house or wife or brothers or parents or children, for the sake of the kingdom of God, who will not get back very much more in this age, and in the age to come eternal life. (Luke 18:29b-30)

These passages would seem very harsh and even repugnant (disciples are called to *hate* their families!) if they were not understood as part of Luke's recurring theme of challenging conventional *oikos* structures and systems. The verses are not an attack on the *people* within one's family, but rather they are intended to challenge listeners to re-think what *oikos* looks like. In particular, they are designed to encourage listeners to consider alternative *oikoi* structures and systems for providing goods and services.[12]

Others have noted that expectations may be different for the current head of an *oikos*, versus adult children within the *oikos*. Whereas both generations are called to change the way that an *oikos* is managed, the current heads of *oikoi* are called to manage change from *within* (e.g., like the head of the *oikos* in the parable of the prodigal son, they are called to manage with compassion; like the heads of *oikoi* in Luke 14, they are called to feed the poor). In contrast, adult children are called to leave their *oikos*, follow Jesus, and learn about and manage to set up alternative *oikoi* characterized by inclusivity where everyone is welcome as a brother and sister in the *oikos* of God.[13]

MASTER-SLAVE RELATIONSHIPS

About a dozen passages in Luke make references to slaves. To be more palatable to twenty-first-century readers, often the word for slave is translated as "servant" (e.g., each of the six times the word "servant" appears in the NRSV translation of Luke, it is translated from a Greek word for slave). Recall from chapter four that whereas the idea of slavery is morally repulsive from a twenty-first-century perspective, this was a bit different in first-century Palestine. As we shall see in Luke slavery was considered to be immoral when it demeaned people and treated them without dignity. That said, in first-century Palestine slaves were often better-off than peasants or freeman who did not enjoy the financial security of belonging to an *oikos*. In other words, in the first century slaves were as "normal" as modern-day employees (who might also be seen as metaphorical slaves of a sort, at least in so far as employers "buy" their services for certain hours during the workweek). For example, as was the norm in first-century Palestine, virtually all the managers described in Luke were slaves.[14]

In several of the passages that mention slaves, they seem to serve more as incidental characters simply doing what is expected of them. For example, a slave invites people to the banquet hosted by a householder (Luke 14:15), a slave serves the returned prodigal son and describes what has happened to his older brother (Luke 15:22,25), and a slave has his ear cut off and subsequently restored when he accompanies the High Priest to see Jesus on the Mount of Olives (Luke 22:50).

In some passages even what appear to be incidental mentions of slaves are noteworthy. For example, it is striking that the first mention in Luke of the word for slave (*doulos*) comes from the mouth of Mary, Jesus' mother, when she refers to herself a "slave" of God whom God has "looked with favor upon" (Luke 1:38, 48). Soon thereafter Simeon, a righteous and devout man, calls *himself* a slave of God (Luke 2:29).[15] Thus, to be a slave of God is a label associated with considerable honor.

Here are five passages describing master-slave relationships in some detail that merit a closer look. As a whole, these passages turn upside-down the conventional first-century understanding of slaves, grant slaves considerable dignity, and even present slaves as role models of servant leadership.[16]

Jesus Heals a Centurion's Valued Slave (Luke 7:1–10)

This passage may have caught the attention of first-century readers because it describes a centurion who goes out of his way to request Jesus to heal his slave. Jesus heals the slave, noting that he has not seen such faith as shown by the centurion in all of Israel. This passage will be examined more closely in chapter nine, but for now note that it describes how the lives of slaves matter.

"Servant Leadership" is Evident When People Serve One Another via Voluntarily Practicing Roles Associated With First-Century Slaves (Luke 12:35–38)

The second passage describes how a master, after returning from a wedding banquet, will be happy when he finds his slaves alert and ready. Then the master will "fasten his belt and have them sit down to eat, and he will come and serve [*diakonesei*] them." In that day serving food was the quintessential act of a slave. When this master serves his slaves, this event turns conventional *oikos* norms upside-down. Of course, this event also foreshadows the well-known occasion where Jesus, hosting his last supper, himself serves (*diakonen*) his disciples (Luke 22:24–28). These passages each point to the goodness in donning the role of a slave.

Managers Should Treat Slaves With Dignity and Respect (Luke 12:41–48)

The third passage, which follows soon after the previous story of the master who served his slaves, is important for our purposes because it explicitly has a manager (*oikonomos*) who acts as a middleman between a master and his slaves:

> And the Lord said, "Who then is the faithful and prudent manager [*oikonomos*] whom his master will put in charge of his [lower] slaves, to give them their allowance of food at the proper time? Blessed is that slave whom his master will find at work when he arrives. Truly I tell you, he will put that one in charge of all his possessions. But if that [managerial] slave says to himself, 'My master is delayed in coming,' and if he begins to beat the other [lower] slaves, men and women, and to eat and drink and get drunk, the master of that [managerial] slave will come on a day when he does not expect him and at an hour that he does not know, and will cut him in pieces, and put him with the unfaithful. That [managerial] slave who knew what his master wanted, but did not prepare himself or do what was wanted, will receive a severe beating. But the one who did not know and did what deserved a beating will receive a light beating. From everyone to whom much has been given, much will be required; and from the one to whom much has been entrusted, even more will be demanded." (Luke 12:41b-48)

This passage is important for two reasons. First, it tells managers that they should treat slaves with dignity and respect, not as mere possessions that can be mistreated. Second, it suggests that it was not unusual for managers to beat slaves; indeed this abuse of authority may have been the default style that managers were expected to follow unless instructed otherwise. The passage blames absentee landlords for this lack of respect in the workplace, and possibly for failing to model such respect themselves.

Slaves are Called to Reject Acquisitive Economics, and Instead to Engage in Sustenance Economics (Luke 17:7–10)

The fourth passage describes what appears to be a simple *oikos* that has perhaps one slave who performs a variety of tasks, such as plowing the field, tending the sheep, and serving the meals. Jesus states that the slave's motivation or reward for performing these tasks does not depend on explicitly receiving thanks from his master. Rather, it seems that the reward is to be inherent in the work itself, the intrinsic satisfaction that comes from tilling the soil, tending for creation, and serving others. Note that these are all hallmarks of meaningful work, and not unlike the work associated with the creation mandates in Genesis, as described in chapter two.

Note also that this intrinsic satisfaction is consistent with the holistic character of sustenance economics, which rejects wheeling and dealing in order to maximize the financial profitability of an *oikos* (acquisitive economics). The end of the passage concludes that the same principle holds true for those who follow Jesus. They are likened to a "worthless" slave. The Greek word for "worthless" is *achreioi*, which can be translated as "unprofitable."[17] In other words, it refers to a slave who refuses to pursue acquisitive economic gain. Rather, the slave is doing simply what he "ought" or was mandated to do, which is to engage in meaningful work and to live in and nurture community. The only other place this word is used in the New Testament is to describe the third slave in the parable of the talents (Matt. 25:30), namely, the manager who refused to participate in the exploitive acquisitive economic practices of his master.

Managers (Slaves) Who Do the Bidding of Exploitive Bosses May Face Injury and Violence (Luke 20:9–19)

The fifth passage where slaves play an instructive role is commonly called the "The parable of the *wicked tenants*" (NRSV). However, as indicated in table 7.1, a heading of "The parable of the *oppressive landlord*" may be more appropriate from a first-century perspective.

A Common Twenty-First-Century Interpretation of the Parable of the Wicked Tenants

The common twenty-first-century interpretation starts with the premise that "this parable is undeniably an allegory."[18] A "parable" is a realistic story that serves to illustrate a moral or religious lesson. An "allegory" is a tale used to convey a meaning that is not literal, usually by showing how the elements of the story signify something else. Although most of the parables in Luke would likely have been interpreted at face value when they were initially heard in the first century, many have since been interpreted as allegories or "theologized."[19] We have already seen evidence of this tendency in the contemporary interpretations of the parable of the ten pounds (where the exploitive nobleman is taken to represent God) and the shrewd manager (where the manager's scattering of resources is not taken to be literally exemplary).

The present parable is seen as an allegory where

1. the man planting the vineyard represents God;[20]
2. the vineyard represents the people of God (Isa. 5:1–7);
3. the tenants are Jewish leaders;
4. the first three *slaves* represent prophets sent by God to Israel; and
5. the "beloved son" represents Jesus (though this latter allusion would certainly not have been readily apparent to Jesus' listeners).

This interpretation goes on to suggest that the Jewish leaders (tenants) will be destroyed because they rejected[21] the prophets (slaves) and kill Jesus (son). This

Table 7.1 Two interpretations of the parable of the wicked tenants/oppressive landlord

Parable of the wicked tenants/ oppressive landlord (Luke 20:9–19)	A common twenty-first-century interpretation	An interpretation via a first-century lens
He began to tell the people this parable: "A man planted a vineyard, and leased it to tenants, and went to another country for a long time.	Jesus told this allegory: "God ['a man'] chose the nation Israel to be the people of God ['vineyard'] and gave it over to Jewish leaders ['tenants'] to manage while God was away for a long time.	Jesus told this parable: "An absentee landowner decided to plant a vineyard—a cash crop—on his (new) land. He leased the land to tenants (possibly the original owners of the land, who had been taxed into bankruptcy).
When the season came, he sent a slave [*doulon*] to the tenants in order that they might give him his share of the produce of the vineyard; but the tenants beat him and sent him away empty-handed. Next he sent another slave [*doulon*]; that one also they beat and insulted and sent away empty-handed. And he sent still a third; this one also they wounded and threw out.	When God sent three prophets ['slaves'] to get God's due from Israel, the prophets were beaten and insulted and sent away empty-handed by Israel's leaders.	When the time came to collect payment from the tenants, the landowner sent three managers [slaves], each of whom were violently rejected by the tenants.
Then the owner of the vineyard said, 'What shall I do? I will send my beloved son; perhaps they will respect him.' But when the tenants saw him, they discussed it among themselves and said, 'This is the heir; let us kill him so that the inheritance may be ours.' So they threw him out of the vineyard and killed him.	When God sent Jesus ['beloved son'], Israel's leaders killed Jesus, hoping to claim God's people for themselves.	Then the landowner sent his son, whom the tenants killed hoping to (re)claim the land.
What then will the owner of the vineyard do to them? He will come and destroy those tenants and give the vineyard to others."	God will respond by destroying the leaders and giving the vineyard to Gentiles.	The landowner will respond by destroying the tenants, and giving the land to others.
When they heard this, they said, "Heaven forbid!"	When the Jewish leaders heard that they would be replaced by the Gentiles, they said: "Heaven forbid."	When the Jewish leaders heard that the land would be given to others, they said: "Heaven forbid."
But he looked at them and said, "What then does this text mean: 'The stone that the builders rejected has become the cornerstone'? [Psalm 118:22] Everyone who falls on that stone will be broken to pieces; and it will crush anyone on whom it falls [Isaiah 8:14–15; Daniel 2:34–35, 44–45].'"	Jesus said: "You have rejected me, but I will become the cornerstone for a new understanding what it means to be God's people. And people who refuse to accept me will fall and be crushed."	Jesus said: "The people who have been marginalized by the elite are the cornerstone in the *oikos* of God. Woe to anyone who oppresses the marginalized people."
When the scribes and chief priests realized that he had told this parable against them, they wanted to lay hands on him at that very hour, but they feared the people.	The Jewish leaders realized this was an attack on their power, and they wanted to get rid of Jesus, but feared the people.	The Jewish leaders realized this parable was against their oppressive practices (as landlords), and they wanted to get rid of Jesus but feared the (oppressed) people.

brings us to the first "lesson" of the passage, namely, that the Jewish leaders who rejected God's prophets and killed God's son will be supplanted.

The parable then goes on to suggest that the vineyard itself will be given to others. This represents the second lesson, namely, that because of the events that have transpired, Gentiles will be given the opportunity to become the people of God.

Finally, a twenty-first-century interpretation assumes that the Jewish leaders listening to Jesus would have recognized all of these allusions and known that the parable was being spoken against them, and that they were like builders who had rejected the prophets and had rejected Jesus. They also recognized that Jesus was saying that he would become the cornerstone for how to understand and worship God in the future, and that anyone who rejects Jesus would be crushed. (Despite the warning, this made the Jewish leaders want to reject Jesus even more, but they didn't dare do so because they feared the people, who presumably had also caught onto all of these allusions.) This brings us to the third lesson, namely, that Jesus was destined to become a foundation for God's people.

An Interpretation of the Parable of the Oppressive Landlord through a First-Century Lens

The meaning of the passage is quite different when interpreted as a realistic parable through a first-century lens. Before beginning the interpretation, consider the following background information regarding vineyards in the first century. First, at that time vineyards were expensive to build and were seen as cash crops, and thus owning a vineyard tended to be attractive to the middling rich who were upwardly mobile (note also that the Jewish leaders of the day would have been considered to be among the middling rich).[22] Second, any new vineyard at that time was likely built on land recently lost by farmers who were no longer able to pay back their debts and taxes.[23] Third, the produce from vineyards was usually seen as being geared for export, reducing availability of locally grown food.[24] And fourth, the structure and nature of the labor required for operating vineyards both created and exploited a class of nonslave laborers.[25]

With this in mind, a first-century interpretation of this passage as a parable (not as an allegory) would suggest that it describes[26]

1. a well-to-do absentee landowner who
2. has transformed existing farmland into a vineyard (a cash crop)
3. where tenants, who are possibly the previous owners of the land who had lost it to the current owner due to debt, rebel
4. against the absentee landholders' managers [slaves][27]
5. and kill his son (who to them represents the future ownership of the land).[28]

The parable describes how the tenants, because they used violence to seek freedom from their oppression, will be destroyed by the landlord's counterattack. This brings us to the first "lesson" of the parable, which is the "futility of violence."[29] Even though it is appropriate for the tenants to seek freedom from oppressive socioeconomic systems, their use of violence to try to resolve the problem is inappropriate and counterproductive.

Because a first-century interpretation is consistent with what is actually happening in the region at the time, it is not surprising that the Jewish leaders recognize that the parable suggests that *they* are acting like estate "builders"[30] who take land from impoverished farmers in order to grow cash crops. The parable then suggests that the estate owners should give their land to others. This brings us to the second key "lesson" of the parable, namely, that the estate should be given to other landless people, so that they may again belong to an *oikos*.[31] The Jewish leaders are aghast at this proposition: "Heaven forbid!"

The passage concludes by suggesting that the working underclass (e.g., landless people without an *oikos*) are the "cornerstone" of the kingdom of God. This interpretation requires a deeper understanding of the verse in Luke 20:17b ("The stone that the builder rejected has become the cornerstone"), which is a quote from Psalm 118:22 ("The stone that the builders rejected has become the chief cornerstone"). Psalm 118, which is the Old Testament chapter most frequently alluded to in the New Testament, was related to the Jewish feast of the Passover, which serves as a reminder of the liberation of the Jewish people from Egypt and return to their homeland. In Psalm 118, the "cornerstone" refers not to an individual person, but rather to a particular people (the nation of Israel), which was being oppressed and marginalized by other nations (i.e., by the "builders" referred to in Psalm 118).[32] Jesus infuriates the Jewish leaders by implying that they are like first-century "builders"[33] who have rejected groups of landless people (the "stone").[34] (For other occasions where "stone" refers to *groups* of nonelite people, see Luke 19:40 and 3:8).[35] This brings us to a third lesson in the parable: it is people without an *oikos* who serve as the cornerstone in the *oikos* of God (see also Luke 3:4b-6; 6:20b). Moreover, anyone who fails to understand this will be broken and crushed. Note that at this point the first lesson becomes paramount, namely, that this "crushing" will not be achieved through violence.

Although the lessons in this passage do not focus on managers specifically, several observations can be made about what managerial life may have been like in a conventional first-century *oikos* of the middling rich who embraced acquisitive economics and patron-client relationships. First, the managers in the parable were doing purely instrumental work; there is no sense that they were somehow contributing to making the world a better place. Second, the vineyard owner seemed to have a conventional top-down relationship with the managers, who were there simply to obey the owner's commands. And third, the managers played the role of enforcers, or as bill collectors, rather than as managers per se. Their work, as brokers working between the vineyard owner and the vineyard workers, did not seem to have much intrinsic meaning. This also got them into trouble with their subordinates. In short, it may not be a stretch to suggest that managers facing such working conditions would have been very receptive to a different approach to management.

Taken together, these passages about masters and slaves make three important statements, each of which challenges first-century norms. First, slaves should be recognized as full human beings and worthy of being treated with dignity, often called by God for holy tasks. This was in stark contrast to the norms of the day, where slaves were seen as little more than their master's possessions (Aristotle). Second, exemplary leaders are those who willingly don the role of a slave and serve their followers. Again, this was in stark contrast to the norms of the day, where slaves worked to serve their masters, not vice versa. And third, according to Luke, slaves should perform inherently meaningful work (like tilling the ground), and not become instruments of financial wealth creation (woe to slaves who do the bidding of exploitive masters). Again, this stood in contrast to the acquisitive economic norms of the day, where masters saw slaves as instruments for wealth creation.

Summary

With regard to managing the three key relationships within organizations, this analysis of the Gospel of Luke can be summarized as follows:

- Wives should not play a second-class role to husbands—both have equally important contributions to make to the *oikos*.
- Adult children are encouraged to leave the security of their parents' *oikos*, and to become members of new forms of *oikos* that include marginalized societal members.
- Slaves should be treated with dignity, and organizational members should serve one other (as slaves) regardless of their position in the *oikos*.

Reflection Point: Connecting Contemporary Research and Luke's Passages about Managing Relationships *within* Organizations

What happens when these ideas drawn from Luke are put into practice? Although Luke describes a wide range of goods and services producing organizations, it might be especially interesting to note how these three main principles in Luke might apply in religious organizations, and in particular in Christian congregations. First, about 8 percent of congregations in the United States are led by women. Compared to their male counterparts, female pastors tend to spend more time in prayer and to place more emphasis in their work on promoting justice and the rights of minorities, helping people, promoting equality, education, and in general applying religion to various social problems (e.g., poverty, environmental issues, and human dignity).[36] Second, with regard to leaving parental congregations in order to start new ones, the little research there is on this topic suggests that it may be reenergizing for a congregation's doors to be closed once it's been around for a generation (e.g., 40–50 years) and for its members to start new congregations.[37] This is in part because the process of institutionalization makes it difficult for congregations to keep up with the times: just as a congregation's financial-giving patterns do not keep up with inflation over time, the same may be true for keeping up with the needs in their larger community. And third, servant leadership within congregations has been found to be related positively to: followers' faith maturity, satisfaction, and sense of empowerment; leaders' effectiveness and job satisfaction; trust within the organization and toward the leader; and church health and growth (but not financial growth).[38]

8

Passages about Managing Money (*Chrematistics*)

It has been suggested that Luke consistently talks about money, but Luke does not talk about money consistently.[1] The analysis in this chapter will argue that this is only half-true. It is true that Luke has a lot to say about money. Luke makes over 50 mentions of words such as "rich/es" (15 total mentions), "money" (7), "coinage"[2] (16), "wealth" (4), and "poor" (11). A total of 18 passages, listed in table 8.1, mention at least one of these words.

However, in examining these 18 passages, it seems that Luke may be much more consistent in what it says about money than others have thought. Table 8.1 lists all 18 passages in Luke that talk about money and divides them into two halves: 9 passages that do not use the word "rich" (*plousious, ploutountas, ploutou*), and 9 passages that do. It turns out that the teachings *within* each half are quite consistent, though the themes *across* the two halves may appear to be at odds. On the one hand, the passages about money that do not mention the word "rich" seem to suggest that money is an appropriate part of everyday life (e.g., natural *chrematistics*). Indeed, in these passages money can be seen to be used to facilitate work associated with the kingdom of God. On the other hand, the passages that do mention the word "rich" disparage great financial wealth (e.g., unnatural *chrematistics*), and call for rich people to sell all their possessions and give their money to the poor. In these passages the emphasis seems to be on reducing inequitable gaps between the rich and the poor.

These differences are signaled right from the beginning of Luke. Consider the negative bias that is evident the first three times Luke mentions the word "rich": (1) Jesus' mother states, "[T]he Mighty One has sent the rich away empty" (Luke 1:46–55); (2) Jesus early on in his ministry says, "[W]oe to you who are rich" (Luke 6:20–26); and (3) Jesus describes riches as metaphorical thorns that choke and prevent the maturation of the "seeds" of the word of God (Luke 8:4–15). This negative bias to the rich is also implied in the positive bias to the poor, which is evident in the first three mentions of the word "poor" in Luke: (1) "The Spirit of the Lord is upon me, because he has anointed me to bring good news to the poor" (Luke 4:18); (2) "Blessed are you who are poor, for yours is the kingdom of God" (Luke 6:20); (3) "[T]he poor have good news brought to them" (Luke 7:22).

Taken together, the parallelism between these first six mentions of rich and poor seem to suggest that riches stand in the way of receiving Jesus' message, whereas at its core his message provides great benefit to the poor. Moreover, it is striking how financial economic concerns (rich versus poor) play such a central and prominent

Table 8.1 Passages that make reference to money in the Gospel of Luke

Passages with keywords: money/riches/ wealth/coinage/ poor	Key ideas in passages that:	
	Refer to someone who is rich (all these passages mention the word "rich;" *plousious, ploutountas, ploutou*).	Do *not* make reference to someone who is rich (these passages do not mention the word "rich" but do mention the other words related to money).
Luke 1:46–55; Rich	Jesus' mother Mary states: "[T]he Mighty One . . . has sent the rich away empty."	
Luke 3:10–14; Money		John tells the crowd to share extra clothing and food, and tells soldiers to be satisfied with their wages and not attempt to extort money.
Luke 4:18–19; Poor		The Spirit of the Lord has anointed Jesus to bring good news to the poor.
Luke 6:20–26; Rich, poor	Jesus states: "[W]oe to you who are rich."	
Luke 7:18–23; Poor		The poor have good news brought to them.
Luke 7:36–50; Coinage		For both the cancellation of financial debts and for the forgiveness of sins, the greater the amount that has been forgiven the greater the love for the forgiver.
Luke 8: 4–15; Riches	Riches are like thorns that choke and prevent the maturation of the seeds of the word of God.	
Luke 9:1–4; Money		When Jesus sends out his 12 disciples to proclaim the kingdom of God they are not to take along any money.
Luke 10:29–37; Coinage		The innkeeper is paid by the Good Samaritan to nurse the robbery victim back to health.
Luke 12:13–48; Rich (2x), poor	Focusing on securing (long-term) financial security for oneself (and one's *oikos*) gets in the way of being "rich toward God."	
Luke 14:7–33; Rich, poor (2x)	When hosting a banquet, practice benefaction by inviting people who cannot repay you; discipleship requires leaving the financial security of a conventional *oikos*.	
Luke 15:8–10; Coinage (3x)		If you lose money, seek it, and when you find it rejoice with your friends in your *oikos*.
Luke 16:1–31; Rich (5x), money, wealth (3x), poor (2x)	It is commendable for managers to deliberately scatter their master's resources; members of a rich *oikos* who fail to share with the poor will face torment in the future.	
Luke 18:18–30; Rich, wealth, money, poor	To be saved/enter the kingdom of God requires leaving behind the financial security of a conventional *oikos*.	
Luke 19:1–27; Rich, money (2x), coinage (9x), poor	Salvation comes to the *oikos* of a rich chief tax collector who gives half his possessions to the poor and repays fourfold anyone he has defrauded; managers in a conventional *oikos* who refuse to widen the gap between the rich and the poor may face harsh consequences.	

Continued

Table 8.1 Continued

Passages with keywords: money/riches/ wealth/coinage/ poor	Key ideas in passages that:	
	Refer to someone who is rich (all these passages mention the word "rich;" *plousious, ploutountas, ploutou*).	Do *not* make reference to someone who is rich (these passages do not mention the word "rich" but do mention the other words related to money).
Luke 20:20–26; Coinage		"[G]ive to the emperor the things that are the emperor's."
Luke 20:45–21:4; Rich, coinage, poor (2x),	Even generous rich people who donate a lot of money to the temple give less than a poor widow who donates two small copper coins.	
Luke 22:1–6; Money		Judas accepts payment to betray Jesus.

role in Luke. Of course, financial management (*chrematistics*) was also a primary concern for managers in the first century, as illustrated by the tension between acquisitive economics (associated with the pursuit of riches) versus sustenance economics (where money is a means to nurture community). The remainder of this chapter will compare and contrast these two groups of passages.

Although the analysis here will draw attention to the implications of these passages for managing money (*chrematistics*), before proceeding it is instructive to note that in the first century the terms "rich" and "poor" did not refer merely to someone's economic status. For example, the word "rich" generally referred as much to social capital as to financial wealth. To be rich was to have social standing that provided "the power or capacity to take from someone who is weak what was rightfully not yours."[3] Similarly, to be "poor" meant to lack social capital or to have been marginalized (e.g., to lack full membership in an *oikos*). This lack of social standing could be due to injustice or to misfortune (e.g., a widow who had no sons might be considered poor, even if she had financial wealth). To be clear, lack of social standing often resulted in financial poverty. In sum, it may be more accurate to translate the word "rich" as "greed" (e.g., think of acquisitive economics) and to translate the word "poor" as "socially unfortunate" (e.g., think of social outcasts).[4]

PASSAGES THAT DO *NOT* USE THE WORD "RICH"
(SUSTENANCE ECONOMICS)

Taken as a whole, the nine passages about money that do not use the word "rich" seem to describe the use of money in ways that are consistent with sustenance economics, that is, money is a means to facilitate exchange between different people or *oikoi*. As we shall see, some of these passages have a very holistic emphasis on using finances to restore people to an *oikos*, that is, to move them from the margins of society to the center.

1. *John the Baptist tells listeners to share extra clothing and food, and tells soldiers to be satisfied with their pay and not attempt to extort extra money (Luke 3:10–14).* In short, this passage encourages people to act as benefactors to the relatively poor, and to find contentment in adequate pay.

2. *Jesus has come to bring good news to those who are poor, and release to those who are oppressed (Luke 4:18–19).* This passage is Jesus' inaugural sermon, and thus an especially important passage in Luke. The significance of the passage for the present discussion becomes clearer when stated in obverse: Jesus has not come to give more riches and power to people who use them in ways that serve to impoverish and oppress others. This challenges first-century norms regarding acquisitive economics (i.e., the conventional norm where the rich get richer by using money to make more money) and patron-client relationships (i.e., the conventional norm was that if you have opportunity to help someone out, you have a duty to your *oikos* to make sure the recipient of your aid becomes a client indebted to you). In contrast, Jesus has come to help the poor to be released from their poverty and oppression.

3. *Jesus restores people to community (Luke 7:22–23).* Recall that in first-century Palestine people who were sick and outcasts were not considered to be full members of the community. With Jesus "the blind receive their sight, the lame walk, the lepers are cleansed, the deaf hear, the dead are raised, the poor have good news brought to them." In other words, Jesus restores the marginalized to become full contributing members of society and *oikoi*.

4. *Jesus notes that the greater the size of a financial debt that one person (e.g., a patron) forgives of another (e.g., a client), the greater will be the love of the client for the patron (Luke 7:36–50).* This passage is not inconsistent with Aristotle's further observation that the greater also will be the love of the benefactor for one who is forgiven.[5] In short, financial management that goes against acquisitive economics (i.e., by reducing debts and also undermining conventional patron-client relationships) fosters community and mutual love between benefactor/recipient.

5. *Jesus fosters mutual interdependence when he tells his followers not to bring along their own financial resources as they travel to different villages to serve others (Luke 9:1–4; see also Luke 10:1–12).* There may be at least two reasons for Jesus' counsel in this passage. First, this creates situations where householders in the host villages feel compelled to show hospitality to the "strangers" among them, which is a virtue that Jesus is trying to develop among everyone (consistent with sustenance economics and God's benefaction). Second, and probably of greater importance, this creates a condition of mutual interdependence between Jesus' disciples and the people whom they are serving. It seems that Jesus goes out of his way to set up structures and systems that undermine the patron-client model of that time. Jesus does not want his followers to use money to become like "patrons" who create indebted "clients."

6. *Jesus praises the example of the Good Samaritan, who pays the innkeeper to care for a robbery victim (Luke 10:29–37).* This story provides an excellent example of sustenance economics at its best, as well as the refusal to become a patron to a client. Money is used to help a needy person become restored back to health. And in this particular parable, the medium is also the message insofar as the Samaritan himself was an outsider helping out his fellow outsider.[6]

7. *Celebrate with your neighbors if you find money that you had lost (Luke 15:8–10).* As with many of the other passages in this group, these verses points to the everydayness of money. The passage describes a woman who finds a lost coin and then celebrates by inviting her friends and neighbors for a community-enhancing party at her *oikos* (sustenance economics).

8. *Give to the emperor the things that are the emperor's, and to God the things that are God's (Luke 20:20–26).* This has been a notoriously difficult, multilayered passage to unravel. For present purposes, it is sufficient to note that Jesus seems to be saying

it is appropriate to pay taxes if you can afford to do so without compromising your ability to live up to God's ideals.

9. *Finally, in a less positive example, Judas Iscariot (the treasurer among Jesus' 12 disciples) accepts payment by chief priests and temple police to betray Jesus (Luke 22:1–6).* This illustrates how money can be used to pay for someone's services. What makes this passage of particular interest is that it seems Judas was not initially looking for payment—"he consented" to be paid—and that by accepting payment he had essentially yielded to temptation to make his betrayal an act of financial gain.

PASSAGES ABOUT MONEY THAT *DO* USE THE WORD "RICH" (ACQUISITIVE ECONOMICS)

Whereas the nine passages that do *not* use the word "rich" generally illustrate how money can be used in a manner consistent with sustenance economics, the nine passages that *do* use the word "rich" are more concerned with money associated with acquisitive economics. We have already briefly looked at the first three of these nine passages, and seen how in Luke's Gospel

- the rich are sent away empty-handed rather than acquiring more (Luke 1:46–55; the Mighty One has "brought down the powerful from their thrones, and lifted up the lowly; he has filled the hungry with good things, and sent the rich away empty");
- the rich will not get to acquire more (Luke 6:20–26; "But woe to you who are rich, for you have received your consolation"); and
- rich people can be "choked by their riches" (Luke 8:4–15).

In each of the remaining six passages in this group, a manager or an *oikos* master plays a central role. Before looking at these six passages separately note that, by way of a quick overview, in *each* one rich people are encouraged to be freed from their possessions (e.g., to get rid of wealth gained via acquisitive economics).

- "Sell your possessions . . . For where your treasure is, there your heart will be also" (Luke 12:32–34).
- "So, therefore, none of you can become my disciple if you do not give up all your possessions" (Luke 14:33).[7]
- "And I tell you, make friends for yourselves by means of dishonest wealth [i.e., take wealth generated via acquisitive economics and use it toward sustenance economic goals] so that when it is gone, they may welcome you into the eternal homes" (Luke 16:9).
- "Sell all that you own and distribute the money to the poor, and you will have treasure in heaven; then come, follow me" (Luke 18:22).
- Zacchaeus stood there and said to the Lord, "Look, half of my possessions, Lord, I will give to the poor; and if I have defrauded anyone of anything, I will pay back four times as much." Then Jesus said to him, "Today salvation has come to this house" (Luke 19:8–9).
- He [Jesus] said, "Truly I tell you, this poor widow has put in more [money into the temple treasury] than all of them [rich people]; for all of them have contributed out of their abundance, but she out of her poverty has put in all she had to live on" (Luke 21:3–4).

1. *Teachings showing the folly of hoarding wealth, and the merit of sharing wealth and treating others with respect (Luke 12:13–48).* It is helpful to divide this passage into three different subsections. The first of these (Luke 12:13–21) highlights the owner of a large agricultural estate who has benefitted from a very good crop year. Rather than consider sharing his windfall with those less fortunate than he, he builds larger barns to store his possessions saying: "I will say to my soul, Soul, you have ample goods laid up for many years; relax, eat, drink, be merry." But the man dies that very night and Jesus concludes: "So it is with those who store up treasures for themselves but are not rich toward God." Echoing Aristotle's views on how the desire for an "easy life" may undermine a "good life," this parable teaches listeners not to be concerned by maximizing how much financial wealth they will get from their *oikos*—"for one's life does not consist in the abundance of possessions"—but rather to be concerned about the genuinely "good" life.[8]

The next subsection in this passage serves as a bit of a counterbalance (Luke 12:22–34). It describes how the natural order of creation is sustainable without a spirit of acquisitiveness: "[D]o not keep striving for what you are to eat and what you are to drink, and do not keep worrying. For it is the nations of the world that strive after all these things, and your Father knows that you need them" (Luke 12:29–30). Jesus proclaims that when people (plural) seek first God's kingdom and thus live according to God's ways, then this will result in everyone (plural) having their daily needs met (Luke 12:31).[9] Put differently, when people work in the way of sustenance economics, then everyone can have a good life.

This passage ends with two stories that have already discussed the previous chapter. The first describes a master who returns from a wedding banquet, finds his slaves ready and alert, and then proceeds to serve them (Luke 12:35–40). The second describes how managers who treat their workers with dignity and respect will be rewarded (Luke 12:41–48). Taken together, these passages encourage managers to work hard, respecting and acting as servants toward those whom they manage. This leads to a virtuous cycle: the more people are given, the more they can give to others.[10]

2. *Teachings about sharing resources with people who do not belong to an* oikos *(Luke 14:7–33).* It is also helpful to divide this passage into three different subsections. The first section underscores how rich people should not be concerned with enhancing their wealth and standing among their peers, but rather focus on including those "*oikos*-less" people who cannot repay them (Luke 14:7–14). In the first century a common way of improving one's status was to host banquets, so that guests would become indebted to the host (e.g., in a sense the host would become a "patron" and the guests would become "clients"). In contrast to such self-serving use of wealth, Jesus says:

> When you give a luncheon or a dinner, do not invite your friends or your brothers or your relatives or rich neighbors, in case they may invite you in return, and you would be repaid. But when you give a banquet, invite the poor, the crippled, the lame, and the blind. And you will be blessed, because they cannot repay you, for you will be repaid at the resurrection of the righteous. (Luke 14:12b-14)

That these teachings promote community-enhancing sustenance economics, and go against acquisitive economics, is underscored in the next subsection (Luke 14:15–22). This builds on the previous verses, and describes how the host of a great feast invites the poor, the crippled, the blind, and the lame (again, these are all *oikos*-less people who cannot possibly repay him with a return invitation).

And the final subsection in this passage (Luke 14:25–33), which has also been alluded to in an earlier chapter, links the ideas of leaving the security of an existing *oikos* (v. 25–26) with making plans for alternative *oikoi* (v. 28–32) based on holistic sustenance economics (v 27, 33).

3. *Obstacles to sharing resources with others (Luke 16:1–31)*. This passage also lends itself to be divided into three subsections. The first is the parable of the shrewd manager, discussed in chapter five, which encourages managers to challenge acquisitive economic norms and instead "scatter" riches entrusted to them for the benefit of the larger community (Luke 16:1–13). However, even in this story about a manager who serves as a positive role model, the manager finds himself out of a job, possibly due to peer pressure facing his master to have him fired.

The second subsection provides a short transition where we find Jesus saying: "You [leaders who love money] are those who justify yourselves in the sight of others; but God knows your hearts; for what is prized by human beings [e.g., acquisitive economics] is an abomination in the sight of others" (Luke 16:14–18). Here seeking status among peers is the obstacle to managing money in a praiseworthy way. One cannot serve both God and wealth.

In the third subsection of this passage (Luke 16:19–31), we read about a rich son from a large *oikos* who failed to share its resources with poor people like a man named Lazarus "who longed to satisfy his hunger with what fell from the rich man's table" (Luke 16:21). After both the rich son and Lazarus die, the son finds himself being tormented in Hades when across a chasm he sees Lazarus alongside Abraham in a better place. The son begs Abraham to send Lazarus back to his father's *oikos* to warn them and save them from their impending torment if they don't change their ways. Abraham tells the rich man: "If they do not listen to Moses and the prophets, neither will they be convinced even if someone rises from the dead."[11] Here the so-called good things in life (v. 25; including fine linen and sumptuous feasts, v. 19) stand as an obstacle to responding even to those who lie in need right outside of one's *oikos*.

4. *Traditional norms related to honoring one's parents can get in the way of sharing possessions (Luke 18:18–30)*. This passage, which was looked at in chapter seven, describes the rich man who wants to inherit eternal life, who honors his parents, and whom Jesus tells to "[s]ell all you own and distribute the money to the poor." When the man becomes sad at the thought of this,[12] Jesus observes: "How hard it is for those who have wealth to enter the kingdom of God! Indeed, it is easier for a camel to go through the eye of a needle than for someone who is rich to enter the kingdom of God" (Luke 18:25).[13] The passage concludes by affirming people who, for the sake of the kingdom of God, have left behind their conventional *oikos*.

5. *Experimenting with alternative structures and systems may result in salvation for the* oikos, *but challenging the status quo can also lead to death (Luke 19:1–27)*. This passage can be divided into two subsections. The first section may be the most interesting, because it seems to be the exception that proves the rule regarding rich people. This passage describes a rich chief tax collector[14] named Zacchaeus who welcomes Jesus as a guest into his *oikos*, much to the chagrin of the people who looked down upon the sinful tax collector (tax collectors were considered to be outside of the house of Israel). Zacchaeus announces that he will give half his possessions to the poor, and will pay back fourfold anyone whom he has defrauded. Jesus responds: "Today salvation has come to this house, because he too is a son of Abraham. For the

Son of Man came to seek out and to save the lost" (Luke 19:9b, 10). Thus, whereas the other passages in this grouping hammer home the idea that riches impede living a truly good life because rich people tend to focus on money (i.e., "You cannot serve two masters"), this passage describes that when rich people finally "get it"—when they catch on to the foolhardiness of acquisitive economics and instead act in ways that enhance sustenance economics—then their *oikos* can experience salvation.

Indeed, as if to underscore that salvation is solidly related to socioeconomic concerns, and not only with other-worldly spiritual concerns, this passage is the only one in all of Luke where Jesus himself uses the word "salvation." Moreover, Jesus says that salvation can come to an *oikos*, apparently in response to the structures and systems it uses to scatter its money. In contrast, Jesus never says that salvation (noun) comes to a person (though individuals may be saved—verb). This suggests that anyone interested in understanding salvation would be wise to think long and hard about how their organizational finances are managed. This will be discussed further in chapter eleven.

This powerful story of salvation coming to the *oikos* of Zacchaeus appears right before the parable of the ten pounds, which was discussed in chapter six (Luke 19:11–27). Certainly placing it in this context—namely that salvation comes when the head of an *oikos* gives away half of his possessions and pays back fourfold anyone whom they have defrauded—provides additional support for the first-century interpretation of the parable of the pounds discussed earlier. In particular, after highlighting how salvation comes from sustenance economic management (i.e., Zacchaeus), it seems unlikely that the very next parable would describe how acquisitive economic practices are holy.

6. *Alternative structures and systems for financing the temple treasury need to be developed (Luke 20:45–21:4).* The final passage in this group starts with Jesus saying that religious leaders who seek honor and status also "devour widows' houses [*oikias*]." He then watches as rich people place large donations into the temple treasury, and sees a poor widow who puts in two small copper coins.[15] Jesus says: "Truly I tell you, this poor widow has put in more than all of them; for all them have contributed out of their abundance, but she out of her poverty has put in all she had to live on" (Luke 21:3–4). Regardless of whether Jesus considers the poor woman's donation to be praiseworthy or lamentable,[16] everyone can agree that Jesus is calling on listeners to replace status quo treasury practices with alternative structures and systems that help people like this widow escape her poverty.

SUMMARY

As a whole, these passages are consistent in suggesting that managers are to reject acquisitive economics and embrace sustenance economics.[17] This is evident in how the passages

- have a negative bias toward the rich (Luke 1:52; 6:24; 8:14), and toward systems that create large gaps between the rich and the poor (Luke 4:18; 6:20; 7:22);
- promote the restoration of poor people to the community (Luke 7:22–23, 36–50);
- promote hospitality, sharing with needy strangers (Luke 9:1–4; 10:1–12);
- promote the sharing of surplus resources, rather than use them for one's own financial gain (Luke 3:10–11);

- teach people not to use their power to exploit others for their own financial gain (Luke 3:12–14);
- encourage rich people to let go of their possessions and share with the poor (Luke 12:32–34; 14:33; 18:22; 19:1–10)[18];
- encourage listeners to seek out and share resources with people who cannot possibly repay them financially (Luke 14:7–24); and
- encourage listeners to experiment with nonconventional ways of managing their *oikos* in order to benefit the needy (Luke 16:1–13; 19:1–10; 21:1–4).

In the words of the parable of the shrewd manager, Jesus challenges managers to find creative ways to deliberately "scatter" surplus organizational resources. More generally, listeners are encouraged to leave behind conventional *oikos* structures and systems (and possessions) and to choose radical alternative forms of goods and services producing organizations that include people at the margins of society. In modern terms, Jesus calls for an approach to *oikos* management that is less materialistic (financial well-being is not unimportant, but it should not be seen as more important than social, spiritual, and physical well-being) and less individualistic (individual needs are not unimportant, but they should not be seen as more important than community needs, and particularly the needs of the marginalized).

Several passages describe creative and meaningful ways in which the rich can help decrease the gap between the rich and the poor. The parable of the shrewd manager had already been discussed in chapter five, and in this chapter we examined the example of Zacchaeus who implements new structures and systems that decrease the gap between the rich and the poor (he gives half his money to the poor) and that promote justice and fairness (he repays fourfold anyone he has defrauded). Note how these two exemplars are interesting because in each the manager of an *oikos* is at the center of actively reducing the gap between rich and poor. However, in neither case has the *oikos* been shut down or the gap been removed altogether (e.g., Zacchaeus is still a chief tax collector and would thus still be managing a large *oikos*, and the shrewd manager did not scatter *all* of his master's resources). Indeed, the merit of having "surplus" resources for philanthropic purposes is evident in many of the other passages (e.g., Samaritan pays the innkeeper, an extra cloak is given to someone who has none). The goal does not seem to be creating financial equality between the rich and the poor, but rather *reducing* the inequities between them. This can occur in at least two ways: (1) philanthropy (giving away wealth to the poor), and (2) creating new kinds of goods and services producing organizations (removing people from the margins by including them in an *oikos*). In any case, the emphasis seems to be more on *moving* in the right direction rather than *having arrived* at a destination; on *becoming* rather than on having *become*; on moving away from acquisitive economics and moving toward sustenance economics. This emphasis on the *process* of managing in the right direction is highlighted in part five.

REFLECTION POINT: CONNECTING CONTEMPORARY RESEARCH AND LUKE'S PASSAGES ABOUT MANAGING MONEY

Does money buy happiness? On this question contemporary research lends empirical support to the passages in Luke. There is general agreement among researchers that money does increase happiness, *but only for the very poor* who do not have enough money to meet their basic needs of food and shelter. Beyond this, the effect of additional riches is unclear. A growing body of research indicates that materialistic people tend to have lower satisfaction in life, poorer interpersonal relationships, and increased mental disorders.[19] Other studies suggest that having more than enough money has virtually no effect on happiness, and yet other research suggests that money indeed can buy happiness *if you give it away*. Foreshadowing some of the ideas in the next chapter, a series of studies show people are happier if they spend money on gifts or for charities rather than on themselves; workers who receive a profit-sharing bonus are happier if they give some of the bonus to others instead of keeping it all for themselves; and students who are given $20 and told to spend it on others are happier at the end of the day than students who are instructed to spend it on themselves.[20]

9

PASSAGES ABOUT MANAGING
RELATIONSHIPS *BETWEEN* ORGANIZATIONS

Recall that the terms "patron" and "benefactor" were both prevalent in the first century, and often appear to have been used interchangeably, but that there were important differences between them. The Roman version of patron-client relationships, where the benefactor had a duty to create long-term clients who were subservient to the patron, was dominant. However, the older Greek understanding of benefaction as giving resources for the good of the larger community without expecting anything in return had not been forgotten (e.g., Seneca).[1]

There are many references to benefaction and/or patron-client dynamics evident in Luke. For example, Danker (1982) cites 241 verses that allude to benefaction, including many of the healings and banquets. The following example, which we have already looked at earlier, is illustrative of an ongoing emphasis on upturning conventional views regarding patron-client relationships:

> When you give a luncheon or a dinner, do not invite your friends or your brothers or your relatives or rich neighbors, in case they may invite you in return, and you would be repaid. But when you give a banquet, invite the poor, the crippled, the lame, and the blind. And you will be blessed, because they cannot repay you, for you will be repaid at the resurrection of the righteous. (Luke 14:12b–14)
>
> Jesus here urges a break with the system of reciprocities in which a gift is always repaid by the recipient . . . This statement represents an important transformation of the very basis for patronage . . . "Giving" shall no longer be used to create clients, and thus the very basis for patronage is taken away . . . [I]n God's household . . . wealth, status and power [no longer] determine social relations.[2]

Another signpost passage that has a lot to say about patron-client relationships is found in the very first words Jesus speaks at the beginning of his public ministry: "The Spirit of the Lord is upon me, because he has anointed me to bring good news to the poor. He has sent me to proclaim release to the captives and recovery of sight to the blind, to let the oppressed go free, to proclaim the year of the Lord's favor" (Luke 4:18–19).

It is instructive to note that the final phrase of this passage, "the year of the Lord's favor," refers to the Old Testament idea of Jubilee living (see Isa. 61, Lev. 25[3]), which listeners would have recognized as general reference to doing away with patron-client relationships: "[T]he dawn of God's new age,"[4] a time associated with setting slaves free, cancelling debts, of returning land to its original *oikos* under Moses.[5]

In other words, from the start Jesus has a clear focus on overcoming political and socioeconomic structures and systems that oppress people.[6]

This is consistent with Luke's passages on indebtedness, which lies at the core of the patron-client relationship. In each case where Luke talks about indebtedness and being obligated (*opheilo*) to another party, the emphasis is on forgiving or removing those debts (Luke 7:41; 11:4; 16:5, 7; 17:10). The most well-known example of this is the Lord's Prayer, which says: "And forgive us our sins, for we ourselves forgive everyone [financially] indebted to us" (Luke 11:4). This is consistent with the parable of the shrewd manager we examined in chapter five, where the manager is praised for forgiving some of the debts others owed to his master (Luke 16:1ff).

Among the dozens of passages that could be examined in this chapter, we will focus on three that stand out for having particularly plentiful evidence of patron-client relations[7]: (1) the story of the centurion who wanted Jesus to heal his slave (Luke 7:1–10); (2) Jesus sends his followers on a peace mission (Luke 10:1–20); and (3) Jesus' description of how to be great (Luke 17:11–19). Other well-known passages where benevolence is clearly evident include the parable of the Good Samaritan (Luke 10:29–37; whom Danker [1982: 339] calls "The Beneficent Samaritan") and the story of Zacchaeus (Luke 19:1–10).

JESUS HEALS A CENTURION'S SLAVE (LUKE 7:1–10)

The passage where Jesus heals the slave of a centurion displays classic evidence of patron-client relations: A "patron" (i.e., the centurion) who has built a Jewish synagogue asks his "clients" (i.e., the religious leaders) to act as brokers to have his slave healed by Jesus. The passage is particularly striking for how the story takes several twists and turns that undermine traditional first-century patron-client relations. As shown in table 9.1, the first time this happens is when the patron seems to become a client of Jesus (i.e., when the patron calls Jesus "Lord").[8] The second happens when Jesus declines the opportunity to become a patron, but proceeds to heal the slave without any sense of future indebtedness on behalf of the centurion.

In other words, the centurion could have asked to be treated as a patron thanks to his building of the synagogue, but he chose not to. Similarly, Jesus could have accepted the opportunity to be treated as a patron for healing the centurion's slave, but he also chose not to. Instead the passage reframes patron-client relations. In the passage the centurion's benefaction is disconnected from the healing of his slave, just as Jesus' benefaction is disconnected from any subsequent obligations from the centurion (or his slave). "Thus ends the story of not one but two benefactors,"[9] and of no indebted clients per se.

JESUS SENDS HIS FOLLOWERS ON A PEACE MISSION
(LUKE 10:1–20; COMPARE 19:11–27)

Although it might not be self-evident to contemporary readers, scholars agree that the passage where Jesus sends 70 (or 72) followers on a mission (Luke 10:1–20) has a lot to say about patron-client relations. This passage is particularly interesting for our present study because it parallels the parable of the ten pounds, which is its chiastic "twin" based on the way the narrative structure of Luke has been organized (this chiastic relationship will be described in much greater depth in chapter thirteen). Using a linguistic formula that would have been easily recognized in the first

Table 9.1 Jesus heals a centurion's slave (Luke 7:1–10)

Passage (Luke 7:1–10)	Implications for patron–client relations
After Jesus had finished all his sayings in the hearing of the people, he entered Capernaum. A centurion there had a slave whom he valued highly, and who was ill and close to death.	These opening verses establish that there is a centurion (a potential "patron" figure) who has a need (thus making him a potential "client," if someone can meet his need).
When he heard about Jesus, he sent some Jewish elders to him, asking him to come and heal his slave.	The centurion acts as a patron when he sends his "clients" (Jewish elders) to act as "brokers" and approach Jesus on his behalf.
When they came to Jesus, they appealed to him earnestly, saying, "He is worthy of having you do this for him, for he loves our people, and it is he who built our synagogue for us."	This provides confirmation that the centurion has acted as a patron to the Jewish people of Capernaum, who therefore feel indebted to him.
And Jesus went with them,	So far the story is consistent with first-century norms, and Jesus seems poised to honor the centurion's request to heal the slave.
but when he was not far from the house, the centurion sent friends to say to him, "Lord, do not trouble yourself, for I am not worthy to have you come under my roof; therefore I did not presume to come to you. But only speak the word, and let my servant be healed.	Here the narrative takes an unexpected turn. When the centurion calls Jesus "Lord" it seems to suggest that Jesus was being given the role of "patron" and the centurion was accepting the role of the "client."
For I also am a man set under authority, with soldiers under me; and I say to one, 'Go,' and he goes, and to another, 'Come,' and he comes, and to my slave, 'Do this,' and the slave does it."	The centurion presumes that Jesus has authority over sickness and death, lending support to the idea that Jesus has become the patron in the narrative, and the centurion is poised to become an indebted client.
When Jesus heard this he was amazed at him, and turning to the crowd that followed him, he said, "I tell you, not even in Israel have I found such faith."	Then the story takes another countercultural turn. Jesus totally deflects the patron–client paradigm, and rejects the opportunity to become patron to a subservient client. Instead, Jesus draws attention to the faith of the centurion. There is no indication given that Jesus expects the centurion to become his client—rather Jesus praises the centurion for having greater faith than anyone in Israel.
When those who had been sent returned to the house [oikos], they found the slave in good health.	It is fitting that a restored oikos is an outcome of this act of healing, and of subverting patron–client relations.

century as an obvious example of patron-client relations, both passages describe a "patron" who sends his "clients" on a mission.[10] Moreover, as shown in table 9.2, the distinct differences between the two stories serve to highlight how Jesus' approach transforms the conventional patron-client relations evident in the parable of the ten pounds.

In terms of patron-client relations, the focus of the parable of the ten pounds is on the nobleman seeking royal power (a hallmark of conventional patron-client relations) to further his acquisitive economic agenda. The conventional nature of the nobleman's approach to patron-client relations is evident in how he uses power to coerce and lord it over others in ways that widen the gap between the rich and the poor. In contrast, a central point in the sending of the 70 is the emphasis on Jesus' followers acting in accordance with and facilitating God's benefaction. God's benefaction is evident in how the kingdom is brought near to the people, how it is invitational, and how it restores people to community (benefaction and sustenance economics). In both passages *oikoi* play a prominent role: the Luke 19 passage emphasizes exploitative financial dealings between *oikoi*, whereas the Luke 10 passage emphasizes the transformative work of peacemaking taking place within *oikoi*.

Because the managers in Luke 19 are given significant sums of money, they have opportunities to become patrons to others. Indeed, in a sense their master has tasked them with lording it over and exploiting others. In contrast, because the followers in Luke 10 are penniless, they need to rely on the benefaction of their host *oikoi* for food and shelter.[11] Of course, at the same time Jesus' followers in Luke 10 are bringing peace and healing to the people, but doing so in a way that does not turn the villagers into indebted clients. This subversion of the traditional patron-client paradigm is also echoed in the following passage.

HOW TO BECOME THE GREATEST (LUKE 22:24–30)

The final passage to be discussed here—Luke 22:24–30—is the most direct and explicit in terms of offering an alternative to conventional patron-client relationships. In particular, the passage says that true greatness comes not from lording it over others as in the patron-client approach, but rather from serving one another as in the benefaction model. Let us consider the entire passage in some detail.

> A dispute also arose among them [i.e., Jesus' disciples] as to which one of them was to be regarded as the greatest. But he [Jesus] said to them, "The kings [*basileus*] of the Gentiles lord it over [*kurieuousin*, to rule over, dominate] them; and those in authority over them are called benefactors [*euergetai*]. But not so with you; rather the greatest among you must become like the youngest, and the leader [*hegoumenos*] like one who serves. For who is greater, the one who is at the table or the one who serves? Is it not the one at the table? But I am among you as one who serves. You are those who have stood by me in my trials; and I confer on you, just as my Father has conferred on me, a kingdom, so that you may eat and drink at my table in my kingdom, and you will sit on thrones judging the twelve tribes of Israel." (Luke 22:24–30)

The passage starts with Jesus explicitly using terms associated with classic patron-client relationships, describing how the emperor and his client-kings lord it over (*kurieuousin*) the people, and describing them as so-called benefactors (*euergetai*). Jesus then rejects the conventional patron-client model, and replaces it with a model where the leaders are to become like servants, just as Jesus did by his own example.

Table 9.2 Parallelisms between Luke 10:1–20 and Luke 19:11–27, highlighting implications for patron-client relations

Luke 10:1–20 (a passage that describes what benefaction looks like as an alternative to patron-client relations)	Luke 19:11–27 (a parallel passage that illustrates conventional patron-client relations)	Hallmarks of benefaction (versus patron-client relations)
Jesus sends out his followers in *groups of two* (fosters mutual accountability).	A nobleman sends out his managers to work *individually* (consistent with traditional understanding of "brokers").	Work in groups (rather than individuals).
Jesus explicitly instructs followers *not to bring any money*, but instead asks them to bring peace to other *oikoi* (this explicitly prevents any possibility of acquisitive economics, but instead focuses on benevolent sustenance economics).	The nobleman gives his managers money and instructs them to "do business" with other *oikoi* (this is explicitly consistent with the agenda of acquisitive economics, as the managers are instructed to use money to make money).	Avoid reliance on money when dealing with other *oikoi* (rather than making money the focal point of interactions).
Jesus' followers travel to other villages in order to bring the kingdom of God close to the people (shares royal power among the people).	The nobleman travels to a distant country in order to get royal power for himself (consistent with conventional patron-client model).	Empower people via benefaction (rather than perpetuate hierarchical patron-client power structures).
Jesus instructs his followers to respect the wishes of others who choose not to receive peace/curing (Jesus' message is invitational).	The nobleman's clients try to prevent him from receiving royal power (although on the face it there are checks-and-balances to prevent oppressive rulers from being empowered, these safeguards clearly were not functional in this case).	Be invitational (rather than coercive).
The followers follow Jesus' instructions and return with joy.	The first two managers follow the nobleman's command and make profits.	
Jesus rewards his followers by giving them *authority and power over evil* (perhaps becoming brokers of a different sort).	Nobleman rewards profitable managers by giving them *authority over cities* (consistent with and enhancing their role as broker).	Seek authority over evil structures and systems (rather than authority over people).
Jesus *rejoices* with his followers (their names are written in heaven), and *laments* when others refuse to accept their invitational message of peace.	Nobleman *rejoices* with his profitable managers, but *punishes* the third manager who did not engage in acquisitive economics, and *slaughters* others who do not want him to rule over them (use of coercive force by rulers was not unusual, and indeed is what Jesus himself faces in the next verses of Luke).	Rejoice with instances of benefaction (rather than perpetuate a coercive patron-client paradigm).

The Greek word choice for leader in this passage (*hegoumenos*, which appears only in this verse in all of Luke) points to the distinctive feature of the kind of leadership Jesus wants his disciples to aspire to—it is a leadership that deliberately considers the views of others and does not lord it over others.[12] The passage ends with Jesus using the image of an *oikos*—where people eat and drink together as equals at a table—as illustrative of what an alternative to patron-client relationships looks like. In this alternative kingdom or *oikos*, leadership and judgment come from the perspective of those who follow Jesus' beneficent example of serving others at the table. This is consistent with the idea of "servant leadership," which was evident in our analysis of what Luke says about servants and slaves; leaders are sensitive to the position of the least powerful in society.

Taken together, the message in this passage is pretty straightforward. The alternative to conventional patron-client relationships is genuine benefaction, which is evident when people serve others as exemplified by Jesus, not out of a desire to lord it over others or to develop clients or to seek honor for oneself. This is the sign of true greatness.[13]

SUMMARY

Luke has much to say about patron-client relationships, and the passages that deal with this most transparently have a clear theme of wanting to transform this oppressive first-century Roman institution.[14] Luke seeks to undermine structures and systems that perpetuate the elite and demean the poor; there is a clear and consistent emphasis on releasing clients from their indebtedness.

In particular, Luke opposes acts of what we might call "counterfeit benevolence," which serves to subordinate recipients and make them subservient to so-called benefactors. Jesus condemns acts of counterfeit benevolence that are based on self-interests and which develop or perpetuate status differences. Rather, Jesus promotes what we might call acts of "genuine benevolence," such as are consistent with the spirit of God's benefaction.

Taken together, with regard to managing relationships between organizations, Luke

- discourages using resources to "lord it over others" (i.e., do not use resources to make others dependent on you or indebted to you; Luke 10:1–11; 22:24–30);
- encourages forgiving debts, "leveling the playing field," treating others with dignity, giving benefits without expecting a self-interested return (Luke 7:1–10); and
- calls for the deliberate inclusion of marginalized groups in society, people who are unable to pay back (i.e., Luke favors generalized reciprocity, nontransactional thinking; Luke 14:12–15).

REFLECTION POINT: CONNECTING CONTEMPORARY RESEARCH AND LUKE'S PASSAGES ABOUT MANAGING RELATIONSHIPS *BETWEEN* ORGANIZATIONS

Are the rich acting more as "patrons" or as "benefactors" toward the most vulnerable people in today's world? Not unlike first-century Palestine, today about 70 percent of the world's starving people are farmers who work on one of its five hundred million small-scale farms (less than five acres/two hectares in size). There are two proven ways in which people from high-income groups can help to double the output on these farms. The first is by using so-called Green Revolution 2.0 industrial agriculture technologies, which also creates opportunities for companies to make profits by providing farm inputs such as seed, fertilizer, pesticides, and so on. The second way is to use sustainable agriculture techniques, which would lower farmers' production costs in the long term, and increase the quality of soil, water, and air. The first approach is more likely to create patron-client relationships, where farmers become dependent on large corporations. The second approach is more in line with benefaction, where people in high-income countries help to provide knowledge resources for farmers in low-income countries. The first approach is consistent with research in the (acquisitive economic) "Bottom of the Pyramid" paradigm that would make farmers dependent on outside suppliers and is favored by governments in some high-income countries. The second approach is consistent with sustenance economics and with the desires of the farmers in low-income countries.[15]

FINAL COMMENTS ON PART THREE

Because the three chapters in part three have used Aristotle's ideas about *oikonomia*, *chrematistics*, and benefaction to describe what Luke says about management, it is worth reviewing how the Gospel of Luke differs from *both* Aristotle *and* from conventional first-century views.

First, the Gospel of Luke has a primary concern for the 10 percent of the population that lies outside the conventional *oikos* structures. That same concern is not evident in conventional first-century norms or in Aristotle's understanding of *oikonomia*. Also, Luke gives much greater status to the role of "slaves" than evident in conventional first-century norms and Aristotle, elevating them to full moral beings with deliberative capacity and even to role models of servant leadership. Finally, Luke's emphasis on *oikoi* where membership is based on shared commitments without regard for biological kinship—what sociologists call a "fictive family"—also differs from Artistotle and from first-century norms.

Second, the Gospel of Luke shares Aristotle's disdain for "unnatural *chrematistics*" (acquisitive economics) that characterized first-century norms. However, by emphasizing the need to create *oikoi* that include the marginalized, Luke enlarges Aristotle's understanding of "natural *chrematistics*" (sustenance economics). In particular, Luke's understanding of sustainable economics is more holistic and reaches across broader segments of the community (and even to other nations and peoples).

Third, the Gospel of Luke denounces conventional first-century Roman patron-client relations, promoting instead something much closer to Aristotle's classic idea of benefaction where benefits are provided without self-interested "strings attached." However, whereas Aristotle's benefaction focuses primarily on benefits provided to people of equal socioeconomic status, Luke describes benefaction especially for the poor and marginalized. That said, insofar as Luke describes treating the poor and marginalized as social peers, then there would be overlap with Aristotle.

IV

NEW WAY OF SEEING: MANAGEMENT, THE KINGDOM OF GOD, SALVATION, AND THE HOLY SPIRIT

The previous chapters have introduced and developed a conceptual framework based on a first-century understanding of management to guide our study of Luke. In particular, we have looked at the three elements that characterize first-century management—managing relationships *within* organizations, managing money, and managing relationships *between* organizations—and examined what Luke says on these topics. For our understanding of managing relationships within organizations (*oikonomia*) we looked at passages that described relationships between three sets of members of the *oikos* (i.e., husband-wife, parent-child, and master-slave/servant). For understanding what Luke says about managing money (*chrematistics*), we examined passages that talked about financial resources. For our understanding of managing relationships between organizations, we looked at passages that referred to patron-client relationships and benefaction and described relationships among parties of different status.

Overall these analyses demonstrate that Luke has a lot to say about management, even though this has been for the most part overlooked in the past. Indeed, after becoming aware of the three elements that characterize first-century management, it becomes virtually impossible to read Luke without seeing the Gospel as an indictment of the status quo, and a trumpet call for alternative socioeconomic structures and systems.[1] What is particularly striking is not only the volume of the material in Luke—over 100 households, over 50 references to money and wealth, and over 200 allusions to benefaction—but also the consistency of the message. Women and men are equally important in the *oikos*, parents and children should find ways to overcome shortcomings of the *oikos* structures and seek to develop new structures, slaves are used as role models for servant leadership, acquisitive economics are deplored in favor of sustenance economics, and conventional patron-client relationships should be replaced by genuine benefaction as demonstrated by Jesus and God.

Part four has what may at first appear to be a more other-worldly, and less managerial, focus. It will examine three major themes in Luke with an eye to drawing out their implications for management theory and practice. Each of the three themes—Luke's emphasis on the kingdom of God, salvation, and the Holy Spirit—have long been identified as being of special importance in Luke. As we shall see, each of these themes is profoundly related to what Luke says about management.

This focus on three major themes in Luke offers two important benefits. First, it compels us to consider the meaning of management from a more holistic perspective than contemporary management scholars and practitioners are accustomed to. Management is not merely about producing and distributing goods and services—it is also about the meaning of life and, in Luke's case, the meaning of Jesus' life. While this may be off-putting to some management scholars who seek to be "objective" and to "separate church and state," it will be a relief to others who recognize that management is never value-neutral nor should it be thought of as something separate from one's understanding of the cosmic. Just as we are prone to forget that the ancient idea of *oikos* goes beyond interpersonal relationships but also includes the production of goods and services, so also we forget that modern organizations go beyond the production of goods and services but also include interpersonal and spiritual relationships.

Recall that in the first century it would have been inconceivable to suggest that management ideas could somehow be separated from one's understanding of God, spirituality, and religion. At that time people had a holistic view of the world, and for them it would have been impossible to separate the economic realm from the social realm from the political realm from the religious realm.[2] Thus, for this book to purport to examine what Luke says about management without taking into account ideas that us moderns tend to relegate to a private religious realm—the kingdom of God, salvation, and the Holy Spirit—would do a disservice to the Lukan text. Luke could not have conceived of management apart from other religious ideas. As a bonus, developing an understanding of management that integrates Luke's theological concepts provides an important service to modern scholars who take seriously the "theological turn" and seek to think about management from a postsecular perspective.

Second, although not a motivating reason to view these themes through a managerial lens, it is noteworthy that doing so may also represent a helpful contribution to the biblical and theological literatures related to the kingdom of God, salvation, and the Holy Spirit. While it may seem presumptuous to say so, perhaps these literatures could benefit from the perspective of a management outsider to help them to connect in new ways with important contemporary social institutions and questions, especially concerning the economic role of organizations.

Thus, the next three chapters will consider how

- the kingdom of God may shed light on what sort of managerial character God models, and provide a framework for understanding and developing alternative *oikos* structures and systems (chapter ten);
- the understanding of salvation may have as much to do with emancipatory organizational structures and systems as it does with achieving a heavenly afterlife (chapter eleven); and
- the Holy Spirit can be considered a necessary "broker" for managers to sustainably implement the alternative structures and systems described in Luke (chapter twelve).

10

THE KINGDOM OF GOD IS ENACTED AND MANIFEST IN ORGANIZATIONAL SETTINGS

Thus far our analysis has shown that the Gospel of Luke is quite relevant for management issues. In particular, we have found that Luke is consistently quite critical of conventional first-century practices related to *oikos*, acquisitive economics, and Roman patron-client relations. However, while it is one thing to critique the status quo, it is quite another matter to articulate what a new-and-improved approach to management might look like. At its best "pro-testing" conventional management must go beyond challenging existing structures and systems; it must begin to spell out and promote improved alternative structures and systems.[1] As it turns out, Luke's descriptions of the "kingdom of God" (KOG)—a central theme in Luke—actually go to some length to spell out the hallmarks of a new-and-improved approach to management.[2]

As has been discussed earlier in the book, many scholars have agreed with Max Weber's compelling argument in *The Protestant Ethic and the Spirit of Capitalism* that an understanding of the kingdom of God based on the Protestant ethic has had an important influence on the development of contemporary management theory. Even so, an increasing number of recent management scholars contend that, rather than support conventional management theory and practice, *biblical* teachings about the KOG may point to an *alternative* paradigm.[3] The goal in this chapter is to review the idea of the KOG, to review the passages in Luke that talk about the KOG, and then draw out implications for management theory and practice.

WHAT IS THE KOG?

Even though scholars agree that Jesus teaches about the kingdom of God more often than any other topic,[4] there is considerable disagreement about what exactly the kingdom of God refers to. There are four basic dimensions or questions of how KOG can be interpreted that are of particular importance for our study. This analysis presents these four dimensions as "either/or" statements (in order to draw attention to differing emphases in the first versus the twenty-first centuries), but the dimensions could also be thought of as "both/and" statements (e.g., the KOG is *both* coming in the future *and* already evident in the present).

1. Is the KOG coming in the future, or is it already evident in the present?
2. Does the KOG refer primarily to a spiritual realm, or is it also relevant in the earthly realm?
3. Is the KOG evident when God reigns over passive citizens, or are its members actively involved in managing in the KOG?
4. Are KOG benefits exclusively for its members, or are KOG benefits available to everyone?

A popular twenty-first-century understanding of the KOG would lean toward the first interpretation along each of these four dimensions. Thus, from such twenty-first-century perspective, *the KOG refers to a heavenly place in the afterlife where God is in charge and takes care of everything for those who believe in Jesus.* However, this interpretation would have been quite foreign to people in first-century Palestine. Let's look at each dimension in turn.

First, very few contemporary scholars think that KOG refers only to the future, with most suggesting it is primarily a present phenomenon or holding a "both/and" view.[5] There is some consensus that the future reality of the KOG in its fullness is what empowers people to put glimpses of it into practice in the present.[6]

Second, while everyone would agree that the KOG is inherently spiritual, recall that in the first century people did not segregate spiritual religious matters from everyday economic matters. This is illustrated by the fact that virtually every coin minted in the Roman Empire had a picture of the emperor and the inscription "Son of God."[7] When first-century listeners heard the phrase "kingdom of God" it would have been entirely natural for them to contrast it with the "kingdom of the Roman emperor" that they were currently experiencing. More to the point, they would have expected the KOG to provide an alternative to the current regime that was characterized by managerial structures and systems consistent with patron-client relations and the *oikos* of the emperor. It seems unlikely that first-century people would have thought of the KOG as a future event of no relevance for managing their everyday lives. For example, the Jews had been waiting for years for a Messiah to come as soon as possible to help escape the oppression of the Romans and invoke a new era of God's reign on earth. Jesus himself taught his disciples to pray for the kingdom to come on earth as it is in heaven.

Thus, to be spiritual meant putting KOG principles into practice. Similarly, putting into practice management and economic principles consistent with KOG principles is synonymous with being spiritual according to the KOG. This sounds foreign to modern ears, not only because we have compartmentalized spirituality to a realm apart from everyday life, but also because of how we think about the word "kingdom." Scholars agree that the word "kingdom" (*baselia*) does not mean what twenty-first-century readers might assume, namely, a geographical region that is ruled by a king. Rather, the Greek word *baselia* might be better translated as the "reign" of God, or, in more contemporary language, the particular "managerial approach" preferred by God.[8]

Third, God is in charge of the KOG, but the biblical record is also very clear that people are invited to be active participants in managing in the KOG. This is evident in the creation mandates discussed in chapter two (e.g., God gives humankind dominion to manage earth in a way consistent with God's management style), in the very first instance where God's people have their own king (who is to rule with God as role model), and in the Gospel of Luke (where the KOG is enacted and manifest in everyday *oikos* settings). This may be the most important dimension for present purposes, because it is clear how a popular understanding of the KOG (as something that happens in the future in an other-worldly spiritual realm) would deflect attention away from people's responsibility to actively reflect KOG in their daily lives.

Fourth and finally, Luke is also clear that the KOG is for the people of Israel, for the followers of Jesus, and for everyone else. Indeed, there are many instances where Jesus proclaims the KOG and shares its benefits with people who are not his followers (e.g., the Roman centurion in Luke 7:1-10; see also Luke 10:8-9, 13:29–30).

Thus, in contrast to a popularized twenty-first-century understanding of KOG, for present purposes a first-century understanding might be more along the following lines: *The KOG refers to instances here on earth (and in heaven) where people actively relate to one another in ways that are consistent with God's way of managing.*[9] These instances are simultaneously spiritual and earthly, are informed and empowered by knowing that the future full consummation of a KOG is already assured, are consistent with God's reign, and are freely available to all humankind.

MAIN THEMES IN LUKE'S KOG PASSAGES

There are 32 mentions of the KOG in Luke (this does not include mentions of only "kingdom" or only "God"). These 32 mentions are found in 21 distinct passages (i.e., some of these passages have multiple mentions of KOG). As described here, these 21 passages can be sorted into four different groupings based on their (a) audience and their (b) content.

Group #1: Passages that Proclaim Core KOG Attributes to Crowds

Crowds form the audience in each of the four passages in the first group, which all appear relatively early in Luke. They are striking in that they provide relatively simple and unadorned statements about core ideas in the KOG, and are all addressed to a crowd of people.

1. But he said to them [*crowd*], "I must proclaim the good news of the kingdom of God to the other cities also; for I was sent for this purpose" (Luke 4:43).
2. I tell you [*crowd*], among those born of women no one is greater than John; yet the least in the kingdom of God is greater than he (Luke 7:28).
3. When the *crowds* found out about it, they followed him; and he welcomed them, and spoke to them about the kingdom of God, and healed those who needed to be cured (Luke 9:11).
4. But if it is by the finger of God that I cast out the demons, then the kingdom of God has come to you [*crowd*] (Luke 11:20).

Luke's first mention of KOG points to its inclusiveness; Jesus must proclaim the KOG to people from all cities and towns (Luke 4:43). The second passage in this group points to the KOG's upside-down nature, where the least are the greatest (Luke 7:28). The final two passages in this group emphasize how Jesus heals people, and thereby restores them into community (Luke 9:11; 11:20).[10] Note also the theme of benevolence implicit in each of these passages, where the KOG is proclaimed and communities are restored without regard to prior faith or approval (generalized reciprocity).

Taken together, these passages introduce the reader to the basic ideas or message of the KOG: everyone is welcome to join, it is countercultural, and it is associated with healing/restoration in everyday life. These themes are elaborated upon in other parts of Luke.

Group #2: Passages That Describe How KOG Ideas are Learned by Disciples

Whereas the passages in the first group have crowds *passively* receiving the KOG, the five passages in this group have *disciples* (i.e., literally, "students") *actively* learning about the KOG.

5. Then he looked up at his *disciples* and said: "Blessed are you who are poor, for yours is the kingdom of God" (Luke 6:20).
6. Soon afterwards he went on through cities and villages, proclaiming and bringing the good news of the kingdom of God. The twelve were with him, as well as some women . . . He [Jesus] said, "To you [*disciples*] it has been given to know the *secrets* of the kingdom of God; but to others I speak in parables, so that 'looking they may not perceive, and listening they may not understand'" (Luke 8:1–10).
7. "But truly I tell you [*disciples*], there are some standing here who will not taste death before they see the kingdom of God" (Luke 9:27).
8. But Jesus called for them and said [to the *disciples*], "Let the little children come to me, and do not stop them; for it is to such as these that the kingdom of God belongs. Truly I tell you, whoever does not receive the kingdom of God as a little child will never enter it" (Luke 18:16–17).
9. "So also, when you [*disciples*] see these things taking place, you know that the kingdom of God is near" (Luke 21:31).

In sum, in these passages disciples learn about the KOG by observing how Jesus proclaims the KOG to the crowds (Luke 8:1) and by receiving instruction geared toward them, which is not available to the crowds (Luke 6:20; 8:10). This includes learning the hallmarks and signs of the KOG coming (Luke 9:27; 21:31). Disciples must receive the KOG as a little child, open-minded and trusting, or they will never enter it (Luke 18:17).

Group #3: Passages That Describe How the KOG is Enacted by Followers

The four passages in the third group describe how the KOG is enacted or proclaimed by followers. Note that, whereas the nine passages in the first two groups seem to take place in an outdoor setting with little reference to *oikoi*, the passages in this third group make explicit reference to *oikoi* or take place in an oikos setting.

10. [A]nd he sent them [*the twelve apostles*] out [to *oikoi*] to proclaim the kingdom of God and to heal (Luke 9:2).

11. To another [potential follower] he said, "Follow me." But he said, "Lord, first let me go and bury my father." But Jesus said to him, "Let the dead bury their own dead; but as for you, go and proclaim the kingdom of God." Another said, "I will follow you, Lord; but let me first say farewell to those at my home [*oikon*]." Jesus said to him, "No one who puts a hand to the plough and looks back is fit for the kingdom of God." (Luke 9:59–62)

12. After this the Lord appointed *seventy others* and sent them on ahead of him in pairs to every town and place where he himself intended to go. He said to them, "Whatever house you enter, first say, 'Peace to this house [*oiko*]!' . . . cure the sick who are there, and say to them, 'The kingdom of God has come near to you.' But whenever you enter a town and they do not welcome you, go out into its streets and say, 'Even the dust of your town that clings to our feet, we wipe off in protest against you. Yet know this: the kingdom of God has come near'" (Luke 10:1–11).

13. When the hour came, he took his place at the table [in an *oikos*], and the *apostles* with him. He said to them, "I have eagerly desired to eat this Passover with you before I suffer; for I tell you, I will not eat it until it is fulfilled in the kingdom of God." Then he took a cup, and after giving thanks he said, "Take this and divide it among yourselves; for I tell you that from now on I will not drink of the fruit of the vine until the kingdom of God comes" (Luke 22:14–20).

It is noteworthy that *oikoi* play an important role in each of these passages about what it means for followers to enact the KOG. For example, consider the second passage in this group, which describes how challenging it can be to go from being a *disciple* (group #2) to becoming *follower* (group #3). This passage describes people who say they want to be followers but then are unwilling to act on their convictions. The passage suggests that the transition between being *disciples* of Jesus and becoming *followers* of Jesus requires giving up the status and security of one's conventional *oikos*.

This larger idea that followers enact KOG principles within an *oikos* is also clearly evident in the two passages where Jesus sends his followers to villages to proclaim the KOG, bring peace, and cure the sick to restore them to community (Luke 9:1–6; 10:1–11). In both these passages Jesus instructs his followers to depend on the hospitality/benefaction of their hosts: "Whatever house [*oikian*] you enter, stay there, and leave from there" (Luke 9:4; cf. Luke 10:7). These passages are consistent with the idea that the KOG is enacted when people who lack an *oikos* (e.g., the sick, and the wandering peacemakers) are welcomed into an existing *oikos*.

The final passage in this group is perhaps the most well-known, and an *oikos* plays an even more central role (Luke 22:14–20). In this passage, often called the Last Supper, Jesus takes the role of an *oikos* master as he hosts a Passover meal for his apostles (celebrating Israel's liberation from oppression in Egypt). In first-century Palestine, eating together was an act that erased status differences among participants, which Jesus clearly further reinforces when he washes the feet of his disciples (Jesus, the leader, becomes like a slave to his apostles). Eating meals together was also a prototypical act of being an *oikos* (e.g., recall also that the etymology of the word "company" means to "share bread together"). However, in the case of the Last Supper, this was clearly not a conventional kinship-based *oikos*—it was an alternative *oikos* comprised of members who had voluntarily given up their own conventional *oikoi*.

More to the point, the passage suggests that at the heart of following Jesus is a call to remember Jesus especially at meal times, which serves to symbolically underscore his interest in establishing inclusive *oikos* structures and systems. Jesus tells his followers to share bread and wine in remembrance of him.[11] This table fellowship is striking because it really means that Jesus' followers are establishing their own *oikos*, consistent with their membership in the *oikos* of God. A hallmark of following Jesus is remembering him by sharing meals with people of any status who want to join this KOG *oikos*.

Group #4: Passages That Describe KOG Outcomes for a Variety of Stakeholders, Including the Social Elite

The remaining eight passages all make explicit mention of the social elite, but they also address people from all walks of life.[12] As with the previous group of passages, *oikoi* are emphasized in at least six of these eight passages.[13] In general, the passages point to outcomes associated with KOG practices that challenge institutional norms.

14. He [Jesus] said therefore [to the *leader of a synagogue* and others], "What is the kingdom of God like? And to what should I compare it? It is like a mustard seed that someone took and sowed in the garden; it grew and became a tree, and the birds of the air made nests in its branches." And again he said, "To what should I compare the kingdom of God? It is like yeast that a woman took and mixed in with three measures of flour until all of it was leavened" (Luke 13:18–21; note the *oikos* setting for the gardener and baker; as will be explained more fully later in the chapter, note also how planting a forbidden weed has positive outcomes for the birds, and how using "impure" yeast has positive outcomes for the hungry).

15. "There will be weeping and gnashing of teeth when you [people on the way to Jerusalem] see *Abraham and Isaac and Jacob and all the prophets* in the kingdom of God, and you yourselves thrown out. Then people will come from east and west, from north and south, and will eat in the kingdom of God. Indeed, some are last who will be first, and some are first who will be last" (Luke 13:28–30; note that the meal takes place in an *oikos* setting, and the outcome is positive for world peace).

16. He [Jesus] said also to the one [*leader of the Pharisees*] who had invited him, "When you give a luncheon or a dinner, do not invite your friends or your brothers or your relatives or rich neighbors, in case they may invite you in return, and you would be repaid. But when you give a banquet, invite the poor, the crippled, the lame, and the blind. And you will be blessed, because they cannot repay you, for you will be repaid at the resurrection of the righteous." One of the dinner guests, on hearing this, said to him, "Blessed is anyone who will eat bread in the kingdom of God!" (Luke 14:12–15; note that the meal takes place in an *oikos* setting, and the outcome is positive for social outcasts).

17. [Jesus said to *Pharisees*] "The law and the prophets were in effect until John came; since then the good news of the kingdom of God is proclaimed, and everyone tries to enter it by force [alternative translation: everyone is strongly urged to enter it]" (Luke 16:16; note the metaphorical allusion to entering into an *oikos*, and the positive outcomes for the indebted people described in the previous verses).

18. Once Jesus was asked by the *Pharisees* when the kingdom of God was coming, and he answered, "The kingdom of God is not coming with things that can be observed; nor will they say, 'Look, here it is!' or 'There it is!' For, in fact, the

kingdom of God is among you" (Luke 17:20–21; note that the word "among" has been interpreted to mean "in the house [*oikos*] of,"[14] and the positive outcome for ten healed lepers in the previous verses).

19. Jesus looked at him [a *very rich ruler*] and said, "How hard it is for those who have wealth to enter the kingdom of God! Indeed, it is easier for a camel to go through the eye of a needle than for someone who is rich to enter the kingdom of God." . . . And he said to them [those who heard it], "Truly I tell you, there is no one who has left house [*oikian*] or wife or brothers or parents or children, for the sake of the kingdom of God, who will not get back very much more in this age, and in the age to come eternal life" (Luke 18:24–30; note the importance of leaving one's conventional *oikoi*, and the positive outcome of eternal life).

20. As they [*Zacchaeus* and many others] were listening to this, he went on to tell a parable, because he was near Jerusalem, and because they supposed that the kingdom of God was to appear immediately (Luke 19:11; note that this verse serves as the transition between the *oikos* of Zacchaeus and the *oikos* of the nobleman; note also the positive outcomes for the poor and mistreated in the previous verses).

21. Now there was a good and righteous man named *Joseph*, who, though *a member of the council*, had not agreed to their plan and action. He came from the Jewish town of Arimathea, and he was waiting expectantly for the kingdom of God. This man went to Pilate and asked for the body of Jesus. Then he took it, wrapped it in a linen cloth, and laid it in a rock-hewn tomb where no one had ever been laid (Luke 23:50–53; note how Joseph is part of the ruling *oikos* and the tomb is Jesus' final "house" here on earth, so to speak; Jesus' eventual resurrection from this tomb serves as a positive outcome for his followers).

The emphasis on *oikoi* in these passages is especially noteworthy. Remembering that there was also an emphasis on *oikos* in the previous grouping of passages, this has an important and clear implication: *In Luke, the* oikos *is the primary setting where the KOG is put into practice and its outcomes are observed.*[15] Put more starkly in management terms, the KOG is primarily enacted and manifest in goods and services producing organizations. As a result, for example, it should not come as a surprise that as the KOG message spread, it traveled from "house to house" (Acts 20:20). Clearly, the KOG is closely linked to *oikos* management.

Perhaps the first passage in this group is the most important (Luke 13:18–21). This passage is noteworthy for three reasons. First, it is the only passage where the text explicitly says: "The kingdom of God is like . . ." Second, it lies exactly at the midpoint of the 21 KOG passages in Luke.[16] And third, as depicted in table 10.1, it seems to encapsulate a simple sequential "formula" for KOG management that itself reflects the four thematic groupings that characterize Luke's KOG passages, as follows:

1. a core/countercultural KOG idea →
2. is taken up/learned/gathered by members of an *oikos* who →
3. find ways to enact the KOG in their daily work and →
4. await expected results (which are beneficial beyond the boundaries of their *oikos*).

Note that table 10.1 also highlights differences between a common twenty-first- versus a plausible first-century interpretation of these two KOG parables. First, twenty-

Table 10.1 The four main elements of KOG teachings evident in two central KOG parables

Thematic grouping	Parable of mustard seed (Luke 13:18–19)	Parable of yeast (Luke 13:20–21)	Common twenty-first-century interpretations	Plausible first-century interpretation of mustard seed parable	Plausible first-century interpretation of yeast parable
1. Core KOG idea	He [Jesus] said therefore, "What is the kingdom of God like? And to what should I compare it? It is like a mustard seed . . .	And again he [Jesus] said, "To what should I compare the kingdom of God? It is like yeast . . .	The KOG is like a small idea with great growth potential . . .	The KOG is like a mustard seed, a small substance that has great growth potential and is *countercultural* ("Rabbinic tradition forbade the sowing of mustard in gardens" because this weed germinated as soon as it hit the ground; Oakman, 1986: 124) . . .	The KOG is like yeast, a small substance with great growth potential that is *countercultural* (among Jesus' Jewish listeners at that time yeast was "a symbol of corruption, while unleaven stood for what is holy" [Funk, Scott, & Butts, 1988: 34; cited in Longenecker, 2000: 141]) . . .
2. Learn about KOG	that someone took and . . .	that a woman took and . . .	that an individual (typically not seen as being connected to an *oikos*) grasped and . . .	that a member of an *oikos* (farm) purposefully gathered and . . .	that a member of an *oikos* (bakery) purposefully gathered and . . .
3. Enact KOG	sowed in the garden;	mixed in with three measures of flour until . . .	put into action . . .	deliberately planted in the ground (a countercultural act);	deliberately embedded into 13.3 liters of flour (a countercultural act);
4. KOG outcomes	it grew and became a tree, and the birds of the air made nests in its branches."	all of it was leavened."	to make a large material change for the good.	it grew into a tree where the birds could find sustenance and refuge (ecologically sustainable outcome, but lowered *oikos* profits).	it rose to become enough bread to feed many people (perhaps especially people from outside the *oikos*).

first-century interpretations rarely note the countercultural implications of mustard seeds or yeast.[17] Second, twenty-first-century interpretations typically divorce these passages from their *oikos* context, whereas this would hardly be possible in the first century because an individual's identity was wholly dependent on the identity of their *oikos*. And third, whereas both first- and twenty-first-century listeners would catch onto the principle that what appears to be a small change can yield big outcomes, twenty-first-century readers are less likely to see, for example, that the resulting vegetable garden lowered the profitability of the *oikos* but was benevolent vis-à-vis the natural environment (e.g., provide a perch for the lowly birds). Note also that both passages have an emphasis on food (an important symbol in KOG). Taken together, the two parables in this passage suggest that the KOG is evident when followers challenge institutional norms and thereby facilitate positive outcomes for others.

The second passage in this group (Luke 13:28–30) also places emphasis on the imagery of sharing food in an *oikos*, and recalls themes associated with the Last Supper. The KOG is evident when meals are shared by people coming from all four directions ("from east and west, from north and south") and status differentials will be minimized (last will be first, first will be last).

This is echoed in the third passage, where Jesus instructs the host of a banquet to invite *oikos*-less people, instead of rich people who can repay them (Luke 14:12–15). In sum, the first three passages in this group share on emphasis on the countercultural nature of the KOG, and indicate that the KOG is evident when people from all walks of life eat together (share an *oikos* meal), share the same status, and act benevolently to each other and nature.

The fourth passage in this group (Luke 16:14–18) follows right after the parable of the shrewd manager where Jesus praises a manager who scatters wealth (Luke 16:1–13; see chapter five). In this passage Jesus urges Pharisees—who are called "lovers of money" and who ridicule Jesus for his praise of the shrewd manager's scattering of resources—to put aside acquisitive economic *oikos* practices and enter into the KOG.[18]

The fifth passage in this group (Luke 17:20–21) draws attention to the fact that the KOG is already present in the world. Some scholars have suggested that the phrase "the kingdom of God is among you" can be taken to mean that the KOG is in your domain or "in the house of."[19] In the present context the KOG is evident in the previous verses where Jesus restores ten lepers to community (Luke 17:11–19). And just like only one of the ten healed lepers returned to thank Jesus, so also even though the KOG is already present not everyone can "see" it.

The sixth passage (Luke 18:24–30), which has also already been discussed in chapter seven, describes how a hallmark of the KOG is the evening out of resources in society that occurs when the rich (and others) leave their conventional *oikos* in order to belong to a new *oikos*.

The seventh passage (Luke 19:11–27) describes how Jesus' disciples expected the KOG to "appear immediately," perhaps partly because in the preceding passage salvation had come to the *oikos* of Zacchaeus, an unlikely candidate (Luke 19:1–10). However, the disciples are then told about the so-called nobleman in the parable of the ten pounds, whose actions are opposite to KOG teachings (Luke 19:11–27). For every Zacchaeus who "gets" the KOG there are many others like the exploitive nobleman and his obedient managers who don't (though glimpses of the KOG are evident in the actions of the third manager; see chapter six).

The eighth and final passage in this section (Luke 23:50–53) underscores the theme that the KOG can be recognized by people from all walks of life (e.g., the farmer who sows the mustard seed, the woman who bakes leavened bread, the Samaritan leper who returns to thank Jesus, the nobleman's manager who refuses to exploit others, and the shrewd manager who uses acquisitive economic wealth benevolently). In this passage we find Joseph of Arimathea, a member of the Sanhedrin, the ruling group of religious elders who were opponents of Jesus. After Jesus has died, Joseph asks Pilate (the local Roman governor) for Jesus' body, wraps it in a linen cloth, and lays it in a rock-hewn tomb—Jesus' final "home" or so Joseph thought.

Summary

This analysis of Luke's KOG passages has several implications for management. As a whole the passages lend support to a first-century understanding where the *KOG can be seen in instances here on earth (and in heaven) where people actively relate to one another in ways that are consistent with God's way of managing.* These instances are simultaneously spiritual and earthly, are informed and empowered by knowing that the future full consummation of a KOG is already assured, are consistent with God's reign, and are freely available to all humankind.

Of particular interest is the observation that the *oikos* is the primary setting in Luke where the KOG is enacted and manifest. This suggests that managers can play a central role in the enactment and manifestation of the KOG. To manage organizations here on earth in ways consistent with KOG principles as they are in heaven is a fully spiritual phenomenon.

Taken together, the 21 KOG passages point to the following four "modes" of management associated with the KOG:

1. The KOG approach is for everyone (the crowds). Everyone is to benefit from KOG management, not just those who abide by its principles. Everyone is welcome into countercultural communities where there are no status differences.
2. The KOG approach is taught and learned. KOG management is characterized by committed study, open-mindedness, and learning from mentors and role models (the primary exemplar in Luke is the life and teachings of Jesus, but people can also learn from one another).
3. The KOG approach is enacted. Followers who enact KOG principles willingly give up conventional sources of security, emphasize benefaction, and develop alternative forms of *oikoi* where everyone is treated with dignity (especially including people who do not belong to a conventional *oikos*).
4. The KOG approach can be observed in outcomes. KOG management is evident in equitable relationships (e.g., men and women, master-slave), sharing (especially when it concerns basic needs, such as meals), sustenance economic practices (e.g., plant trees for the birds, shrewd manager, third manager in the parable of the ten pounds), and surprising role models (e.g., Zacchaeus, Joseph of Arimathea).

Finally, it is also helpful to consider the implications of the KOG passages explicitly in terms of the three-dimensional first-century lens. With regard to

1. managing relationships *within* organizations, the passages point to the importance of treating everyone with dignity (e.g., sharing *oikos* meals together as equals in remembrance of Jesus and in anticipation of the KOG; Luke 22:14–18; cf. 23:51);
2. managing money, the passages point to subverting conventional financial management norms by being willing to voluntarily lower *oikos* productivity for

the sake of the natural environment (Luke 13:18–21) and thwarting acquisitive economic pressure despite personal risk (passages before and after Luke 19:11)[20]; and

3. managing relationships with outsiders, the passages encourage the practice of inclusive benefaction, evident in hosting banquets for people from all four corners and from the margins of society (Luke 13:28–30; 14:12–15) and in bringing peace, curing the sick, and proclaiming the KOG in others' *oikoi* (Luke 9:1–6; 10:1–11).

REFLECTION POINT: CONNECTING CONTEMPORARY RESEARCH AND LUKE'S PASSAGES ON THE KOG

How does a KOG approach to management compare with the sorts of approaches to nonconventional management that scholars are increasingly calling for?[21] As Gary Hamel puts it, there is a growing consensus that the time has come to replace conventional Management 1.0 with a qualitatively different Management 2.0 approach. Some hallmarks characterizing what a new-and-improved "Management 2.0" might look like emerged from a conference of 25 leading management scholars and practitioners—including Gary Hamel, Henry Mintzberg, Jeffrey Pfeffer, Chris Argyris, Peter Senge, Eric Abrahamson, and C. K. Prahalad—who recently met to "spur the reinvention of management in the twenty-first century." The group emphasized the importance of reconstructing the philosophical foundations of management, explicitly noting the importance of drawing lessons from fields like theology. While there are certainly differences between KOG management and what this group was calling for, there is also considerable overlap, as evident in looking at their ideas through the three-dimensional lens. First, *in terms of managing relationships within organizations*, the group called for designing organizations where: "power flows up from the bottom and leaders emerge instead of being appointed"; goal setting is "distributed through a process in which the share of voice is a function of insight, not power"; fear is reduced and trust is increased; and empowerment is accorded to "employees whose emotional equity is invested in the future rather than the past." Second, *in terms of managing money*, the group called for the development of "holistic performance measures," noting that conventional "performance metrics must be recast" and, in particular, pointing to the need to stretch perspectives and time frames toward discovering "alternatives to compensation and reward systems that encourage managers to sacrifice long-term goals for short-term gains." "Tomorrow's management systems must give as much credence to such timeless human ideals as beauty, justice, and community as they do to the traditional goals of efficiency, advantage, and profit." Finally, hallmarks of *managing relationships with outsiders* are captured in the group's first two "grand challenges": (1) *Ensure that the work of management serves a higher purpose. Management, both in theory and practice, must orient itself to the achievement of noble, socially significant goals.* ["Most companies strive to maximize shareholder wealth—a goal that is inadequate in many respects."] (2) *"Fully embed the ideas of community and citizenship in management systems.* There's a need for processes and practices that reflect the interdependence of all stakeholder groups." The group also called for decision-making processes that "exploit the collective wisdom of the entire organization and beyond."

11

Salvation is Facilitated when People are Saved *from* Oppressive Structures and Systems, and are Saved *for* Work in Liberating Organizational Structures and Systems

According to Max Weber, the question of suffering, and thus of salvation, has been central to the origin and development of religion throughout the history of humankind. For him salvation refers to transcendent ways for humankind to be liberated from suffering. He notes that the meaning of salvation has changed through the course of history both within and across religions, and that people's understanding salvation informs how they manage and organize (and vice versa).[1]

In a paper with my coauthor Elden Wiebe, we trace how changing views of salvation within Western Christianity over the past two millennia have been manifest in changes in organization and management practices.[2] We suggest that humanity's age-old pursuit of salvation pervades the contemporary management literature, though it is rarely referred to in religious terms, nor typically called "salvation." Rather, it is more likely to be called "emancipation," escaping the "iron cage," "self-actualization," "empowerment," and so on.[3] Even ideas like "sustainable development," and "corporate social responsibility" have echoes of the ancient ideas of "salvation"—that is, they address how people can reduce the suffering associated with the status quo.[4]

What is Salvation?

Despite it being a central feature of Christianity, there is a lack of consensus on the meaning of salvation[5] and it has been oft-noted that there has been great variation in how the meaning of salvation has been interpreted over the past two thousand years. Similar to the KOG, there are four basic dimensions or questions of how salvation can be interpreted that are of particular importance for our study. Again, this analysis will present these four dimensions as "either/or" statements in order to draw attention to differing emphases in the first versus the twenty-first centuries, but the dimensions could also be thought of as "both/and" statements (e.g., salvation is concerned with both a future *and* the present life).

1. Is salvation primarily concerned with the afterlife, or is its emphasis on the present?
2. Does salvation refer primarily to a spiritual realm, or is it also relevant in the earthly realm?
3. Is salvation something provided to passive recipients, or does salvation involve the active participation of those who are saved?
4. Is salvation primarily a personal (individual) concern, or is it a social (corporate) phenomenon?

A popular twenty-first-century understanding of salvation would lean toward the first interpretation along each of these four dimensions. Thus, from a popular twenty-first-century perspective, the understanding of salvation is evident in the following paraphrased interpretation of John 3:16: "*God loved the world so much that God sent Jesus—God's only son—to die on the cross as an atonement for people's sins, so that every individual who believes in Jesus will have everlasting life.*" In this paraphrase the emphasis is on the afterlife and a spiritual realm (Jesus brings everlasting life), on a passive role for recipients (Jesus died for humankind and people simply need to accept this), and on individuals (every individual who believes is saved).

However, this twenty-first-century interpretation would have been quite foreign to people in first-century Palestine, especially readers of Luke, who might begin by noting the implications of *oikos*[6] embedded in John 3:16: "*Just as Jesus left his Father's* oikos *to bring salvation to people (especially for the 'lost') via setting up KOG structures and systems, so also Jesus calls his listeners to leave their childhood* oikos *and establish new forms of inclusive* oikos *(especially for the 'outcast') consistent with the KOG.*" Compared to the more popular twenty-first-century understanding, such a first-century understanding places greater emphasis on the present and the earthly realm (salvation provides community for everyone, especially marginalized people), on an active role for recipients (Jesus demonstrates a new way of living as a model for followers), and on social groups (salvation is evident in new *oikos* structures and systems). Let's look at each dimension in turn.

First, the majority of Luke's references to salvation indicate that it is already visible and present (e.g., Luke 2:30; 7:50; 8:48; 17:17; 18:42: 19:9).[7] This emphasis on the present is especially notable in the meaning of healings Jesus performs, where he saves people from their illnesses and thus their social marginalization. It is underscored by expressions like "this day" a savior is born (Luke 2:11) and "today" salvation has come to this *oikos* (Luke 19:9).[8]

Second, as in the case of our discussion of the meaning of the KOG, the tendency in the twenty-first-century to separate spiritual ideas like "salvation" from everyday life would have been foreign in the first century. In the first century, salvation would be expected to be evident in everyday life. This is not to deny the spiritual nature of salvation, but simply to note again that in the first century people did not segregate spiritual religious matters from everyday economic matters. For example, the Roman emperor was commonly called the "Savior" thanks to him providing so-called Roman peace (*pax Romana*) to his conquered peoples.[9] Thus, when first-century listeners heard about Jesus described as "Savior" it would have been entirely natural for them to contrast his salvation with the kind of "salvation" they were currently experiencing under the Romans. In other words, they would have expected Jesus to provide an alternative to the current regime's structures and systems. In particular, the Jews had been waiting years for a Messiah to help them escape from the oppression of the Romans and to invoke a new era of God's reign on earth. In short, it seems unlikely that first-century people would have thought of salvation narrowly as a spiritual event of no relevance to their everyday lives.

Third, Luke and early theologians emphasized that the modality through which Jesus provides salvation is to follow his example as role model, rather than via his sacrificial death on the cross.[10] Thus, in the first century people were not primarily seen as passive recipients of salvation, but rather as being given the opportunity to actively participate in redeemed structures and systems. This emphasis on the importance of Jesus as a role model for how his followers ought to live is also evident in church leaders writing about salvation in the second and early third century.[11]

Fourth and finally, Luke consistently draws attention to the corporate social nature of salvation. When salvation (noun) is mentioned in Luke, it is always for an identifiable group of people (e.g., Jesus says: "Today salvation has come to this *oikos*," Luke 19:9). And when being saved (verb) is mentioned, it either identifies individuals being saved *from oikos*-lessness (e.g., social outcasts are reinstated into community) or saved *for* developing life-giving inclusive forms of community/*oikos* (e.g., walk away from conventional *oikoi* and start countercultural *oikoi*). This emphasis on *oikoi* and community is consistent with the first-century understanding that salvation was linked to challenging unjust social systems and structures (especially among the Jews), rather than focused on individual piety. Indeed, Jesus' death on the cross is itself clear testament that his teachings had important sociopolitical implications, indicating that Jesus was seen as a subversive threat to the political elite of his day.[12] This countercultural social dimension of salvation would also have been an ongoing reality for the early church, when it was often persecuted by imperial Rome.

Main Themes in Luke's Salvation Passages

Luke is known for its emphasis on the theme of salvation, which with 25 mentions is referred to more often in Luke than in any other Gospel (17 mentions are in the form of a verb, 8 in the form of a noun). Moreover, Luke is the only synoptic Gospel where Jesus is called the Savior (*soter*), which was a term used frequently in the Greco-Roman world to refer to emperors, gods, statesmen, philosophers, and physicians.[13] In order to interpret what Luke means by salvation, it is helpful to note two things.

First, in first-century Palestine salvation generally emphasized either being saved *from* oppression, or being saved *for* new ways of living. The idea of being saved *from* oppression is related to the Jewish understanding of salvation as deliverance from enemies and a restoration of Israel to its rightful place in the world. Most notably, in the first century the Jews were longing to be freed from oppressive Roman structures and systems, just as the Jews had been liberated from Egyptian domination centuries earlier.[14] The emphasis on being saved *for* new ways of living is related to the Greco-Roman view that associated salvation with the bestowal of blessings, which could include the bestowal of life-giving structures and systems.[15]

Second, Luke uses the *noun* form of salvation (e.g., savior, salvation) differently than the *verb* form (to be saved). As shown in table 11.1, seven of Luke's eight uses of the *noun* form of salvation occur prior to Jesus' baptism (Luke 3:21), and in each case it refers to a *group* of people (e.g., *oikos* of David, gentiles, all people) receiving both dimensions of salvation (i.e., being saved *from* oppression, and being saved *for* new ways of living). In contrast, all 17 subsequent uses of the *verb* form refer to *individuals* being saved, and typically emphasize only one dimension (individuals are either saved from, or saved for).[16] Moreover, as shown in table 11.2 later in this

Table 11.1 Mentions in Luke of the noun forms of "salvation," "savior," and "to be saved"

Key verses in passage	Saved *from* . . . oppression, exclusion, *oikos*-lessness	Saved *for* . . . new blessings, inclusive *oikos*	Salvation for whom?
a. Mentions prior to Jesus starting his public ministry			
My spirit rejoices in God my **Savior** [*soteri*] . . . (Luke 1:46–55)	. . . he has brought down the powerful from their thrones	. . . and lifted up the lowly, he has filled the hungry with good things	. . . he has helped his servant [the people of] *Israel*
"[The Lord God] has raised up a mighty **savior** [*soterias*] . . . (Luke 1:67–79)	. . . that we would be **saved** [*soterian*] from our enemies	. . . to give knowledge of **salvation** [*soterias*] to his people . . . to guide our feet into the way of peace.	. . . *The Lord God of Israel* . . . has raised up a mighty savior *for us in the house of his servant David* . . .
To you is born this day in the city of David a **Savior** [*soter*], (Luke 2:11)	who is the Messiah [allusion to Jewish understanding of savior],	the Lord [allusion to Greek understanding of savior].	
. . . for my eyes have seen your **salvation** [*soterion*], (Luke 2:25–35)	. . . for glory to your people Israel [allusion to Jewish understanding of savior]	. . . a light of revelation to the Gentiles	. . . Good news of great joy for *all people* . . . which you have prepared for *all peoples*
. . . and all flesh shall see the **salvation** [*soterion*] of God. (Luke 3:6)	. . . every mountain and hill shall be made low, the crooked shall be made straight,	. . . and the rough ways made smooth	and *all flesh* shall see the **salvation** of God.
b. Mentions after Jesus starts his public ministry			
Then Jesus said to him [Zacchaeus], "Today **salvation** [*soteria*] has come to this house, (Luke 19:1–9)	because he too is a son of Abraham." [Zacchaeus is restored to the house of Israel; also, the poor and the defrauded experience freedom from oppression].	. . . Zacchaeus stood there and said to the Lord, "Look, half my possessions, Lord, I will give to the poor; and if I have defrauded anyone of anything, I will pay back four times as much" [a radical way of managing an *oikos*].	. . . Today **salvation** has come to *this house* [and thus, by example, a sign for anyone else who wishes to have salvation come to their *oikos*].

chapter, in passages where the individual is *identified* (e.g., a man with a withered hand, a prostitute, a Samaritan leper) they are usually being *saved from* oppression (e.g., Jesus heals them and they are restored to community). In passages where the individuals being saved are not specified (e.g., "generic" followers of Jesus), they are usually being *saved for* something (e.g., to establish a new kind of *oikos*). We will look at each of these different types of passages in turn.

Passages That Refer to Salvation as a Noun

As shown in table 11.1, the passages that use the noun form of salvation all offer salvation to a group of people, and each encompassed *both* the idea of being saved from *and* the idea of being saved for. People are saved *from* oppressive and powerful leaders, from enemies, from obstacles, and from being treated as social outcasts. People are saved *for* good things, for the way of peace, revelation, straight paths, and new *oikos* structures that are beneficent and just.

This dual emphasis is sometimes built into the progression of a passage, as is illustrated by the following quote from Zechariah, the father of John the Baptist. Zechariah's prophecy begins by emphasizing the traditional Hebrew understanding of salvation as being delivered from enemies (being redeemed/rescued from the hands of enemies), and ends with an emphasis on going forward in a new way (to give knowledge, to guide feet into the way of peace):

> Part A—Saved *from*: "Blessed be the Lord God of Israel, for he has looked favorably on his people and redeemed them. He has raised up a mighty savior for us in the house of his servant David, as he spoke through the mouth of his holy prophets from of old, that we would be *saved from our enemies* and from the hand of all who hate us. Thus he has shown the mercy promised to our ancestors, and has remembered his holy covenant, the oath that he swore to our ancestor Abraham, to grant us that we, being *rescued from the hands of our enemies*, might serve him without fear, in holiness and righteousness before him all our days . . .
>
> Part B—Saved *for*: And you, child, will be called the prophet of the Most High; for you will go before the Lord to prepare his ways, to *give knowledge of salvation* to his people by the forgiveness of their sins. By the tender mercy of our God, the dawn from on high will break upon us, to *give light* to those who sit in darkness and in the shadow of death, to *guide our feet into the way of peace*." (Luke 1:67–79; emphasis added here)

A condensed version of this twofold emphasis is evident in the passage where the angel announces to the shepherds: "To you is born this day in the city of David a Savior, who is the *Messiah* [Hebrew emphasis, did not use Greek word 'Christ'], the Lord [Greek word, *kurios*]" (Luke 2:11).[17]

Passages That Describe *Identified* Individuals Being Saved (Verb)

The passages that use the noun form of salvation typically describe it as something that occurs at a group level and they tend to emphasize *both* its saved from (restorative) and its saved for (transformative) dimensions (table 11.1). As shown in table 11.2, this is notably different from the passages that use the verb form of being saved, which tend to describe individuals who are *either* being saved from (restorative) or being saved for (transformative). In particular, passages that describe *identified* individuals who are saved tend to be consistent with the Jewish idea of being saved from

Table 11.2 Mentions in Luke of the verb forms of "to be saved"

Key verses in passage	Saved from . . . oppression, exclusion, *oikos*-lessness	Saved for . . . new blessings, inclusive *oikos*	Salvation for whom?
a. Mentions that identify a specific (oikos-less) person being saved			
Then Jesus said to them, "I ask you, is it lawful to do good or to do harm on the sabbath, to **save** [*sosai*] life or to destroy it?" (Luke 6:9)	Withered hand, and thus restored to community (freed from oppressive Sabbath laws)		Man with withered hand
And he said to the woman, "Your faith has **saved** [*sesoken*] you; go in peace." (Luke 7:50)	Guilt, and thus restored to community		Prostitute
Those who had seen it told them how the one who had been possessed by demons had been healed [*esothe*]. (Luke 8:36)	Demon-possession, and thus restored to community (returns to his *oikos*)		Man with demons
He said to her, "Daughter, your faith has made you well [*sesoken*]; go in peace." (Luke 8:48)	Bleeding, and thus restored to community		A woman who had been bleeding
When Jesus heard this, he replied, "Do not fear. Only believe, and she will be **saved** [*sothesetai*]." (Luke 8:50)	Death, and thus restored as member of her household		Daughter of synagogue leader
Then he said to him, "Get up and go on your way; your faith has made you well [*sesoken*]." (Luke 17:19)	Leprosy, and thus restored to community		Samaritan leper
Jesus said to him, "Receive your sight; your faith has **saved** [*sesoken*] you." (Luke 18:42)	Blindness, and thus restored to community		Blind man on road to Jericho
b. Mentions that do not identify a specific person being saved (generic)			
The ones on the path ["bad soil"] are those who have heard; then the devil comes and takes away the word from their hearts, so that they may not believe and be **saved** [*sothosin*]. (Luke 8:12)		Grow in "good soil" in which to implement godly ideas/bear fruit	Listeners who hear the word, hold it in their hearts, bear fruit, and have a long-term orientation

Scripture			
For those who want to **save** [*sosai*] their life will lose it, and those who lose their life for my sake will **save** [*sosei*] it. (Luke 9:24)		Following Jesus' way	Listeners who take up their cross (thereby leaving conventional *oikos*) and join Jesus' *oikos*
Someone asked him, "Lord, will only a few be **saved** [*sozomenoi*]?" He said to them, "Strive to enter the narrow door; for many, I tell you, will try to enter and not be able." (Luke 13:23)		Enter new *oikos*	Listeners who deliberately choose to enter new forms of *oikos* associated with KOG
Those who heard it said, "Then who can be **saved** [*sothenai*]?" (Luke 18:26)		New *oikos*	Listeners who leave their conventional *oikos* for the sake of KOG
For the Son of Man came to seek out and to **save** [*sosai*] the lost." (Luke 19:10)	Jesus previously saved people and then permitted them to be restored to community.	New ways of *oikos* management	Zacchaeus and others

Refers to individuals who had previously already been saved from oppression |
| And the people stood by, watching; but the leaders scoffed at him, saying, "He **saved** [*sosen*] others; let him **save** [*sosato*] himself if he is the Messiah of God, his chosen one!" . . . "If you are the King of the Jews, **save** [*soson*] yourself!" . . . One of the criminals who were hanged there kept deriding him and saying, "Are you not the Messiah? **Save** [*soson*] yourself and us!" (Luke 23:32–43) | Jesus and the two criminals are *not* saved from crucifixion | "Paradise" (literally, "garden" = image of a new creation) | Jesus and criminal alongside him are not saved from crucifixion, but are saved for paradise |

being outcasts and restored to community (table 11.2a). Here the crippled, guilty, mentally ill, sick, dead, lepers, and the blind are healed and thus restored to (conventional?) community. In contrast, passages that provide *general teachings* about unidentified individuals being saved tend to emphasize the bestowal of new blessings and the introduction of transformed communities and *oikoi* (table 11.2b). Here the emphasis is on creating good soil, following Jesus' way, and promoting alternative forms of *oikos*.

The seven passages in table 11.2a identify specific individuals who are restored to community/released from oppression. A common theme for each of these individuals is that they start off as social outcasts of some sort, and in each case Jesus saves them to become members of conventional communities. Recall that in first-century Palestine, the sick, the prostitutes, the demon-possessed, criminals, and so on were all denied access to the *oikos* of Israel. They were considered too impure to be full members of their parental *oikos* or of the house of Israel. In each of these passages Jesus heals[18] or forgives such individuals, and thereby restores them to the community that has oppressed them.[19] This is consistent with Jewish expectations of a savior. However, whereas the Jews expected a savior who would save the Jewish people from *foreign* oppressors like the Romans, in these passages Luke describes a savior who saves people from conventional "local" customs that result in oppression and marginalization.

Finally, note that the identified people who are saved in Luke are not passive (i.e., table 11.2a), but rather in almost every case they show some initiative. The man with the withered hand sought out Jesus' teachings and made himself available to Jesus (Luke 6:6–9); the prostitute washed Jesus' feet and anointed him with oil (Luke 7:37–38); the bleeding woman reached out to touch Jesus, even though she was ritually unclean and should not have done so (Luke 8:44); the lepers approached Jesus and asked him for mercy and followed his instruction to show themselves to the high priests (Luke 17:12–14); the blind man shouted out to Jesus asking him for mercy, even when the crowd ordered him to be quiet (Luke 18:35–43); and the criminal recognizes that Jesus had done nothing wrong and asked for Jesus to remember him (Luke 23:40–42).[20]

In sum, these passages in table 11.2a describe instances where Jesus heals specifically identified individuals and restores them to community, and in this way they are saved from oppression.

Passages That Describe *Unidentified* Individuals Being Saved (Verb)

The remaining six passages that use the verb form of "to save" tend not to focus on one particular person being, but instead provide a more encompassing teaching about being saved (see table 11.2b). In contrast to the passages in table 11.2a, the passages in table 11.2b generally tend to place greater emphasis on being saved *for* ("undergoing transformation") versus as saved *from* ("overcoming oppression"). In each passage in table 11.2b, the person being saved enjoys blessings from God, and often these blessings allude to new life-giving social structures. These blessings include being in settings where the word of God can flourish such as:

- "good soil," versus settings characterized by acquisitive economics (Luke 8:4–15);
- "finding one's true self" in a KOG-like *oikos*, versus being caught in conventional systems (Luke 9:23–27);

- entering the narrow door into an inclusive *oikos* comprised of people from around the world, versus conventional *oikoi* where relative social status is revered (Luke 13:22–30); and
- reaping the "eternal life" that comes from choosing KOG structures, versus conventional ones (Luke 18:18–30).

Taken together, the two groups of passages represented in tables 11.2a and b can be seen as two sides of the same coin. Whereas table 11.2a describes *oikos*-less people who are saved when they are restored to community, table 11.2b describes people are saved when they voluntarily leave their conventional *oikos* in order to create more inclusive, life-giving structures and systems. What the two groups of passages share in common is finding ways to include marginalized people in an *oikos*, either by saving outsiders so that they can participate in conventional *oikos* (table 11.2a), or by transforming the *oikos* so that everyone who was previously marginalized is now welcomed (table 11.2b). We will now briefly look at each passage in table 11.2b.

The parable of the soils (Luke 8:4–15). This passage describes how "good soil" facilitates salvation. It describes a farmer who sows seed (which represents the word of God) in four different kinds of soils, with four different results.

1. Some seed falls on the path and is trampled on. This represents the many people who hear God's word, but the Devil comes and takes away the word from their hearts so that they may not believe nor be saved.
2. Some seed falls among the rocks, where they grow but then wither for lack of moisture. This represents those people who received the word with joy, but they believe for only a short while and then fall away in a time of testing because they lack root.
3. Some seed falls among the thorns and is choked by them. This represents people who hear the word but the fruit does not mature because they are choked by the cares and riches and pleasures of life.
4. Some seed falls on good soil where it grows and produces hundredfold. This represents people who: (a) hear the word, (b) hold it fast in an honest and good heart (an internal disposition), (c) bear fruit, and (d) show patient endurance.[21]

Overall, the parable suggests that the likelihood of people being saved is linked to the kind of conditions they are surrounded by. In particular, listeners should be thankful for good soil that allows them to reap the benefits of increased understanding of the word of God. In contrast, people in an *oikos* where they face acquisitive economic pressures and temptations are less likely to experience salvation, akin to the seeds that fall among the thorns and thus are "choked by the cares and riches and pleasures of life" (Luke 8:14). The implications for first-century managers are threefold: (1) be thankful for *oikoi* with "good soil" (structures and systems); (2) insofar as you have a choice, be careful when choosing the kind of *oikos* you work in; and (3) cultivate/nurture the "soil" in the *oikos* where you work.

The paradox about saving one's life (Luke 9:23b-27). The second passage is worth quoting in full because of its double reference to being saved, and because of its link to other issues of interest to management:

> If any want to become my followers, let them deny themselves and take up their cross daily and follow me. For those who want to *save* their life will lose it, and those who lose their life for my sake will *save* it. What does it profit them if they gain the whole world,

but lose or forfeit themselves? Those who are ashamed of me and of my words, of them the Son of Man will be ashamed when he comes in his glory and the glory of the Father and of the holy angels. But truly I tell you, there are some standing here who will not taste death before they see the kingdom of God. (Luke 9:23b-27; emphasis added)

The passage starts by calling listeners to "deny themselves" and to "take up their cross daily" and follow the example of Jesus.[22] In the first century to deny oneself meant to deny one's primary relationships, especially within their *oikos* because these relationships were what made up one's identity. Such a denial of these relationships is also echoed in the idea of carrying one's cross day by day. In the first century, to carry a cross meant to have been condemned for failing to uphold the dominant sociopolitical expectations. In particular, in legal terms such condemned persons had forfeited their estates (*oikos*, wealth) and were denied burial (a crucial element of honor and social status in the first century). In the context of the Roman world, the metaphor of carrying one's cross was consistent with the rejection of conventional status and wealth.[23]

The second sentence in this passage, then, could be paraphrased as follows:

> People who want to *save* their current lifestyles (in particular, people who strive to belong to a conventional *oikos*, and who value acquisitive economics and honor) will lose the opportunity to live as fully as God intends. In contrast, people who are willing to be *saved* from conventional lifestyles for my sake will experience the intended meaning of life as practiced in the structures and systems associated with the kingdom of God.

This message is echoed in the subsequent verses, which explicitly describe the folly of seeking financial profits and of living in ways that do not honor God. The final verse suggests that "being saved" in this radical way is associated with seeing the kingdom of God here on earth. Thus, taken together, this passage suggests that *being saved involves turning one's back to conventional expressions of financial security and status, and instead choosing to participate in countercultural KOG structures and systems.*

The narrow door (Luke 13:22–30). In the third of these general teachings, Jesus is asked whether only a few will be saved. Jesus' response suggests that being saved has something to do with becoming a member of an *oikos* managed according to KOG teachings. In particular, he suggests that being saved requires people to come forward on their own accord and enter the KOG *oikos* of their own accord (i.e., enter through the narrow door, one by one). People in the crowd who merely listen to Jesus' teachings but fail to act on them[24] will not enter. Those who have the greatest status by conventional standards often refuse to enter the KOG *oikos*, whereas those who seem to have the lowest status will enter first. In sum, *people from all four corners of the world are welcome to enter the narrow door in order participate in the KOG* oikos *and be saved.*

To be saved involves leaving one's conventional oikos *(Luke 18:18–30).* This passage was discussed in chapter seven when discussing managing relationships within *oikoi*. In this passage, Jesus responds to the question of who can be saved by explaining how people who leave their conventional *oikos* for the sake of the KOG will gain much in this age and in the future. This message is consistent with earlier passages.

Jesus is crucified alongside two criminals (Luke 23:32–42). The final passage in table 11.2b is striking for several reasons. First, this passage mentions being saved four times (Luke 23:35, 37, 39), signaling that this is a key passage for understanding salvation. Second, unlike each of the previous occasions where Jesus does save people from oppression, in this passage he saves neither himself nor the criminals beside him from crucifixion. Thus, it seems that Jesus' death on the cross signals a shift toward the transformative side of salvation. This is evident in Jesus' reply to the criminal who asks to be remembered in the KOG: "Truly I tell you, today you will be with me in Paradise" (v. 43). The Greek word for "Paradise" (*paradeiso*) can also be translated as "garden," and is the same word used in Greek translations for the Garden of Eden.[25] Thus, in terms of the overarching creation-fall-salvation-kingdom of God biblical narrative described in chapter two, Jesus' death seems to be linked with ushering in a new kind of garden or *oikos* (i.e., the kingdom of God).[26] This emphasis on new structures and systems is consistent with all the passages in table 11.2b.

This passage also draws attention to what may appear to be a paradoxical core aspect of salvation that is represented by the cross. *Not only does Jesus not save himself from suffering on the cross, Jesus suffers on the cross precisely because he has saved others from suffering* (Luke 23:35). Occasions where Jesus saves others often prompted leaders of the day to become furious at him or make accusations against him or challenge him or laugh at him (e.g., Luke 6:7, 11; 7:39; 8:53). Even many of the people he healed fail to thank him (Luke 7:17), and his disciples were unsure (Luke 8:45). In saving others (i.e., in reducing the suffering of others), Jesus brings suffering onto himself.[27]

Luke's Keystone Passage on Salvation and Being Saved: The Salvation of the *Oikos* of Zacchaeus (Luke 19:1–10)

This final passage serves as a keystone passage for unlocking what Luke says about salvation. The passage starts with Jesus entering Jericho and inviting himself to the *oikos* of a rich man named Zacchaeus. Being a rich chief tax collector in the region, Zacchaeus was in charge of a relatively large *oikos*, with junior tax collectors reporting to him.[28] As a tax collector, Zacchaeus would have been despised and considered to be a social outcast among the Jews.[29] The people who saw Jesus enter the *oikos* of Zacchaeus grumbled: "He [Jesus] has gone to be the guest of one who is a sinner."[30] Zacchaeus says to Jesus:

> "Look, half of my possessions, Lord, I will give to the poor; and if I have defrauded anyone of anything, I will pay back four times as much."[31] Then Jesus said to him, "Today *salvation* [noun] has come to *this house* [*oikos*], because he too is a son of Abraham.[32] For the Son of Man came to seek out and *save* [verb] the lost."[33] (Luke 19:8–10)

Several features make this the most striking of all Luke's passages on salvation and being saved.

- This is the only time where *Jesus* uses the noun "salvation";
- This is the only time the noun "salvation" is mentioned in all of Jesus' public ministry (i.e., after Luke 3:21); and
- This is the only passage anywhere in Luke that mentions *both* "salvation" (noun form) *and* "to be saved" (verb form).

Given the previous stories in Luke's description of Jesus' ministry, the reader would be primed to fully expected Jesus to respond to Zacchaeus by saying something like: "Zacchaeus, your faith has saved you; go in peace" (a phrase Jesus utters on four previous occasions[34]). For the passage to end with Jesus saying, "Today salvation has come to this *oikos*" seems totally unexpected.[35]

The implications for management could not be more striking. The only time Jesus talks about salvation is when the head of a large *oikos* changes the structures and systems of his organization toward KOG principles.[36] These organizational practices facilitate salvation *from* poverty (give half of possessions to the poor), and salvation *for* justice (repay fourfold anyone who has been defrauded). Does salvation have something to do with how people manage their organizations? The answer is a clear and unequivocal yes. Is the way that an *oikos* is managed a concern that is front-and-center for Jesus? It could scarcely be more central.

The passage ends by Jesus saying: "I have come to seek out and save the lost." It is somewhat ambiguous who the "lost" might refer to. Is it "lost" people like Zacchaeus, a tax collector, who can no longer be shut out of the religious community of God's people? Or is it "lost" people like the religious elite, for whom "outsiders" like Zacchaeus provide a model of salvation?[37] In either case, Jesus came to save people from oppression and to save them for alternative ways of managing their *oikos*.[38]

SUMMARY

As a whole, these passages draw considerable attention to *oikoi*, and especially to how salvation is related to the inclusion of marginalized people within *oikoi*, and thus to the role managers can play in facilitating salvation. In particular, salvation and demarginalization are very much related to how organizational boundaries are managed.

On the one hand, Jesus saves specific people by removing the affliction that prevented them from being full members of society (e.g., healing the sick, forgiving the prostitute), thereby bringing them in from the margins. This is an immediate "sign" that points to what sort of outcomes are associated with being saved (i.e., being restored to community).

On the other hand, Jesus calls his followers to establish organizational structures and systems that are inclusive and thereby welcome marginalized people into the *oikos*: "Go out at once into the streets and lanes of the town and bring in the poor, the crippled, the blind, and the lame" (Luke 14:21) (i.e., become a restorative community). This is the work Jesus' disciples are called to do. Note however that this work in reducing the suffering of others, which lies at the core of Jesus' teaching and example, may result in suffering for oneself. Thus, salvation is evident when people manage to create structures and systems that reduce overall suffering, even if they can expect such acts of social nonconformity to prompt their own suffering.

To modern readers the idea that something as "spiritual" as salvation is so thoroughly grounded in something as "earthly" as management and organizational structures and systems may seem foreign. But it would certainly not have been foreign in the first century, a time when the spiritual and religious was very much grounded in the fabric of everyday life. Looking at the passages in Luke from a managerial perspective provides a different lens than people are accustomed to. It points to the importance of making *oikos* boundaries more porous, increasing the scope of who belongs within the *oikos* and informing how to manage relationships with outsiders. It draws attention to the fact that the KOG is to be manifest in how people organize themselves in the everyday world, and that salvation has to do with being freed from oppressive structures and systems, and how participating in inclusive organizations is consistent with KOG principles.

In sum, Luke describes how Jesus came to seek out and save people, to help them escape oppressive situations and to show them glimpses of what KOG organizations might look like (Luke 19:10). The challenge for his followers is to put these KOG principles into practice in their everyday *oikos*. Salvation is evident insofar as this occurs.[39]

REFLECTION POINT: CONNECTING CONTEMPORARY RESEARCH AND LUKE'S PASSAGES ABOUT SALVATION

How does Luke's description of "salvation" compare to the idea of "emancipation," which is probably the closest concept to "salvation" that is discussed in contemporary management research? The two ideas are similar in that each seeks to free people from oppression, each emphasizes putting new structures and systems into practice/praxis, and each has an inherent tension between the individual and the larger group. However, a key difference between the two is that the emancipation literature has a bias toward getting people to act in *their self-interests* (once they recognize oppressive social structures and systems), whereas the description of salvation in Luke has a bias toward getting people to act in *the interests of others* (i.e., others who are oppressed by structures and systems). A second difference is that emancipation, at least in some forms, recognizes that violent means may need to be used to overthrow oppressive regimes, whereas the idea of salvation as expressed in Luke is nonviolent in principle (though it may prompt a violent response from others). Indeed, this lies at the core of Jesus' example in being crucified for daring to challenge the structures and systems of his day that oppressed people at the margins of society.[40]

12

THE HOLY SPIRIT IS KEY TO SALVIFIC KINGDOM OF GOD MANAGEMENT

Given the growing interest in spirituality in management among both scholars and practitioners, one might expect a considerable literature that relates the Holy Spirit to management. However, this is not the case. While there is growing interest in spirituality, it seems that there is little interest in a spirit (or in spirits). For example, in looking among articles and books specifically on spirituality, it is striking how few mentions there are of a specific (external) spirit, or God, or higher power. And in most instances where the word "spirit" is mentioned, rather than refer to the spirit of God, it refers to ideas like the "spirit of capitalism," the human spirit, or team spirit, or a spirit of cooperation. One examination of one hundred books related to "spirituality in organizations" showed that fewer than 20 percent mention God or a higher power. Reference to God, or a spirit, is even lower in scholarly articles on spirituality in secular journals.[1] A similar lack of mention of "spirit" is also evident among consultants in the area.[2]

This lack of mention of a spirit per se may be attributable to several factors. First, insofar as an emphasis on a Holy Spirit or a God suggests that there may be some higher power that people are accountable to, this goes against people's current desire to be independent and be their own boss. People today do not want to be subservient or accountable to an external power that they cannot control.

A second factor that may help to explain why the Holy Spirit is absent in the management literature is related to the view held by some that the Holy Spirit is focused primarily or purely on inward piety. However, others believe that the Spirit is very relevant for everyday and external structures and systems, and some hold a "both/and" view.[3]

As it turns out, on occasions where the Holy Spirit *is* explicitly mentioned in the general management literature, it is typically consistent with the larger view that encompasses structures and systems. For example, Jeff van Duzer and his colleagues talk about the Holy Spirit as being involved in continually realizing Jesus' desired vision of the kingdom of God:

> The totality of the scriptures would seem to affirm that, enabled by the power of the Holy Spirit, it is possible to live out, albeit imperfectly, God's values in the midst of a fallen world both as a means of transformation and as a sign that points to the coming reign of God . . . *by the power of the Spirit, Christians can participate in the actual transformation of the practice of business.* Business activities can be brought more into alignment with godly values. While perhaps never being able to successfully complete

the transformation, much in the scriptures would seem to support the conclusion that significant steps in the right direction can be taken.[4]

The merit of incorporating ideas like the spirit of God in management is consistent with the striking number of leading management scholars and practitioners who are specifically pointing to *theology* as a starting point for developing alternative approaches to management theory.[5] This renewed interest in God within the management literature is consistent with the larger "theological turn" evident among leading philosophers, which frees scholars to develop alternative management theory and practice based on concepts that transcend contemporary management theory. For example, scholars note that it can be difficult to conceive of acts of altruistic benefaction within (secular) contemporary management theory, which is thus forced to use "instrumental language" to try to "justify" benefaction.[6] The theological turn remedies this situation because it opens the door to the *possibility* of altruism and other ideas that are impossible within a secular paradigm based on rational choice theory and consequential utilitarianism. For example, just because altruism cannot be defended from a phenomenological or rational viewpoint does not mean it is not possible. A theological perspective, premised on the assumption that there is a benevolent God, is able to conceive the lure of altruism being no less powerful than the lure of profits.[7] In short, the theological turn permits the development of management theory and practice that takes into account "ideas and ideals" that lie outside of secular paradigms.[8]

Thus the "theological turn" enables us to conceive of a loving God—even if we don't believe that such a god exists—which in turn allows us to imagine and theorize about concepts like altruism and genuine benefaction, concepts that are difficult to conceive within conventional paradigms. Inverting the argument, social structures and systems that enact or provide glimpses of such altruism or genuine benefaction in turn may be seen to point to the existence of a loving God.

Weber foresaw this reembracing of the theological. He argued that the contemporary approach was destined to fail in the long term despite its allure, speculating that change would be triggered by ecological factors (perhaps it would remain "until the last ton of fossilized coal is burnt") or by lack of ultimate meaning associated with the iron cage ("the pursuit of wealth, stripped of its religious and ethical meaning, tends to become associated with purely mundane passions, which often actually gives it the character of sport"). He famously observes that of this secular materialistic-individualistic iron cage it might truly be said: "Specialists *without spirit*, sensualists *without heart*; this nullity imagines that his has attained a level of civilization never before achieved."[9]

WHAT IS THE HOLY SPIRIT?

When it comes to the meaning of the Holy Spirit, there seems to be considerable agreement among first-century Jews and Greco-Romans, and views in the twenty-first century, that the Holy Spirit "is first and foremost the empowering presence and activity of God among and alongside [God's] people."[10] Although the Hebrew Scriptures (Old Testament) do not refer to a "Holy Spirit" per se, they do on 98 occasions refer to "the Spirit of God" or "the Spirit of the Lord," which "is generally an extended expression for God's power or presence by which he accomplishes his divine/ mighty deeds."[11] Within the first-century Jewish tradition "the Spirit was understood almost exclusively as the source of inspired speech, revelation, and esoteric wisdom."[12]

Whereas at least since the age of Romanticism, today we think that new ideas or insights or inspiration might come from within us as individuals, in the first century they were thought to enter from the outside: "Thus, Plato ascribes poetic creativity to being seized by the gods, that is, to a divine influence from outside or to spirit possession."[13] Other New Testament authors write about the fruit and gifts of the Spirit.[14]

Put into management terms, in the first century the Holy Spirit was thought to essentially act as a "broker" between God and people. The Holy Spirit provides access to the voice and power of God, serving as a conduit for God's power or presence by which God's mighty deeds are accomplished. Most contemporary theologians would also consider the Holy Spirit to be a "partner" in the "trinity"—along with God and Jesus—though the Bible does not *explicitly* talk about this trinity. Together these three form the Godhead, an understanding of Divinity that is intrinsically social (versus individualistic) and *oikos*-like (comprised of parent, child, and servant).

There is also general agreement that the Holy Spirit is intimately connected to salvation, and to the kingdom of God. However, the nature of these connections was understood differently in the first century than it is today, in ways that are consistent with differences in how salvation and KOG are understood differently today versus two thousand years ago (described in chapters ten and eleven). In basic terms, a twenty-first-century understanding sees the Holy Spirit as a counselor and sign of personal spiritual salvation and entry into the KOG in the afterlife. In contrast, a first-century understanding sees the Holy Spirit more as an inspiration and *enabler* of social-material salvation and the radical changes associated with the KOG.

MAIN THEMES OF PASSAGES IN LUKE THAT MENTION THE HOLY SPIRIT

Luke mentions the Holy Spirit more than all the three other Gospel writers combined. Luke uses the Greek word for "spirit" (*pneumatos*) 36 times. Of these 36 mentions, 17 refer to the Holy Spirit specifically,[15] which can be divided into two groupings of passages. The first group contains 12 mentions that, taken together, indicate the Holy Spirit has come upon every person in Luke who makes a proclamation about salvation. The second group is made up of 5 mentions that are associated with general teachings about the Holy Spirit. The 19 references to spirits other than the Holy Spirit can be divided into two additional groups. Twelve mentions are in passages that describe how people with unclean spirits are healed, and the remaining 7 mentions are in passages with other meanings of spirit (e.g., such as "giving up one's spirit" when someone dies).[16] The discussion in this chapter will focus on the passages that mention the Holy Spirit, with particular attention to its implications for management.

Group 1: Passages That Indicate That the Holy Spirit Has Come upon Every Character in Luke Who Makes a Proclamation about Salvation

The first few chapters of Luke are filled with passages that say that the Holy Spirit rests upon: John the Baptist (Luke 1:15), Elizabeth the mother of John the Baptist (Luke 1:41), Zechariah the father of John the Baptist (Luke 1:67), Simeon (Luke 2:25–27), Mary the mother of Jesus (Luke 1:35), and of course Jesus himself (Luke 3:22; 4:2, 14, 18).

What is striking about this list of names is that these are also *exactly* the same people who make proclamations about salvation (noun) in Luke. Thus, it seems very clear that Luke makes a strong linkage between salvation and the Holy Spirit—the

Holy Spirit enables the proclamation of salvation. This supports the idea that the Holy Spirit can be seen as the "broker" of salvation. It is through the Holy Spirit that people can be saved. This theme will be elaborated upon in other subgroups.

Perhaps the most noteworthy passage in this group is Jesus' inaugural sermon, referred to in earlier chapters, which sets the tone for the rest of the Gospel: "The Spirit of the Lord is upon me, because he has anointed me to bring good news to the poor. He has sent me to proclaim release to the captives and recovery of sight to the blind, to let the oppressed go free, to proclaim the year of the Lord's favor" (Luke 4:18–19).

This passage is also of particular importance to the understanding of management, because it has central themes of welcoming the marginalized into community, outsiders into the *oikos*, and in particular of allowing clients to escape from under the thumb of patrons. The Spirit of the Lord is front and center in setting this agenda and enabling Jesus to address it. The passage talks about Jesus being "anointed" to bring good news to the poor and blind, release to the captives and oppressed. The interesting thing about this "anointing" is that this is exactly what the Hebrew word "Messiah" and the Greek word "Christ" mean, namely, literally "the anointed one." Thus the passage points precisely to what Jesus has been anointed to do, why he is called the Christ and the Messiah. It is not a stretch to suggest that Jesus' followers who are anointed by the Spirit via baptism would have a similar agenda.

Also, it should come as little surprise that the themes alluded to in this inaugural sermon are entirely consistent with the themes that have been found throughout Luke. These themes subvert conventional structures in order to free the oppressed, point to alternative ways of organizing that foster sustenance economics rather than acquisitive economics, and exemplify benefaction rather than patron-client relationships. This is also entirely consistent with the Jubilatory practices associated with the "year of the Lord's favor" referred to in chapter seven (e.g., see Isa. 61, Lev. 25).

Finally, note that these changes will not be violently wrought. This is implicit in the observation that Jesus avoided reading the final line from the Isaiah 61 passage, which in the whole reads: "to proclaim the year of the Lord's favor, *and the day of vengeance of our God*" (Isa. 61:2). The good news Jesus proclaims is inconsistent with a spirit of vengeance or violence.[17] This refusal to use violence is a hallmark of Jesus' anointing of the Spirit; the Spirit is inviting, not coercive. Jesus has come to exemplify and invite others to help implement life-giving structures and systems for a new era.

Group 2: Passages That Provide General Teachings about the Holy Spirit

The most interesting passage for the present study is a statement from John the Baptist, a man filled with the Holy Spirit who has been experiencing great success preparing the way for Jesus by "proclaiming a baptism of repentance for the forgiveness of sins." When people ask him whether he is the Messiah (i.e., the "anointed one"), "John answered all of them by saying, 'I baptize you with water; but one who is more powerful than I is coming; I am not worthy to untie the thong of his sandals. He will baptize you with the Holy Spirit and fire'"[18] (Luke 3:16).

This passage suggests three things.

1. A special capacity of the Messiah is to baptize people with the Holy Spirit. Even someone like John the Baptist, who himself and whose parents have been filled with the Holy Spirit by God, seems unable to baptize others with the Spirit.

2. The Holy Spirit is central to what the Messiah offers humankind.
3. And it implies that Jesus will be baptizing a lot of people with the Holy Spirit in the Gospel of Luke.

Somewhat oddly, though, nowhere in the Gospel is there any mention of Jesus baptizing anyone with the Holy Spirit. Indeed, in the remainder of Luke after John has made this statement, no one receives the Holy Spirit except for Jesus himself (Luke 3:22). What is going on? Well, it turns out that to find the accounts of people being baptized in the Spirit you need to look in Luke's second volume, Acts, where the Holy Spirit appears 41 times. In fact many people believe that Luke's second volume should be called the Acts of the Holy Spirit.[19]

Just as the Gospel of Luke starts with a flurry of mentions of the Holy Spirit, so also the Holy Spirit plays a prominent role at the beginning of Acts, which starts with the resurrected Jesus giving his apostles instructions through the Holy Spirit (Acts 1:2) saying that "John baptized with water, but you will be baptized with the Holy Spirit not many days from now" (Acts 1:5) and that they will receive power when the Holy Spirit has come upon them (Acts 1:8). After adding a new member to restore their 12-man organization (to replace the departed Judas, one of the original 12; Acts 1:12–26), they were all "filled with the Holy Spirit" (Acts 2:4). This prompts a sermon from the apostle Peter, and the first mention of converts—three thousand—being baptized "in the name of Jesus" and receiving the Holy Spirit (Acts 2:38). Quickly thereafter these followers establish *oikos* structures and systems that embody their own variation of "Today salvation had come to this house" (Jesus' phrase from Luke 19:9):

> All who believed were together and had all things in common; they would sell their possessions and goods and distribute the proceeds to all, as any had need. Day by day, as they spent much time together in the temple, they broke bread at home [*oikon*] and ate their food with glad and generous hearts, praising God and having the goodwill of all the people. And day by day the Lord added to their number those who were being saved. (Acts 2:44–47)

A recent dissertation examining all Luke/Acts passages on the Holy Spirit concludes that:

> for Luke, *the Holy Spirit is the central figure in the formation of a new social identity that affirms yet chastens and transcends ethnic identity.* We have seen that the formation of this trans-ethnic social identity requires both a certain kind of *person* and a certain kind of *group.* The character and characteristics of these persons and this group are, for Luke, entirely Spirit-wrought realities.[20]

Thus, John the Baptist's reference to Jesus' baptism of the Spirit (Luke 3:16) can be seen to foreshadow and be fulfilled in the book of Acts. After Jesus leaves, it is the Holy Spirit that empowers people to be saved, to repent (i.e., turn away from conventional ways of living), and to embrace new ways of living (i.e., new *oikos* structures and systems that provide glimpses of the KOG) as salvation spreads from "house to house" (Acts 2:46; 8:3; 20:20; NRSV translation). This is not something people can sustain based on their own self-discipline alone—*salvation requires the enabling power of the Holy Spirit.*[21] People simply do not have enough willpower to break free from oppressive structures and temptations, especially when those structures reward them with self-interested material and social benefits. People need transcendent revelation and help to develop and implement KOG structures and systems.

These teachings are echoed in the remaining passages in this grouping. It is the Holy Spirit who provides the insight that has eluded those who are traditionally considered to be intelligent and wise (Luke 10:21). It is the Holy Spirit who reveals to people how they should respond when being judged by oppressive rulers and authorities (Luke 12:12). Indeed, without the Holy Spirit, no one can be released or freed from the oppressive structures that characterize the status quo (Luke 12:10).[22]

These passages not only point to the "broker" role of the Holy Spirit to access the benevolence of God, they also point to the benevolence of God in providing the Spirit. This is most explicit in a passage that follows just after Jesus has taught his disciples how to pray:

> So I say to you, Ask, and it will be given you; search, and you will find; knock, and the door will be opened for you. For everyone who asks receives, and everyone who searches finds, and for everyone who knocks, the door will be opened. Is there anyone among you who, if your child asks for a fish, will give a snake instead of a fish? Or if the child asks for an egg, will give a scorpion? If you then, who are evil, know how to give good gifts to your children, how much more will the heavenly Father give the Holy Spirit to those who ask him! (Luke 11:9–13)

This passage describes the Holy Spirit as a gift from a benevolent God available to people who knock on the door of God's *oikos* and enter in.

Group 3: Passages That Describe People With Evil/Unclean Spirits Being Healed

These passages describe situations where Jesus cures people of unclean spirits (e.g., Luke 4:31–37; 6:17–19). The significance of these passages is not so much that Jesus can exorcise demons (again, other first-century people did that too; Luke 11:19), but rather that his cures point to the overarching work Jesus has been anointed by the Holy Spirit to do. Much like the healing passages linked to "being saved" looked at earlier in chapter eleven, it is noteworthy that the people cured of unclean spirits are thereby restored and reintegrated to community.[23] As if to underscore this parallelism, on several occasions being cured from unclean spirits happens along other types of physical healing (e.g., Luke 6:18; 7:21; see also Luke 13:11).

Several of the passages pay particular attention to the *oikos* to illustrate this restorative dimension. The first is a passage we looked at earlier that describes how being healed of evil spirits enabled a homeless Gerasene man become reintegrated in his *oikos* (Luke 8:26–39). Another passage describes how women whom Jesus healed of evil spirits were now using their resources in a sustenance economics way to provide for the needs of Jesus' traveling *oikos* (Luke 8:1–3). And a third passage notes that it is important not only for an *oikos* to be emptied of unclean spirits (akin to being released from oppressive structures and systems), but also to be replaced with a good spirit (akin to being adopting alternative structures and systems) (Luke 11:24–26).

The remaining two passages in this group are interesting because they focus on Jesus' disciples. The first describes a man who asks Jesus' disciples to heal his son, who is intermittently seized by a spirit (Luke 9:37–43). When the man tells Jesus that the disciples were unable to heal the son, Jesus becomes somewhat exasperated[24] and proceeds to heal the boy himself. In the very next chapter Jesus sends his disciples on a mission to bring peace to people's *oikoi*, and when they return they say: "Lord, in your name even the demons submit to us!" Jesus replies: "[D]o not rejoice at this, that the spirits submit to you, but rejoice that your names are written in heaven [i.e., among the citizens of the KOG[25]]" (Luke 10:19–20).

Taken together, these two passages seem to underscore an ongoing theme in Luke. Jesus uses healings and cures in his ministry as a "sign" pointing to the inclusive nature of the KOG and salvation, as a very clear and immediate example of the restorative community that characterizes the KOG and salvation. It seems that he is not so much interested in his disciples engaging in this particular miraculous healing ministry, but more so in having his followers begin to enact the KOG structures and systems that minimize marginalization in the first place. In other words, it is not so important that evil spirits are obedient, it is more important to be living as citizens enacting the structures and systems of the KOG.

Group 4: Passages That Describe Other Meanings of Spirit

Of all the mentions in this group (Luke 1:17, 47, 80; 8:55; 23:46; 24:37, 39) the one of some interest for this study describes what happened at the moment of Jesus' death on the cross: "[T]he curtain [covering the Holy of Holies, the presence of God] in the temple was torn two. Then Jesus, crying with a loud voice, said, 'Father, into your hands I commend *my spirit*.' Having said this, he breathed his last" (Luke 23:45b-46).

This passage may provide a clue as to *how* Jesus enabled his followers to be baptized in the Holy Spirit. The Holy of Holies was the inner sanctum of the Jerusalem Temple, and represented the presence of God. The entrance to this room was covered by a curtain, and could only be entered by the high priest, and could only be entered once a year. At the moment of Jesus' death this curtain separating all the other people from the presence of God was torn into two; a boundary surrounding the figurative *oikos* of God was opened for all to enter. This may symbolically link Jesus' death to enabling everyone to enter into the presence of God via the Holy Spirit. Jesus' exemplary life of countercultural service to the marginalized, culminating in paying the ultimate price of social nonconformity, enables others to gain access to the Holy Spirit so that they too can work toward advocating and implementing social structures and systems that treat everyone with dignity and justice. It is precisely when Jesus is taking his last breath on the cross—that symbol of release from worldly concerns for wealth and status, and the expression of commitment to alternative structures and systems—that the curtain covering the Holy of Holies in Jerusalem's temple is torn into two, thereby releasing the presence of God to everyone.

Moreover, this tearing of the curtain also in effect symbolically tore power away from the high priest and other religious elite (including the emperor). No longer were *they* the "brokers" between the people and the presence of God. Rather, the Holy Spirit (the presence of God) was now free to everyone who was baptized (anointed) to follow Jesus, to proclaim good news to those who are economically impoverished, release to the downtrodden, give sight to the blind, and freedom to the oppressed. Thus, the Holy Spirit serves as a conduit to God's power that helps people to envision and establish communities/*oikoi* that manifest the salvific KOG.

SUMMARY

In sum, the implications for management are clear. Managers cannot sustain salvific KOG structures and system based on their own willpower; they need the enabling power of the Holy Spirit.[26] This enabling power is evident when individuals are healed via the Spirit and thus restored to community, and when inclusive and restorative *oikos* structures and systems are developed and implemented. The Spirit essentially serves as broker between humankind and the power of God. The Spirit is one of the three faces of the Godhead, and allows people to think and act according to transcendent ideals. In terms of the "theological turn" referred to earlier, the Holy Spirit is a means by which managers can integrate altruism, benevolence, and forgiveness into their daily actions.

Reflection Point: Connecting Contemporary Research and Luke's Passages about the Spirit

What are some hallmarks associated with contemporary spiritual managers who seek God's guidance for their work lives? If you were to look at the *empirical* research published on this topic in secular management journals, you would find about a dozen articles. Many of the managers in these articles follow Christianity, but other religions include Buddhism, Confucianism, and Islam. The striking thing about all these articles is the consistency in their findings. Overall managers who communicate relatively frequently with a divine being, seeking guidance for their everyday work lives, embrace nonconventional management theory and practice. In particular, these managers place lower emphasis on things like profit-maximization and self-interests, and greater emphasis on a holistic sense of nurturing community.[27]

Summary of Part Four

This section examined some of the most familiar religious ideas that Luke is known for—the kingdom of God, salvation, and the Holy Spirit—through a first-century lens to draw out implications for management. This proved to be a new way to look at some very familiar themes in Luke. The analysis showed the following:

1. The *oikos* lies at the center of enacting and manifesting the KOG in everyday life. The challenge is to manage and develop organizational structures and systems that are consistent with KOG principles and practices.
2. An important part of salvation has to do with being freed from oppressive social structures and systems, and replacing them with KOG structures and systems. The challenge for managers is to follow the example of Zaccheus, and create forms of *oikoi* that are associated with salvation.
3. The Holy Spirit is essential for this to happen, which forms a central plank in the Luke-Acts narrative. The challenge for managers is to be filled with the Holy Spirit, receive the strength and wisdom to both walk away from oppressive management practices, and to embrace alternative KOG management practices.[28]

The centrality of *oikos* and management for the kingdom of God, salvation, and the Holy Spirit may surprise some readers. After all, management is often characterized as dealing with the instrumental and mundane aspects of life, and thus regarded as the opposite of such transcendent spiritual ideas. Our analysis of Luke calls for much more research and scholarly reflection to focus on the importance of spirit-inspired management for salvation and the kingdom of God.

For some readers, this will be a welcome finding. For example, management scholars seeking to embrace the "theological turn" should be pleased to find so much fodder in the biblical narrative for their endeavor. Hopefully these findings will also help inspire future research examining other sacred writing with a new lens, and find additional relevant material for their quest.

Practitioners seeking to integrate their Christian faith in the workplace should also welcome these findings. Research suggests that managers have often complained that their church does not adequately value or understand their contribution to society. These findings suggest that the opposite should be the case; it seems difficult to *over*state the importance of management for enacting the KOG on earth as it is in heaven!

While the analysis thus far has pointed to hallmarks of nonconventional management consistent with Jesus and his life and teachings, it has not provided much focused analysis on organizational *processes* that characterize *how* this alternative approach can be implemented. Without this "how to" information, first-century readers may have felt overwhelmed by the management ideals described in Luke—it was difficult enough managing within the conventional paradigm, never mind trying to introduce countercultural structures and systems! The next chapter will introduce a process model embedded in Luke that is helpful for moving away from conventional management and toward an approach consistent with the message in Luke.

V

INSTITUTIONAL CHANGE: A FOUR-PHASE "HOW TO" PROCESS MODEL FOR PUTTING INTO PRACTICE MANAGEMENT PRINCIPLES DESCRIBED IN LUKE

Thus far our analysis has demonstrated that Luke has a lot to say about management. In particular, Luke criticizes first-century management practices that emphasize conventional *oikos* relationships, acquisitive economics, and patron-client relationships. In their place, Luke points to a style of management that is based on treating everyone with dignity (especially the oppressed), sustenance economics, and benefaction. Inclusivity is a hallmark of Luke's alternative approach to management, with a particular affinity for structures and systems that serve the marginalized in society. This approach to management also has a close relationship to Luke's description of the kingdom of God, salvation, and the Holy Spirit.

The focus in the previous sections has been on the "what" of management—what are the shortcoming of conventional structures and systems, and what are the hallmarks of redemptive structures and systems—but has not given much attention to the "how" of management. How should the transition away from conventional *oikos* be managed? How can organizations based on position and privilege be replaced by organizations based on inclusiveness and community? How can new institutional norms and customs be implemented that are consistent with the approach to management described in Luke?

Part of the answer comes from paying attention to the sequencing of passages in Luke. Until this point our look at passages has been thematic in nature, with the context being what is known about those themes in first-century Palestine. For example, earlier chapters examined all the passages that refer to one of the three dimensions of *oikonomia*, or all the passages that mention money, or all passages that mention KOG or salvation. While the merits of this approach speak for themselves, biblical scholars also recognize the merits in interpreting any focal passage in light of passages that come immediately before or after it. Passages should not just be interpreted in their historical first-century context, they should also be interpreted according to their narrative context.

The next three chapters provide just such an analysis, focusing especially on the sequential order and meaning of passages that comprise the section of Luke called the "Journey Narrative" (Luke 9:51–19:40). The Journey Narrative is of particular relevance for our study because of this section's emphasis on management issues. For example, as noted in chapter two, the Journey Narrative contains over 70 percent of Luke's mentions of words related to management and organizational resources, even though the Journey Narrative has (only) 38 percent of the total words in Luke.

Moreover, the Journey Narrative contains many of the key passages related to management issues that we have examined so far, including the parable of the ten pounds (Luke 19:11–27), the parable of the shrewd manager (Luke 16:1–13), the account of salvation coming to the *oikos* of Zacchaeus (Luke 19:1–10), and the account of the manager who serves his slaves (Luke 12:35–38).

There is widespread agreement among biblical scholars that the ten chapters of the Journey Narrative constitute an identifiable "central section" of the Gospel. It has been called the "Journey Narrative" because at its

- *start* Jesus sets his face to go to Jerusalem (Luke 9:51);
- *midpoint* Jesus says he must continue on his way to Jerusalem (Luke 13:33–34);
- *end* Jesus arrives in Jerusalem (Luke 19:28).

Chapter thirteen describes how analyzing the Journey Narrative as a literary unit lends support to the idea that embedded within it is a four-phase process model, which provides practical advice for people seeking to manage the journey from conventional toward KOG organizational structures and systems. Put differently, Luke's Journey Narrative describes the *process* by which KOG management is implemented. KOG management is not an event; rather, it is characterized as a journey that is informed by its destination. KOG managers never arrive; rather, KOG management is a process to be savored. The midpoint of the Journey Narrative provides an example of the four-phase model in a nutshell.

Chapter fourteen describes how passages in the first half of the Journey Narrative are sequentially ordered so that readers move through the four-phase model in three complete cycles, and chapter fifteen describes how the passages in the second half of the Journey Narrative are sequenced so that readers move through the four-phase model in three additional cycles (but this time in the reverse direction).

This process model is welcome relief to readers who might feel overwhelmed by the prospect of trying to figure out how to implement KOG structures and systems. It can be tough enough to simply maintain the financial viability of an *oikos* at the best of times, never mind being charged with operationalizing countercultural KOG principles, which seems a daunting task even if enabled by the Holy Spirit.

The four-phase model is a reminder that managers should focus on the *process* of KOG management, not so much on achieving *outcomes* like "perfect" organizational structures and systems. Indeed, Luke suggests that the process may lead to different outcomes, noting that organizational structures that make sense and exemplify the KOG in one setting may not be appropriate in another. For example, sometimes KOG management is evident by refusing to use money to exploit others (parable of the ten pounds), and sometimes it is evident when money is scattered within the larger community (parable of the shrewd manager). Sometimes it is right to sell all your possessions and give the proceeds to the poor (advice to the rich ruler), and sometimes salvation comes to the *oikos* that gives half its money to the poor and repays fourfold anyone it has defrauded (Zacchaeus).

In short, whereas the previous chapters have described the hallmark principles of KOG management, the next three chapters will focus on the *process* of putting these principles into practice. Note that appendix A provides a more detailed analysis and support for the chiasm and four-phase model described in part five, as well as corroborating evidence. That said, the purpose of describing the methodological rigor involved in identifying the four-phase process model is not to "prove" that this is the only way or even the best way to interpret this text, but rather simply to demonstrate that it is a plausible interpretation. In any case, reading the Journey Narrative as having this process model embedded within it offers valuable insights into management issues.

13

A Four-Phase Process Model Embedded in Luke's Journey Narrative

The Chiastic Structure of the Journey Narrative

Recall that, as discussed in chapter two, the Journey Narrative (Luke 9:51–19:40) is the section of Luke that contains most of the passages that have a particular focus on issues related to management.[1] Several other features about this section of Luke are important to understand before examining the four-phase process model embedded within it.

First, although scholars agree that the ten chapters that comprise the Journey Narrative form a clear and recognizable literary unit, they also recognize that the order of passages within it is very difficult to interpret in a linear way. For many years scholars had thought the Journey Narrative simply described Jesus' physical journey from northern Galilee through Samaria and Judea into Jerusalem. However, upon closer inspection it became clear that this was not the description of a simple *geographic* journey. Not only are there few mentions of villages and geographic markers, more tellingly, when villages and markers are mentioned they are often placed in the wrong order for describing a journey from Galilee to Jerusalem. At the same time scholars have found it virtually impossible to find a linear *thematic* progression for the passages within the Journey Narrative. Read linearly from start to finish, there seems little rhyme or reason to the order of the passages, no readily apparent logic or flow, no thematic progression and message.[2] Rather it reads like a series of dialogues and teachings related to issues of everyday life. This is particularly surprising because it is generally agreed that Luke was an excellent author, and he himself explicitly claims to have paid great attention to providing an "orderly account" in the Gospel (Luke 1:3).[3]

Recognizing these difficulties in reading the Journey Narrative geographically and linearly, numerous scholars have argued that the order of the passages in the Journey Narrative may make more sense if they are seen as having been written in the form of a *chiasm* (or a ring structure).[4] A simple chiasm is a text that has an A-B-B'-A' structure.[5] Each "element" in the chiasm may be a word, a phrase, a clause, a story, or even a large narrative section. An example of a short chiasm found in Luke is: *"Indeed, some are [A] last who will be [B] first, and some are [B'] first who will be [A'] last"* (Luke 13:30). An example of a somewhat longer chiasm in Luke is Jesus' inaugural address, which has a strong, rhetorical impact thanks to the symmetrical, chiastic arrangement of its seven elements that draws attention to the quotation from Isaiah, which "lies at the heart of what Jesus' identity and mission are all about" (Luke 4:16b–20a):

A: Jesus stands to read,
    B: the book of Isaiah is given to him,
        C: he opens the book,
            D: he reads from Isaiah the prophet,
        C': he closes the book,
    B': the book is returned to the attendant,
A': Jesus sits down and begins to speak.[6]

Chiasms are evident throughout the Bible and throughout Greco-Roman and other ancient literatures,[7] and students at that time were educated to think and write in chiastic ways. For example, students in Classical Greece and Imperial Rome were taught to memorize their 24 letter alphabet starting simultaneously at the beginning and the end. In English, this would mean learning AZ, BY, CX, DW, EV, FU, and so on. In this way students learned to see endings and beginnings simultaneously—the alpha and omega—and how texts were propelled to and from middles.[8]

Ancient authors used chiasms to add structure, meaning, and focus to narratives, perhaps especially long and complicated narratives. We moderns often forget that two thousand years ago writers did not have access to literary devices like punctuation at the end of sentences, capitalized words at the beginning of sentences, and paragraph structures (and, of course, the idea of dividing biblical books into various chapters and verses did not come until centuries later).[9] Rather, authors like Luke had to rely on other literary devices like chiasms.

As shown in table 13.1 (and described more fully in appendix A), Luke's Journey Narrative has the form of a 25-step chiasm which includes 12 passages before, and 12 passages after, its midpoint passage. The four-phase process model embedded in this rather imposing table will be "unpacked" in this and the next two chapters. Appendix A provides a side-by-side analysis that highlights the parallelism within the chiasm, showing the overlap between each pair of "twinned" passages as the chiasm moves toward the middle from both the beginning and the end.[10] What is of particular interest for the present study is the observation that these 25 elements are arranged so that the reader is guided through three consecutive cycles of a four-phase process model (embedded in the 12 elements found in the first half of the chiasm) before reaching the midpoint of the chiasm, and then the reader returns for an additional three cycles through the four-phase model in the reverse direction (i.e., the 12 elements in the last half of the chiasm).

Brief Description of the Four Phases in the Process Model

In short, as depicted in figure 13.1, the four-phase process model embedded[11] in Luke's Journey Narrative unfolds as follows:

1. *Problem recognition*: A problem associated with conventional practice is identified.
2. *Action response*: Actions are undertaken to try to resolve the problem.
3. *Changed way of seeing*: A new insight or perspective for seeing a situation is achieved.

Table 13.1 An overview of the chiastic structure of Luke's "Journey Narrative," highlighting the six cycles of its embedded four-phase process model

The Samaritan Cycle	A. Problem:	The problem is that Jesus' followers want to destroy a Samaritan village (Samaritans are cultural outsiders).	(9:51-56)
	B. Response:	Jesus asks his followers to leave their own *oikos* and to live for a time as guests in a Samaritan *oikos*.	(9:57-10:20)
	C. Seeing:	People who lived with the Samaritans gain insights that escape conventional wisdom/intelligence.	(10:21-24)
	D. Institutions:	The "Good Samaritan" rejects traditional purity laws, and models life-giving cross-cultural benevolence.	(10:25-37)
The New Rules for the *oikos* Cycle	E. Problem:	Doing conventional *oikos* work (Martha) can distract from and demean listening to Jesus' message (Mary).	(10:38-42)
	F. Response:	Jesus asks his followers to persistently pray that their *oikos* practices become consistent with the KOG.	(11:1-13)
	G. Seeing:	People who hear and obey the word of God are seen as members of God's *oikos*.	(11:14-36)
	H. Institutions:	Jesus presents six institutional norms associated with KOG *oikonomia*.	(11:37-54)
The Yeast Cycle	I. Problem:	When conventional authorities misinterpret Scriptures, it gives rise to oppressive social structures.	(12:1-12)
	J. Response:	Instead of using Scriptures selfishly, Jesus' followers treat everyone in their *oikos* with dignity.	(12:13-48)
	K. Seeing:	Jesus' followers see how interpreting Scriptures on their own corrects their reliance on the elite.	(12:49-13:9)
	L. Institutions:	institutions are redeemed when KOG processes focus on the spirit (vs the letter) of the law.	(13:10-30)
	M. Midpoint: The Response-to-Oppression Cycle: Managing to overcome institutional violence.		**(13:31-35)**
The Benefaction Cycle	L'. Institutions:	Patron-client norms are erased when people share resources with others unable to reciprocate.	(14:1-24)
	K'. Seeing:	Jesus' followers see how taking up their cross corrects a worldview based on status and possessions.	(14:25-35)
	J'. Response:	Instead of focusing on their own well-being, Jesus' followers act to help the lost and lowly.	(15:1-32)
	I'. Problem:	Dominant conventional views of wealth encourage people to serve money versus God.	(16:1-13)
The Justice Cycle	H'. Institutions:	Jesus' followers enact *oikos* based on just sustenance economics, rather than acquisitive economics.	(16:14-17:10)
	G'. Seeing:	Jesus' followers see and praise and rely on God's benevolence, un-blinded by conventional security.	(17:11-37)
	F'. Response:	Jesus' followers persistently act to promote justice for the oppressed, rather than accept the status quo.	(18:1-8)
	E'. Problem:	An elitist 'holier-than-thou' attitude is problematic because it marginalizes others; the humble are justified.	(18:9-17)
The Salvation Cycle	D'. Institutions:	Jesus' followers step outside of social traditions and model new life-giving norms that benefit social outcasts.	(18:18-34)
	C'. Seeing:	People with a social outcast's perspective see Jesus' message of salvation in a way that others don't.	(18:35-43)
	B'. Response:	Managers who follow Jesus' teaching share their wealth and refuse to use money to exploit others.	(19:1-27)
	A'. Problem:	The problem is that mainstream leaders want Jesus' followers to stop proclaiming his socially-disruptive peace.	(19:28-40)

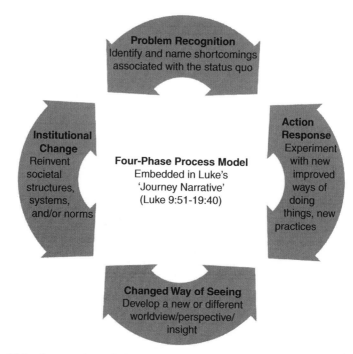

Figure 13.1 An overview of the four-phase process model embedded in the chiastic structure of Luke's "Journey Narrative."

4. *Institutional change:* Attempts are made to change the larger social norms and structures that give rise to the problem.

For example, the process model describes how (1) shortcomings associated with conventional management are (2) addressed via implementing new ways of doing things that in turn (3) result in new insights and (4) the implementation of KOG norms and customs. The model also moves in the reverse direction, namely, describing how (4) KOG institutional norms (3) transform worldviews and (2) result in actions that (1) liberate people from oppression.

This chapter will provide a general description each of these four phases, including a description of the four-phase process in the passage at the midpoint of the chiasm. The next two chapters will then provide a more detailed description of each of the six four-phase cycles embedded in the Journey Narrative.

Phase 1: Problem Recognition

Each phase 1 passage in Luke's Journey Narrative describes a problem and is set up in such a way that Jesus rebukes conventional wisdom. Typically these passages identify dual competing positions, and describe how Jesus takes a countercultural position.[12] For example, Jesus rebukes his disciples rather than the Samaritans who reject them, Jesus rebukes hard-working Martha rather than reclining Mary, and Jesus rebukes the prayer of a conventional religious leader rather than the prayer of a humble tax collector. What is all the more striking is that in the first two cycles Jesus rebukes people who are among his dearest friends—two disciples (James and John), and a friend whom he regularly visits (Martha). This suggests that the four-phase model may be particularly appropriate *within* a KOG *oikos*.

In more general terms, the four-phase process starts when someone becomes aware of a problematic situation. This may be an ethical problem that needs to be solved, or a practical problem in how to manage relationships in a social setting (e.g., racism, widening gap between rich and poor, adherence to dysfunctional *oikos* norms).[13] The descriptions in Luke suggest that it is valuable to name the problem as specifically as possible, and to ground it in specific actions and context. While it may be possible to think about the problem in grand and abstract terms, more often it is best to bring it down to a specific situation.

Phase 2: Action Response

The passages in phase 2 have a focus on seeking new ways of acting that will help to resolve the problems that have been recognized. These passages describe occasions where people experience alternative ways of living, especially where Jesus provides counsel and describes actions that are consistent with KOG-management. As a whole, these passages point to the importance of a giving, benevolent nature. Just as Jesus gave his followers the kingdom and the authority to address issues, so also they are to have a generous giving orientation to others (especially giving financial resources to the poor). Often these passages contain parables that provide "what if" scenarios and lessons grounded in everyday life. What if a rich man stored his crops for selfish reasons, what if an exploitive nobleman went on a journey and gave his managers control over his assets, what if someone who owned one hundred sheep or coins lost one? These are sort of "thought experiments" that encourage people to think through possible actions, and vicariously learn, for example, that what seems obvious in the short term has unanticipated negative outcomes in the longer term.[14]

In general terms, the focus in this phase is on identifying what actions can be taken to address specific problems or issues. The proposed actions need not be the definitive solution, but instead can be seen like mini-experiments that can be learned from. This embracing of experimentation allows problems to be addressed sooner, and facilitates experiential learning. This in turn will help participants to improve their understanding of the issue, and informs subsequent actions as they develop and refine potential solutions. People shouldn't be afraid of making mistakes, so long as they learn from their actions (indeed, there is not perfect action, so people should always be learning).

Phase 3: Changed Way of Seeing

The passages in this phase describe instances of insight and revelation, often literally a new way of seeing and perceiving things. This phase includes the "aha" worldview-changing moments that occur after experiencing the actions in the previous phase. A blind man sees, people "see the light" and learn to "see the [hidden] signs of the kingdom" that are around them.[15]

This new worldview is an important outcome of the experiential knowledge developed in the previous phase. Not only do people's actions address the specific problem they are facing, but their actions also begin to shape the way they see the world and their place in it. This new way of seeing is not so much the result of new cognitive insights, but rather as it comes from engaging in new actions and experiences. "It's been said that the first followers of Jesus didn't *think* themselves into a new way of living; they *lived* themselves into a new way of thinking."[16] This new worldview will make the world appear different than before, and enables people to see it more in ways consistent with the KOG.

Phase 4: Institutional Change

The passages in this phase describe how Jesus challenges the social elite to change existing institutions and norms, toward creating new structures and systems that are consistent with the KOG.[17] Indeed, a striking feature is that *each* one of the six "phase 4" passages starts with Jesus addressing members of the social elite in first-century Palestine, and in each case he promotes new norms and customs that challenge and overcome problems associated with status quo institutions that benefit the social elite.

As shown in figure 13.1, the four-phase process in Luke is presented as a bidirectional loop. In the first half of the Journey Narrative, the process moves "forward" from phase 1 through phase 4 as has just been described (the 12 steps together constitute three consecutive forward cycles through the four phases). In the second half of the Journey Narrative the process is reversed, moving from phase 4 to phase 3 to phase 2 to phase 1. For example, in the "forward" direction issues that need to be addressed (phase 1) prompt new ways of acting (phase 2) and seeing (phase 3), and lead to the development of new social structures and systems (phase 4). In the reverse direction, participating in new social structures and systems (phase 4) can facilitate a new worldview (phase 3) and new actions (phase 2) that resolve problems (phase 1).

It is also worth noting that the four-phase model can be seen as an ongoing process. Learning occurs continuously, with one cycle prompting another, prompting yet another, and so on. The point is not to "arrive" having learned everything there is to know, but rather to discern and learn continuously.

Illustrative Passage: The Four-Phase Process Model Embedded within the Passage at the Midpoint of the Chiasm (Luke 13:31–35)

As depicted in figure 13.2, the passage at the midpoint of the chiasm provides a condensed version of the four-phase process model. Given the importance of midpoint passages in chiasms generally, and the suggestion that a four-phase process model is embedded in the larger Journey Narrative, it should not come as a surprise that the midpoint passage in the Journey Narrative can also be readily interpreted in terms of the four-phase process model.[18]

Phase 1 (Problem Recognition): Herod Wants to Kill Jesus (Luke 13:31)

The key issue to be addressed in this passage reflects an overarching theme within the entire Journey Narrative, namely, corrupt social institutions led by wrong-headed rulers. Such institutionalized power is evident in the starkest way possible in this passage, namely, the coercive power to kill people who disrupt the status quo. Religious leaders (Pharisees) tell Jesus that Herod Antipas (the Roman procurator in Galilee) intends to kill Jesus for his clearly countercultural KOG message: "Get away from here, for Herod wants to kill you" (Luke 13:31). This is no hollow threat, as Herod had already imprisoned and then beheaded John the Baptizer (Luke 3:19–20; 9:9). The problem presented in this passage is that leaders use threats of institutional violence to intimidate others.

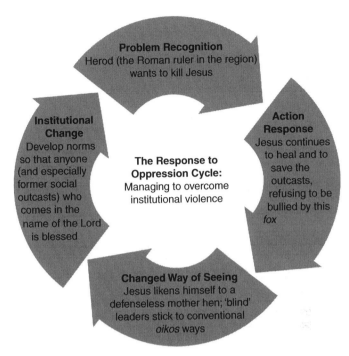

Figure 13.2 The response-to-oppression cycle: managing to overcome institutional violence (Luke 13:31–35).

Phase 2 (Action Response): Jesus Continues to Heal and to Save the Outcasts, Refusing to be Bullied by This Fox (Luke 13:32–33)

Jesus responds by saying that he will continue to act as he has been—with a focus on healing outcasts—as he makes his way to Jerusalem.[19] Jesus will not let corrupt institutional powers intimidate him. More generally, the passage may also provide two helpful tips regarding *how* to avoid being intimidated by violent institutions. Jesus says: "Go and tell that fox for me, 'Listen, I am casting out demons and performing cures today and tomorrow, and on the third day I finish my work. Yet today, tomorrow, and the next day I must be on my way, because it is impossible for a prophet to be killed outside of Jerusalem'" (Luke 13:32b–33).

First, in his act of civil disobedience Jesus refuses to consider authorities like Herod to be more significant than they are. Jesus does ingratiate himself to unjust authorities. This is evident in calling Herod a fox, an unflattering term that suggests conventional leaders like Herod do not play a central role in KOG structures and systems.[20] Jesus does not expect Herod's support in promoting countercultural ideas.

Second, Jesus' response suggests that he will methodically continue on with his ministry. Jesus refuses to be intimidated by institutionalized violence: despite what they might think, political authorities like Herod are not in charge. Violence cannot quash Jesus or his message. Rather, love prevails. Day by day, step by step, and action by action, glimpses of the KOG can be manifest on earth as it is in heaven.[21] He will continue to work on behalf of social outcasts and the marginalized, those who may not belong to an *oikos* (e.g., the demon-possessed, the sick).

Phase 3 (Changed Way of Seeing): Jesus Likens Himself to a Defenseless Mother Hen, But "Blind" Leaders Stick to Conventional *Oikos* Ways (Luke 13:34–35a)

Jesus sees himself in what is clearly a novel and countercultural way, namely, as a defenseless mother hen who seeks to gather in, nurture, and protect all her children. "Jerusalem, Jerusalem, the city that kills the prophets and stones those who are sent to it! How often have I desired to gather your children together as a hen gathers her brood under her wings, and you were not willing! See, your house [*oikos*] is left to you" (Luke 13:34–35a). Few commentators note the fact this is a female image and one of nonviolence, which stands in stark contrast to and is vulnerable to Herod the fox.[22] In any case, Jesus' countercultural message remains foreign not only to Herod, but also to conventional civic-religious leaders like the Pharisees, who can "see" only the status quo way of managing their *oikos*.[23]

Phase 4 (Institutional Change): Develop Norms So That Anyone (and Especially Social Outcasts) Who Comes in the Name of the Lord is Blessed (Luke 13:35b)

Jesus longs for the day when people say, "Blessed is the one who comes in the name of the Lord." There is some debate as to what this phrase might mean, but there is general agreement among biblical scholars that it is a direct allusion to Psalm 118:26,[24] which says: "Blessed is the one who comes in the name of the Lord. We bless you from the house of the Lord."

As we found out in earlier chapters, Psalm 118 is the most-cited Old Testament chapter in the New Testament, and it is generally accepted that in the original Psalm "the one who comes in the name of the Lord" does not refer to an individual person, but rather to a group of people who have been treated as social outcasts.[25] Thus, in Luke 13:35 Jesus is longing for the day when social norms will not allow people to be treated as social outcasts—instead, everyone will be treated with dignity and be blessed. In short, Jesus longs for institutional structures and systems consistent with his message of salvation, the KOG, benefaction, and sustenance economics: *these* are the hallmarks of the *oikos* of the Lord (Psalm 118:26b).

SUMMARY

This chapter argues that the Journey Narrative section of Luke—which contains most of Luke's material directly relevant to management—is written in the form of a 25-passage chiasm that has embedded within it a four-phase process model that describes *how* to implement KOG management. The midpoint passage of the chiasm not only illustrates the four-phase process model, but also points to an ongoing thematic emphasis in the Journey Narrative on the importance of addressing institutional norms and structures (which is exactly what Jesus was anointed to do). However, those new structures should not be *imposed* on others (because this would transform them into oppressive structures), nor should they be introduced violently. Jesus refused to use physical force to overcome oppression, but rather modeled how to become released from oppressive powers by taking up his cross (moral force).[26] The four-phase process model found in Luke's Journey Narrative is offered as a viable framework for followers to implement KOG structures and systems. The next two chapters will describe how the four-phase process model is evident in the first half (chapter fourteen) and second half (chapter fifteen) of the Journey Narrative.

REFLECTION POINT: CONNECTING CONTEMPORARY RESEARCH AND LUKE'S FOUR-PHASE PROCESS MODEL

Is the four-phase process model embedded in the Journey Narrative similar to process models in the contemporary management literature? It turns out there are several four-phase organizational learning models that are similar. Perhaps the most analogous model builds on the work of scholars like Chris Argyris and Richard Nielsen and their description of "triple-loop" learning.[27] Phase 1 (problem recognition) corresponds to the situation that triggers the need or basis for learning: there is a problem or error that needs to be resolved. Phase 2 (action response) corresponds to the *single-loop learning* that occurs when people change their *actions* to resolve a specific problem. This is the most basic type of learning. Phase 3 (changed way of seeing) corresponds to what has been called *double-loop learning,* which occurs when people change their values or worldviews to align with the new behaviors associated with the second phase. Thus, change occurs not only at the basic level of people's actions (single-loop), but also in terms of their deeper governing ethics and underlying views and beliefs. Finally, phase 4 (institutional change) corresponds to *triple-loop learning,* which goes beyond the learning that occurs at the level of people's actions (single-loop) and their values and worldviews (double-loop); rather, triple-loop learning occurs at the level of social traditions and norms embedded in *institutional structures and systems.* Triple-loop learning is the deepest form of organizational learning, and it can also feed back (or feed forward, depending on your perspective) by shaping people's worldviews and actions.

14

LUKE'S THREE "FORWARD" CYCLES
THROUGH THE FOUR-PHASE
PROCESS MODEL

Recall that the Journey Narrative goes through six complete "cycles" of the four-phase process, the first three times forward, and then three times in reverse. An overview of these six cycles is provided in the previous chapter, and summarized in figure 13.1 and table 13.1. While it may be tedious to provide a detailed examination of each of the six cycles, there is merit in providing a brief description of each. This chapter will describe the three cycles of the four-phase process that occur in the first half of the Journey Narrative, and chapter fifteen will describe the three cycles through the four-phase process that occur in the second half of the Journey Narrative.

CYCLE #1: THE SAMARITAN CYCLE: MANAGING RELATIONSHIPS WITH CULTURAL OUTSIDERS (LUKE 9:51–10:37)

As depicted in figure 14.1, the overarching theme for the first cycle, dubbed the "Samaritan cycle," is on how to relate to cultural outsiders (i.e., people who belong to a different culture). In particular, the passages in this cycle focus on the relationship between Jews and Samaritans. These two groups had a long-standing history of animosity, even though Samaritans were sometimes considered half-Jews. Both groups worshiped the same God (Yahweh), but the Samaritans placed particular emphasis on the Pentateuch (first five books of the Old Testament) and had different views of the Messiah.

Phase 1 (Problem Recognition): The Problem is That Jesus' Followers Want to Destroy a Samaritan Village (Luke 9:51–56)

If you wanted to travel from Galilee to Jerusalem, the most direct route would be through Samaria. But, because of the rivalry and animosity between Samaritans and Jews, and especially on the hot button topic of whether Jerusalem or Mount Gerezim was God's holy place, Galileans would generally not take this direct route, preferring instead to make a detour around Samaria to get to Jerusalem. So it is a bit surprising that Jesus sent his disciples ahead of him into a Samaritan village, but it is not surprising that the Samaritans did not welcome them when they found out Jesus

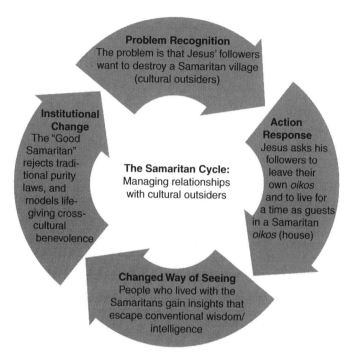

Figure 14.1 The Samaritan cycle: managing relationships with cultural outsiders (Luke 9:51–10:37).

was headed for Jerusalem. And perhaps it is not entirely suprising that James and John would have been quick to judge the Samaritans who refused to welcome Jesus into their village. The disciples ask Jesus: "Do you want us to command fire to come down from heaven and consume them?" (Luke 9:54).[1] Jesus rebukes his disciples for their unneighborly outburst (Luke 9:55), admonishing them for their desire to use violence against the Samaritans.

This first passage sets up the Samaritan cycle by pointing to two inter-related problems: the Samaritans are unwilling to receive Jesus, and perhaps more importantly, the disciples have a bad attitude and desire for vengeance against the Samaritans. By way of foreshadowing, at the completion of this cycle (phase 4) a Samaritan is presented as a role model of someone who is a good neighbor. How did Jesus deal with this problematic animosity between Jews and Samaritans?

Phase 2 (Action Response): Jesus Asks His Followers to Leave Their Own *Oikos,* and to Live for a Time as Guests in a Samaritan *Oikos* (Luke 9:57–10:20)

The second phase begins with a reminder that following Jesus is not an experiment to be taken half-heartedly; it requires leaving behind conventional *oikos* structures and systems. The passage then goes on to describe one way that Jesus addresses the problem of lack of respect for outsiders. Essentially, Jesus asks 70 of his followers to give up the comforts and security associated with their current *oikos,* and instead rely on the hospitality of their Samaritan neighbors for a time.[2] Moreover, he deliberately disallows his followers to "buy" their way into the favor of the Samaritans: he tells them not to bring along any money. Jesus goes on to instruct his envoys to heal people in the villages and to bring them peace. Surely part of that peace includes fostering a sense of mutual respect among Jews and Samaritans.

A fascinating aspect about this passage is that it can be seen as a sort of social experiment, where the first "pilot project" had already been carried out earlier with a smaller number of participants (12 disciples; Luke 9:1–6).[3] Even so, there is no indication that Jesus knew how successful the current mission with 70 participants would be. Indeed, he spends several verses telling his followers how to respond to various scenarios, in particular explaining what to do if they were not welcomed into the Samaritans' *oikoi*.

When the 70 return from their mission with joy and report that people were freed from evil spirits, Jesus notes that he had seen Satan fall from heaven like a flash of lightning. What does it mean? Perhaps partly it means that evil forces fall when people are willing to leave their comfort zones; when, instead of asking for fire to come down from heaven to consume people whom they have traditionally seen as enemies, they visit these so-called enemies and accept their hospitality. Experimenting with new ways of acting can have powerful unanticipated consequences.

Phase 3 (Changed Way of Seeing): People Who Lived with the Samaritans Gain Insights That Escape Conventional Wisdom/Intelligence (Luke 10:21–24)

The experience of ministering to and accepting the hospitality of their Samaritan neighbors (and other villages) undoubtedly had a profound effect on Jesus' followers. Their new experiences prompt Jesus to rejoice in the Holy Spirit because they were able to see things that remain hidden even to the wise and intelligent who are bound by their traditions. By defying traditional practices people can often see the folly of those traditions. (This may be especially true when defying norms that serve the interests of and are perpetuated by elites in the status quo.) This experiential learning provides a new vantage point, a new perspective, a worldview that lies outside of anything that can be fathomed or experienced within their previous comfort zones. Such an enlarged worldview provides insight into what the KOG might look like, and is far removed from that of kings in this world who are preoccupied with their own vested interests. "Then turning to the disciples, Jesus said to them privately, 'Blessed are the eyes that see what you see! For I tell you that many prophets and kings desired to see what you see, but did not see it, and to hear what you hear, but did not near it'" (Luke 10:23–24).

Phase 4 (Institutional Change): The "Good Samaritan" Rejects Traditional Purity Laws, and He Models Life-Giving Cross-Cultural Benevolence (Luke 10:25–37)

This new way of seeing brings brand new meaning to God's Law, a radical new understanding to what it means to love God with all one's heart, soul, strength, and mind. When the lawyer asks Jesus what he must do to inherit eternal life, Jesus tells him he must love his neighbor as himself. When the lawyer asks what is meant by the term "neighbor," Jesus clearly explains that the term includes people who are cultural outsiders, people who seem to be impure by conventional religious standards.

Jesus tells him the story of a man who had been robbed and left on the road for dead. When religious leaders (a priest and a Levite) see the beaten man, they pass by on the other side. To have touched the man would have made them religiously impure for the time being. However when a Samaritan—a cultural outsider—passes by, he provides help. He puts bandages on him and takes him to an inn where he pays the innkeeper in advance to take care of him until he recovers from the beating. The Samaritan is an example of what it means to love your neighbor, and Jesus tells his listeners to "Go and do likewise."

This teaching clearly challenges core norms and institutions of the day, violating fundamental conventional ideas about what it means to be pure and loving. The spirit of God's Law is fundamentally transformative, and its fulfillment is partly evident when traditional enemies (including Samaritans and other outsiders) are recognized as neighbors, who are to be loved as much as one's own. God's Law is not evident by avoiding "impure people" (as the priest and Levite did when they avoided the robbery victim), but rather by helping the needy. It is this sort of genuine benefaction that is exemplified by the Good Samaritan in this passage.

The implications for management of this first cycle are straightforward. The first phase calls people to rebuke anyone who exhibits attitudes that denigrate people who are cultural outsiders or come from a competing *oikos* or background, perhaps especially when such an attitude is exhibited by a close friend or colleague. The second phase recognizes that giving up conventional views is not easy, but rather calls for deliberately developing and implementing new practices that permit, in this case, treating enemies as neighbors. These new structures and systems need not be foolproof, and it is good to consider contingency plans in case they do not work as planned. Phase 3 suggests that once people experience such alternatives they will be transformed, they will have new ways of looking at the world. This will, in phase 4, prompt them to want to change fundamental institutional structures and systems, so that they manifest a fuller expression of God's Law.

Cycle #2: New House Rules Cycle: Managing Relationships within the *Oikos* (Luke 10:38–11:54)

Whereas the first cycle focused on managing relationships with cultural outsiders—from competing *oikoi*, so to speak—the theme in the second cycle focuses on relationships within one's *oikos* (figure 14.2).

Phase 1 (Problem Recognition): Doing Conventional *Oikos* Work (Martha) Can Distract from and Demean Listening to Jesus' Message (Mary) (Luke 10:38–42)

The issue addressed in this cycle is related to conventional *oikos* practices. The cycle starts with Jesus visiting his friends Mary and Martha. Martha stays true to the conventional role of hostess by doing many tasks, while Mary sits down and listens to what Jesus is saying. When Martha complains to Jesus that Mary is breaking norms and is not helping her, Jesus surprisingly rebukes Martha. Jesus tells her that Mary made the better choice while she (Martha) was worried and distracted by many things. Jesus is saying that conventional *oikos* roles, rules, and norms can get in the way of important things.[4] In short, the problem is that adherence to conventional

Problem Recognition
Doing conventional *oikos* work (Martha) can distract from and demean listening to Jesus' message (Mary)

Institutional Change
Jesus presents six institutional norms asso-ciated with KOG *oiko-nomia* (which contrast the status quo's six woes)

New Rules for the *Oikos* Cycle:
Managing relationships within the *oikos*

Action Response
Jesus asks his followers to persistently pray that their *oikos* practices become consis-tent with the KOG

Changed Way of Seeing
People who hear and obey the word of God are seen as members of God's *oikos*

Figure 14.2 New rules for the *oikos* cycle: managing relationships within the *oikos* (Luke 10:38–11:54).

oikos work can distract people from listening to others, and that it can lead to feelings of superiority and blame.

Phase 2 (Action Response): Jesus Asks His Followers to Persistently Pray That Their *Oikos* Practices Become Consistent With the KOG (Luke 11:1–13)

This phase starts with what has become known as the Lord's Prayer. A quick over-view of the Lord's Prayer, and how it may have been interpreted differently via a first-century management lens than it generally is today, is provided in table 14.1.

Overall, a first-century interpretation of the Lord's Prayer through a manage-ment lens suggests it says a lot about how to manage an *oikos* in countercultural ways that: truly honor the founder's name (e.g., God as mentor); seek to emulate KOG structures and systems; look after the daily needs of members; refuse to enter into patron-client relationships; and shun acquisitive economics. The act of repeating this prayer regularly provides an important time of meditating and listening to what it means to manage an *oikos* in KOG ways. Recall that praying is not only talking to God, but it is also listening to God through the Spirit.

The remaining verses in this phase continue to focus on the *oikos*, looking at the benevolent sharing of organizational resources, both *within* and *between* organiza-tions (Luke 11:5–13). The gist of these verses counsels listeners to give resources

Table 14.1   A first- and a twenty-first-century paraphrase of the Lord's Prayer

Lord's Prayer (Luke 11:2b-4)	A typical twenty-first-century interpretation/paraphrase	An interpretation/paraphrase via a first-century management lens
Father, hallowed be thy name.	Because you are our holy Father, we get to enjoy an intimate parent-child relationship with you.	As the founder of the *oikos* that we belong to, help us to act in ways that truly bring honor to your name.
Your kingdom come.	We look forward to a heavenly afterlife.	May your managerial structures and systems come to earth as they are in heaven.
Give us each day our daily bread.	Ensure that our needs are met.	You are a benevolent God; please ensure that the daily needs of *oikos* members are met (and help us not unnecessarily store up food for the long term, or think that our ability to do so makes us less dependent on you).
And forgive us our sins, for we ourselves forgive everyone indebted to us.	And forgive us our sins, just as we forgive others when they have wronged us.	And forgive us our sins, for we follow your benevolent example and forgive the (financial) debts of all our clients (thereby transforming these former clients into friends).
And do not bring us to the time of trial.	And don't let us get into situations where our faith in you is weakened.	And help us to avoid social structures and systems where we may be tempted to act according to acquisitive economics, or where we are tempted to become patrons to clients.

to neighbors who need them (even if it is inconvenient to do so), just as they would do the same for young children within their own *oikos* (and just as the benevolent heavenly Father does for the members of God's *oikos*): "Ask, and it shall be given to you; search, and you will find; knock, and the [*oikos*] door will be opened for you" (Luke 11:9).

Phase 3 (Changed Way of Seeing): People Who Hear and Obey the Word of God are Seen as Members of God's *Oikos* (Luke 11:14–36)

This phase contrasts and compares competing views regarding how to interpret Jesus' actions. First, the passage starts with Jesus healing a mute man and restoring him to community, which some observers see as having been done by the power of God, while others see it as having been done by the power of Beelzebul (the ruler of the demons). Which of these two "kingdoms" do people see Jesus as belonging to?[5] Moreover, which of these two kingdoms do Jesus' opponents belong to? People should beware of what kind of spirit they welcome into their *oikos* (Luke 11:24).

Second, Jesus contrasts and compares a conventional *oikos* with the *oikos* of God. When Jesus is told that the womb of his biological mother is blessed (or, truly happy[6]), he replies, "Blessed rather are those who hear the word of God and obey it!" (Luke 11:28). Rather than thinking of *oikos* only in conventional terms, Jesus introduces an alternative way of seeing *oikos* that welcomes everyone who chooses to join. Membership in this alternative *oikos* does not depend on one's birth family, but rather on the choices one makes.

Finally, just as on past occasions when God has provided signs for the people, people can see (or fail to see) the signs Jesus provides. Seeing the signs will serve to bring light to one's entire *oikos* for all who enter, whereas failing to see the signs results in darkness (Luke 11:36).

In sum, Jesus offers a vision of a KOG *oikos* that transcends conventional and biological understandings, and all those who recognize the signs he offers will live in a new light.

Phase 4 (Institutional Change): Jesus Presents Six Institutional Norms Associated With KOG *Oikonomia* (Which Contrast to the Status Quo's Six Woes) (Luke 11:37–54)

If readers considered Jesus' rebuffing of Martha's concerns in phase 1 of this cycle to be somewhat rude, they would certainly see Jesus in phase 4 as especially rude and dismissive of conventional *oikos* norms. Like all phase 4 passages, this one starts with Jesus interacting with a member of the dominant societal elite. In this case a Pharisee invites Jesus to dinner. Jesus accepts the invitation, but then proceeds to undermine basic first-century social conventions in ways that would insult his host. This starts as soon as Jesus takes his place at the table without washing his hands (which would be seen as an insult to his host; hand-washing was seen as a boundary-making/-keeping device), and then proceeds as Jesus makes a series of insulting observations about his hosts (a rude outburst that went against the social norms of the day). In short, Jesus is undermining conventional *oikos* practices and customs,[7] and is calling religious leaders to adopt a different approach in their roles as *oikonomia* in the larger community. In particular, Jesus offers six specific suggestions for these institutional leaders, elaborated and highlighted as below. Woe to those who follow the conventional custom of

1. tithing mint and rue and herbs of all kinds; it is much more important to practice justice and the love of God;
2. seeking to be treated honorably by others (especially at public events); it is much more important to treat others with dignity and honor (especially those at society's margins);
3. focusing on the superficial pursuit of correct outward behavior; it is much more important to deal with any "hidden" inner corruption;[8]
4. creating burdensome rules to draw out the true goodness in others; it is much more important to provide the necessary support to help them (e.g., including creating appropriate structures and systems);
5. attending to the tombs of prophets; it is better to focus instead on their teachings (or you are just as guilty as your ancestors who killed the prophets because of their countercultural teachings); and
6. taking away the "key of knowledge" and thereby hindering the ability of others to enter the *oikos* of God (and refusing to enter it yourself); it is better to provide the key of knowledge so that everyone may enter into the *oikos* of God.

Of these six "woes," perhaps the final one is the most intriguing for our study of Luke on management. What exactly is the "key of knowledge," and the door to what *oikos* does it open? While this is not made explicit in the text, the implicit message is clear: the key opens the door to entering a KOG *oikos*, and it calls for the powerful elite to create new institutions that serve the interests of the marginalized. Or, to paraphrase and elaborate what Jesus told Martha in phase 1 of this cycle: "Don't be distracted by conventional tasks and customs that seem to be important; instead, listen up and institute counter-cultural norms like Mary." This means imitating the benevolence of God in *oikos* management (phase 2), and thereby identifying with the *oikos* of God rather than the *oikos* of Beelzebul (phase 3).

In sum, the message of cycle #2 suggests that, even at their best, conventional *oikos* structures and systems fall short. There is nothing inherently wrong with Martha having worked on *oikos* tasks, but her instrumental focus got in the way of enjoying relationships (phase 1). Experiment daily with finding ways to imitate God's benevolence in *oikos* life, via forgiving debts and walking away from acquisitive economics and patron-client relationships (phase 2). This will enlighten your views and help you to differentiate between good and evil (phase 3). And it will help you to develop and implement new norms and understandings to guide institutions (phase 4; though it is probably still a good idea to wash your hands before meals and to avoid insulting your hosts).

CYCLE #3: THE YEAST CYCLE: MANAGING RELATIONSHIPS REGARDING THE INTERPRETATION OF SCRIPTURES (LUKE 12:1–13:30)

Just as the first cycle was framed by mentions of Samaritans (in first and fourth phases), this third cycle is framed by the idea of "yeast" (appears in first and fourth

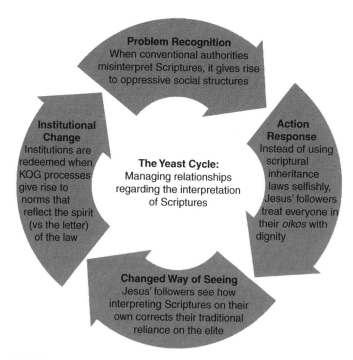

Figure 14.3 The yeast cycle: managing relationships regarding the interpretation of Scriptures (Luke 12:1–13:30).

cycle) (figure 14.3). And just as the mention of Samaritans symbolized "social outcasts" or members of competing *oikoi*, so also in this cycle the word "yeast" is used metaphorically to refer to core religious ideas. In terms of the present study, bad yeast gives rise to oppression, and good yeast gives rise to KOG management.

Phase 1 (Problem Recognition): When Conventional Authorities Misinterpret Scriptures, it Gives Rise to Oppressive Social Structures (Luke 12:1–12)

This cycle starts with Jesus warning his listeners about the "yeast" of their leaders, that is, their "hypocrisy." Note that the interpretation of the Greek word for hypocrisy (*hupokrisis*) should not be taken to mean that the leaders were play-acting or were acting differently from what they knew to be correct. Rather, as in its use in the Hebrew Scriptures, the term refers to having a misdirected understanding of God's purposes and hence being unable to discern the authentic meaning of Scripture.[9] Thus, Jesus is telling his listeners to beware of authorities—even the most well-intentioned religious authorities of the day (e.g., the Pharisees)—because the institutions that they govern are based on a faulty interpretation of Scripture.[10]

Phase 2 (Action Response): Instead of Using Scriptural Inheritance Laws Selfishly, Jesus' Followers Treat Everyone in Their *Oikos* With Dignity (Luke 12:13–48)

This phase starts with a listener, who wants his brother to divide the inheritance of their family *oikos* with him, asking Jesus to essentially interpret the Hebrew Scriptures related to inheritance laws. Such was not an unusual request to be made of a "teacher" (literally, *rabbi*).[11] However Jesus refuses to play the role of "judge and arbiter," alluding to the accusation uttered against Moses who had inappropriately used violence to try and enact justice (see Exod. 2:14, and Acts 7:27). The encounter ends with Jesus drawing attention to the underlying *spirit* of Scriptures, and deflecting attention away from figuring out ways to interpret the *letter* of the law to increase one's financial well-being: "Take care! Be on your guard against all kinds of greed[12]; for one's life does not consist in the abundance of possessions" (Luke 12:15).

After this introduction, the passage continues with Jesus providing a sort of "thought experiment" regarding what happens when people act in conventional ways with *oikos* wealth. He tells the story of a wealthy man who, after a great harvest, stores up his riches for his retirement saying to himself: "'Soul, you have ample goods laid up for many years; relax, eat, drink and be merry.' But God said to him: 'You fool![13] This very night your life will demanded of you. And the things you have prepared, whose will they be?' So it is with those who store up treasures for themselves but are not rich toward God" (Luke 12:19b–21).

After exposing the emptiness of the conventional practices of the wealthy, Jesus then describes countercultural practices and role models, starting with a well-known passage that encourages listeners to rely upon (and model) the benevolence of God:

> Consider the lilies, how they grow; they neither toil nor spin; yet I tell you, even Solomon in all his glory was not clothed like one of these . . . Do not be afraid, little flock, for it is your Father's good pleasure to give you the kingdom. Sell your possessions, and give alms. Make purses for yourselves that do not wear out, an unfailing

treasure in heaven, where no thief comes near and no moth destroys. For where your treasure is, there your heart will be also. (Luke 12:27, 32–34)

Clearly this counsel to sell possessions counters acquisitive economics, and such almsgiving counters the indebtedness associated with patron-client relations.

This phase concludes with reference to the practices of several countercultural *oikos* role models, including the owner of a household who serves his slaves (Luke 12:37), and a manager who places the needs of the people he manages higher than his own wants (Luke 12:42, 45). Managers and the social elite are called to act responsibly with the resources and opportunities entrusted to them: "From everyone to whom much has been given, much will be required; and from those to whom much has been entrusted, even more will be demanded" (Luke 12:48).[14]

Phase 3 (Changed Way of Seeing): Jesus' Followers See How Interpreting Scriptures on Their Own Corrects Their Traditional Reliance on the Elite (Luke 12:49–13:9)

This passage starts with Jesus describing how he came to bring fire to the earth. In the Hebrew Scriptures fire is a symbol of discernment and purification, which could be used to unveil the misunderstandings promoted by hypocritical religious leaders: "Is not my word like fire, says the LORD, and like a hammer that breaks a rock in pieces? See, therefore, I am against the [hypocritical] prophets, says the LORD, who steal my words from one another" (Jer. 23:29, 30). Jesus then describes how he is pressing on toward experiencing a kind of baptism—apparently different from his baptism by John, recorded in Luke 3:16—perhaps the sort of cleansing not uncommon at that time associated with entering "a new state of life" or "a new community."[15] In short, Jesus is ushering in a new era when the views of hypocritical religious leaders are replaced by a new vision of community.

Jesus' new vision will necessarily disrupt conventional social structures, including power relationships in the conventional *oikos* (Luke 12:51–53). The emphasis on a new way of seeing is even more explicit in the subsequent verses, where Jesus encourages readers to read the signs of the times and act according to their new understandings:

He also said to the crowds, When you see a cloud rising in the west, you immediately say, "It is going to rain"; and so it happens. And when you see the south wind blowing, you say, "There will be scorching heat"; and it happens. You hypocrites [people who fail to understand the Scriptures]! You know how to interpret the appearance of earth and sky, but why do you not know how to interpret the present time? (Luke 12:54–56)

The concluding verses in the passage focus on the implications of this new way of seeing vis-à-vis relationships with authority figures. First, listeners are called to avoid conventional judges altogether (Luke 12:58). Second, listeners are told that the acts of the conventional authorities should not be seen as representing God's judgment (Luke 13:1–3; nor should accidents be interpreted as representing God's judgment, Luke 13:4–5); rather, listeners should transform the way they see the world. Finally, listeners should be willing to challenge authority figures, and be willing to do the work required to support what they believe to be right. This final point foreshadows the next phase.

Phase 4 (Institutional Change): Institutions are Redeemed When KOG Processes Give Rise to Norms That Reflect the Spirit (versus the Letter) of the Law (Luke 13:10–30)

This phase starts with Jesus teaching in a synagogue where he gets into trouble with the leader. Jesus first challenges the religious elite's overemphasis on rules when he heals a woman on the sabbath. When this raises the ire of the leadership, Jesus points to the shortcomings of conventional religious rules:

> "You hypocrites [i.e., people who fail to understand the Hebrew Scriptures]! Does not each of you on the sabbath untie his ox or his donkey from the manger, and lead it away to give it water? And ought not this woman, a daughter of Abraham whom Satan bound for eighteen long years, be set free from this bondage on the sabbath day?" When he said this, all his opponents were put to shame; and the entire crowd was rejoicing at all the wonderful things that he was doing. (Luke 13:15b–17)

Thereupon Jesus describes how the KOG subverts conventional institutional (religious) norms. This includes, as described in chapter ten, breaking rabbinic tradition by planting a weed like a mustard seed so that the birds have a place to call home. And it includes inserting (religiously impure) yeast into dough to feed many people. Of course, this reference of yeast is of particular note because in the first phase of this cycle Jesus warned about the yeast of the leaders, which is their hypocrisy (i.e., lack of understanding of the Scriptures). Now in this phase 4 passage Jesus inverts the imagery, saying that just as a *lack* of understanding of Scriptures can yield corrupt social institutions, so also properly interpreted Scripture can serve as yeast to help to redeem those very same institutions.

The passage ends with a teaching about the establishment of an *oikos* based on KOG teachings. The countercultural nature of this *oikos* is illustrated by its unusual entry point (a narrow door, versus a conventional door) and by its inclusive nature ("people will come from the east and west, north and south, and will eat in the kingdom of God"; Luke 13:29). Many people, including the religious leaders who have a long and committed history of conventional interpretations of Scripture, will not be able to comprehend and thus fail to enter this countercultural KOG *oikos*: "Indeed, some who are last will be first, and some are first who will be last" (Luke 13:30).

REFLECTION POINT: CONNECTING CONTEMPORARY RESEARCH AND LUKE'S FORWARD-MOVING FOUR-PHASE MODEL

Are there modern-day events described in the management literature akin to the four-phase process evident in the first half of the Journey Narrative? It turns out there are many.[16] For an example related to the exclusion/inclusion of cultural outsiders, consider the Mission Church in a large southwestern US city, which had a tradition of segregation between its members and African Americans (e.g., the church building had a chapel nameplate honoring a former church leader and grand dragon of the KKK, an organization known for oppressing of African Americans). Phase 1 (problem recognition) occurred when young adults in the church recognized needs among homeless African Americans who lived in the downtown neighborhood of the historic Mission Church. Phase 2 (action response) started when the young adults started serving breakfast to homeless people in that neighborhood. Phase 3 (changed way of seeing) was evident when other church members began to volunteer their professional services (optometry, medical, dental) to the homeless people, and when Mission Church's homeless neighbors began to see the church as a welcoming place and began to participate in worship services. Phase 4 (institutional change) was evident when the nameplate honoring the former KKK leader was melted into a communion chalice and given to an all-black sister congregation, when homeless people began to serve others as ushers and choir members, and when infrastructure and resources for the poor and marginalized were greatly increased.

15

LUKE'S THREE "REVERSE" CYCLES THROUGH THE FOUR-PHASE PROCESS MODEL

Given the parallelism built into a chiastic structure, it comes as no surprise that the three cycles in the first half of the Journey Narrative are "mirrored" and thus go in the "reverse" direction in its second half. Thus, the presentation of the three cycles in this chapter will describe how institutional changes have an effect on new ways of seeing, which in turn has an effect on actions and problem recognition. Also, as expected, thanks to the chiastic structure of the Journey Narrative, there is considerable overlap in the thematic content of the three cycles in this chapter and in the previous chapter.

CYCLE #4: THE BENEFACTION CYCLE: MANAGING RELATIONSHIPS BETWEEN PATRONS AND CLIENTS (LUKE 14:1–16:13)

The passages in this cycle describe how subverting conventional patron-client institutions results in new ways of seeing the world, which results in new ways of managing *oikoi* and helps to recognize the fundamental problem related to trying to serve both God and money (figure 15.1).

Phase 4 (Institutional Change): Patron-Client Norms are Erased When People Share Resources with Others Who are Unable to Reciprocate (Luke 14:1–24)

The setting of this passage is Jesus having a meal in the *oikos* of a leading Pharisee along with other persons of high social status (Pharisees and lawyers).[1] The passage begins by addressing two related hallmark conventional institutional norms: acquisitive economics and patron-client relations. First, Jesus heals a man who had edema (dropsy), a disease where the body swells due to excessive fluids, which, in antiquity, was used metaphorically to refer to money-lovers.[2] Second, Jesus criticizes the conventional custom steeped in the patron-client paradigm where, at events like wedding banquets, people seek seats that provide the highest social status possible. Jesus says that people should rather choose a seat of lowest honor (with the possibility of subsequently being "promoted" to a seat of higher honor by the host): "For all who exalt themselves will be humbled, and those who humble themselves will be exalted" (Luke 14:11).

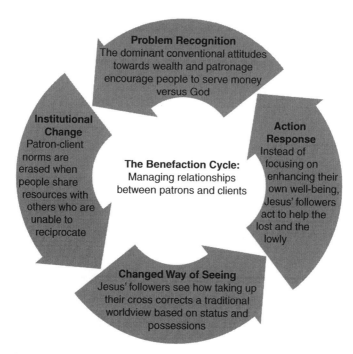

Figure 15.1 The benefaction cycle: managing relationships between patrons and clients (Luke 14:1–16:13).

Jesus then proceeds to describe countercultural institutional norms. He begins by telling his host:

> When you give a luncheon or a dinner, do not invite your friends or your brothers or your relatives or rich neighbors, in case they may invite you in return, and you would be repaid. But when you give a banquet, invite the poor, the crippled, the lame, and the blind.[3] And you will be blessed, because they cannot repay you,[4] for you will be repaid at the resurrection of the righteous. (Luke 14:12b–14)

He goes on to describe a situation where this new institutional norm has been put into practice.[5] A well-to-do man was hosting a great dinner, but after his first invitations had been rejected by people who had "metaphorical dropsy" (e.g., a absentee landowner who had to check out a new purchase of land, a rich farmer who had to check out his new yoke of five oxen,[6] and a newlywed), the man asked his slave to invite people from the margins of society:

> "Go out at once into the streets and lanes of the town and bring in the poor, the crippled, the blind, and the lame." And the slave said, "Sir, what you ordered has been done, and there is still room." Then the master said to the slave, "Go out into the roads and lanes, and compel people to come in, so that my house [*oikos*] may be filled. For I tell you, none of those who were invited will taste my dinner." (Luke 14:21b–24)

This passage is about countercultural institutional norms, of someone who was "toppling the familiar world of the ancient Mediterranean, overturning its socially constructed reality and replacing it with what must have been regarded as a scandalous alternative."[7]

Phase 3 (Changed Way of Seeing): Jesus' Followers See How Taking Up Their Cross Corrects a Traditional Worldview Based on Status and Possessions (Luke 14:25–35)

This phase describes hallmarks of the worldview associated with the new institutional norms presented in the previous phase. First and foremost, these norms result in a new way of seeing *oikos*, where the *oikos* of God displaces conventional views (Luke 14:26). Second, a hallmark of being Jesus' disciple is not characterized by becoming a member of a (new) religious social *elite*, but rather by renouncing elitism altogether and instead willingly paying the price of social nonconformity via carrying the cross (Luke 14:27). This view of carrying one's cross, described more fully in chapter eleven, provides an essential corrective to conventional ways of seeing status and possessions. Third, becoming a disciple of Jesus is characterized not by gaining possessions and status, but rather by giving up all one's possessions (Luke 14:33).

Members of such a new *oikos* must be committed to its guiding vision, one that disassociates itself from acquisitive economics and patron-client relations. Just as conventional rich people would only build a tower if they had enough money,[8] and conventional kings would only enter into a war if they had a large enough army, so also Jesus' would-be disciples should pursue membership in the *oikos* of God only if they are willing to commit to the vision associated with giving up their possessions: "Let anyone with ears to hear listen!" (Luke 14:35).

Phase 2 (Action Response): Instead of Focusing on Enhancing Their Own Well-Being, Jesus' Followers Act to Help the Lost and the Lowly (Luke 15:1–32)

This phase starts with conventional leaders complaining that Jesus welcomes sinners and eats with them. The term "sinner" in Luke typically refers to "persons whose primary attribute is that they cannot be included among the [conventionally defined] righteous and are therefore persons of low socio-religious status counted among the excluded, even damned."[9] Whereas conventional status seekers would try to enhance their own well-being by deliberately distancing themselves from sinners and tax collectors, Jesus welcomes them. This is consistent with Jesus having come to save the lost and the lowly, and to restore them to community/*oikos*.

The phase proceeds to describe three related parables that all share the same format: (i) a main character loses something, (ii) then recovers it, and (iii) then celebrates the restoration with the larger community. In the first parable a relatively well-to-do shepherd with one hundred sheep loses one, finds it, and then celebrates with his *oikos* and friends. In the second, a widow with ten silver coins loses one, finds it, and then celebrates with her *oikos* and friends. In the third, a rich man with two sons "loses" one who asks for an early inheritance and spends it all abroad in reckless living, finds him when the son returns, and then celebrates with his *oikos* and friends. The core message of each parable is in regaining what has been lost and in the celebration that occurs at the end, which is likened to the great rejoicing that takes place in heaven when the "lost" are recovered and community is enhanced.[10]

Phase 1 (Problem Recognition): The Dominant Conventional Attitudes toward Wealth and Patronage Encourage People to Serve Money versus God (Luke 16:1–13)

This phase contains the parable of the shrewd manager, which has been discussed at length in chapter five. In the context of the four-phase model, the parable describes how the shrewd manager, and his rich master, address the most vexing of problems facing the social elite with regard to acquisitive economics: "You cannot serve God and wealth" (Luke 16:13). And even when, as in the case in the parable, a patron supports a manager who scatters wealth to his clients, both can still expect negative peer pressure from other rich patrons (Luke 16:1). In short, it can be difficult even (especially?) for patrons to escape the social pressures to be servants of money/wealth/Mammon. Refusing to "use money to make money" is foreign to the acquisitive economics patron-client paradigm, and patrons who act benevolently toward clients will be accused of "wasting" or "squandering" their money.

CYCLE #5: THE JUSTICE CYCLE: MANAGING RELATIONSHIPS WITH THE SOCIAL ELITE (LUKE 16:14–18:17)

Unlike the previous four cycles, the passages in cycle 5 (and in cycle 6) can easily be seen to provide a "dual track" analysis within each of the four phases. What this means is that each phase describes two parallel views—a conventional view and a KOG view—within each of the four phases. In cycle 5, called the justice cyle, this means describing

- two approaches to *oikonomia* in phase 4 (the conventional approach of the rich man who excludes Lazarus, versus the KOG approach where members of an *oikos* do what they ought instead of focusing on acquisitive economics);
- two views of religious approval in phase 3 (being content with legitimation from conventional religious leaders, versus being thankful to Jesus);
- two approaches to justice in phase 2 (ambivalence versus persistence); and
- two basic attitudes to God in phase 1 (self-satisfaction for meeting conventional religious expectations, versus humility and contriteness).

Taken as a whole, this fifth cycle suggests that the kind of institutional norms that are in place in phase 4 (conventional versus KOG) influences how people see the world in phase 3, which in turn influences how people act vis-à-vis justice in phase 2, and their attitude toward God in phase 1 (figure 15.2). In the first "track" conventional institutions (phase 4) are associated with a desire for approval from conventional religious leaders (phase 3) and ambivalence about social justice (phase 2) and a self-satisfied demeanor when having met conventional religious expectations (phase 1). In the second track a sustenance economics approach to managing one's *oikos* (phase 4) is associated with a thankful outlook (phase 3) and persistent work for justice (phase 2) and a spirit of humility (phase 1).

Phase 4 (Institutional Change): Jesus' Followers Enact *Oikoi* Based on Just Sustenance Economics, Rather Than on Acquisitive Economics (Luke 16:14 through to 17:10)

Cycle 5 starts with Jesus criticizing the Pharisees for following institutional norms that render them "lovers of money" and caring too much about outward appearances

Figure 15.2 The justice cycle: managing relationships with the social elite (Luke 16:14–18:17).

(and forgetting that "God knows your hearts"). After explaining that his message is entirely consistent with a correct interpretation of God's Law and the prophets, Jesus goes on to tell the story about Lazarus, which describes how one's approach to *oikos* management can have implications not only for others in society, but also for the afterlife. It suggests that people like the rich man, with access to the scriptures, should know better than to follow conventional management practices. God is benevolent and wants the best for humankind, but if humankind refuses to listen to God then there will be consequences. Moreover, managers should beware if they endorse structures and systems that cause others—especially the powerless—to stumble. "It would be better for you if a millstone were hung around your neck and you were thrown into the sea than for you to cause one of these little ones to stumble" (Luke 17:2). But the passage also offers considerable hope for people who see the error of their ways and strive to mend them, and points to new kinds of institutional norms: "If another disciple sins, you must rebuke the offender, and if there is repentance, you must forgive. And if the same person sins against you seven times a day, and turns back to you seven times and says, 'I repent,' you must forgive" (Luke 17:3, 4).

In contrast to the *oikos* of the rich man in the story of Lazarus, Jesus goes on to describe a second *oikos*, one organized according to countercultural institutional norms. In this radical *oikos* members are not driven by acquisitive economics, but instead do the things they "ought to have done" consistent with KOG economics (Luke 17:7–10).[11] Thus, phase four describes two approaches to *oikos* management: a conventional one and one more consistent with KOG principles.

Phase 3 (Changed Way of Seeing): Jesus' Followers See and Praise and Rely upon God's Benevolence, Unblinded by Conventional Sources of Security (Luke 17:11–37)

This phase begins with Jesus healing ten lepers who, because their leprosy made them unclean according to conventional religious laws, had been forced to live outside of a village as social outcasts.[12] Jesus tells the lepers to show themselves to the priests so that they can be recognized as ceremonially cleansed members of the community. Nine of the lepers are more than content with being reinstituted into the community whose laws had labeled them as outcasts in the first place. However, the tenth leper "saw" (Luke 17:15) what happened, and returned to give thanks to Jesus. He recognized the benevolence of God that is all around for everyone to see, though many remain blind to it. The passage then goes on to describe Jesus talking to the Pharisees, thereby showing how difficult it is for some to see the KOG even though it is already present and among them (e.g., the healing of the lepers could be seen as a sign of the KOG). The KOG cannot be seen through conventional lenses.

In short, how people see Jesus in turn determines whether they are able to see signs of the KOG all around them. Over time the KOG will light up the whole world for everyone to see, but in the meantime people will be oppressed by conventional views and structures of power. This is not the first time that people have had a difficult time seeing beyond a conventional worldview—no one believed Noah until the rains came, nor Lot until the day he left Sodom. Those who seek to secure and justify their lives with conventional means will fail to live fully, but those who lose their conventional lives may truly live.

Phase 2 (Action Response): Jesus' Followers Persistently Act to Promote Justice for the Oppressed, Rather Than Accept the Status Quo (Luke 18:1–8)

This passage presents a parable with two main actors. The first actor is a judge and, akin to the Pharisees in the previous two phases, this conventional leader has little concern for the institutionalized woes of those at the margins of society—he neither fears God nor has respect for people. Indeed when the second actor in the parable, a widow, comes to the judge saying: "Grant me justice against my opponent [likely someone of higher social status than her]" the judge refuses to grant justice (Luke 18:3). But the widow refuses to give up. She has hope that the judge will grant justice if she persists with her request, so she keeps working at it. Because the judge finds her persistence trying, he finally concedes to her repeated efforts: "[B]ecause this widow keeps bothering me, I will give her justice, so that she may not wear me out by continually coming" (Luke 18:5).

Has the judge seen the light, and now become a champion for the poor? Probably not. Has the widow's little experiment, to test whether persistence pays off, been rewarded? Definitely. And if persistence pays off with a conventional judge, surely God will grant justice to and provide help for those who cry out to God.

Phase 1 (Problem Recognition): An Elitist "Holier-Than-Thou" Attitude is Problematic Because it Marginalizes Others; the Humble are Justified (Luke 18:9–17)

This phase also presents a parable with two main actors, again paralleling the sets of two actors in the previous three phases. The first actor is a Pharisee, who seems quite self-satisfied with his standing within the conventional religious system, as is evident in his prayer at the temple:

> God, I thank you that I am not like other people: thieves, rogues, adulterers, or even like this tax collector. I fast twice a week [i.e., I do not limit my fasting to only pre-scribed days]; I give a tenth of *all* my income [i.e., I do not limit myself to tithing only what I myself produce, as the law requires].[13] (Luke 18:11b–12).

In short, this Pharisee perceives himself to act in ways that go above and beyond the minimums prescribed in the religious laws. Ironically, in describing this he explicitly distances himself from others, especially social outcasts and expendables. This is a telling observation of what is problematic with a conventional interpretation of scrip-ture, one where members of the social elite invariably marginalize others.

The second actor is the tax collector whom the Pharisee has referred to, who is also at the temple praying: "The tax collector, standing for off, would not even look up to heaven, but was beating his breast and saying, 'God, be merciful to me, a sinner!'" (Luke 18:13). Jesus says that the tax collector went home justified, but not the Pharisee: "for all who exalt themselves will be humbled, but all who humble themselves will be exalted" (Luke 18:14). The passage concludes with Jesus saying that the KOG belongs to people who receive it like little children, like people who need to (re)learn what it means to be human, willing to unlearn conventional ways and to embrace KOG ways.

CYCLE #6: THE SALVATION CYCLE: MANAGING RELATIONSHIPS WITH SOCIAL OUTCASTS (LUKE 18:18–19:40)

Recall that as with cycle 5, cycle 6 offers a "dual-track" run through the four phases. Taken together, the phases in this cycle demonstrate that, because they define who is a social outcast, institutional structures and systems do matter. Cycle 6 shows how following conventional institutional norms will lead down one path that cre-ates social outcasts, and following alternative KOG norms will lead down another path that redeems social outcasts. In the conventional track, when institutions like those associated with the conventional rich ruler in phase 4 prevail, people will see Jesus of Nazareth as (merely) a wise teacher (Phase 3), entrepreneurial activities will seek continued political and financial economic success like the nobleman and his managers (Phase 2), and Jesus will not be lauded as a king who ushers in a new kind of peace (Phase 1). The KOG track is evident in examples like the disciples who have walked away from conventional *oikos* institutions and instead opted for structures and systems that are more life-giving (phase 4), in people who see Jesus as a savior who offers new ways of living (phase 3), in people who do experiments where they unilaterally share money with the poor and repay people who have been wronged (phase 2), and in people who accept Jesus as a king who ushers in a new kind of peace/salvation (Phase 1) (figure 15.3).

Phase 4 (Institutional Change): Jesus' Followers Step Outside of Social Traditions and Model New Life-Giving Norms That Benefit Social Outcasts (Luke 18:18–34)

This phase starts with the story of a rich ruler who wants to know what he must do to inherit eternal life. This ruler seems to be about as good[14] as could be hoped for within a conventional approach. He takes conventional norms seriously: he does not

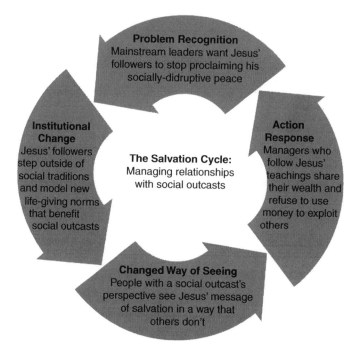

Figure 15.3 The salvation cycle: managing relationships with social outcasts (Luke 18:1–19:40).

steal, lie, murder, or commit adultery. For goodness sake, he even honors his mother and father. How much more wholesome can you get?

Well, it turns out you *can* get more wholesome. Jesus suggests there is only one thing lacking, namely, the ruler should sell everything he has, give the money to the poor, and follow Jesus. We have already learned in chapter seven how this would challenge the conventional meaning of the commandments of the Hebrew Scriptures, perhaps most notably flying in the face of the conventional meaning of what it means to honor one's mother and father.

Interestingly, Luke leaves it somewhat ambiguous as to what the rich ruler does. We read that the ruler is sad. This has often been interpreted to mean that he is sad because he is unwilling to sell all his possessions, possibly because this would counter the conventional interpretation of the commandments he had followed since his youth. Alternatively, perhaps in that encounter with Jesus the ruler realizes in an instant the folly of the conventional paradigm, and he is sad because he has wasted so much of his life pursuing a somewhat hollow understanding of the commandments. An understanding that has neglected the poor and lowly.

In any case, the passage makes very clear that it is difficult for people who are powerful or rich, thanks to their status, to enter the kingdom of God—"it is easier for a camel to go through the eye of a needle than for someone who is rich to enter the kingdom of God" (Luke 18:25). Those who heard Jesus explaining how this exemplary conventional ruler fell short asked: "Then who can be saved?" (Luke 18:26).

With regard to the second "track," the passage continues with Jesus affirm-ing disciples who have left behind their conventional *oikos* in order to follow KOG norms. Thus, the verses in this phase set up two kinds of *oikos*: the first is evident in the rich ruler who honors his parents in a conventional way, and the second is evident in disciples who leave their conventional *oikos* in order to establish a new *oikos* with Jesus and thereby receive eternal life (Luke 18:30).

The passage ends on what may seem like a bit of an odd note. Jesus tells his 12 dis-ciples that once they get to Jerusalem he will be handed to the Gentiles, arrested, mocked, flogged, killed, and raised on the third day. In short, he will become a social outcast, and then he will be raised from the dead. But the 12 disciples simply don't get it: "But they understood nothing about all these things; in fact, what he said was hidden from them, and they did not grasp what was said" (Luke 18:34). This raises at least two questions. Why did Jesus bother telling his disciples this even though he presumably knew they would not be able to understand it? And why was it worth including in Luke's Gospel? The answer may have something to do with the fact that Jesus is signaling that his manner of death and resurrection are inextricably related to institutional structures and systems. In one sense this is self-evident: it was the elite within the institutions of first-century Palestine who had the power to decide who was a social outcast worthy of crucifixion. These verses show how Jesus' death is related to fallen institutions and, perhaps more importantly, how Jesus' res-urrection calls for the reinvention of those institutions.

Phase 3 (Changed Way of Seeing): People With a Social Outcast's Perspective See Jesus' Message of Salvation in a Way That Others Don't (Luke 18:35–43)

Building on the two types of *oikos* identified in Phase 4, this passage describes two possible ways that people interpret who Jesus is. On the one hand you have people like the rich young ruler and others like him who see Jesus merely as "Jesus of Nazareth," a wise teacher who has important things to say (Luke 18:37). On the other hand you have people like the blind man who see Jesus as the "Son of David" (i.e., the long awaited savior who would deliver Israel from her enemies and establish an eternal reign) (Luke 18:38).[15] Members of this latter group, often social outcasts who are ordered to be quiet by "those in front," recognize that Jesus represents a new of seeing: "[A]ll the people, *when they saw it*, praised God" (Luke 18:43).

Phase 2 (Action Response): Managers Who Follow Jesus' Teachings Share Their Wealth and Refuse to Use Money to Exploit Others (Luke 19:1–27)

The two passages in this phase, which have been described at some length earlier in the book, again describe the two kinds of people identified in phases 4 and 3. On the one hand, Zacchaeus understands who Jesus is, and responds accordingly, and Jesus says that salvation has come to his *oikos*. The nobleman in the parable of the ten pounds, on the other hand, is the worst kind of leader within the conventional paradigm, who takes what does not belong to him, and who promotes structures and systems where the rich get richer and the poor get poorer (and who punishes the poor and slaughters his enemies). The contrast between Zacchaeus and the noble-man is highlighted by placing the two passages side by side.[16]

Phase 1 (Problem Recognition): Mainstream Leaders Want Jesus' Followers to Stop Proclaiming his Socially Disruptive Peace (Luke 19:28–40)

Again, here we meet the two kinds of people that appear in each of the previous phases. On the one hand is the *oikos* master who is happy to share his donkey with Jesus, and the multitude who acknowledge Jesus as savior when they shout: "Blessed is the king who comes in the name of the Lord! Peace in heaven, and glory in the highest heaven!" (Luke 19:38). These people recognize that Jesus represents a different kind of king, and offers a qualitatively different kind of peace than the *pax Romana* offered by the Roman emperor.[17] They remember all the deeds Jesus has performed that helped the social outcasts, as is evident in their reference to Psalm 118.[18] On the other hand are the Pharisees, who still don't get it, whom Jesus rebukes after they suggest he order the crowds to be silent. The Pharisees are rightly afraid that people and structures and systems that benefit the social outcasts will usher in a kind of peace that disrupts the status quo and will be perceived as a threat by conventional leaders.

REFLECTION POINT: CONNECTING CONTEMPORARY RESEARCH AND LUKE'S FOUR-PHASE MODEL IN REVERSE

Is this reverse order of Luke's four-phase model evident in the business world today? Yes it is, and glimpses of it can be seen in the studies that examine deinstitutionalization, social movements, and structuration theory.[19] One particularly relevant example comes from BankBoston's creation of the First Community Bank of Boston, which is well-known for demonstrating how banking in the inner-city can be profitable. Phase 4 (institutional change) was evident when US government regulations made it illegal for banks to participate in "redlining," so named because banks drew red lines on maps around the borders of poor neighborhoods where they were reluctant to provide loans to people. Phase 3 (changed way of seeing) occurred in 1980, when a report by the US Federal Reserve clearly showed that banks in Boston were guilty of underserving poor neighborhoods, and moreover that this was discriminating against African Americans. This was a revelation to executives at BankBoston who, until that point, had not "seen" that the problem of redlining truly was occurring. Phase 2 (action response) was evident when BankBoston experimented by developing nonconventional ways to measure credit for people in poor neighborhoods, and then began to provide loans to them. In contrast, at this same time other banks were closing their inner-city branches. First Community Bank of Boston was established in the late 1980s, making healthy profits within five years, and attracted visitors from over 50 other banks seeking to learn how to serve the poor profitably. Phase 1 (problem recognition) was evident in the constant tension facing the First Community Bank because it was going against the norms of the conventional banking industry. As testament to this tension, First Community Bank was eliminated some time after BankBoston (then Fleet) was acquired by Bank of America.

SUMMARY OF PART FIVE

Despite its apparent simplicity and elegance, the four-phase process model embedded in the Journey Narrative encompasses many of the key ideas that have been discussed in earlier chapters. This model is valuable because it provides a *practical* process by which the ideas regarding KOG management and salvation introduced earlier can be implemented. In this way it is helpful to think of the process model as providing a *means* toward a larger end; it is a means for putting KOG ideals into practice.

For example, although the basic first-century understanding of salvation described in Luke—that is, being released from oppression, and implementing alternative structures and systems that facilitate emancipation—is clearly very inviting, it can also seem overwhelming to put into practice. Indeed, managers have a tough enough time designing and implementing changes that fine-tune the status quo, how can they ever manage transformational change on the level of salvation? The four-phase process can help to break this down into a more manageable step-by-step ongoing process. For example, people *can* (1) identify specific issues to be addressed, (2) develop experiments to address these situations, and (3) experience changed worldviews that (4) eventually inform institutional change. Luke never suggests that such changes will be easy or happen overnight. Indeed, this will be a challenging process, and sometimes glimpses of KOG management will be fleeting.

That said, it may not be entirely helpful to think of the process model as merely the *means* to an end. Rather, in many ways working through the model is an end in and of itself. Salvation is not about having implemented some "perfected" structures and systems, but rather it is about the *process* of implementing evermore KOG-like structures and systems. In the language of Luke, the process of salvation is in the journey, not in arriving at the destination.

As a final comment, readers may find it interesting to note that the layout of this book roughly follows the four-phase model embedded in the Journey Narrative.

Phase 1 (problem recognition) was evident in part two, which, using a first-century management lens, provided an interpretation of two key management parables—the parable of the shrewd manager and the parable of the ten pounds—that essentially pointed to possible problems associated with conventional twenty-first-century interpretations of these parables. These first-century interpretations may have initially come across as odd or perhaps even off-putting for modern readers. Jesus praises a manager for unilaterally scattering the rich man's resources? It is better to keep money out of circulation than to use it to make more money? These countercultural interpretations seemed to promote managerial behavior that was dishonest, and perhaps even illegal.

Phase 2 (action response) was evident in part three, which used the first-century lens to identify and analyze *all* the passages in Luke that explicitly deal with first-century management issues (i.e., husband-wife, parent-child, master-slave, money, benefaction/patron-client relationships). This little experiment to test the basic findings from part two provided overwhelming confirmation for the countercultural first-century interpretation. The "problematic" interpretations of the parable of the shrewd manager and the ten pounds were entirely consistent with the overarching teachings on these topics in Luke.

Phase 3 (changed way of seeing) was evident in part four where the analysis, based on a first-century understanding of management, resulted in a new way of seeing other overarching themes in the Gospel message. In particular, this prompted a new way of seeing what Luke says about the kingdom of God, salvation, and the Holy Spirit. This showed that organizational structures and systems play a central role in enacting the KOG and facilitating salvation, and that the Holy Spirit played an important role in sustaining these.

Phase 4 (institutional change) was evident in part five, which examined the four-phase process model embedded in Luke's Journey Narrative. The process model identified discrete steps that can be taken to challenge conventional institutional norms, structures and systems, and to replace these with radical institutions based on benefaction and sustenance economics. In particular the Journey Narrative describes instances where the four-phase model is useful for finding more KOG-like ways to manage relationships: within the *oikos*, with cultural outsiders and social outcasts, with the social elite and between patrons and clients, and with regards to interpreting scriptures. Indeed, adoption of this four-phase process model itself can be seen as an institutional change.

VI

IMPLICATIONS FOR TWENTY-FIRST-CENTURY MANAGEMENT THEORY AND PRACTICE

By way of a quick review, thus far we examined what the Gospel of Luke says about the management of goods and services producing organizations via a first-century managerial lens. This involved gathering ideas and frameworks and debates about management that were current in the first century, and using them to identify and interpret relevant passages in Luke. In this way we looked at key relationships within the ancient *oikos* (husband-wife, parent-child, master-slave), considered two basic ways of managing money (e.g., acquisitive economics versus sustenance economics), and examined key dimensions of relationships between different goods and services producing organizations (e.g., patron-client relations versus classical benefaction). We found that Luke consistently criticizes conventional management practices, and promotes an alternative approach.

We also examined key themes that Luke is noted for (kingdom of God, salvation, Holy Spirit) through a managerial lens. Here we found that the teachings in each of these areas have strong implications for management: the KOG is primarily enacted and evident in *oikos* settings that are consistent with countercultural organizing principles; salvation is evident when people are freed from oppressive structures and systems and freed to participate in KOG-like organizations and institutions; and the Holy Spirit is essential for all this to happen.

Finally we examined the literary unit at the heart of Luke's passages about management—namely, the Journey Narrative, a sort of "management manual"—using first-century literary tools. We found that embedded within the chiastic Journey Narrative is a four-phase process model that provides a practical way to put KOG management into practice. In particular, this model underscores the importance of social institutions. It describes a process people can use to develop KOG-inspired structures and systems that facilitate salvation. It helps to undermine conventional structures and systems that lead people into temptation associated with acquisitive economics and patron-client relationships.

This final part of the book, rather than continue to examine how a first-century management lens can serve to interpret the Gospel of Luke, will use the understanding of management described in Luke as a lens to interpret contemporary management theory and practice. Drawing on a historically grounded exemplar like Luke to use as an "ideal-type" is a time-honored and valuable way for conceptualizing and developing management theory and practice.[1] Of course, developing such countercultural management theory and practice is much more complex and challenging than can be accomplished in a single book. Even so, there is merit in presenting a basic outline of what such theory might look like. That is the task for chapters sixteen through eighteen.

This task is not of little significance. For example, recall that Max Weber argued that modern problems could be overcome by appealing to ancient ideals and prophets, such as the ones associated with a biblical understanding of Jesus. If this is true, then the present study may be of great interest for many people, ranging from management philosophers contemplating the "theological turn" all the way to practitioners out to save the world. The goal in this section will be to take the approach to management championed in the Gospel of Luke—here called "KOG management" for short—and use it as a lens to both: (a) critique conventional contemporary management theory and practice; and (b) highlight and develop alternative management theory and practice. This section will be organized according to the three main levels of analysis presented in the earlier chapters:

> Chapter sixteen: Managing relationships *within* organizations—organizational structure, motivation, and leadership
>
> Chapter seventeen: Managing money—economics, finance, and accounting
>
> Chapter eighteen: Managing relationships *between* organizations—marketing, supply chain, and strategy

Within each of these three levels of analysis some of the most popular and influential conventional theories will be presented, and will be used as a springboard to sketch out in broad brush strokes what alternative KOG-management theory and practice might look like. Of particular interest, each chapter will include real-world examples of how four-phase change processes, akin to those embedded in Luke's Journey Narrative, have helped practicing managers to implement such alternative practices.[2]

In short, the goal is to contrast and compare KOG management with contemporary organization theory and practice, and to begin to speculate what modern management theory and practice based on a first-century KOG ethic might look like.[3]

MANAGING RELATIONSHIPS *WITHIN* ORGANIZATIONS: ORGANIZATIONAL STRUCTURE, MOTIVATION, AND LEADERSHIP

When it comes to managing relationships within the organization, the message in Luke has the following three key themes:

1. *Everyone is to be treated with dignity* (e.g., in first-century terms, rather than men lording it over women, women and men are treated more as equals, with women often having a leadership role in the *oikos*).
2. *Organizational boundaries are to be porous and welcoming* (e.g., in first-century terms, rather than adult children having a primary focus on enhancing the security of their *oikos* and thereby honoring their parents, adult children are challenged to leave the security of their *oikos* to establish new inclusive forms of *oikos* where everyone is welcome to find security).
3. When looking for leadership within an organization, particular attention should be given to those who do the basic work of the organization (e.g., in first-century terms, rather that masters exploiting their slaves, slaves are held up as role models of "servant leadership").

In general terms, the KOG is present when people are saved from oppressive structures and systems, when social outcasts are welcome from all corners of the world and everyone is treated with dignity, and when people serve one another. These are the kinds of institutional structures that will lead people away from the temptations associated with self-interested acquisitive economics.

These three themes have key implications for contemporary management theory and practice. We will look at this in terms of three main topics: (i) the fundamentals of organizational structure; (ii) motivation; and (iii) leadership.

THE FUNDAMENTALS OF ORGANIZATIONAL STRUCTURE

At its most basic level, the essence of organizing has four basic elements as shown in table 16.1. Building on work by Max Weber coupled with a radical theology of management, table 16.1 also shows how conventional management theory addresses each of the four basic issues, and contrasts this with how they might look under

Table 16.1   Four fundamental elements of organizational structure

Four fundamental elements of organizing	How these elements are addressed in conventional management theory	A KOG-management approach to addressing these elements
1. The overall work of the organization is broken down into appropriate tasks	*Standardization* (developing uniform practices for organizational members to follow in doing their jobs) ensures that work activities are being completed in the best way	*Experimentation* (an ongoing voluntary implementation of new ways of performing tasks on a trial basis) ensures that work activities are completed in the best way
2. Members know what their specific subtasks are	*Specialization* (grouping standardized organizational tasks into separate jobs) ensures that members know what subtasks they should perform	*Sensitization* (searching for and responding to needs and opportunities to improve the status quo) ensures that members know what subtasks they should perform
3. Members know whom they should defer to	*Centralization* (having decision-making authority rest with managers at the top of an organization's hierarchy) ensures orderly deference among members	*Dignification* (treating *everyone* with dignity and respect in community) ensures orderly deference among members
4. Members' task performance fits together meaningfully with their coworkers	*Departmentalization* (grouping members and resources together to achieve the work of the larger organization) ensures that members work together harmoniously	*Participation* (mutuality and giving stakeholders a voice in how the organization is managed and how jobs are performed) ensures that members work together harmoniously

KOG management.[1] We will not repeat the content of table 16.1, but do note that the conventional approach offers a more static response to the four fundamentals, whereas the KOG approach is more dynamic and processual.

Practitioner Example

While the four basic fundamentals of organizing listed in table 16.1 will be familiar to most readers, it is worthwhile to illustrate how an organization can move from a conventional toward a more KOG management approach. Consider Semco, a business that produces marine pumps for Brazil's shipping industry.[2] Ricardo Semler took over this company from his father as a 21-year-old. At the time Semco employed about a hundred people and generated about $4 million in annual revenue. The company was managed in a fairly conventional way, with formal rules, well-developed operating standards, detailed job descriptions, and a fairly centralized authority structure with a well-developed departmental structure. In short, Semco's structures and systems had been developed fully enough for the father to hand it over to a 21-year-old.

Ricardo Semler, however, did not particularly like how the company was run. As a previous summer employee in Semco's purchasing department, he asked himself: "How can I spend the rest of my life doing this? How can I stomach years of babysitting people to make sure they clock in on time? Why is this worth doing?" So, when he took over the firm he discarded the formalized rules and regulations that had been the result of years of *standardization*. Even though the company has since grown to over $200 million in annual revenue and three thousand employees, its manual has cartoons and is a mere 20 pages long. Indeed, the company even lacks a written mission statement, preferring instead to foster *experimentation*. Minutes are seldom taken at meetings in Semco, because once things get written down and codified they can reduce future experimentation. Semler wants activity at Semco to be guided by standards that are fluid and constantly (re)constructed by its members.

Specialization is also downplayed; there are no job descriptions at Semco. However, it does have a "Lost in Space" program, which recognizes that young employees often do not know what they want to do. Semco allows new recruits to roam through the company for a year, moving to a different unit whenever they want to, looking for what they want to do. Semler himself does not have an office and spends little time at work, choosing instead to seek a wide variety of inputs and stimuli. These practices create occasions for everyone to become *sensitized* to needs and opportunities that otherwise might be overlooked.

Centralization is also downplayed at Semco; it still has only three levels of hierarchy. Ricardo Semler is one of six "counselors" (top management), who take turns leading the company for six months at a time. Workers in Semco set their own salaries, choose their own work hours, and select their own managers. Workers trust one another and are treated with *dignity*. According to Semler: "Most of our programs are based on the notion of giving employees control over their own lives. In a word, we hire adults, and then we treat them like adults."[3]

Finally, regarding *departmentalization*, Semco's large departments have been dismantled. Semler prefers smaller, more autonomous units no larger than 150 members, where everyone knows that their *participation* matters and how their work contributes to and fits in with that of their coworkers. This emphasis on participation is consistent with Semler's commitment to democracy, which is a watchword at Semco.

In short, Ricardo Semler enjoys being a countercultural manager, and he intends to keep it that way. Semco has had an excellent growth rate, but Semler is also clear that profits and growth are not his primary goals. He states:

> I can honestly say that our growth, profit, and the number of people we employ are secondary concerns. Outsiders clamor to know these things because they want to quantify our business. These are the yardsticks they turn to first. That's one reason we're still privately held. I don't want Semco to be burdened with the ninety-day mind-set of most stock market analysts. It would undermine our solidity and force us to dance to the tune we don't really want to hear—a Wall Street waltz that starts each day with an opening bell and ends with the thump of the closing gavel.[4]

> Profit beyond the minimum is not essential for survival. In any event, an organization doesn't really need profit beyond what is vital for working capital and the small growth that is essential for keeping up with the customers and competition. Excess profit only creates another imbalance. To be sure, it enables the owner or CEO to commission a yacht. But then employees will wonder why they should work so the owner can buy a boat.[5]

Semler enjoys demonstrating that organizations can thrive when managers treat people with dignity, when trust and participation are fostered, when experimentation and ongoing learning are valued, and when members are sensitive to needs and opportunities in the larger community. For Semler, these are genuine *fund*amentals of organizing. His approach has impressed his peers, evident in the fact that a poll of fifty-two thousand Brazilian executives has repeatedly chosen him to be business leader of the year.

MOTIVATION

The message in Luke demands rethinking some of the foundational research and theory that has shaped the contemporary motivation literature. This is perhaps nowhere more clear than in Abraham Maslow's "hierarchy of needs" theory, which remains one of the best-known and most important theories in motivation.[6] According to Maslow, people are motivated to satisfy five need levels, starting with the most basic needs and moving up the hierarchy.

1. Physiological (food, clothing, shelter, and physical needs that people seek to satisfy);
2. Safety (security, stability, and protection from harm);
3. Love (to be accepted by peers or to belong to a group);
4. Esteem (recognition and respect from peers); and
5. Self-actualization (achieving one's full potential).

He suggested that these needs can be placed in a hierarchy, and the key to motivating others is to see which needs they have. Thus, people who do not have their physiological needs met will be motivated to work hard when their effort is rewarded with food and shelter. People who have their physiological needs met but not their safety needs will be motivated to work hard when their effort is rewarded with increased security and stability. And so on.

Of course, the message of Luke would challenge the thinking behind this theory on several fronts. First, Maslow's model seems to be quite consistent with conventional patron-client thinking—as long as the basic needs of the masses are in jeopardy, they will work hard for absentee landlords and emperors who provide such basic needs. From a KOG-management perspective even (especially?) the poor should be treated with dignity and have opportunities to meet their basic needs, if necessary thanks to the benefaction of others. Second, Maslow's model implicitly dehumanizes the part of society that is poor and on the margins, implying, for example, that their need for love is less salient than the need for love of the relatively well-to-do. In contrast, in Luke it is the slaves and those who "take up their cross" who are presented as the most loving and most likely to treat others with dignity. Third, Maslow's model has an individualistic bias insofar as the idea of "*self*-actualization" lies at the top of the hierarchy. In contrast, from a Lukan perspective the pinnacle of salvation comes in a community setting.

What is particularly surprising is that Maslow's model continues to be so popular, even though empirical research does not support it.[7] This may be telling in two ways. First, the popularity of Maslow's model suggests that its implicit values resonate so well with other conventional management thinking that people are drawn toward it. Second, the fact that the model has not received empirical support suggest that, even though decades of teaching it should have resulted in a self-fulfilling prophecy, the model may be so foreign to innate human nature that even people who are attracted to the model do not behave according to it. Rather, subsequent research indicates that people's needs are much more holistic. Everyone deserves to be treated with dignity, everyone has needs for love and relationship and growth.[8]

Practitioner Example

For an example of what can happen when workers are treated with dignity as whole people, rather than as merely workers who need to be motivated to work hard, consider the story of James Despain. Despain worked as manager of Caterpillar Inc.'s three-thousand-member Track-Type Tractors division, and he describes the process of moving from a conventionally managed organization to one whose values were more in line with KOG management principles. The business was known for its poorly motivated workforce and for its antagonistic union-management relations. This began to change when Despain emphasized treating employees with dignity, as whole people to be trusted rather than as individual workers to be instrumentally motivated. Here is part of the story of this turnaround, in the words of James Despain in his book . . . *And Dignity for all*, presented in terms of the four-phase process model[9]:

> *Phase 1 (problem recognition): Low morale/motivation/productivity in workforce.* "I contemplated the *lack of motivation* of the workforce."
>
> *Phase 2 (action response): Trust and treat everyone with dignity.* "The road to change for me began with the value of Trust. My epiphany was the realization that for my entire life I had trusted no one. I had been taught not to—not purposely, but in subtle ways. Over many years, I was encouraged to write things down for the purpose of 'proving' my innocence later if conflict or failure should occur. I had learned to not discuss certain things with certain people, to 'spin' information to make things seem better, and to never fully admit being responsible for mistakes or failure. And I was a very good student. After struggling most of one night with *what I should do,* I decided to trust everyone—everyone. I decided to share what I knew without thinking of any particular motive for sharing. If I were going to get hurt from this, then hurt I would get."
>
> *Phase 3 (changed way of seeing): Treating people with dignity = liberation.* "This decision at this moment liberated me! From then on, *I saw people differently.* I began to care for them and was willing to listen to them without judgment. Later I would *see* how feelings of trust would permeate our organization and would *witness* the power of it."
>
> *Phase 4 (institutional change): New holistic values in the organization.* "Instead of being forceful or loud in an effort to get our individual ways, we started to listen, really listen, to what others were trying to say. Instead of hurting feelings as sensitive issues surfaced, we began to practice real respect. We lost our need for ownership of ideas and began giving meaningful recognition to others. Our *collective ideas* were more innovative and powerful."

Eventually antagonistic union-management relations improved, and hourly and salaried members began to treat each other with respect and dignity. Everyone at Caterpillar changed, from top managers to hourly workers. Soon employees' approval of management rose by more than 30 percent, there was a 25 percent increase in employee participation, satisfaction, and accountability, and their identification with the organization's goals jumped by 40 percent. Before long the division, which had been losing tens of millions of dollars a year, was again profitable.

LEADERSHIP

The message in Luke also points to a need to rethink some of the foundational research and theory that has shaped the leadership literature. Let us consider two key leader behaviors that have been identified in the literature: (1) leaders initiate structure for subordinates (i.e., leaders exhibit concern for accomplishing the task), and (2) leaders show consideration to subordinates (i.e., leaders exhibit concern for people and interpersonal relationships).[10] These two behaviors form the basis for what is perhaps the most popular leadership model among practitioners,[11] situational leadership, which suggests that the most effective leaders change their frequency of these two behaviors in a way that is situation-appropriate, as determined by the followers' (1) technical ability and (2) motivation. This results in four types of leader behavior, as described in table 16.2.

Table 16.2   Basic overview of conventional situational leadership theory

HIGH *Need for a leader to provide considerate, supportive and relationship-oriented behavior in order to improve a subordinate's motivation*	*Supporting* (sustain high productivity): when followers have high technical ability but low motivation, it is effective for leaders to exhibit low concern for task (i.e., followers don't need to be taught what to do) but show high concern for people (i.e., motivate followers).	*Coaching* (address weaknesses in followers): when followers have low technical ability and low motivation, it is effective for leaders to exhibit high concern for task (i.e., teach followers what to do) and high concern for people (i.e., motivate followers).
LOW	*Delegating* (optimize efficiency): when followers have technical ability and are committed to the task, it is effective for leaders to exhibit low concern for task (i.e., followers already know what to do) and low concern for people (i.e., followers don't need to be motivated).	*Directing* (improve productivity immediately): when followers have low technical ability but high motivation, it is effective for leaders to exhibit high concern for task (i.e., teach followers what to do) but show low concern for people (i.e., followers don't need to be motivated).

LOW   HIGH

Need for a leader to provide directive, task-oriented, job-centered, initiating structure behavior in order to improve a subordinate's ability

In a nutshell, conventional situational leadership theory suggests that managers need to be able to perform each of the four combinations of behaviors—supporting, coaching, directing, and delegating—and must choose which one is the most appropriate based on the situation they are facing.

From a KOG-management perspective, this model has shortcomings on several fronts. First, the model focuses on how leaders can maximize followers' productivity. There is little in Luke to support the contention that maximizing productivity should be the *primary* goal of leadership. Indeed, there are many other things that would be higher priorities from a KOG-management perspective, such as including outcasts. Productivity is valued, it is just not the most important goal.

Second, conventional situational leadership theory presumes that leaders know best how to perform the work tasks of organizational members. Again, a KOG-management perspective would not presume this, and indeed often Luke seems to suggest that workers are better-suited than masters in deciding how to perform a task.[12] More importantly, from a KOG-management perspective this top-down direction is questionable in the first place. Recall Luke's emphasis is on servant leadership (i.e., precisely those who do not lord it over others). And as described in chapter nine, the only time Jesus uses the term "leader" to refer to his followers is also the only time he uses the word *hegoumenos*, which refers to a style of leadership that deliberately takes into the account the views of others.[13]

Third, conventional situational leadership theory assumes that the optimal amount of *consideration* shown to others depends on (1) their needs and (2) whether it will enhance productivity.[14] As we have seen, from a KOG-management perspective (1) everyone should be treated with dignity and consideration, especially those who are outcasts, (2) even if it does not enhance productivity.

That said, there is some evidence within Luke supporting the basic idea of a (non-conventional) situational leadership model. One indicator is that different leadership terms are sometimes used to describe Jesus, depending on the situation. Most notably, Jesus is referred to as "master" only in specific kinds of situations. On each of the six occasions where the disciples call Jesus "master" (*epistates*[15]), it is "always in contexts where they exhibit a lack of comprehension."[16] It is almost as though, when the disciples seem helpless and perplexed, they revert to asking Jesus to don the role of "master" to help them out. For example, in one case Simon lowers his fishing net despite being confused by Jesus' request (Luke 5:5); in another the disciples awaken Jesus when they are at their wit's end in the middle of a storm at sea (Luke 8:24); in another Peter points to the awkwardness of Jesus' question "Who touched me?" when walking through the middle of a crowd (Luke 8:45); in another the disciples inappropriately want to build a dwelling place for Jesus, Moses, and Elijah (Luke 9:33); and in the final one they are perplexed when an outsider performs wonders in Jesus' name (Luke 9:49). On the whole, the passages seem to suggest that the disciples ask Jesus to act as a "master" in situations where they are confused.

A second indicator of a possible situational leadership model embedded in Luke is related to the observation that there were four different modes of KOG passages: proclamation of core KOG attributes, teaching/learning KOG ideas, enacting the KOG, and enjoying KOG outcomes (see chapter ten). It may be that each of the modes of God's reign is associated with a different aspect of leading. Thus, proclaiming is appropriate when people are unfamiliar with the KOG, teaching/learning is appropriate when people are interested in finding out more, enacting is appropriate when people are ready and wanting to implement ideas, and enjoying outcomes is appropriate when KOG actions are manifest.

A third indicator, not inconsistent with the four KOG types of passages, is observable in patterns evident in the passages in Luke where the Greek word *kurios* (= lord, master) is used to describe God and Jesus. As shown in appendix B, the 79 mentions of Jesus ($N = 45$) and God ($N = 34$) as *kurios* (lord) can be grouped into four different situational modes as follows:

1. Being prepared/preparing the way for the KOG (19 mentions);
2. Learning/teaching KOG ways (17 mentions)[17];
3. Implementing countercultural KOG ideas (21 mentions); and
4. Facilitating/enjoying KOG outcomes (22 mentions).

Of course, these passages await much deeper analysis than has been provided here and in appendix B, but taken together even this simple analysis suggests that grounded in Luke may be a fourfold situational leadership model along two dimensions. The first dimension refers to the type of knowledge that is lacking among followers and/or being offered by the leader: cognitive or experiential. For example, the modes of "being prepared/preparing the way" and "learning/teaching KOG ways" generally place greater emphasis on *cognitive* knowledge, whereas the modes of "implementing KOG ideas" and "facilitating/enjoying KOG outcomes" generally place greater emphasis on *experiential* knowledge.

The second dimension refers to the nature of the commitment that followers exhibit toward the KOG: passive or active. For example, it could be argued that the modes of "being prepared/preparing the way" and "enjoying KOG outcomes" may generally require relatively *passive* commitment, whereas the modes of "learning/teaching KOG ways" and "implementing KOG ideas" generally requires relatively *active* commitment. When these two dimensions are crossed, it results in a

Table 16.3   A situational leadership model based on Luke

Cognitive *Nature of learning or knowledge (lacking in followers, and/or offered by leader)*		Be prepared/Prepare the way for KOG	Learn/Teach KOG principles
Experiential		Facilitate/Enjoy KOG outcomes	Implement KOG ideas/Challenge traditions

Passive   *Active*

Nature of commitment to participate
(desired by followers, and/or offered by leaders)

situational leadership model shown in table 16.3, which points to the following four different kinds of behavior.

First, it is appropriate for leaders to exhibit *preparedness* behavior in situations where others are not aware of or particularly committed to KOG principles. In this quadrant leaders simply show and tell others about KOG principles. The main leadership activity is information sharing and modeling, which occurs in an invitational and noncoercive manner.

Second, leaders emphasize *teaching/learning* behavior when others have indicated an active interest to learn more about KOG ways. Leaders engage in deliberate teaching to followers who are motivated to learn about KOG, but who lack the knowledge about how to implement it. Most of the teaching/learning in this stage is cognitive, and may involve describing cases where glimpses of the KOG are evident.

Third, leaders emphasize *implementing* behavior when others are ready to enact KOG ways in real-world settings. Here the emphasis shifts from cognitive ideas toward experiential practices. Leaders encourage and support followers who wish to put their KOG knowledge into practice. This has a self-propelling nature, as the experiences themselves lead to new insights and ideas, which help to inform structures and systems as they continue to be improved. Here members become full participants in KOG management, and begin to more fully experience the salvation that Luke describes.

Finally, KOG leaders must also know when to *enjoy* and *facilitate* highly visible KOG outcomes. While every day can be characterized by acts of benefaction and of sharing meals together in a KOG-*oikos*, not every day can or should be a banquet or large-scale scattering of resources. These significant actions are an important part of KOG leadership, which informs and facilitates each of the other three situations. For example, when the poor and marginalized are invited to KOG banquets, they may still be uninformed of KOG ideas and thus their commitment to the KOG may be quite passive. But it may spark an interest in them, or in other observers, to find out more.

Practitioner Example

The servant leadership literature provides a four-step change method that is very similar to the four-phase process found in Luke (and has some overlap with the situational leadership model presented in table 16.3). In particular, KOG-management ideas are very evident in the management style of Robert Greenleaf, who has been credited with coining the term "servant leadership." Greenleaf deliberately used a four-part "friendly disentangling" method while working as a senior manager at AT&T.[18] Here is an example of how Greenleaf used this method to solve the problem of women being underrepresented among telephone line installers at AT&T.

Phase 1 (Problem Recognition): AT&T Hiring Practices Discriminate against Women

For Greenleaf, identifying the problem to be resolved (phase 1) was closely linked with encouraging institutional change (phase 4). The injustice Greenleaf noticed was that women were underrepresented in AT&T's workforce. However, rather than blame individual managers for causing the problem, Greenleaf recognized that the problem was due to the traditional culture and values at AT&T. Indeed, he recognized that he himself was part of the shared culture and institutional norms that did not treat women justly.[19]

Phase 2 (Action Response): Place the Issue on the Agenda, and Invite Managers to Understand the Problem and to Suggest Actions That Might Help to Resolve it

As in Luke's model, the second part of the friendly disentangling model has an invitational quality. Greenleaf did not pretend that he had the solution—he deliberately invited others to participate in developing a solution.[20] Rather than call a meeting and demand that managers correct the problem, Greenleaf adopted an inclusive and dignifying approach when he discussed the issue with managers who were responsible for making hiring decisions. Greenleaf did not use his hierarchical authority as a senior manager to impose solutions. When Greenleaf met with these managers, he deliberately started each conversation by discussing shared experiences and friendships at AT&T, and how well they had been able to work together in the past. This provided the context for the "experiments" that were developed.

Phase 3 (Changed Way of Seeing): See Tasks in a New Light

At the core of the servant leadership "disentangling" process is fostering the ability in others to see how current problems are "entangled" or embedded in current norms and organizational cultures, and then to see possible solutions from the perspective of new norms and organizational cultures. Greenleaf invited the managers to discuss the specific traditions and structures that gave rise to the problem, and on this basis to develop ways to address it. In this particular example, managers suggested that women were rarely hired because the job demanded regularly lifting 50-pound rolls of telephone wire—which was too heavy for most women—and they saw that this problem could be resolved by providing the wire in smaller 25-pound rolls.

Phase 4 (Institutional Change): Redesign Operations and Systems

Greenleaf provided his support to any managers willing to experimentally implement changes to AT&T's structures and systems. Managers willing to experiment with 25-pound rolls were invited to do so. As the merits of this new approach became evident throughout the organization, it became institutionalized in its operations. In the end more women were hired, and the men were also happier to have lighter loads to carry.

MANAGING MONEY: ECONOMICS, FINANCE, AND ACCOUNTING

Ever since Aristotle differentiated between acquisitive economics (i.e., "unnatural *chrematistics*," using money to make money) and sustenance economics (i.e., "natural *chrematistics*," using money merely as a mechanism to facilitate the flow of goods and services), management thinkers and practitioners have debated the merits of the two approaches. Recall that the analysis of passages in Luke on this matter pointed to a consistent and clear message.

On the one hand, in each passage where money is mentioned without reference to wide disparities in financial well-being, money is treated as a normal part of everyday life. This suggests that it is entirely appropriate to use money in ways consistent with sustenance economics.

On the other hand, in seven of the nine passages where the word "rich" is used, the riches are seen in a negative light. The rich are repeatedly encouraged to share their wealth with others in order to decrease the gap between the rich and the poor. The only two passages where the "rich" are described favorably is when their resources are shared with the poor: (1) a rich man commends his manager for shrewdly scattering some of the rich man's wealth (Luke 16:1–13); and (2) Jesus says that salvation has come to the *oikos* of a rich tax collector named Zacchaeus who has promised to give half his possessions to the poor and to repay fourfold anyone he has defrauded (Luke 19:1–10).[1] It merits noting that on both these occasions where rich people are praised, the *oikos* of the rich is still financially viable—that is, the rich do not "sell all their possessions" as repeated elsewhere in Luke. It seems that running a financially viable and sustainable *oikos* is not frowned upon (indeed, it can be a good thing that is associated with salvation). The problem occurs when money becomes an end in itself, or when it results in wide gaps between the rich and the poor, or when its primary use is to make more money.

The possible implications of this analysis for managing money in today's world are manifold, but this chapter will briefly highlight only three areas: economics, finance, and accounting.

ECONOMICS

Luke challenges fundamental assumptions that undergird contemporary economic theory. For example, whereas Aristotle's formulation of acquisitive economic theory assumed (merely) that economic actors behave out of unquenchable financial self-interest, this has since been amped up in two of the leading contemporary economic theories in management. Agency theory and transaction cost theory are both built on the assumption that people will act opportunistically, that is, these theories assume "self-interest seeking with guile."[2] In contrast, Luke calls people not to take advantage of others, and indeed calls managers to be shrewd on behalf of the disadvantaged.

Research has shown that when people learn to assume that economic actors are self-interested, and when the theories they are taught are consistent with this assumption, then they themselves become more self-interested. Put differently, teaching an acquisitive economic ethic acts as a self-fulfilling prophecy.[3] On a more positive note, research has also shown that by teaching students countercultural ways to manage, ways that do not make the same assumptions about self-interests and materialism, students become less individualistic and less materialistic.[4] The Gospel of Luke calls for the development of sustenance economic theory based on a cooperativeness ethic, where actors trust one another to do what is best for the whole. And why not? Is it not much more life-giving to assume that people will act in their mutual interests? And for most of the history of humankind it has been natural to share possessions, rather than to hoard them.[5]

Practitioner Example

Aaron Feuerstein, past owner and CEO of Malden Mills Industries in Lawrence, Massachusetts, is an example of a manager whose economic ethic corresponds to KOG management.[6] When most of the Malden Mills factory burnt to the ground in December 1995, the then seventy-year-old Feuerstein could have taken the $300 million insurance money and enjoyed retirement. Or, he could have followed the lead of others in his industry and taken the money to rebuild the factory in the south where labor costs were lower. Consider what actually happened, as seen through the lens of the four-phase process model.

Phase 1 (Problem Recognition): A Fire Burns Down a Factory That Employs Three Thousand Workers in a Needy Community
Rather than view the fire as a business problem (i.e., related to acquisitive economics) with an obvious business solution (move south), Feuerstein viewed it through a more holistic lens (sustenance economics). For him the problem was that three thousand workers in an economically depressed community were out of a job.

Phase 2 (Action Response): Factory Owner Pays Workers While Rebuilding the Factory
For Feuerstein, the appropriate response to the problem was to rebuild the factory on the same site, even though the insurance covered only three-quarters of the reconstruction costs. He also voluntarily kept all three thousand employees on the payroll during reconstruction. Clearly Feuerstein, who found guidance in Jewish moral law and tradition, placed a high value on community: "I simply felt an obligation to the entire community that relies on our presence here in Lawrence; it would have been unconscionable to put three thousand people out on the streets."[7]

Phase 3 (Changed Way of Seeing): This Radical Act Attracts Media Attention and Appreciation for a Nonconventional Way of Managing
Feuerstein's willingness to use his financial resources to nurture community in a countercultural way captured the imagination of a lot of people: "I got a lot of publicity. And I don't think it speaks well for our times . . . At the time in America of our greatest prosperity, the god of money has taken over to an extreme." By

his actions people could see how businesses can be managed based on sustenance economic principles.

Phase 4 (Institutional Change): Customers and Suppliers Go Out of Their Way to Support This Company

Feuerstein's actions created a lot of goodwill for Malden Mills. When he reopened the factory, customers sought out his product. Suppliers, buyers, and employees all went the extra mile to try to support the company through tough times. Even so, KOG management is no guarantee for financial success (nor is management based on conventional acquisitive economic principles). Successive warm winters and cheaper overseas goods conspired to reduce the sales of its fleece products, and Malden Mills was forced into bankruptcy in 2001.[8]

FINANCE

KOG management does not mix well with the acquisitive economic assumptions that characterize conventional financial practice. For example, KOG management would not approve of buying and selling stocks and shares with the express and *primary* purpose of making money. This message is clear in the parable of the ten pounds (Luke 19:11–17), where the people who manage to make five- and tenfold profits are associated with exploitation. There is nothing commendable about the success and political power such people achieve.

Of course, as a result of globalization and changes in commerce and technology the world today is much more complex than the world was two thousand years ago, and commentators have developed all sorts of arguments to explain why acquisitive economics is actually a good thing for society. In its basic form, this line of argument goes back at least as far as Adam Smith's popularized idea of the "invisible hand."[9] Regardless of the theoretical merit of such arguments, in practice it is quite clear that over the past 50 years, coinciding with an increasing emphasis on acquisitive economics, there has been a widening disparity between the rich and the poor within firms, within nations, and across nations.[10] Few investors (or scholars) would intentionally worsen the relative lot of the least privileged in our world. And yet, very discomfortingly, a growing amount of data suggest that this may be exactly what is happening via conventional financial systems, institutions, and theories.

Especially troubling from a KOG-management perspective is that the vast majority of money being traded, and much of the profit being generated, fails to contribute to any real sense of productivity. For example, even though the finance industry accounts for less than 10 percent of the value added in the US economy, it has accounted for about 30 percent of all US domestic profits since 2005.[11] As the financial crisis of 2008 shows, this trading can have devastating effects on the lives of people and nations who are mere pawns in financial games being played from afar.[12]

KOG management offers a different approach to "business-as-usual" and to the "common sense" that characterizes contemporary finance. For example, consider the conventional versus KOG views on the following "axioms of finance."[13]

1. The time value of money

   Conventional view: a dollar received today is worth more than a dollar received tomorrow

   KOG view: a dollar spent today on a worthwhile cause (e.g., to save a life) is worth more than a dollar received or spent tomorrow

2. Efficient capital markets
   Conventional view: "the price of an asset reflects all the relevant information that is available about the intrinsic value of the asset"[14]
   KOG view: it is folly to think that financial capital markets can provide a complete measure of any firm's true or intrinsic value; just as a family heirloom may be priceless to its members, even though its financial market value can be pegged at $30, so also the "true" or full value of a firm may be far greater (or less) than its market value

3. Risk return trade-off
   Conventional view: investors will only accept extra risk if there is a potentially higher *financial* pay-off
   KOG view: investors are willing to take on additional risk if they expect additional *non-financial* returns (e.g., if an investment supports sustainable development)

4. The agency problem
   Conventional view: managers are tempted to maximize their own self-interests rather than the financial interests of shareholders
   KOG view: managers are more likely to act in the interests of other stakeholders (e.g., employees, customers, suppliers, neighbors) compared to the absentee owners[15]

Practitioner Example

Perhaps the most notable contemporary example of an organization that has successfully incorporated ideas consistent with KOG management in the financial sector is the Grameen Bank founded by Mohammad Yunus. His description of the founding and development of the Grameen Bank dovetails nicely with the four-phase process model, and also has some interesting similarities with the Samaritan cycle described earlier (especially in phases 2 and 3).[16]

Phase 1 (Problem Recognition): Conventional Economic Theory is Failing the Poor
The story starts in 1974, when an estimated 1.5 million people in Bangladesh died in a famine. Yunus had begun teaching economics at a university in Bangladesh, having just graduated with a PhD in the United States. Even with his newly minted PhD in hand, Yunus felt totally helpless to offer any solutions to the people waiting to die all around him. *"I felt that whatever I had learned, whatever I was teaching was all make-believe stories, with no meaning for people's lives."*

Phase 2 (Action Response): Walk Alongside and Learn from Suffering People
So Yunus left his academic theories, and went to visit with the people in the village adjacent to the university campus, trying to better understand why there was so much suffering and death, and what he could *do* to prevent it. Yunus learned many things by talking to the villagers, and a key turning point came when he met a woman who made beautiful bamboo stools but earned only two cents a day. He couldn't understand how she could earn so little. She explained to him that she didn't have enough money (about 20 cents) to purchase the raw material she needed to make the stools, so she had to depend on a "trader" to loan her the money to buy the bamboo. The trader did this on the condition that she would sell him the finished stool at a price that he set. She was essentially in bonded labor to the trader. Yunus wanted to find out how common this situation was. He and a student spent several days talking to people in the village, and found that there were 42 people facing the same problem, and that they in total needed 27

dollars. Yunus felt ashamed of being a member of society that would allow this to happen.

To kind of escape that shame, *I took the money out of my pocket and gave it* to my student. I said: "You take this money and give it to those 42 people that we met and tell them this is a loan, that they can pay me back whenever they are able to. In the meantime, they can sell their product wherever they can get a good price."

Phase 3 (Changed Way of Seeing): Recognize Need for an Alternative Approach to Financing

The 42 villagers who received the money were excited, and *"seeing that excitement"* made Yunus think about what his next steps should be. He approached the bank on the university campus, and told the manager the story about the 42 villagers, asking whether the bank might lend money to other poor people he had met in the village. The manager said that this would be impossible because the bank's rules would not allow it, explaining that the poor did not have any collateral to offer and that lending such a small amount would not be worthwhile for the bank. The manager suggested Yunus approach officials higher up the banking hierarchy, but everyone Yunus spoke to told him the same thing, even when Yunus offered to guarantee the loan.

When every one of the 42 people repaid Yunus's loan in full, he went back to the bankers and said, *"Look,* they paid back, so there's no problem." But the bankers refused to provide loans, claiming this village was unusual. So Yunus hurriedly repeated the experiment in a second village, but the bankers still didn't believe it. Then he did it in five villages, ten, twenty, fifty, one hundred villages, but the bankers still refused to believe. "Luckily, I was not trained that way so *I could believe whatever I am seeing,* as it revealed itself. But their minds, *their eyes were blinded by the knowledge they had.*"

Phase 4 (Institutional Change): Starting a New Bank

"Finally I had the thought: why am I trying to convince *them?* I am totally convinced that poor people can take money and pay back. *Why don't we set up a separate bank?*" It took him two years to convince the government, but finally in 1983 they became a formal independent bank (*Grameen* means "village"). What started in 1974 as a loan of 27 dollars to 42 people had grown into providing one billion dollars in loans by 1994. And by 2006, when Yunus and Grameen were awarded the Nobel Peace Prize, Grameen had disbursed over US$ 5.7 billion, had 6.6 million borrowers (over 95 percent of whom are women),[17] and had almost twenty thousand employees in over two thousand branches[18] working in over seventy thousand villages. Its loan recovery rate is over 98 percent, and it has made a profit almost every year since its inception. In short, the simple idea of providing credit to the world's poorest microentrepreneurs has proven to be enormously effective. Almost 70 percent of the poor who have borrowed from Grameen are now out of poverty. With success like this, little wonder that over one hundred million people worldwide were involved with microcredit programs when 2005 was declared as the "Year of Microcredit." Lessons from the Grameen model, and its related businesses, are now being used to develop other like-minded businesses.[19]

It is interesting to note that microfinancing charges interest on the money it loans out, which seems inconsistent with the antiusury sentiments in scriptures. That said, two comments are in order. First, Grameen is not motivated by acquisitive economics (lending money to make money for itself); rather it is motivated by sustenance economics (lending money to help so-called clients—but with the express purpose of freeing these clients from poverty). Second, it has been noted that providing funding without charging interest to recipients can be dysfunctional for the recipients, perhaps especially when the benefactors who supply the resources are "face-less" to the recipients. Such recipients often become dependent on their "patrons" and remain stuck in their role at the margins of society. In a modern context treating someone with dignity (as a full person) is consistent with setting up institutional structures that expect them to contribute to helping other "outcasts" in society over time. Third, for the very poor, the payback for such external funding can be "in kind." A viable example of this occurs when impoverished farmers contribute the labor required to build sand dams that will allow them to grow crops, and external benefactors contribute the required construction materials.

ACCOUNTING

Just as a KOG approach to management provides a new way of thinking about the economics and finance, so also it provides a new way of thinking about the four conventional assumptions that underpin the Generally Accepted Accounting Principles (GAAP)[20] (see table 17.1). It may be tempting to think of accounting as "value neutral" and totally "objective." But, as with any theory, accounting also has an underlying moral point of view that influences how it is put into practice. The main four GAAP assumptions are economic entity, unit of measure, periodic reporting, and going-concern.[21]

The economic entity assumption specifies the focus of the accounting activity: where does one draw the boundaries around the organization that is being held accountable? Are owners included or not? If the organization engages in activities that result in pollution costs that need to be borne by society, should that be reflected in its accounting statements? A conventional twenty-first-century perspective separates an organization's business activities from its owners, which in turn separates a firm's activities from the larger community. In contrast, a KOG approach tends to have a broader view, one that takes into account externalities that would be disregarded by a conventional approach.[22]

The unit of measure assumption identifies the yardstick or criterion to be used in accounting. From a conventional approach, "money" provides the only appropriate basis for accounting measurement and analysis, partly because it allows diverse information to be aggregated and summarized. However, this focus on money (especially coupled with acquisitive economics) can easily result in commodification and oppression of the relatively poor and powerless.[23] In contrast, from a KOG perspective there are multiple bottom lines; put simply, organizations should be accountable for more than merely financial performance (e.g., *chrematistics* should be subservient to *oikonomia*). Performance from a sustenance economic perspective includes "living well" by nurturing meaningful community and relationships, practicing and facilitating the practice of virtues, and so on. For example, from a conventional twenty-first-century approach a particular entity may be seen as a marginal contributor because of poor financial performance, but in fact it may play an important role in the healthy functioning of the larger community (e.g., the value of Malden Mills to the community was far greater than its financial "book value"). Similarly, a specific firm may be doing very well by conventional financial measures, but when negative

Table 17.1   Two approaches to the four basic GAAP assumptions

Assumption	Conventional twenty-first-century perspective	Based on a KOG ethic
1. *Entity:* Describes the "boundaries" around the organization (e.g., what/who is in/ excluded in the accounting).	For accounting purposes, employees, suppliers, customers, and neighbors are "external" to the organization. Transactions are recorded as transfers of wealth between the organization and these external members. The assets and liabilities of the organization do not include the well-being of these external parties.	For accounting purposes, the organization includes employees, suppliers, customers, and neighbors. The organization's effect on the well-being of these parties is considered as part of the performance of the organization.
2. *Unit of measure:* What is/are the measures used in accounting for the activity of the entity.	Consistent with an acquisitive economics perspective, the unit of measure is money, and the organization is accountable to maximize its financial resources. This can lead to commodification.	Consistent with a sustenance economics perspective, there are multiple measures of well-being: financial, social, ecological, spiritual, aesthetic. This can lead to complexity.
3. *Periodic reporting:* How frequently are accounting reports provided?	Reporting is linear according to calendar time (usually quarterly), serving the interests of short-term investors and the stock market.	Reporting takes into account the natural rhythms of organizational life, serving the interests of long-term investors (e.g., rather than prepare a premature quarterly report, wait the additional two weeks required to complete a big project).
4. *Going concern assumption:* What criteria do accountants use to determine whether an entity is viable?	The assessment of whether an organization is financially viable (i) has a short-term time horizon (one year), (ii) focuses on financial measures, and (iii) is at the level of analysis of the single entity (ignoring long-term nonfinancial externalities).	The assessment of whether an organization is holistically sustainable (i) has a long-term time horizon (e.g., considers effects on future generations), (ii) takes into account multiple forms of well-being, and (iii) considers contributions and drawbacks of the entity in the context of its larger social and ecological systems.

externalities are taken into account (e.g., long-term pollution costs, mental health of employees, etc.) it may be a bankrupt organization in terms of sustenance economics (e.g., some of the banks prior to the 2008 recession). Rather than try to measure everything in term of financial measures, KOG management is comfortable with the messiness of developing and using many different measures, and does not shy away from some things that cannot be easily measured.[24]

The periodic reporting assumption considers the frequency and timing of accounting reports. Conventional accounting emphasizes quarterly and annual reports, geared to meet the expectations of financial markets whose investors who are interested in maximizing short-term financial gains. Rather than force data into calendar-determined time slots, a KOG approach places greater emphasis on accounting and reports to be structured to make sense within the workflow of organizations and to meet the needs of long-term investors.[25]

The going concern assumption is concerned with the criteria to be used to determine whether an organization is viable. A conventional approach focuses on the financial viability of an entity for the coming year. A KOG approach considers the holistic viability of an entity within its community for the indefinite future.

Practitioner Example

The final example comes from the "Economy of Communion" (EOC), a group of 750 businesses around the world who seek to put into practice the teachings of the gospel. The EOC is related to the Focolare, the largest lay movement in the Catholic Church with over four million people involved in over 180 countries. The Focolare can be seen as a variation of a "house church." Its basic institutional structure is the local "focolares" or "houses," usually comprised of five–eight people who have made a lifelong commitment to Focolare, most of whom work outside the house.[26] The word "focolare" means "hearth," and symbolically refers to a gathering place for family and friends, sharing food and stories.[27]

The Focolare and EOC are of particular relevance for the present study because of their explicit grounding in Luke's writings, because their historical development can be used to think about the two dimensions of salvation (being saved *from*, and saved *for*) and as an example of the four-phase process model, and because of their relationship to the development of an alternative approach to accounting.[28] Let us begin by using the four-phase model to provide a brief history of the founding of Focolare, drawing attention to its emphasis on saving people *from* oppression.

Phase 1 (Problem Recognition): Need to Save People from Suffering Caused by Institutional Violence

The problem that triggered the formation of the Focolare Movement was the suffering of people living in and around Trent, Italy, during the bombing of World War II.[29]

Phase 2 (Action Response): Start-Up a Beneficent Oikos

Upon recognizing the gravity of the problem, Chiara Lubich (the then 23-year-old founder of the Focolare Movement): (1) left her family as it was escaping Trent during the bombing[30]; (2) returned to Trent to start a new "family" in an apartment with her friends (called the "focolare"), who started to (3) "give away all of their possessions to the poor, keeping only the essentials for survival."[31]

Phase 3 (Changed Way of Seeing): Others are Inspired to be Beneficent

When other people saw what the Focolare members were doing to help the poor, they "began to change how they viewed reality."[32] Suddenly all sorts of people began to bring things to the Focolare for redistribution, including firewood, food, and clothing. This "was seen as Providence: a visible sign of God's blessing" and benefaction.[33]

Phase 4 (Institutional Change): The Focolare Movement Became an Official Part of the Catholic Church

After the war, the message of the Focolare spread in a way reminiscent of the message of the early church, house-to-house, from Trent to other nearby regions, and finally to the ends of the earth.[34] The Vatican approved of the Focolare Movement for the first time in 1963 and provided final approval in 1990, which encouraged the

Focolare to expand further. The Focolare's radical vision of living according to the Gospel clearly involved working to change social and political institutions toward the emancipation for the poor.[35] For Lubich it was key to recognize that, because possessions are a means of connecting with other people, the distribution of wealth (and the understanding of economics more generally) is an inherently spiritual matter.[36] Expressed in terms of the four conventional assumptions of the GAAP, it is clear that the Focolare Movement does not

1. draw a tight boundary around its core members (instead, the Focolare "entity" includes the poorest in society);
2. fixate on money to measure worth (instead, the Focolare are quick to share all sorts of resources, recognizing that financial well-being is but one form of well-being);
3. march to the beat of rigid periodic reporting (instead, the Focolare share on an 'as needed' or 'as able' basis); and
4. seek to be judged a financially viable "going concern" for one year by conventional measures (its core members make a lifelong commitment to Focolare).

After the Focolare Movement itself had been well established, it in turn gave birth to the "Economy of Communion" (EOC), which can be seen to have developed via its own cycle through the four-phase process model.

Phase 1 (Problem Recognition): Need to Save People for Life-Giving Work
By the early 1990s Chiara Lubich noted that although the Focolare movement was good at saving people *from* poverty, it needed to get better at saving people *for* creating goods and services. Of course, an emphasis on the redistribution of goods would continue to be appropriate at times such as were evident in the creation of the Focolare Movement (e.g., it can save people *from* oppression), but Lubich realized that this model of *oikos* did little to address important root causes of oppression and inequality, such as low wages, economic rationalization, and unemployment. The need was to create goods and services producing organizations that overcome negative externalities and create positive ones. In other words, instead of focus only on the *re*distribution of "surplus" goods, there was a need for "redeemed" forms of organizations involved in the *creation* of "surplus" goods.[37]

Phase 2 (Action Response): Start-Up the EOC
In 1991 Chiara Lubich presented the basic idea and some key guiding principles for the formation of the EOC.[38]

1. *Profit sharing.* The first EOC principle was to divide business profits into three: the first part was to be kept for reinvestment in the firm, the second part given to the poor, and the third part used to develop educational structures that promote a "culture of giving."
2. *Widespread ownership.* A second key principle was that the ownership of businesses should be widespread in order to give many people a chance to participate.
3. *Business parks.* This principle, related to the idea of "model towns," was consistent with Chiara Lubich's view that the Focolare's practice of "spirituality of unity" should include developing community-level social structures and institutions that reflect a biblical vision of how the world can work.

4. *Global networks.* The EOC project should be a global effort and span a wide range of economic sectors, and a global body should decide how to distribute the profits donated to the poor.[39]

Phase 3 (Changed Way of Seeing): Economic Life and Spiritual Life are One

Participating in the EOC changed the way businesspeople saw their business. They began to see their economic enterprise as wholly spiritual, and their spiritual lives as manifest in economics. They saw that their business can become places where the kingdom of God is enacted, based on relationships built on mutual respect and love. For EOC members "the business itself became the central focus for living out the spirituality" and members saw "their businesses as playing a critical role in transforming modern society into one that is more equitable and just."[40]

Phase 4 (Institutional Change): New Management Norms and Practices

The EOC now has over 750 participating firms, and research shows that their new ways of seeing[41] have led to new institutions and norms within EOC organizations. These can be briefly reviewed in terms of the three-dimensional management lens.

1. *Changed ways of managing relationships* within *organizations.* Managers of EOC firms identify various nonconventional ways of managing relationships within their organizations. This includes adopting recruitment policies that target people at the margins of society,[42] sharing the decision-making process throughout the firm, and more generally, building relationships with others first as "people" instead of as "task-completers."

2. *Managing money.* Like the Focolare Movement more generally, members of EOC firms challenge conventional GAAP assumptions and norms. EOC firms see their "entity" as extending far beyond their walls, see money as merely one measure of performance,[43] are not beholden to linear financial reporting,[44] and have a going concern assumption that extends far beyond one year. The day-to-day management practices associated with EOC point to an emphasis on sustenance economics. For example, in terms of pay structure, EOC firms emphasize paying a living wage and reducing the gap between the rich and the poor.[45] Similarly, EOC firms not only share profits with the poor in other parts of the world, they also have programs in place designed to help fellow members who may be facing hardships. Finally, reflecting the fact that profit-maximization is not their primary concern, EOC firms emphasize taking "externalities" into account in their financial management practices (e.g., EOC firms are more likely to pay their taxes and to pay "extra" costs to secure environmentally friendly resources and energy).[46]

3. *Managing relationships with other organizations.* Consistent with taking externalities into account, paying their taxes and choosing environmentally friendly suppliers, EOC firms are less likely to see customers merely as a source of revenue to maximize profits—rather they are valued for their personal relationships.[47] Similarly, EOC firms have a nonconventional way of treating their competitors. By way of foreshadowing the discussion in the next chapter, consider the following (chiastically structured) experience told by an EOC member in a Brazilian medical supply business.

Many business have tried to copy our way of working. Our competitors are shocked by the fact that we are happy to show them how we work—and they try to do the same. They don't manage to copy our way of working, however, because it is not a formula that says "do this" "do that" . . . it is a way of being, a way of acting.

Phase 1 (problem recognition): Aggressive competitor. Last year there was a competitor who tried to attack us on every corner . . . creating a very difficult situation for our business.

Phase 2 (action response): Help the aggressive competitor. At a certain point, the law in Brazil changed and it was a very important change. In order to help this other business, we faxed the news to them.

Phase 3 (changed way of seeing): The competitor sees you as a friend (and recommends a helpful consultant). The business owner was so struck by our gesture that he not only wanted to reestablish his friendship with us, but he offered to help us in areas that we find difficult.

Phase 4 (institutional change): Improved organizational structures and systems (via consultant). It was through him that we had the idea of getting in a consultancy—the best decision that we ever made.

Phase 3' (changed way of seeing): Consultant sees EOC firm as admirable. That consultant was so impressed by how we run our business that

Phase 2' (action response): Consultant freely offers help. he goes out of his way to help us in whatever way he can.

Phase 1' (problem recognition): Aggressive competitor? This all started through responding to the aggression of our competitors with a different attitude.[48]

Managing Relationships *between* Organizations: Marketing, Supply Chain, and Strategy

In first-century Palestine patron-client relationships were the dominant paradigm for managing relationships between organizations. In short, the goal and duty of managers from relatively powerful goods and services producing organizations was to sustain and increase the power of their *oikos* via becoming "patrons" to outside "clients" who had relatively less power. Luke clearly and consistently speaks against such patron-client relationships, and presents a model of benefaction where the relatively powerful share resources with the relatively powerless without lording it over them. Similarly, Luke consistently favors sustenance economics over acquisitive economics.

This chapter looks at three contemporary business functions that have a focus on managing relationships with others outside the boundaries of an organization—marketing, supply chain management, and business strategy—and contrasts and compares the conventional versus a KOG approach to each.

Marketing

In modern-day usage, the term "client" is most likely to be used in marketing. In simple terms, marketing is concerned with ensuring that there are clients who will purchase the goods and services that an organization offers. Thus, marketing lies at the interface between an organization and its clients, and informs what kinds of goods and services are produced, how these goods and services are promoted in the marketplace, and how they are delivered to clients.

It is worth noting that the meaning of "market" has changed since the first century. At that time a market was where everyone knew your name and belonged to the same local community. The "market" was a place where members of a community would gather, visit, and arrange to buy and sell goods and services. People in the market were neighbors, and a healthy community market was one where people treated one another with dignity and respect. Antagonism and dysfunctional status differentials would be created if one neighbor were to start to make exceptional profits due to having a virtual "monopoly" (which is what having a unique product or service that others couldn't imitate was called prior to being dubbed a "competitive advantage"). This is a variation of the sentiment captured in the slogan: "You cannot get rich in a small town because there are too many people watching."[1] Today the word "market" has the opposite connotation, where everyone is anonymous and decisions are made purely based on financial criteria and acquisitive economics.

The marketing function has been famously broken down into four elements called the four P's of marketing—Product, Price, Place (Distribution), and Promotion—which have been presented to generations of students as an "article of faith, a prayer to be learned."[2] The way that these four P's are understood and managed differs between a conventional and a KOG approach. Here is a quick look at each "P" from both a conventional approach and a KOG perspective.[3]

Product refers to specific goods and services that an organization offers to clients.

> From a conventional perspective, organizations should provide goods and services that have features that satisfy customer needs or wants. Ideal products are desired by customers but are not available elsewhere.

> From a KOG perspective, product goes beyond the specific good or service offered by an organization. Rather, the "product" includes the relationships and connections formed among organizations and people in the creation, distribution, and usage of the product. Ideally products nurture community and help the needy.

Price refers to the amount paid by a client for a product.

> From a conventional perspective price refers to the financial amount clients are willing to pay for a product. Ideal products are in such great demand that they can command a high "mark-up" (i.e., the difference between the financial costs to produce a product versus the price at which it can be sold).

> From a KOG perspective price goes beyond merely the financial price that consumers pay for a product or service. Rather, price also includes its externalities (i.e., social costs and benefits not reflected in the sticker price). Ideal products have financial prices that reflect their true overall costs (e.g., the price paid for shipping a product includes the financial costs to clean up the environment due to pollution caused by the shipping).

Place refers to the location of an organization in the distribution network.

> From a conventional perspective, place focuses on the competitive advantage an organization can achieve in selling its products thanks to its "location" in the distribution network. Ideal locations are client-friendly, either physically (e.g., a retail store located in a high traffic area but with convenient parking) or virtually (e.g., iTunes' ease of downloading songs).

> From a KOG perspective, rather than see the organization as a separate self-centered entity that is trying to out-compete others, the organization is seen as part of a larger network that is cooperating with others and working as partners with suppliers and distributors. Ideal places/networks are characterized by trust and mutual fulfillment.

Promotion refers to how the organization communicates information about the product to others.

> From a conventional perspective promotion focuses on communication designed to sell products (e.g., advertising, sales). Ideal promotion strategies are low-cost and have high-impact (e.g., word of mouth, unsolicited testimonials from trusted sources).

> From a KOG perspective promotion goes beyond simply "selling" products and pushing information (in one-to-many transactions, or in a one-to-one relationship). Rather, a KOG approach intentionally fosters multidirectional listening and advanced

collaboration. Ideal communication enables others in the network play a key role in "co-creating" products and services.

Practitioner Example

An inspiring example of a KOG approach to marketing is evident at the Wiens Family Farm, owned and operated in Canada by Dan and Wilma Wiens. Consider how the four-phase process model helped to give shape to the KOG marketing approach at the Farm.[4]

Phase 1 (Problem Recognition): Dan and Wilma Recognize Inherent Problems in the Global Agri-food System

The process started when Dan and Wilma lived in Swaziland, Africa, where Dan worked in the field of agricultural development. While solving world food issues is a complex and far-ranging issue, Dan became convinced that part of the solution was to grow food as locally for consumers as practical and in an environmentally friendly manner. Moreover, not only was this important for Africans, but it was also important for people in high-income countries. A world where control over agricultural inputs (e.g., seeds, fertilizers, equipment) and outputs (sales of commodities, distribution) is dominated by multinationals offers little opportunity for the five hundred million small-scale farms on this planet to flourish. In first-century terms, the acquisitive economic aspirations of such huge patrons simply outweigh possible benefits for small-scale farmer clients.

Phase 2 (Action Response): Start a Small-Scale Organic Vegetable Farm for a Local Market in Canada

To begin to develop a partial solution to some of the problems they recognized, when Dan and Wilma moved back to their small farm in Canada they started growing organic vegetables and selling them at the local farmers' market.

For them the "product" was far more than tasty tomatoes or crunchy carrots—it was also about being good stewards of the land (nurturing the soil) and developing relationships between rural and urban people.

In terms of "promotion," at this time Dan invited a support group of like-minded people from all walks of life to help give shape to the Wiens Family Farm. After several meetings, this group developed the idea of "Shared Farming," where city people could purchase in advance "shares" of the farm produce. The purpose of Shared Farming was to provide a viable, environmentally friendly, community-enhancing way of doing agriculture that can be duplicated by others.

This support group helped to develop ideas about "place" and for distributing the vegetables. In this model each sharer is supplied with a "blue box" full of vegetables on a weekly basis, which is delivered to several centrally located neighborhood "depots" where sharers pick-up their veggies and also drop-off compost materials to be used on the farm. Depots included sharers' driveways, garages, and the farm itself.

Phase 3 (Changed Way of Seeing): Consumers See Vegetables in a New Light

Within a couple of days of a short article appearing in the local paper describing this new Shared Farm, Dan and Wilma's phone was ringing off the hook, and they had well over two hundred sharers plus many more on a "waiting list." It seems that this little experiment called Shared Farming, envisioned by a group of people, had captured the imagination of many other people. As the slogan goes, "It's not just about vegetables." Rather, many people began to see that Shared Farming is a step toward developing a food system that is more just, and that respects the land, and that fosters dignity and community among and between rural and urban people.

Phase 4 (Institutional Change): The Development of Shared Farming

Dan and Wilma continued seeking counsel from sharers. This might happen when sharers volunteered at the farm, at annual fall pot-luck events with sharers at the farm, with questionnaires distributed in the blue boxes, or at special meetings. At one meeting after the first year of operations, Dan asked his sharers to set the "price" of a share. Dan and Wilma had set the share price in the first year, but wanted to give this responsibility to sharers: "These are our friends, and we're sure they will treat us fairly." After receiving information about the expenses involved in running the farm, sharers decided to increase the price of shares by 40 percent.

The Shared Farming movement has grown beyond the Wiens Family Farm. This includes activities on the farm itself, which in recent years has included university students living and working on the farm during the summer, and the establishment of a spiritual retreat center. Dan and Wilma have also helped start several similar farms. One such farm run by Salvadorean refugees provided both employment plus varieties of vegetables unavailable at regular grocery stores. The Wiens' have also helped to find agricultural land for underemployed inner-city people to grow vegetables. Finally, Dan has been invited to give presentation at events in other provinces, where the idea of Shared Farming has inspired creation of similar farms.

SUPPLY CHAIN MANAGEMENT

Supply chain management also has a focus on relationships between organizations, and specifically on ensuring that organizations find optimal ways to acquire the supplies that they need from other organizations. This includes *strategic purchasing* (e.g., supplier selection, evaluation, and development; single versus multiple sourcing) and the management of relationships with other organizations (e.g., supplier partnerships).[5]

A hallmark characteristic of a conventional approach is embedded in the very name of this area, namely, its emphasis on a "value chain" approach. Value chains have a linear focus, moving from an organization's input to its conversion processes to its outputs. This is sometimes called "cradle-to-grave" thinking, where an organization uses raw materials ("cradle") as inputs for their products and services, and after being used up its products eventually find their way into a landfill ("grave"). In contrast, a KOG approach has more of a "value cycle" perspective. This is sometimes called "cradle-to-cradle" thinking, where an organization's outputs are designed to eventually turn into inputs. The value cycle approach is particularly relevant in terms of its ecological advantages. Rather than allow resources or products to end up as "waste," the value cycle approach ensures that they are recycled and become future inputs, either for their own organizations or for others.

The short-sightedness of chain-like thinking is evident in various ways where organizations fail to consider implications beyond the first-order relationships with their suppliers or customers. For example, by always looking for the lowest-cost supplier without concern for the implications of this approach, businesses' actions can result in promoting poor-paying jobs with unsafe working conditions (including overseas suppliers who operate sweatshops). They fail to see how this can unintentionally lead to fewer customers able to afford their products, higher production costs due to lost time and accidents in the workplace, and greater costs on the environment due to pollution associated with international shipping.[6]

Taken together, conventional versus KOG approaches use different criteria for choosing and managing relationships with suppliers. For example, a conventional perspective would choose suppliers who offer the best combination of: (a) financial price (influenced by factors like just-in-time delivery, which helps to minimize inventory costs); (b) products that meet the required technical specifications; and (c) dependable delivery (e.g., on-time delivery, reliable transportation network). In contrast, a KOG perspective would choose suppliers who offer the best combination of: (a) low total overall costs (i.e., including "externalities"); (b) products that meet technical and socioecological specifications; and (c) dependable and environmentally friendly delivery.

Practitioner Example

Perhaps the best-known example of a business that is implementing practices consistent with value cycle thinking is Interface Inc., the world's largest supplier of modular carpeting with over $1 billion in annual sales.[7] We will use the four-phase framework to describe how the thinking about supply chains changed in this company.

Phase 1 (Problem Recognition): Interface was Plundering the Earth
The process started in 1990 when its late CEO Ray C. Anderson, who had founded the company in 1969, was asked by salespeople to give a presentation on the company's environmental vision. Having no such vision, Anderson read Paul Hawken's book *The Ecology of Commerce*, and was embarrassed to discover that over 5 billion pounds of carpet in landfills came from Interface, and that it had used 1.2 trillion pounds of the earth's stored natural capital in the previous year alone. "I was running a company that was plundering the earth . . . some day people like me will be put in jail!"[8] He talked about the planet earth being perhaps the most rare resource in the universe, and that humankind had better be a good steward of it.

Phase 2 (Action Response): Reduce, Reuse, Recycle
At first Interface simply followed the mantra of the day—reduce, reuse, recycle—but this soon grew into a much more ambitious vision.

Phase 3 (Changed Way of Seeing): To Climb Higher Than Mount Everest
Soon a desire to think in terms of value cycles became a central vision for the company. The twofold goal is for the company to (1) reduce its ecological footprint to zero (i.e., to create zero waste), and (2) transform existing "waste" created by other organizations into valued inputs. This emphasis on going beyond simply being environmentally neutral is why Anderson likened the vision to climbing higher than Mount Everest.

Phase 4 (Institutional Change): A Value Cycle Company
The changes in Interface can be seen in three general areas of operation. First is Interface's success at minimizing its inputs and waste. In the first year of its

initiative Interface increased its sales by about 20 percent without any increase in its resource inputs. Part of Interface's success comes from designing new products that use less material without compromising quality. Also, using a program called QUEST (quality utilizing employees' suggestions and teamwork), Interface was able to reduce total waste in its global business by 40 percent in the first three years, which saved the company $67 million dollars (that money helped to pay for other changes at Interface). The goal is to reduce waste by 50 percent every three years, which is related to its goal of eliminating toxic waste altogether by 2020. Other goals include using resource-efficient transportation and using only renewable energy (e.g., use solar power rather than oil). This is related to Interface's goal to redesign commerce so that it is based on the overall *cost* of natural resources, not the financial *price*. For example, Anderson noted that like everyone else Interface pays the market *price* for oil, but it does not pay for *costs* like damage due to global warming in severe weather, and health costs due to toxic emissions.

The second area of operations where this new way of thinking about supplies is evident is on the restorative side of its strategy, which includes enabling other stakeholders to become more ecologically sustainable. For example, Interface's "Cool Blue" initiative allows it to become "waste positive" by reclaiming the waste of other organizations and people, thus in effect reducing the total amount of waste in society. Interface also provides education and offers other products and services that help stakeholders to become more sustainable. For example, Anderson helped Walmart CEO Mike Duke develop his sustainability vision. Of course, the company also has a focus on reducing its customers' waste, a key stakeholder, by having used carpets returned to Interface where they are recycled (rather than thrown in a land fill). This "cradle-to-cradle" thinking helps Interface to lower its inputs. Interface was a pioneer by developing its "Evergreen Lease" where, instead of buying carpets, customers perpetually lease the service of carpeting (and Interface cleans and replaces carpet tiles as necessary).

A third element of the Interface's approach is in an area that Anderson calls the "soft side" of the business, which he linked to the need for spirituality in business: "The growing field of spirituality (a term that, frankly, turned me off when I first heard it, because I associated it with religiosity) in business is a cornerstone of the next industrial revolution." Anderson recognized the importance of promoting social equity in his organization and in the larger world, but he confessed that personally he was not as passionate about this issue as he is about the ecological environment. As a result, he was very glad that others in the company rallied to the cause of social equity issues with the same passion he showed to the environment. For example, rather than yield to the temptation of exploiting workers in Asia to supply high-income markets, Interface builds and operates those factories to the same high standards as in North America, Europe, and Australia. Interface has also successfully found ways to provide jobs in poor communities (Harlem, New York City) and encourages its members to become involved in communities.

Within four years after introducing this new approach Interface was listed on the *Fortune 100* list of "Best Companies to Work For"—the company had doubled its employment, and had tripled its profits. By 2007 its use of fossil fuels was down 45 percent, net greenhouse gas production was down 60 percent, contribution to landfills down 80 percent, and its carpet-manufacturing used only 33 percent of the water it had used before.

Strategy

In twenty-first-century management theory and practice, competitive strategy is the dominant paradigm for managing relationships with other organizations. Much like patron-client relationships, competitive strategy theory makes it the goal and duty of managers to use their organizational resources to sustain and increase their power over other stakeholders.

Michael Porter's theory of competitive advantage is the most well-known and influential variation of this conventional view.[9] His theory is designed to maximize the financial performance of an organization (acquisitive economics), in part by maximizing the control it has over its key external stakeholders (akin to the patron-client paradigm). Porter has developed a five forces framework for understanding industry structure. In a nutshell, financial success is more likely in industries with low: (1) supplier power (i.e., there are numerous suppliers); (2) buyer power (there are numerous customers); (3) threat of substitutes (there are few substitutes, or the use of substitutes requires extra resources); (4) threat of entrants (e.g., there are high capital requirements to start a new firm in the industry); and (5) intensity rivalry (e.g., there is a lot of differentiation among firms in the industry, so that firms face little direction competition).

A conventional twenty-first-century strategy focuses on how managers serve their organization's acquisitive economic interests by using Porter's five competitive forces to gain relative advantage over external stakeholders. In contrast, theory and practice based on KOG management would focus on five parallel factors that managers can use to serve the overall well-being of the community (see table 18.1). From a

Table 18.1 A conventional versus a KOG management approach to five external relationships

A conventional approach enhances one's power and competitiveness via reducing:	A KOG-management approach nurtures community via enhancing:
1. Supplier power (i.e., how much influence suppliers have over an organization; supplier power is low when there are many potential suppliers to choose from)	*1. Relationships with suppliers, and seeking to include* "new" suppliers of resources (human and other) that were previously underutilized (e.g., by engaging former "outcasts")
2. Buyer power (i.e., how much influence customers have on an organization; buyer power is low if there are many potential customers)	*2. Customers' capacity to meet community needs, even if* this means that the focal organization decreases its size (e.g., rich absentee landowners return land to the peasants currently leasing it)
3. Substitutes (i.e., products or services that are similar or that meet the same needs of a customer, but come from a different industry)	*3. Substitutes that promote overall well-being* (e.g., as a substitute for the status that comes from financial wealth, the shrewd manager provides his master with honor from others that comes from benefaction)
4. Threat of new entrants (i.e., conditions that make it easy for other organizations to enter or compete in a particular industry)	*4. Bridge-building among organizations that serves the* larger community (e.g., the Samaritan cycle overcomes animosity and removes barriers that prevent beneficence and cooperation among competing *oikoi*)
5. Rivalry intensity (i.e., the intensity of competition among existing organizations in an industry)	*5. Mutually beneficial interdependence that serves the* larger community (e.g., Jesus points to a centurion and a tax collector whose actions serve the larger community)

conventional perspective, the KOG approach will appear as nonsensical gibberish, because of its very different starting point.

Suppliers and Buyers

Rather than assume that *suppliers* will try to charge the highest price possible (opportunism) and that *buyers* will take advantage of you if they can, a KOG approach treats suppliers and buyers as neighbors and fellow community members in both the short and the long term. The goal is not to achieve monetary advantage over other *oikoi* in the short term whenever possible, but rather to build long-term trusting relationships whenever possible, especially by finding ways to engage previously underutilized resources (e.g., findings ways to bring "outcasts" back into the community). This might even mean reducing the debt of current customers (e.g., parable of shrewd manager) or losing current customers altogether (e.g., returning your land to former "clients" who have leased it from you).

Example from the Fashion Industry in New York City

Are such countercultural practices even possible in the dog-eat-dog world of competitive business? Yes, according to a study of a part of the fashion design and manufacturing industry in New York City. The study found that managers often looked out for the concerns of their suppliers and customers rather than simply to maximize their short-term or narrow economic gain. In other words, managers in this industry valued sustenance economics, neighborliness, and trust. For example, because negotiating contracts and specifying their content take time away from a quick response in the marketplace and the ability to make timely changes, many orders were placed and delivered before any prices had been set. Suppliers and buyers trusted that, when all was said and done, they would be able to agree upon a mutually satisfactory price. They also accommodated one another in other ways. For example, during slow times a buyer might place orders sooner than usual in order to create work for a supplier. Working in such a climate of neighborliness and trust creates a sense of satisfaction and mutual concern, where people respect one another's needs and knowledge (which often cannot be codified ahead of time in a contract). On the rare occasions where a firm's manager tried to take un-neighborly advantage of this trusting community—such as when the manager refused to pay a fair higher price for above-contract services—then that manager was unlikely to be included in the community for long.[10]

Substitutes and the Threat of New Entrants

Rather than feel threatened by another *oikos* that offers similar products or services, a KOG-management approach welcomes such substitutes insofar as they enhance community. For example, the parable of the shrewd manager shows how the honor that comes from sharing one's wealth can serve as a substitute for the status that comes from adding riches to riches. Along the same lines, rather than seek to insulate current *oikoi* from outsiders, Luke describes how Jesus deliberately sought to build bridges between groups. For example, Jesus sent his disciples in groups of two to teach and learn from Samaritan villages, and he offered freedom from oppressive structures and systems to everyone, not only the Jews.

Example from Shared Farming

Consider again the Wiens Family Farm. Having more sharers than he could accommodate did not cause Dan to bask in his position of relative power in the marketplace (e.g., no one else was offering a similar service). Rather, Dan used his position as an opportunity to teach others about Shared Farming. He offered workshops on his farm and across the prairie provinces and beyond, telling people about Shared Farming and sharing his knowledge about how to grow vegetables organically on the Canadian prairies. Dan was thrilled when dozens of new Shared Farms opened up in the region, including half a dozen in his own hometown. He was especially happy for a Shared Farm run by new immigrants, where they could grow food from their home country. And he has helped find land for a Community Food Club, where people from the inner-city can come and grow their own vegetables. Finally, he is thrilled when his former sharers quit because they are inspired to grow their own vegetables in their own backyards or in community gardens. In short, Dan welcomes competitors, substitutes, and new entrants because his goal is to foster sustainable living.[11]

Rivalry Intensity

Finally, rather than trying to prevent rivalry intensity, KOG management seeks to enhance beneficial mutual interdependence among organizations. This is because it is based on a cooperativeness ethic, rather than a competitive one.[12] The goal is not for each organization to maximize its financial well-being (acquisitive economics), but rather to work together to nurture a healthy community (sustenance economics).

Example from Virginia Poultry Processors

Such a cooperative ethic is evident in the New York fashion industry and in the story of Dan Wiens and Shared Farming. Another example occurred in a community in Virginia after a poultry processing plant burned down. Managers of a competing poultry processor in the community could have taken advantage of the situation by purchasing poultry from their competitor's suppliers at reduced rates, and by selling processed poultry at increased prices to their competitor's buyers. Instead, while the first firm rebuilt its plant, managers at the second plant invited their competitor to bring in a second shift to utilize their undamaged facilities. These nonconventional managers were more interested in nurturing overall community than in improving their short-term financial return.[13]

Practitioner Example

The transition from a conventional toward a KOG-management approach to strategy seems daunting. It involves not only a single organization, but by its nature includes other stakeholders and organizations in the community. The EOC described in chapter seventeen provides one example of how this can take place. Another example comes from Kalundborg, Denmark, where Porter's five competitive forces are being used as levers to nurture community.

Phase 1 (Problem Recognition): An Organization Discards as "Waste" Resources That Others Find Valuable

The process all started when the coal-fired Aesnes Power Plant recognized that the "waste" heat it had been pouring as condensed water into a nearby fjord was in fact a valuable resource. Not only was pouring the heat down the fjord ecologically irresponsible, it was also a missed opportunity to generate funds to recoup the cost of creating the heat in the first place.

Phase 2 (Action Response): Supply the Valuable "Waste" to Another Organization
To address this problem managers at Aesnes began to sell the heat directly to the nearby Statoil refinery and to the Novo Nordisk pharmaceutical firm. This resulted in a win-win-win situation: less wasted heat for the ecological environment, more funds for Aesnes, a more environmentally friendly source of heat for Statoil and Novo Nordisk, and the formation of new mutually beneficial relationships among neighboring *oikoi*.

Phase 3 (Changed Way of Seeing): Other Organizations in the Community Begin to See Their "Waste" in a New Light, and Recognize its Value.
The "experiment" of participating in the redemption of Aesnes's "waste" heat prompted other organizations to look anew at their "waste," and to think about how it could become a valuable input to others in their larger community.

Phase 4 (Institutional Change): Decreased Waste via Increased Mutual Interdependence
As shown in figure 18.1, soon Statoil refinery installed a mechanism to remove sulfur from its "wasted" gas. It then sold the "new" sulfur to the Kemira chemical company, and sold the cleaner burning gas to the Gyproc sheetrock factory and to Aesnes (which resulted in burning thirty thousand fewer tons of coal). When Aesnes began removing sulfur from its smokestacks it produced calcium sulfate, which it sold to Gyproc for use in place of mined gypsum. The "waste" fly ash from Aesnes coal generation began to be utilized for concrete production and road construction. Soon Aesnes was able to provide surplus heat to residents of the town (enabling them to shut off thirty-five hundred oil-burning heating systems), to a fish farm, and to

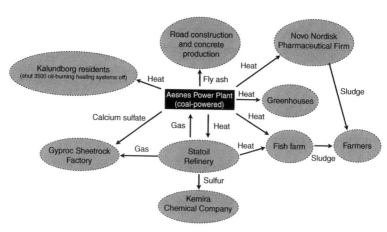

Figure 18.1   Transformation of previous "waste" within a community of organizations.

greenhouses. In time "waste" heat from Statoil was transferred to the fish farm, which produced and sold about two hundred tons of turbot in the French market. In turn sludge from the fish farm was provided as fertilizer by farmers, who also received sludge from the Novo Nordisk pharmaceutical firm.[14]

The Kalundborg example provides a nice illustration of differences between a conventional and a KOG approach to managing an organization's external relationships:

Suppliers: Whereas a conventional approach seeks to minimize dependence on suppliers, a KOG approach welcomes becoming dependent on suppliers who provide inputs that were previously considered "waste" or underutilized resources (e.g., managers of greenhouses in the community were happy to depend on "waste" heat supplied by the Aesnes Power Plant).

Buyers: Whereas a conventional approach seeks to minimize the power that buyers have over a firm, a KOG approach welcomes becoming dependent on specific buyers in order to nurture community or transform waste (e.g., Novo Nordisk's primary motive to provide previously wasted sludge to farmers was not to increase its power over farmers, but rather to foster environmental sustainability while simultaneously helping farmers meet their needs for fertilizer).

Substitutes: Whereas a conventional approach seeks to minimize competition from substitutes, a KOG approach embraces substitutes that enhance overall community well-being (e.g., Statoil welcomed the "substitute" heat provided by Aesnes to what had been thirty-five hundred oil-burning customers; in the same way community well-being was enhanced when Statoil provided waste gas that served as a "substitute" for burning thirty thousand tons of coal at Aesnes).

Entry barriers: Whereas a conventional approach seeks to erect entry barriers that make it difficult for others to compete, a KOG approach welcomes removing barriers that prevent firms from cooperating with each other (e.g., barriers to cooperation were removed with technology that permitted Statoil's "waste" sulfur gas to become a new source of sulfur for Kemira and of cleaner burning gas for Gyproc).

Rivalry: Finally, whereas a conventional approach seeks to decrease rivalry intensity via having a company differentiate itself from other organizations, a KOG approach welcomes increased mutually beneficial interdependence across organizations (e.g., Aesnes and Statoil cooperated to provide their "waste" heat for a fish farm, which in turn provides fertilizer for farmers).

In sum, whereas a conventional use of the five forces model seeks to achieve patron-client-like relationships with stakeholders in order to achieve sustainable *competitive* advantage, a KOG use of the model seeks to achieve sustainable *mutually* advantageous and beneficial relationships. The five forces are similar, but the manner in which they are used is quite different. Note also how the Kalundborg example focused on ecological goals, but the same five forces can also be used to think about other goals, such as achieving sustainable social justice. For example, Pura Vida and Starbucks are examples of organizations that promote "fair trade" coffee that pay extra funds to their suppliers (i.e., coffee growers) in order to ensure that they earn a living wage. Ten Thousand Villages is another example of a KOG management that provides buyers with products supplied by craftspeople in low-income countries who have earned an adequate livelihood.

SUMMARY OF PART SIX

Of course a book like this cannot begin to rewrite more than a century of modern organization management theory and practice. It can, however, begin to sketch out in broad terms what such theory and practice might look like if it were consistent with the teachings embedded in the Gospel of Luke. And perhaps more importantly, it can highlight glimpses of KOG management in contemporary goods and services producing organizations.

Final Thoughts

The basic premise of this book is both simple and profound. It is simple because it sought to interpret the Gospel of Luke through a first-century management lens. After describing the basic contours of such a lens (i.e., the hallmarks of conventional first-century *oikonomia*, *chrematistics*, and benefaction/patron-client relationships), the content of the Gospel was examined to see what it said about management. The message throughout Luke is quite consistent: goods and services producing organizations should be designed so that everyone is treated with dignity (with special attention to including former outcasts), money should be managed to nurture community consistent with sustenance economics, and external relationships should be characterized by benefaction. Using this same lens to look at some broader themes in Luke showed that the kingdom of God is often enacted and manifest in goods and services producing organizations, that salvation often involves being freed from oppressive organizational practices and embracing redemptive alternatives, and that the Holy Spirit plays a key role in facilitating the development of such inclusive radical *oikoi*. Finally, embedded in Luke's Journey Narrative is four-phase process model, a veritable "how to guide" explaining how to transition from conventional to countercultural *oikos* practices. While these ideas are nuanced and elegant, they are also is some sense simple. Indeed, once equipped with a first-century management lens, it would be difficult for readers *not* to see these basic principles in the Gospel of Luke.

The Radical Nature of Luke's Message

The message of the book is also profound as it offers truly "radical" findings, in at least four senses of that word.[1] The adjective *radical* comes from the Latin *radicalis*, meaning "of or relating to the root."[2] The Gospel of Luke is literally radical in so far it was written in the first century, and thus represents a root document for describing "basic, fundamental" aspects of Jesus' life and teachings. Analyzing Luke's Gospel is qualitatively different than analyzing, say, the writings of Max Weber or Martin Luther or John Calvin or papal encyclicals. This is not to suggest that examinations of such subsequent writing is somehow inferior, but rather simply to say that it is literally more "radical" to go back to first-century documents that lie at the root of understandings of Jesus' life and teachings.

Luke's message is also radical in a second sense of the word, which over time has come to be used "to describe something that was extremely different from the usual." Such a countercultural quality is very evident in the message in Luke, especially as it applies to management theory and practice.[3] Moreover, Luke's message was radical not only for its first-century context (e.g., role of women, adult children, slaves, acquisitive economics, patron-client relations), but also for the twenty-first century (e.g., role of women, widening gap between the rich and the poor, acquisitive economics, competitive advantage). In short, Luke describes an alternative moral point of view to the materialistic-individualistic hallmarks that characterize the present status quo. This countercultural dimension may be a surprise to anyone who had assumed both that (i) a Protestant ethic underpins conventional management theory and practice and (ii) this Protestant ethic is consistent with a first-century understanding of the Gospel of Luke.[4]

Third, the noun *radical* has come to be used to describe any person who seeks to reform society's (dysfunctional) institutionalized norms and practices. Again, this is an accurate description of Jesus as presented in Luke, and also consistent with what Jesus' followers are called to emulate. Jesus' followers are called to opt out of the conventional pursuit of financial and social gain (this is what it means to metaphorically take up one's cross), and instead to develop alternative organizational forms (this is a focal point of teachings about salvation and the KOG). How societies' goods and services producing organizations are managed and how they relate to one another are of profound concern in Luke. Luke promotes new institutional norms that are characterized by treating others with dignity (especially social outcasts), sustenance economics (where there are multiple forms of well-being for multiple stakeholders), and mutual benefaction. In addition, Luke contains a practical four-phase "how to" process model that shows how social institutions are linked to problems and vice versa.[5] Of course, this is not to suggest that radical change agents should expect an easy ride. Quite the contrary. The radical institutional norms and practices described in Luke were threatening in the first century, and are threatening today, for people who have a stake in the status quo.[6] Indeed Jesus represented such a threat to the institutions and leaders of his day that they killed him. Perhaps one of the most important aspects of Luke's radical message is that such institutional change is not to be achieved by violence (e.g., Jesus did not call on an army to defend him), but rather by nonviolently resisting oppressive practices and modeling life-giving practices. This brings us to the fourth dimension of how Luke's message is radical.

Finally, and perhaps most importantly for Weber and other contemporary scholars and practitioners, Luke's message is radical in the sense that it *frees* management theory and practice from the "iron cage" (the word *eradicate* also comes from the Latin word for "root"). The radical freedom described in Luke is qualitatively different from other kinds of freedom in at least three distinct but interrelated ways. First, the radical freedom in Luke is invitational, not coercive. This may be its most countercultural quality by first-century standards, where people expected freedom from oppression to come via might and violence. Certainly this latter approach was the basis of the "freedom" offered by the Roman Empire for its subjected people, and it was also the means of freedom expected by Jewish people who were waiting for a Messiah to help them become free from Rome's tyranny.

Second, this radical freedom is based on changing the metric used to measure success. The goal is not to replace one tyrant/cultural group who is lording it over others with another. Rather, the goal is to cease having anyone lord it over others. Using first-century language, the goal is not to replace one patron with another, the goal is to stop having patron-client relationships altogether. Rather than assume an acquisitive economic paradigm where the *oikos* with the most clients or money "wins," Luke's radical message suggest that everyone is free to live according to a sustenance economic paradigm where members of *oikoi* voluntarily work toward mutual beneficence. The four-phase model provides a process to describe how such changes can be attempted and implemented on an incremental basis. Of course, such changes may face resistance, but they also provide glimpses of what the world could be like.[7]

Third, this radical freedom is based on a holistic worldview that suggests that the spiritual and material world are tightly linked. This may be its most countercultural quality by twenty-first-century standards, where the two have been segregated and defined as mutually exclusive.[8] This relinking of the spiritual and the everyday will resonate deeply with readers who have long known that what goes on inside goods and services producing organizations is of great spiritual meaning. Within the Christian tradition this meaning has often been rendered invisible in previous interpretations of biblical scriptures, perhaps especially when they fail to recognize the *oikos* as the primary goods and services producing organization in biblical times. This reconnection may be especially interesting among scholars and students of business interested in the so-called theological turn. Regardless of whether such readers are committed to the biblical narrative as a normative faith document, the fact that the Gospel of Luke has a lot to say about how the idea of "a loving God" has implications for management and organization theory provides welcome fodder for future research. Of course, the implications of this need to be plumbed much more deeply than was possible in this book, but I trust that its basic frameworks and insights offer strong scaffolding for such future research.

BACK TO WEBER'S *PROTESTANT ETHIC*

By way of completing the circle started in the introduction—which suggested that this book could be seen to continue where Weber's influential work *The Protestant Ethic and the Spirit of Capitalism* had finished—note how each of the four aspects of Luke's radical message for the first and twenty-first centuries are entirely relevant to Weber's ideas. First, consistent with Weber's observations, going back to the roots of the Christian teachings has helped to identify teachings that can form the basis for the kind of "a great rebirth of old ideas and ideals" of which Weber spoke. The analysis presented here suggests that reading Luke through a first-century lens contributes potentially valuable ideas to a discussion of management-related issues that dates back at least as far as Aristotle.

Second, again consistent with Weber's speculation, Luke's message about management theory and practice is indeed countercultural to the "Protestant ethic." By the time Weber was writing (1903–1904) he had already observed that the "Protestant ethic" had long been secularized, and that any attempts by radical religious voices to influence economic life were being actively resisted.[9] The materialist-individualist moral point of view and theory and practices associated with the (secularized) Protestant ethic had become institutionalized and thoroughly engrained in "the modern economic order. This order is now bound to the technical and economic conditions of machine production which to-day determine the lives of all the individuals who are born into this mechanism, not only those directly concerned with economic acquisition, with irresistible force."[10]

This brings us to the third point, namely, that Weber would have welcomed the fact that Luke's message has a lot to say about changing institutional norms and practices. It is unclear whether Weber would have held out any hope that a society based on sustenance economics and benefaction would be workable. But given his penchant for "ideal types," it seems reasonable to suggest that he would have welcomed the conceptual frameworks based on Luke to contemplate such matters.

Moreover, it seems especially likely that he would have been intrigued by micro-communities where radical norms and practices were becoming institutionalized, perhaps especially among organizations in the (Catholic) Focolare's "Economy of Communion."

Finally, even though he was agnostic, Weber may well have welcomed how Luke's radical message reintegrates the spiritual and the material. After all, recall that he had found the separation of these two realms particularly problematic—"Specialists without spirit, sensualists without heart: this nullity imagines that it has attained a level of civilization never before achieved"[11]—and that he had noted that escape from the "iron cage" might come from a prophet (literally, a messenger from God). These views are also consistent with Weber's contention that religious ideas "are in themselves, that is beyond doubt, the most powerful plastic elements of national character, and contain a law of development and a compelling force entirely their own."[12] Taken together, this suggests that Weber would have welcomed the reintegration of spirituality into management theory and practice, and moreover that for him this would have been the most likely avenue to escape the iron cage.

FUTURE RESEARCH

As already alluded to, if taken seriously a study like this can lend support to and point to a wide range of questions for future research, including the following.

What Factors Explain the Shift in Values within Western Christianity over Time?

The analysis in this book demonstrates that the popular twenty-first-century interpretation of Luke differs substantially from an interpretation based on a first-century management lens. How did this happen? For example, how did we move from a first-century interpretation of the parable of the ten pounds (where the third manager is the hero, and the first two managers are villains) to a twenty-first-century understanding (where the third manager is the villain, and the first two managers are heroes)? Two historical events of particular importance in explaining these shifts are well-known. First, when Christianity became the official religion of the Roman Empire under the Emperor Constantine in fourth century, it lost its subversive edge as it was reinvented to be subservient to the empire.[13] Second, further changes were triggered when the Protestant Reformation challenged the Roman Catholic church in the sixteenth century. According to Weber, two hallmarks of the Protestant ethic were its emphasis on materialism (wealth as a sign of God's blessing) and individualism (people were called and saved based on their own works), both of which do not square with our analysis of Luke.[14]

Research specifically linking changes over time in biblical interpretation, and their implications for organization and management theory and practice, is underdeveloped. However, there is a rich storehouse of historical information that scholars interested in this question can draw upon. For example, in a recent study Elden Wiebe and I examine how the meaning of salvation has changed from the first century to the present time, and trace the relationships to management theory and practice as the shifts occur.[15] In that study we refer to three Weberian dimensions of salvation: modality, instantiation, and locus of ethical activity. First, whereas in the first century the *modality* of salvation emphasized Jesus as role model, this changed in the post-Constantine era with the increasing emphasis on Jesus as sacrifice. Second, whereas in the first century the *instantiation* of salvation placed relative emphasis on it being evident in this world (e.g., in how the *oikos* of Zacchaeus was managed), this changed post-Constantine with increasing emphasis on the afterlife.[16] And third, whereas the early church emphasized a <u>social</u> *locus of ethical* activity, this changed with the Reformation's emphasis on <u>individual</u> calling. In terms of implications for management and *oikos*, whereas the first-century church's understanding of salvation was manifest in the so-called Jerusalem Love Community (see Epistle of James, opening chapters of Acts), in the post-Constantine era it was manifest in increasing emphasis on centralization and rationalization (e.g., St. Benedicts Rules of monastery[17]), and in the post-Reformation it became evident in the idea of being true to individual calling, which results in material well-being (e.g., Josiah Wedgwood).[18]

Is the Message of the Gospel of Luke Consistent With the Rest of the Bible?

Is the radical message about management described here unique to Luke, or is consistent with other biblical scriptures, particularly those that were influenced by Jesus' life and teachings (i.e., the New Testament)? It may be that other scriptures lend support to more conventional ideas about management theory and practice.

Scholars wishing to look at this question may find it fruitful to start by examining the Epistle of James, notable because it was probably the earliest written of the books in the New Testament, and because it has a lot to say about management theory and practice.[19] This epistle, possibly written by Jesus' brother James, describes how Jesus' earliest followers organized themselves according to what has been called the "Jerusalem Love Community." A central teaching in James—and the one that would eventually irk Martin Luther so much as to move the Epistle of James toward the back of the New Testament—was the idea that faith without works is dead:

> What good is it, my brothers and sisters, if you say you have faith but do not have works? Can faith save you? If a brother or sister is naked and lacks daily food, and one of you says to them, "Go in peace; keep warm and eat your fill," and yet you do not supply their bodily needs, what good is that? . . . For just as the body without the spirit is dead, so faith without works is also dead. (James 2: 14–26)

James criticizes the dominant social and organizational practices in first-century Palestine (e.g., unnatural *chrematistics*, widening gap between the rich and the poor, indebtedness, exclusive *oikoi* that do not accept the "unclean" sick and foreigners), and describes the hallmarks of the Jerusalem Love Community (rich sharing with the poor with no strings attached, people treating one another with dignity, inclusiveness that goes beyond kinship groups). The Jerusalem Love Community welcomed the outcasts (i.e., the poor, the dispossessed, and others who lack the security of belonging to an *oikos*). James (the author) was eventually killed by leaders of the status quo, possibly in part because the Jerusalem Love Community undermined conventional patron-client relationships and meanings of *oikos*.

Also, scholars interested in examining whether Luke's message is consistent with other New Testament authors should take a close look at the writings of Paul, a key leader and biblical author in the early church. A particularly interesting and relevant place to start might be to contrast and compare a conventional understanding of "charismatic" leadership (as formulated by Max Weber) versus a Pauline understanding of *charisma* ("a gift of grace from God").[20] Paul's writings provide an important starting point for understanding the term not only in the Christian tradition, but in ancient writings more generally. Paul's 16 references to charisma are more than the total of all known mentions prior to him.[21] Similarly Max Weber, aware of Paul's usage, wrote about "charismatic" leadership at a time when this term was not used at all in popular culture, nor the social sciences, and rarely in theological writings. Weber defined charisma as referring to "a certain quality of individual personality by virtue of which he [*sic*] is set apart from ordinary men and treated as endowed with supernatural, superhuman . . . exceptional powers or qualities . . . not accessible to the ordinary person."[22] Weber's definition, which seems made-to-measure for developing a conventional spiritually informed understanding leaders, has proven enticing for many scholars in the area. That said, Weber's understanding of charismatic leadership differs starkly from Paul's (and Luke's) ideas. Unlike Paul, Weber sees charisma

- as a form of authority, and one of three ways to acquire legitimate domination (versus Paul's view, which saw charisma as unrelated to authority);
- as distributed to a select few people (versus being given to everyone in the community);
- as belonging to the gift-holder (versus being grounded in a larger community); and
- as referring especially to supernatural abilities (versus referring to everyday tasks);
- as ethically neutral (versus being normed by love to build community).

In sum, compared to Weber, Paul's idea of *charisma* was much more universal (*charismata* are distributed to all people), diverse (there are a wide variety of gifts), united (the gifts are tied to the Spirit, Lord, and God), communal (they serve to nurture community), egalitarian (gifts have equal value, though they are different), mediated by the Holy Spirit, and bounded by love. From this perspective, a Pauline model of charismatic leadership would draw attention to serving and building up the community, to be used interdependently with other gifts, and to manifest love as exemplified by Jesus. In short, Paul's understanding of charisma differs radically from Weber's description of charismatic leadership. However, a Pauline understanding of charismatic leadership would be entirely consistent with Luke's description about leadership as *hegoumenon*, and the idea that different leadership gifts (often held by different people) will be appropriate for use in different situations to nurture an *oikos* and the larger community.

What are the Implications for Readers Who Take These Radical Findings to Heart?

The analysis and findings presented here may have profound practical implications for readers who strive to integrate their work and biblical teachings. Ideas like management and business have largely been marginalized in theology and biblical studies, perhaps an unintended result of translating the ubiquitous biblical *oikos* as "house" and forgetting that it refers to the primary goods and services producing organization in biblical times. Thinking of *oikos* as "home" and "nuclear family" results in hiding the many references to organizational management in the scriptures, and has made it easier to think of business as a "secular" endeavor that has little to do with the "spiritual" message of the Gospel.

Analyzing the Gospel through a first-century management lens takes management from the sidelines and puts it smack dab in the middle of the highway. Far from being a secular or nonsacred choresome part of life that has little to do with spiritual or transcendent matters, managing the everyday organizations that produce the goods and services needed by humankind lies near the heart of Godly living. It is *the* primary setting where people enact and see the kingdom of God, and it is the only setting where Jesus said salvation has come.

The final three chapters provided glimpses of KOG management evident in contemporary *oikoi*. These are businesses where people are treated with dignity as whole human beings, rather than as cogs in a wheel where the amount of consideration they are shown is dependent on the expected return in financial performance. These are businesses where sustenance economics trump acquisitive economics. These organizations foster communities characterized by mutual interdependence, rather than seeking to lord it over one another toward achieving competitive advantage. These contemporary examples illustrate that implementing KOG-management principles is quite do-able. Step-by-step, day-by-day, everyone has the opportunity to follow the four-phase process model to nurture community and to help the socially marginalized.[23]

Many Other Research Questions

Of course, there are more questions for future research raised here than can be mentioned. These include: What are key similarities and differences between the findings in the present study and the founding values of the world's other major religions? How might the three-dimensional lens be used by social scientists to study other first-century writings and institutions? What are the implications of the findings presented here for the management of congregations and para-church organizations, or for nonprofit and nongovernmental organizations? What are the implications for theologies of work, salvation, the kingdom of God, and the Holy Spirit? And so on.

In conclusion, this book does not purport to argue that a first-century management lens provides the only way or the best way to interpret the Gospel of Luke. Rather, the book presents a compelling argument that such a lens makes a valuable contribution, and is of particular relevance given the growing size of organizations and role of managers in first-century Palestine. And such a lens seems especially useful for any reader seeking to glean timeless wisdom from these ancient writings for today, given the increased power of managers and organizations in the twenty-first century. In any case, failing to use this lens is tantamount to turning a blind eye toward the implications of the Gospel to the activities humankind spends most of its waking time involved in.

Appendix A

Analysis of the Chiasm in Luke's Journey Narrative

A rigorous process was used to identify and lend support to the 25-element chiasm embedded in Luke's Journey Narrative. This appendix (and exhibit A1) will

1. describe how the Journey Narrative is consistent with the general characteristics of a chiasm;
2. identify and provide empirical support for the specific breakpoints and 12 pairs of twinned passages in the chiasm;
3. identify and provide empirical support for the four-phase process model embedded in the chiasm; and
4. provide corroborating evidence from other parts of Luke's writing and the first century that lends support to the model.

Confirmation That Luke's "Journey Narrative" Meets the General Criteria of Being a Chiasm

A number of scholars have developed criteria for evaluating the presence of chiasms,[1] which can be summarized into five general characteristics of a chiasm. Luke's Journey Narrative clearly satisfies these five general criteria:

1. Scholars agree that the structure of the Journey Narrative text *is* problematic (e.g., it is clearly not structured in the form of a geographical journey).
2. Other biblical commentators (including those not interested in chiasms) *have* called attention to parallelisms in the two halves of the Travel Narrative text (e.g., this is most evident in the two parallel references to *"What must I do to inherit eternal life?"* found both in both Luke 10:25ff and in Luke 18:18ff).
3. Scholars agree that the Journey Narrative chiasm is much longer than a three-part ABA format.[2]
4. The midpoint passage of the Journey Narrative chiasm *is* worthy to be considered a climax in light of its theological significance (the midpoint foreshadows Jesus' death in Jerusalem, and encapsulates Jesus' countercultural message and others' opposition to it, Luke 13:31–35; *"Yet today, tomorrow, and the next day I must be on my way. Because it is impossible for a prophet to be killed outside of Jerusalem.' Jerusalem, Jerusalem, the city that kills the prophets and stones those who are sent to it!"* Luke 13:33,34a).
5. The theme at the midpoint—with its focus on journeying to Jerusalem—is also prominent in the first and last part of the chiasm (the chiasm starts with *"When*

the days drew near for him to be taken up, he set his face to go to Jerusalem" Luke 9:51; and finishes with *"After he said this, he went on ahead, going up to Jerusalem"* Luke 19:28).

Identification of Specific Breakpoints and Parallel Passages of the Journey Narrative Chiasm

Having established that it is plausible that the Journey Narrative is written in the form of a chiasm, it is appropriate to apply a set of three criteria developed by scholars to identify the breakpoints and the parallel "elements" within a chiasm. The first step in this process was to create a printed copy of the Journey Narrative with headings and chapter and verse markers removed, and then providing it to each of five researchers familiar with chiastic structures who were asked to independently read the Journey Narrative and to identify its natural breakpoints (e.g., including change of location, change of audience, repetition of certain transition words, use of summarizing remarks to signal the end of a sections, and so on). This helped to meet the criterion that the overall text has been divided into its separate passages at natural breakpoints that would be agreed upon even by others who do not argue that the Journey Narrative text is written in chiastic form (i.e., the proposed chiasm does not violate the structure of the text). These breakpoints were then recorded onto a spreadsheet, which provided the basis for the next step in the process.

Based on these breakpoints, and attending to thematic similarities in possible parallel passages that constitute the chiasm, the lead researcher then developed a first draft of the possible chiastic structure of the Journey Narrative. This draft, which raised uncertainties and questions and variations, was then provided to the other researchers who eventually met to make final decisions about how to subdivide the Journey Narrative chiasm into its separate passages. At the end of the process the researchers were surprised to find that each half of the chiasm had 12 passages (this was a "pleasant" surprise because "12" is a recurring biblical number, as in, e.g., the 12 Apostles of Christ and the 12 tribes of Israel).[3] While it may seem unimaginable to modern readers that people two millennia ago would have been sensitive to finding 12 sets of parallel passages in such a long chiastic text, note that it corresponds exactly to the 12 pairs of the 24 letters in the alphabet that students would have learned at that time (which they learned in chiastic form), and that chiasms with 24 "elements" in ancient texts are not unheard of.[4]

With breakpoints established, the next criteria for establishing the existence of a chiasm involves demonstrating that there is similar thematic and/or linguistic content across the paired "twin" passages (i.e., determine whether there are similarities between the first and last passage, between the second and second-last passage, and so on). Each pair was analyzed to identify and document common themes (see table A.1 for a side-by-side analysis of common themes in each chiastic pair). Similarly, each pair was also analyzed for parallels and similarities in linguistic/verbal content (e.g., both use identical catchwords or grammar), aware that these should involve central or dominant imagery or key terminology (i.e., not include trivial or peripheral language) and that these keywords should not be regularly found elsewhere within the overall chiasm.[5]

As a final step to examine the validity of this chiasm, an experiment was designed to test whether "naïve" readers of the chiasm would also place the passages in the same "pairings" as in the proposed chiasm. As described in appendix A1 in greater

Table A.1 Overview of the parallel passages associated with the six cycles of the four-phase process model in Luke's Journey Narrative

Cycle 1: The Samaritan cycle—Managing relationships with cultural outsiders (passages #1–4)	Cycle 6: The salvation cycle—Managing relationships with social outcasts (passages #21–24)
Phase 1: Problem recognition (Luke 9:51–56) • Jesus begins his journey to Jerusalem • Jesus sends messengers to a Samaritan village ahead of them to make ready for him • The Samaritans in the village reject the messengers • Two disciples, James and John, ask Jesus whether they should command fire to come down from heaven and consume the Samaritans • Jesus rebukes his disciples for their judgmental attitude toward the Samaritan people	Phase 1: Problem recognition (Luke 19:28–40) • Jesus prepares to enter Jerusalem • Jesus sends messengers to village ahead of them to ask a man for a donkey to make ready for him • The man in the village accepts the messengers' request, and Jesus rides the donkey into Jerusalem amid cheering from a multitude of people • The Pharisees ask Jesus to order the people to stop saying things like: "Blessed is the king who comes in the name of the Lord!" • Jesus rebuffs the Pharisees for their judgmental lack of understanding: "I tell you, if these [crowds] were silent, the stones would shout out!"
Phase 2: Action response (Luke 9:57–10:20) *Story #1: Describes people who wish to experiment with following Jesus, but who remain committed to conventional oikos ways* • Jesus is on the road • A potential follower says, "I will follow you wherever you go." • Jesus says he has no *oikos*: "Foxes have holes, and birds of the air have nests; but the Son of Man has nowhere to lay his head." • Another potential follower asks to first go back to his *oikos* and bury his father, but Jesus says "Let the dead bury their own dead" [thus Jesus counters traditional standards of honor] • A third potential follower reverts to traditional *oikos* norms by saying, "I will follow you, but let me first say farewell to those at my home." • Jesus says that people who revert back to traditional *oikos* structures and systems are not fit for the kingdom of God *Story #2: Jesus sends 70 followers on a mission, providing instruction and correctives, and then appraises the results of this little experiment* • Jesus is on his way to Jerusalem [where he will die on the cross] • Jesus appoints 70 followers with a task to prepare others for his arrival • Jesus sends the 70 out in groups of two • Jesus tells the 70 not to bring their purse [money] • The 70 are told to bring peace to others' *oikoi*, to cure the sick, and to tell them the KOG is near • Jesus puts contingency plans into place to be used in villages who do not welcome the 70; Jesus notes that villages who reject his followers also thereby reject Jesus and God • The 70 who follow Jesus' instruction are given authority over the power of the enemy, but villages who reject Jesus' message will face a judgment (they will be rejected by the one who sent Jesus)	Phase 2: Action response (Luke 19:1–27) *Story #1: Describes someone who wishes to experiment with following Jesus, and who implements oikos practices consistent with KOG* • Jesus is on the road (entering Jericho) • Zacchaeus follows Jesus wherever he goes as he walks through Jericho • Jesus says he wants to visit Zacchaeus's *oikos*: "Zacchaeus, hurry and come down [from the perch in that tree]; for I must stay at your house today." • Observers grumble that Jesus should know better than go the *oikos* of a sinner [thus Jesus counters traditional standards of honor] • Zacchaeus changes the structures and systems in his *oikos*, giving half the money to the poor and repaying fourfold anyone who has been defrauded • Jesus says that salvation has come to this countercultural *oikos*, for the Son of Man has come to seek out and to save the lost *Story #2: A nobleman sends 10 managers on a mission, providing instruction and correctives, and then appraises the results of this little experiment* • A nobleman is on his way to the emperor to get more power for himself • The nobleman appoints ten slaves with a task that will prepare for the nobleman's return • The nobleman sends his slaves out individually • The nobleman gives each follower a pound [money] • The 10 are told to use their pounds to make money from others' houses • A contingency plan is put into action by subjects who do not welcome the nobleman's rule; they travel to Rome to ask the emperor to reject the nobleman's request for more power • The slaves who obey the nobleman are rewarded with power over cities, but the slaves who refuse to participate in the nobleman's acquisitive economic power-seeking behavior are impoverished; others who opposed the nobleman are slaughtered

Continued

Table A.1 Continued

Cycle 1: The Samaritan cycle—Managing relationships with cultural outsiders (passages #1–4)	Cycle 6: The salvation cycle—Managing relationships with social outcasts (passages #21–24)
Phase 3: Changed way of seeing (Luke 10:21–24) • People traditionally considered to be wise and intelligent, such as prophets and kings, are unable to see the Father because they refuse to see Jesus as the Son • It is Jesus' disciples and the very young who can see that Jesus is the Son, and who are thus able to see the Father	Phase 3: Changed way of seeing (Luke 18:35–43) • Most people recognize Jesus' lineage only as someone who comes from Nazareth, and thus are unable to see him as the Messiah • It is a blind man who can see that Jesus is the merciful Son of David [i.e., the Messiah who will release people from oppressive rulers and ideas]
Phase 4: Institutional change (Luke 10:25–37) • A lawyer asks Jesus "What must I do to inherit eternal life?" • Jesus poses a counterquestion: What do you read in the law? • A fivefold response to the original question is offered: "You shall love the Lord your God with: —all your heart, —and with all you soul, —and with all your strength, —and with all you mind; —and you shall love your neighbor as yourself." • The reply from the lawyer—"Who is my neighbor?"—elicits a follow-up response from Jesus • A lowly Samaritan who shows mercy does a better job fulfilling the Law than priests and Levites whose adherence to keeping religious purity laws prevents them from helping the needy	Phase 4: Institutional change (Luke 18:18–34) • A certain ruler asks Jesus "What must I do to inherit eternal life?" • Jesus poses a counterquestion: Why do you call me good? No one is good but God alone. • A fivefold response to the original question is offered: "You know the commandments: —you shall not commit adultery; —you shall not murder; —you shall not steal; —you shall not bear false witness; —honor your mother and father." • The reply from the ruler—"I have kept all these since my youth"—elicits a follow-up response from Jesus • People who choose not to be beholden to traditional *oikos* structures and systems "get" the kingdom of God and get much more than people with high status within traditional social structures

Cycle 2: The new rules for the *oikos* cycle—Managing relationships within the *oikos* (passages #5–8)	Cycle 5: The justice cycle—Managing relationships with the social elite (passages #17–20)
Phase 1: Problem recognition (Luke 10:38–42) • Two women (Martha and Mary) host Jesus in their house • One woman (Martha) does all the things expected of her (e.g., the tasks of a hostess) • The other women (Mary) fails to perform her traditional household duties, and instead sits at Jesus' feet and listens to him • The first woman (Martha) notes that she is doing all the housework, and tells Jesus that she would like Mary to join her and help • The story has a countercultural ending because Jesus says Mary made a better choice (Martha was too distracted by housework)	Phase 1: Problem recognition (Luke 18:9–17) • Two men (a Pharisee and a tax collector) go to pray in the house of God • One man (Pharisee) does all the things expected of him (e.g., fasting, tithing) • The other man (tax collector) fails to perform his traditional religious duties, and instead beats his breast and asks God for mercy • The first man (Pharisee) notes that he is doing all the right things, and thanks God that he is not like other people (like the tax collector) • The story has a countercultural ending because Jesus says the humble tax collector went home more justified than the Pharisee (the Pharisee was too busy exalting himself); whoever does not humble themselves as a little child will not enter the KOG

Phase 2: Action response (Luke 11:1–13)
• Jesus teaches his disciples how to pray
• Jesus teaches them a prayer that has four components:
  i. acknowledge God as holy, head of *oikos*
  ii. desire to have everyone's daily needs met
	Phase 2: Action response (Luke 18:1–8)
	• Jesus teaches his disciples about their need to pray
	• Jesus tells a parable about an unjust judge who has four characteristics:
	  i. the judge has no fear of God
	  ii. the judge has no respect for people's daily needs

Continued

iii. forgive sin/debts (even though retaining the debt would, in conventional eyes, be just)
iv. ask to avoid situations where you are tempted to follow conventional norms
- People will give bread to persistent neighbors who need it
- Parents give children the needs they ask for

Phase 3: Changed way of seeing (Luke 11:14–36)
- Jesus heals a mute who begins to speak (and the crowds are amazed)
- Jesus invites exorcists to determine whether healing was by God or Beelzebul
- People ask Jesus for sign that he is from God (versus from Beelzebul ruler of demons)
- Jesus will be a sign for this generation:
  i. just as Jonah was a sign for the Ninevites
  ii. even greater than the sign of the queen of the south found in Solomon
- Contrast between a body full of light (good) versus darkness (bad)

Phase 4: Institutional change (Luke 11:37–54)
- Jesus tells Pharisees that they care too much about external show ("but inside you are full of greed and wickedness")
- Jesus identifies six woeful shortcomings of religious leaders' norms:
  i. tithing without practicing justice/love
  ii. seeking best seats for self rather than seeking to honor others
  iii. inadvertently dishonoring the dead
  iv. creating burdensome rules ostensibly to bring out the true goodness in others
  v. failing to follow the teachings of prophets
  vi. withholding the key of knowledge
- Ends with observation that the religious leaders took offense at Jesus, cross-examined him, and sought to catch him in something he might say

iii. the judge grants justice to a widow because she persisted (even though he initially refused)
iv. the judge wants to avoid situations where he is "worn out" by persistent justice-seekers
- Unjust judge granted justice to the persistent widow
- God grants justice to those who ask for it

Phase 3: Changed way of seeing (Luke 17:11–37)
- Jesus heals ten lepers who call out for healing (but only one returned to give thanks)
- Jesus sends the healed lepers to the priests to get them to authorize that they were clean
- Jesus says that KOG is not coming with things [signs] that can be observed
- Jesus will be rejected by this generation:
  i. just as the people did not listen to Noah
  ii. just like the people of Sodom the day that Lot left
- Contrast between losing your life (good to give) versus trying to make it secure (bad to be selfish)

Phase 4: Institutional change (Luke 16:14–17:10)
- Jesus tells Pharisees ("lovers of money") that they care too much about external show ("but God knows your hearts")
- Jesus describes shortcomings of a certain rich *oikos* that has six brothers who are guilty of:
  i. failing to share with the poor/tithe
  ii. taking best seats for self and having the poor man Lazarus sit with the dogs
  iii. knowingly dishonoring the poor
  iv. failing to remove burdens for Lazarus, eventually causing him to die
  v. failing to follow the teachings of prophets
  vi. being oblivious to the key of knowledge (mercy)
- Ends with the story of an *oikos* where the manager does not demand acquisitive economic behavior from members, but rather where everyone does what they ought to

---

Cycle 3: The yeast cycle—Managing relationships regarding the interpretation of Scriptures (passage #9–12)

Cycle 4: The benefaction cycle—Managing relationships between patrons and clients (passages #13–16)

Phase 1: Problem recognition (Luke 12:1–12)
- Jesus tells listeners to beware of the yeast (hypocrisy) of the Pharisees: "nothing is secret that will not become known" (Luke 12:2)
- Listeners are told to be accountable: "even the hairs of your head are all counted"
- People who acknowledge Jesus before others will be forgiven [and forgiving]
- Don't worry about defending your countercultural actions to authorities, the Holy Spirit will teach what you ought to say

Phase 1: Problem recognition (Luke 16:1–13)
- Jesus tells story about a rich man who was made aware of that his resources were being scattered by the (shrewd) manager
- The manager is called to give an accounting of his actions
- The manager acknowledges that what he must do for others is be forgiving [and forgiven]
- The manager does not worry about how he will defend his countercultural actions to his boss; the boss commends the manager
- No *oikos* member can serve both God and money; you will either hate one and love the other, or be devoted to one and despise the other

Continued

Table A.1   Continued

Cycle 3: The yeast cycle—Managing relationships regarding the interpretation of Scriptures (passage #9–12)	Cycle 4: The benefaction cycle—Managing relationships between patrons and clients (passages #13–16)

Phase 2: Action response (Luke 12:13–48)
- Don't seek to maximize the inheritance money you get from your *oikos*: "Be on guard against all sorts of greed, for one's life does not consist in the abundance of possessions."
- Jesus tells parable of a householder who hoards up his *oikos* money for himself
- Do not worry about your personal wants, but instead ensure that everyone's needs are met

- Be ready for the return of the master
- Woe to the manager who abuses his position, but blessed is the manager who authentically serves the needs of the holistic *oikos* rather than their own wants

Phase 3: Changed way of seeing (Luke 12:49–13:9)
- Jesus disrupts conventional views of *oikos*: "From now on five in one household will be divided, . . . father against son and son against father, mother against daughter and daughter against mother."
- Be prepared, read the signs of the KOG just as you read other signs: "He said also to the crowds: When you see a cloud rising in the west, you immediately say, 'It is going to rain'; and so it happens. And when you see the south wind blowing, you say, 'There will be scorching heat'; and it happens."

- If you fail to make peace with your neighbors, it'll cost you every last penny
- A fig tree that does not produce figs is (eventually) cut down

Phase 4: Institutional change (Luke 13:10–30)
- Jesus heals a crippled women on the sabbath in the synagogue
- The synagogue leaders becomes indignant, saying such work should not be done on the sabbath
- Jesus says to them: "Does not each of you on the sabbath untie his ox or his donkey from the manger, and lead it away to give it water?"
- Do countercultural things like:
  —plant mustard seeds (weeds) in garden
  —add yeast (impure) to your dough
- Jesus likens the KOG to a place where "people will come from the east and west, from north and south, and will eat in the kingdom of God. Indeed, some are last who will be first, and some are first who will be last."

Phase 2: Action response (Luke 15:1–32)
- Any joy that comes from recovering 1 or 10 percent of lost *oikos* assets, or even keeping all your *oikos* assets, pales in comparison to the joy in heaven when one sinner repents
- Jesus tells parable about a son who squanders his *oikos* inheritance on himself
- Even foreigners helped the son (who had squandered his resources fulfilling his wants) to meet his basic needs
- The master was ready for the return of his son
- Woe to the older son who loyally obeyed all the conventional norms, but even so failed to authentically serve the needs of the holistic *oikos* rather than his own wants

Phase 3: Changed way of seeing (Luke 14:25–35)
- Jesus disrupts conventional views *oikos*: "Whoever comes to me and does not hate father and mother, wife and children, brothers and sisters, yes, and even life itself, cannot be my disciple."

- Be prepared, read the signs of the KOG just as you read other signs: "what king, going out to wage war against another king, will not sit down first and consider whether he is able with ten thousand to oppose the one who comes against him with twenty thousand? If he cannot, then, while the other is still far away, he sends a delegation and asks for the terms of peace."
- If you want to become Jesus' disciple, you must give up all your possessions
- Salt that does not taste salty is thrown away

Phase 4: Institutional change (Luke 14:1–24)
- Jesus heals a man with edema (dropsy) on the sabbath in the house of a leading Pharisee
- When Jesus asked whether it is lawful to cure people on the sabbath, the assembled lawyers and Pharisees refuse to answer
- Jesus says to them: "If one of you has a child or an ox that has fallen into a well, will you not immediately pull it out on a sabbath day?"
- Do countercultural things like:
  —sit beneath your status at a banquet
  —invite social outcasts to your *oikos*
- Jesus likens the KOG to a banquet that includes "the poor, the crippled, the lame, and the blind . . . Then the master said . . . 'For I tell you none of those who were invited [prior to these outcasts] will taste my dinner.'"

detail, this experiment involved removing all headings and chapter/verse markings from each of the 24 passages in the chiasm. The first 12 passages were then placed in random order and printed out on 12 separate "cards" numbered from #1 through #12. The last 12 passages were also placed in random order, and printed out on separate cards numbered #13–24. The 30 participants in the study were then asked to find one "match" for each of the first 12 passages from among the second 12 passages. If the passages in the first half of the chiasm were unrelated to the ones in the second half, we would expect them to be matched "correctly" only 8 percent of the time (i.e., one-twelfth). However, on average the participants paired the passages in the way we predicted 47 percent of the time, a statistically significant finding.[6]

These results are striking, especially in light of the conservative nature of our experiment design: (a) our readers did not look at the passages in their original language, so may have missed some clues for matching pairs; (b) our readers were not trained to identify chiasms, and so may have missed some clues for matching; and perhaps most importantly, (c) the passages in our experiment were placed in random order, whereas in the original text readers aware that they are reading a chiasm have the advantage of knowing the sequential ordering of passages, which would have provided even more guidance for connecting the pairs.

Evidence of a Recurring Four-Phase Model

The pairings identified in the chiasm provide a partial explanation for the sequencing of the Journey Narrative passages (i.e., the first passage "matches" the last passage, the second passage matches the second last passage, and so on). However this still does not provide a rationale behind the *sequencing* of the 12 passages *within* each half of the chiasm (recall that they do not follow a simple or linear geographic or thematic progression). It seems unlikely that the passages would have been arranged in random order, especially given Luke's self-identified preoccupation with providing an "orderly account" for his reader (Luke 1:3).[7]

As it turns out, perhaps the reason it has been difficult to unlock the rationale for the ordering of the passages is because scholars have been using linear and Western ways of reading the text, rather than interpreting it as a cyclical model within a chiastic structure. Perhaps it should not come as a surprise when, upon closer inspection of the Journey Narrative chiasm, its narrative structure can be shown to point to a recurring four-phase process model. Consistent with the criteria to establish a chiasm generally, support for the four-phase process model is evident in word choice, themes, breakpoints, and in the passage that lies at the midpoint of the chiasm.

Keywords and Themes in Each of the Four Phases

Just as use of keywords helps to identify chiastic pairs generally, so also keywords help to identify important themes shared by the six passages that represent each of the four phases in the Journey Narrative. (Note that the keyword analyses were done in Greek, but the English words are reported here for reader-friendliness). To find these keywords the focus was limited to words that are relatively meaningful (e.g., the analysis did not consider common often used words such as "I," "you," "he," "she," or "we"[8]). Each of the 16 keywords listed in the table A.2 was mentioned an average of 13 times in the Journey Narrative (and not more than 31 times; as a whole this equals about 0.3 percent of the total number of words in the Journey Narrative),

Table A.2 Thematic keywords associated with each of the four phases: total number of mentions in each phase, frequency scores, and dominance ratio

Keywords, by phase	Number of mentions of keywords in each phase				Frequency ratio = # mentions/# words in phase				Dominance Ratio = frequency in focal phase/ frequency other three phases
	Phase 1	Phase 2	Phase 3	Phase 4	Phase 1 (1276 words)	Phase 2 (3067 words)	Phase 3 (2016 words)	Phase 4 (2747 words)	
1a. Disciple/student (*mathetes*)	7	3	5	1	**.55%**	.10%	.25%	.04%	4.8
1b. Two (*duo*)	**4**	5	4	1	**.31**	.16	.20	.04	2.5
1c. To rebuke (*epitimeson*)	**3**	0	1	1	**.23**	0	.05	.04	9.2
Total for phase 1 keywords	*14*	*8*	*10*	*3*	*1.10*	*.26*	*.50*	*.11*	*4.1*
2a. To give (*didomi*)	1	**22**	5	3	.08	**.72**	.25	.11	4.8
2b. To find (*heurisko*)	2	**14**	5	0	.16	**.46**	.25	0	3.9
2c. Proverb/poem/parable (*parabole*)	1	**5**	1	1	.08	**.16**	.5	.04	3.3
Total for phase 2 keywords	*4*	*41*	*11*	*4*	*.31*	*1.33*	*.55*	*.15*	*4.2*
3a. To hear, to heed, to obey (*akouo*)	3	6	**8**	7	.24	.20	**.40**	.26	1.8
3b. To see (*horao*)	3	5	**8**	9	.24	.16	**.40**	.33	1.7
3c. To receive sight (*anablepsis*)	0	1	**3**	0	0	.03	**.15**	0	10.6
Total for phase 3 keywords	*6*	*12*	*19*	*16*	*.47*	*.39*	*.94*	*.58*	*2.0*
4a. Law, principle (*nomos*)	0	0	0	**3**	0	0	0	**.11**	n/a
4b. Lawyer; trained in law (*nomikos*)	0	0	0	**5**	0	0	0	**.18**	n/a
4c. Rich (*plousios*)	1	2	0	**6**	.08	.07	0	**.22**	4.6
4d. Poor (*ptochos*)	0	1	0	**5**	0	.03	0	**.18**	11.6
4e. Place, position; opportunity (*topos*)	0	3	1	**6**	0	.10	.05	**.22**	3.5
Total for phase 4 keywords	*1*	*6*	*1*	*25*	*.08*	*.20*	*.05*	*.91*	*7.2*

and each word was mentioned in at least three of the six passages that together make up a phase. As shown in the "Dominance ratio" scores, the words were more than four times as likely to be in the phases they are associated with than in any one other phases in the Journey Narrative. Taken together, these words help to point to the distinct themes that characterize the passages within each phase.

Phase 1 (Problem Recognition)

The three keywords associated with the first phase—two, disciple, rebuke—are consistent with the overarching idea that passages in this phase tend to describe a situation or an issue where disciples of Jesus are facing two differing views about an issue, and where one of the views is rebuked.[9] Each phase 1 passage in the Journey Narrative has dual competing positions, and describes how Jesus often takes a position that was likely counterintuitive to many of his listeners.

It may be noteworthy that Luke places considerable emphasis on "dialogue" in the passages in the Journey Narrative generally, and in the first phase passages in particular.[10] There tends to be an average of one dialogue for every three verses in phase 1, whereas there is one dialogue every four verses in phases 2 and 4, and one for every six verses in phase 3. Also, of the six phase 1 passages, four of them contain dialogue that is unique to Luke (i.e., it is not found in Matthew or Mark). Also, it seems that the four-phase process is often driven or animated by issues facing a group of Jesus' disciples.

Phase 2 (Action Response)

The three keywords for the second phase—give, find, parable—point to the idea that the second phase deals with actions that respond to the issues raised in the first phase. First, the passages point to the importance of a giving, benevolent spirit. Just as Jesus gave his followers the kingdom and the authority to address issues, so also they are to have a generous giving spirit to others (especially giving financial resources to the poor). Second, these passages talk about seeking solutions, and promise that those who seek will find what they're searching for, and that they will find what has been lost. Third, the passages provide a number of parables that provide "what if" scenarios and lessons grounded in lessons from everyday life.[11]

Phase 3 (Changed Way of Seeing)

The keywords for phase 3—to hear and to see/receive sight—point to this phase being a time of insight and revelation, literally a new way of seeing and perceiving the world. Perhaps the keystone passage that encapsulates the meaning of a new way of seeing and hearing is found in phase 3 of the first cycle:

> At that same hour Jesus rejoiced in the Holy Spirit and said, "I thank you, Father, Lord of heaven and earth, because you have hidden these things from the wise and the intelligent and have revealed them to infants; yes, Father, for such was your gracious will. All things have been handed over to me by my Father; and no one knows who the Son is except the Father, or who the Father is except the Son and anyone to whom the Son chooses to reveal him." Then turning to the disciples, Jesus said to them privately, *"Blessed are the eyes that see what you see! For I tell you that many prophets and kings desired to see what you see, but did not see it, and to hear what you hear, but did not hear it"* (Luke 10:21–24).

Phase 4 (Institutional Change)

The keywords for phase four—law/yer, rich/poor, place/position—point to issues of power and status. In these passages the emphasis is on challenging existing institutions and norms, with the idea of creating new structures and systems that are consistent with Jesus' message. This is illustrated by the emphasis placed on Jesus being tested by lawyers and challenging them, Jesus admonishing the rich to be more generous toward the poor, and Jesus pointing to the folly of caring about status and social position.[12]

Breakpoints between Cycles, and Coherent Themes within Cycles

In addition to pointing to consistencies in word choices and themes *within* each of the four phases described earlier (across the six cycles), a second way to provide support for the four-phase model is to demonstrate that each of the six four-phase cycles can be seen as a coherent literary unit, with a distinct breakpoint separating one cycle from the next.

Perhaps the strongest and most obvious signal that there is a breakpoint between the first and fourth phase of the model is that in *each* of the six cycles phase 4 starts with a reference to Jesus interacting with an elite leader in society.[13] Once this pattern is recognized, it functions as a metaphorical "hard return" on a keyboard signaling time to end one line (or cycle) of thought and to begin a new one. In the first century, such mentions of interaction with members of the elite were sure to catch the attention of readers.

In terms of coherent literary units, each of the six cycles can be seen as having its own theme or "story-line" that flows through each of the four-phases. These are described in some length in chapters fourteen and fifteen, and summarized in table 13.1.

CORROBORATING EVIDENCE: A FOUR-PHASE PROCESS MODEL IN THE EARLY CHURCH?

There is substantial evidence that a four-phase process model is embedded in the Journey Narrative. But is there additional evidence in Luke's writings to corroborate this finding? And, moreover, is there any evidence that this model is used by Jesus' followers, or is it simply the model evident when Jesus went on *his* journey to Jerusalem? Finally, is it even conceivable that first-century listeners would have been attuned to such a four-phase model? Each of these three questions is addressed here.

Evidence of a Similar Four-Phase Process Model in Acts

A good way to begin to answer these questions is by looking at Acts, which is Luke's account of the early church after Jesus' resurrection. As it turns out, a very similar four-phase process model seems to be embedded in the organizing scheme and content of Acts. Consider the following similarities and parallels. To start, note how the geographic organizing structure of the Journey Narrative and Acts are inverted. Recall that the Journey Narrative starts with Jesus located in the northernmost point he ever visited (i.e., around Caesarea Phillippi, a Gentile region just outside the jurisdiction of Herod Antipas) and describes his wanderings through Samaria and Judea and into Jerusalem. The sequential order of this movement is inverted in Acts, which starts with the disciples in Jerusalem and describes how they receive the Holy Spirit as they witness to Jesus in Jerusalem, in all Judea and Samaria, and to the ends of the earth (Acts 1:8).[14]

Table A.3 provides an overview of how the book of Acts can be seen to be written in four sections, organized according to these four concentric geographic circles moving outward from (i) Jerusalem (Acts 1:12–5:42) to (ii) Samaria (Acts 6:1–9:43) to (iii) Judea (Acts 10:1–12:24), and (iv) the rest of the world (Acts 12:25–end).[15] Table A.3 also points to several other differences between each of the four sections, including how each of the story lines within each of the four sections has its own key central cast of characters, and how each section contains one of the only four mention of the Holy Spirit descending and taking possession of human beings where the coming of the Spirit is associated with the gift of speaking in tongues.[16]

Perhaps of greatest interest for present purposes, each of the four sections of Acts can also be seen to contain within it a four-phase process similar to the one Luke embedded in the Journey Narrative. As shown in table A.3, each of the four sections of Acts: (1) starts with a problem or issue to resolve, (2) describes actions designed to resolve the issue, (3) describes a new way of seeing (especially new ways of speaking/interpreting ancient scriptures in light of Jesus), and (4) concludes with a description of a confrontation with authorities.[17]

The *third* of the four sections of Acts described in table A.3 (Acts 10:1 through 12:24) is of particular interest because it describes one of the most significant changes in the early church, as the church abandons traditional aspects of its Jewish heritage and begins to embrace Gentiles as equal members. This transition, which is described in considerable detail and repetition in Acts chapters 10 and 11, can be seen to follow the four-phase process as follows.[18]

Phase 1 (Problem Recognition): Avoid Misguided Attempts to Segregate "Clean" and "Unclean" People (Acts 10:1–16)

The process starts when both Cornelius and Peter independently have what at first seem to be problematic visions while they are praying. Cornelius, a gentile Roman centurion, is the first to receive the vision. Initially the purpose of the vision is unclear, except that he is to send some of his men to Joppa to invite Peter to his house, where Peter would give "a message by which you and your entire *oikos* will be saved" (Acts 11:14). Shortly thereafter Peter is in prayer and receives a vision that he should not to adhere to conventional religious laws about what is clean and unclean (Acts 10:9–16).[19] At first the problem is simply knowing how to respond to these unusual visions, rather than knowing exactly why.

Phase 2 (Action Response): Spend Time in the Oikos of Segregated Groups (Acts 10:17–43)

Both Cornelius and Peter act on their visions, even though they are not at all sure what the outcome of this little experiment might be. Cornelius sends messengers to the *oikos* where Peter is staying to invite him. The Spirit tells Peter to accept the invitation to go to Cornelius's *oikos*, and Peter brings along six of his Jewish friends (Acts 10:17–33). The problem that their actions are addressing becomes clearer when Peter says: "You yourselves know that it is unlawful for a Jew to associate with or to visit a Gentile; but God has shown me that I should not call anyone profane or

Table A.3 How the four-phase process model is embedded within each of the four geographic steps of the "journey" described in Acts (building on Goulder, 1964a)

	Cycle 1: Acts 1:12–5:42	Cycle 2: Acts 6:1–9:43	Cycle 3: Acts 10:1–12:24	Cycle 4: Acts 12:25–end
Geographic center/ Key characters	Jerusalem The Twelve Apostles (esp. Peter and John)	Samaria/periphery of Israel The Seven Deacons (esp. Stephen and Phillip)	Judea Peter (and Cornelius)	Rest of world Paul (and Barnabas, Silas, and Timothy)
1. Problem recognition	The problem is that the disciples are not sure what to do after Jesus' ascension (interestingly, the first step is to reestablish the group of 12 Apostles by choosing a new Treasurer)	The problem is that the widows of "outsiders" (Greek-speaking Jews from outside Palestine) are being neglected in the daily distribution of food in the early church (Acts 6:1)	The problem is that purity laws create segregation between "clean" and "unclean" followers of Jesus (e.g., Gentiles were not yet considered to be full members of the church, Acts 10:1–16)	The problem concerns spreading the word beyond Judea
2. Action response	The disciples begin to model living in a nonconventional *oikos*/intentional community (Acts 2:44–47; 4:32–5:11); (choose Matthias as new Treasurer, Acts 1:23–26)	The group chooses seven deacons (helpers) to resolve the problem (Acts 6:2–7); two of these deacons subsequently also preach the word of God	Cornelius sends people to visit Peter, and Peter and some believers go to visit (unclean) Cornelius and his *oikos*, where Peter speaks to them about God's peace and inclusiveness (Acts 10:17–43)	Send disciples in small groups (in first instance Paul and Barnabas are chosen/"set apart" for the task—Acts 13:2) to different cities to establish local groups of believers
3. New way of seeing (new way of interpreting Scripture via Holy Spirit)	Peter receives Spirit (and gift of tongues) for a new way of interpreting Scripture (Acts 2:4); two longer speeches (Acts 2:14–36; Acts 3:12–26); *New insight highlighted:* Jesus is Messiah who brings a liberating new kind of *oikos* (based on benefaction) (Acts 2:4)	Spirit-filled Stephen gives a speech providing a new way of seeing Jewish history (Acts 6:5,10; 7:1–51); Phillip preaches in Samaria and teaches the Ethiopian treasurer (Acts 8:4–40); *New insight highlighted:* God goes beyond a narrow Jewish interpretation of ancient Scriptures that focus on the Temple in Jerusalem (Acts 8:15)	The Holy Spirit descends upon the Gentiles who speak in tongues (Acts 10:44–48); Peter has a vision that renders purity laws obsolete *New insight highlighted:* The Holy Spirit is available to *all* believers (not only Israel) (Acts 10:46)	Provide message in ways appropriate to the various audiences (e.g., in Athens be sensitive to familiar ways of teaching—Acts 17:16–32). The Holy Spirit comes upon a new "Group of 12" who speak in tongues and join Paul in spreading the word of the Lord to "all the residents of Asia" (Acts 19:6) *New insight highlighted:* The message of Jesus is for the whole world (Acts 19:10)
4. Institutional change (confrontation with authorities)	Jewish authorities (Sanhedrin) twice confront the Apostles: (1) when they threaten the Apostles (Acts 4:1–22) and (2) when they imprison Peter and John, who escape via the Spirit (Acts 5:17–42); Gamaliel argues to leave apostles alone	Jewish authorities (Sanhedrin) stone Stephen to death (Acts 7:54–8:3), but one of the people doing the stoning repents and is "raised up" (Saul/Paul, Acts 9:1–31); the resurrection theme is also evident when Aeneas is healed and when Dorcas is raised from the dead, Acts 9:32–42	Institutional change occurs when church leaders in Jerusalem hear accounts and agree to accept Gentiles as equal members in church (Acts 11:1–18; also, Herod Antipas arrests Peter to please those Jews who still consider Gentiles unclean, but angel helps Peter to escape prison and Herod dies, Acts 12:1–24)	Paul challenges Jewish and Roman authorities and institutions (Acts 21:27–28:31); many allusions to the trials of Paul, indicating that Paul was advocating countercultural norms

unclean. So when I was sent for, I came without objection. Now may I ask why you sent for me?" (Acts 10:28b–29).

*Phase 3 (Changed Way of Seeing): The Holy Spirit is Available to All
Believers (Not Only Israel) (Acts 10:44–48)*

As Peter preached the message of Jesus to these Gentiles they received the Holy Spirit, and all who saw it happen were astounded. Peter remembered the word of the Lord: "John baptized with water, but you will be baptized with the Holy Spirit" (Acts 11:16) and so they were baptized in the name of Jesus Christ.

*Phase 4 (Institutional Change): Gentiles Accepted as Full Members in the Church
(Acts 11:1–18; 12:1–24)*

The cycle ends with a description of institutional change as the church leaders in Jerusalem meet to discuss the whole process and everyone agrees to welcome Gentiles as full members of the church (Acts 11:1–18). At the level of political institutions, though, Herod Antipas (the Roman tetrarch of Galilee and Perea) arrests Peter to the pleasure of Jews who are not followers of Jesus.

Evidence That First-Century Listeners May Have Been Attuned to Such a Process Model

Socrates's dialogic method, arguably his most important contribution to philosophy, may be a similar early analog to the four-step process model embedded in Luke's Journey Narrative.[20] Recall that Socrates (469–399 BCE) lived about four centuries prior to Jesus, and that the Socratic method is considered an early forerunner to today's scientific method. Socrates used his four-step dialogical method to teach and to learn: by continually asking questions to get to the root of an issue, everyone could understand the key dimensions of that issue better. For Socrates, this understanding meant knowledge, which was for him the essence of virtue. He was known for practicing his method with anyone whom he might meet in the marketplace: "If you speak Greek and are willing to talk and reason, you can be Socrates' partner in searching, with the prospect that truth undisclosed to countless ages might be undisclosed here and now, on this spot, in the next forty minutes, between the two of you."[21] Here are the four steps of the Socratic method.[22]

Step 1: Present a Faulty Thesis Statement

In the case of Socrates, this refers to problematic statements that were uttered by someone other than himself. Usually the statements were about truth in the moral domain, dealing with questions like: "what is the way we ought to live?" and "what sort of man should one be, and what should one practice?"[23] The statement should be as specific as possible. Participants in the dialogue must remain open-minded, lest they become defensive and thus stifle learning. In modern applications of this Socratic method, the thesis statement is the identification of an issue or problem to be addressed.

*Step 2: Gather Information About the Statement, and Seek Agreement
on Premises Related to the Statement*

The goal in this step is to deeply understand the statement and the assumptions that it rests upon, and to raise related premises that can be agreed upon. This is an intellectual exercise that does not involve any actions or collecting of empirical data (note how this step is very different from phase 2 of the model embedded in the Journey Narrative).

Step 3: Identify the Shortcomings of the Faulty Thesis Statement by
Demonstrating it to be Inconsistent with Other Agreed Upon Premises
This step may threaten people's way of seeing via "jarring their adherence to some confident dogma by bringing to their awareness its collision with other, no less confident, presumptions of theirs." It is by compelling people to recognize the faultiness of an original thesis statement that they are prepared for the final step.

Step 4: Accept a New-and-Better "True" Thesis Statement
For Socrates, knowledge was the engine of virtue. He believed that once people had a deeper understanding of what was true and ethical, they would act on their understanding and insights. "Thus *elenchus* has a double objective: to discover how every human ought to live *and* to test that single human being who is doing the answering—to find out if he is *living* as one ought to live."

To be clear, no one knows whether Luke and his readers would have been familiar with the four-phase Socratic model as described here (or any other similar model). However, it does seem reasonable to speculate that Luke would have been familiar with some Socratic teachings and methods, and also that he would have expected many of his readers to be familiar with Socrates.[24]

Evidence of the Four-Phase Model in Acts When Paul Walks in the Footsteps of Socrates

Finally, it is noteworthy that Luke seems to allude to the four-step process model precisely where the reader would be most likely to look for it. Namely, when Luke describes the Apostle Paul's trip to Athens (Acts 17:16–32), ample evidence suggests that Luke had Socrates in mind, the greatest philosopher of Athens. This is first evident in the way that this passage starts by describing how Paul spent his days talking to the people whom he happened to meet at the marketplace, which exactly "corresponds to the typical picture of Socrates" and which Luke does not describe happening when Paul visits other cities.[25] It is also evident because this is the only passage where Luke uses the same Greek verb to describe how Paul "argued" in Athens that was used by Plato to describe Socrates's "dialogical technique." "Luke depicts Paul as being involved in dialogical teaching *a la* Socrates with his message." The Acts account can also be seen to start off where the story of Socrates ended up, namely with Paul arguing with philosophers who were members of the *Aereopagus* (the ruling council in Athens that had ordered Socrates's death). Finally, reminiscent of the charge against Socrates that he had been worshipping other gods, "this is exactly the accusation Paul faced in Athens (Acts 17:18–20). The wording of these accusations mirrors the Socrates tradition."

Of course, there are several differences in the stories, an important one being that—unlike Socrates—the apostle Paul escapes with his life. Might Paul's success be partly attributed to the fact that his presentation differed from what would have been consistent with the Socratic method? Put differently, would we expect Paul's reasoning with the intellectual descendants of Socrates to be an occasion where Luke's readers could be reminded of the four-phase process model embedded in the Journey

Narrative? It turns out that the passage in Acts can be seen to unfold in four steps akin to the four-phase process model.

Phase 1 (Problem Recognition): Who is the Unknown God? (Acts 17:22–23)

The beginning of Paul's speech draws attention to the problem of the "unknown god," thereby setting up a dialectic between worshipping "known gods" versus worshipping an "unknown God." Paul seeks to make known the unknown (Acts 17:22–23), and he thereby implicitly rebukes what the Athenians think they know.

> Then Paul stood in front of the Areopagus and said, "Athenians, I see how extremely religious you are in every way. For as I went through the city and looked carefully at the objects of your worship, I found among them an altar with the inscription, 'To an unknown god.' *What therefore you worship as unknown, this I proclaim to you.*" (Acts 17:22–23)

Phase 2 (Action Response): Seek and Find God (Acts 17:24–27)

Paul describes how the God he knows has acted, and how God has set in motion the parameters of this great "experiment" that we call the world, and how in the course of events humankind would search for and find God (v 24–27).

> The God who made the world and everything in it, he who is Lord of heaven and earth, does not live in shrines made by human hands, nor is he served by human hands, as though he needed anything, since he himself gives to all mortals life and breath and all things. From one ancestor he made all nations to inhabit the whole earth, and he allotted the times of their existence and the boundaries of the places where they would live, so that *they would search for God and perhaps grope for him and find him*—though indeed he is not far from each one of us. (Acts 17:24–27)

Phase 3 (Changed Way of Seeing): People are Part of God's Oikos (Acts 17:28–29)

Paul then goes on to interpret Greek poetry in a new way so that others may "see" this previously unknown God (v 28–29). In particular, by seeing themselves as children of God, God can thereby be seen as the head of their *oikos*.

> For "In him we live and move and have our being"; as even some of your own poets have said, "For we too are his offspring." Since *we are God's offspring*, we ought not to think that the deity is like gold, or silver, or stone, an image formed by the art and imagination of mortals. (Acts 17:28–29)

Phase 4 (Institutional Change): Change Your Ways Because Jesus is the Ultimate Judge (Acts 17:30–31)

Paul concludes by challenging the leading philosophers of Athens to change their ways (i.e., to repent).

> While God has overlooked the times of human ignorance, now he commands *all people everywhere to repent*, because he has fixed a day on which he will have the world judged in righteousness by a man whom he has appointed, and of this he has given assurance to all by raising him from the dead. (Acts 17:30–31)

SUMMARY

In short, this appendix describes how the Journey Narrative has been written in the general form of a chiasm, and offers empirical and experimental support for the contention that it contains 12 chiastic pairs. It then describes the linguistic and thematic support for the recurring four-phase process model embedded within the chiasm. It concludes by describing: how a similar four-phase process model is also embedded in the organizing structure of the book of Acts; how the four-phase process was evident when the early church accepted gentiles as full members; how first-century listeners may have been familiar with the idea of multistep processes to discern truth, especially in light of the Socratic method; and how Paul's address before the *Aereopagus* (the same body of leaders that condemned Socrates) is consistent with the four-phase process model.

Exhibit A1

Overview of the Empirical Study Examining the Plausibility of the Chiastic Pairings

Research Design

In order to develop empirical support for the plausibility of the 12 chiastic pairs that were identified in Luke's Journey Narrative, a test was designed that asked participants to sort through the 12 passages from the first half of the Journey Narrative, and to pair them with a matching passage from the second half of the Journey Narrative. (The instructions given to participants are described later in this exhibit.) The research design was very conservative. First, the passages were placed in random order. In their sequential order in the original Journey Narrative, any reader who recognized that the Journey Narrative was written in chiastic form would then be prompted to see how the parallel texts relate to each other. In particular, they would likely find similarities that they perhaps would not have identified as easily otherwise. By placing the 12 passages in both halves of the chiasm in random order, the design of this study did not permit readers to take their cues from the actual order presented in Luke.

Second, the test was conservative because study participants were given the texts in English (NRSV). Because of this, they were unable to see in the original Greek any wordplay and uses of unique or telling linguistic devices that might signal or point to parallel/twin passages.

Third, the test was conservative because study participants were not accustomed to thinking about and finding parallels between passages in this way. Although at the start of the study participants were provided with a short description and some examples for sorting and pairing the passages, readers in the first century would have had training and experience in developing and identifying and thinking about chiasms.

A total of 30 people participated in this study. Each person was paid $30 for participating in a 90-minute exercise. After being welcomed to the session and provided an overview of the study, each participant was asked to read the instructions and then "trained" for the task they would be participating in via a two-sided page of "sample" parallel passages. Each participant was also given a copy of the 12 passages in the first half of the chiasm (Group A), as well as of the 12 passages from the second half (Group B). Each passage was printed on a separate sheet, and participants were asked to pair one passage from Group A with one of the passages from Group B. Results were reported on a two-column sheet.

Findings

The results, shown in table A.4, provide very strong support for the chiasm. If there were no relationship among the different pairs, then readers would be expected to put them in the predicted pairings about 8 percent of the time (i.e., one-twelfth of the time). However, participants in the study placed the passages into the predicted pairs about 45 percent of the time, or more than five times more often than by chance. Moreover, for 9 of the 12 cases (i.e., 75 percent of the time), readers most frequently paired together the two passages predicted by the chiasm. In the remaining 3 cases, the predicted pairing was the second most-frequent twice (tied), and the third most-frequent once.

A chi-square test was used in two ways to determine whether these findings are statistically significant. The first test examined the null hypothesis that the participants' responses were randomly distributed across the various response categories. The null hypothesis could be rejected in 10 of the 12 cases at alpha = .001 level (i.e., the likelihood that they are randomly related is less than one-thousandth). This suggests that the passages are related to each other in a meaningful (nonrandom) way.

Second, the same chi-square test was performed on all the passages after removing the results from the expected pairing. This was to examine whether, after the expected pairings were removed, the remaining pairings were random. In this case we are unable to reject the null hypothesis in 10 of 12 cases, suggesting that the remaining pairings were indeed random.

Taken together, these findings lend strong support to the chiastic pairs that constituted the Journey Narrative. The support is particularly striking given the conservative nature of our research design (e.g., random ordering of the passages, translated text, readers with little chiastic knowledge/experience).

Discussion of the Findings

The strongest results were in the so-called Deuteronomic pillars passages in Pair 4a/4b (90 percent of readers placed them together). This is not entirely surprising because it is also the twin most often referred to in the nonchiastic literature. The next two strongest results were, appropriately, for the opening (83 percent) and closing (77 percent) twinned passages that "frame" the chiasm. This would be consistent with an argument that Luke wanted to underscore where the chiasm started, and where its central turning point was.

The three "weakest" twins (i.e., the passages where the expected pairing was not the pairing readers most frequently pointed to) also warrant special attention (Pairings #2, #5, and #9). One of these (Pair #9) involved the parable of the shrewd manager, which many see as perhaps the most difficult of Jesus' parable to interpret. Another involved the parable of the ten pounds, which may have been difficult to place appropriately (i.e., as twinned with the sending of the 72) because the dominant mainstream twenty-first-century interpretation parable of the pounds is very different than a first-century interpretation. Finally, it is unclear why so many readers missed the third pairing (#5), because the parallels seem quite evident at face value, even in the English translation.

Table A.4 Frequency of pairing (a) the 12 passages in the first half of the chiasm with (b) their parallel passages in the second half

	1a	2a	3a	4a	5a	6a	7a	8a	9a	10a	11a	12a	chi-sq	sig at a=.001
1b	25	2	1	0	0	0	0	0	2	0	0	0	220.1	yes
2b	0	4	0	0	3	0	1	5	4	11	0	2	44.3	yes
3b	1	2	10	0	4	1	2	2	8	0	0	0	46.1	yes
4b	0	1	0	27	1	0	0	0	1	0	0	0	259.3	yes
5b	0	0	12	0	6	6	0	3	2	0	0	0	68.1	yes
6b	1	1	1	0	3	21	0	0	1	0	2	0	149.7	yes
7b	2	3	1	1	0	0	13	2	0	0	4	4	67.5	yes
8b	0	1	1	0	0	1	2	9	6	6	3	1	36.5	yes
9b	0	4	1	1	2	0	5	4	5	6	2	0	22.7	no
10b	1	4	1	1	5	1	2	3	1	6	5	0	16.5	no
11b	0	8	1	0	4	0	2	0	0	1	14	0	81.3	yes
12b	0	0	0	0	2	0	3	2	0	0	0	23	188	yes

Instructions Provided to Study Participants

In this exercise you will be given 24 passages taken from the Bible. Each passage is written on a separate sheet, and each sheet is numbered randomly for identification purposes. Of these 24 passages, the passages #1 through #12 are labeled as "Group A," and the passages #13 through #24 are labeled as "Group B."

Your task is to read the passages, and link each with one other passage so that in the end you form 12 "matching pairs." In each pair, one passage should come from Group A and the other from Group B.

The pairs may be similar in *theme* (e.g., both passages are about healing, both describe God's mercy), *structure* (e.g., a passage where Jesus talks with three women is paired with a passage where Jesus talks to three men; or two passages are linked where Jesus enters a town at the beginning and leaves at the end of each passage), or *wording* (e.g., both passages talk about "lambs" and "wolves").

The exercise has been divided into three steps:

Step 1: Read each passage

Please feel free to make notes on the sheets to remind yourself about key *themes, structures,* or *words* that you notice in each passage. As you do this keep in mind the following:

a) *Themes* need not be intricate; for example, "Jesus teaching on Baptism" or "Jesus in the Temple" could both be considered themes. Often the parallel themes in the passages may be "mirror images" of each other. For example, in one passage Jesus may tell a story of a man who asks for healing but receives salvation, and in its paired passage there may be a man who asks for salvation but gets healed. One passage teaches about the love of God, and the other tells about the ways of Satan. In one passage Jesus tells a parable about an escape from captivity, in another he instructs his disciples how to prepare for Passover.

b) *Structures* can also be rather simple constructions and you need not try to find elaborately built systems of argument. Often paired passages are similar in length and format, and they progress through a similar sequence of ideas/steps from the beginning of the passage to its end. For example, each passage may start with Jesus teaching on fasting, then Jesus going into the wilderness, then Jesus visiting a poor person. Again, sometimes the structures of two paired passages may mirror each other. For example, in one passage Jesus enters a home where he is served a meal, in another he tells a parable of someone who is kicked out of a village for eating unclean food.

c) Key *words* can be the most tricky to judge in terms of relevance. The parallel words may be very unique ("baptism of the spirit") or quite common, and often have simple opposites (e.g., "high" versus "low," "on" versus "off," "young" versus "old"). Pay particular attention to key words or themes that do not appear in the other passages you were provided.

As you will be able to see from the "sample" paired passages on the attached sheet, parallels can range from quite strong to relatively weak. Agreement in theme, structure, and wording often do not exist together, rather one or two of these concepts are generally present in passages that end up being paralleled. Keep this in mind as you complete the exercise.

Step 2: Once you've read and become familiar with each passage,
start sorting them into pairs

You may find some pairs very easily. Remember that for each pairing, one passage should come from "Group A" and the other passage from "Group B." Look for shared themes and words, similar structures and format, remembering that sometimes the parallel passages are mirror images of one another. Move the sheets around until you are comfortable with the pairings you have found. There are no right or wrong answers—we are looking for how you would match-up the passages into pairs.

Step 3: Record your pairings

Please use the "Response Sheet" provided here. Record the "Passage numbers" shown at the top of each passage corresponding to your 12 paired passages. It does not matter which order you list the pairs, so long each pair's passage numbers are entered on the same row. [Participants were provided with a response sheet that had three columns labeled as follows: "Pairing;" "Passage Number (from 'Group A')," and "Passage Number (from 'Group B')." Beneath these three columns were 12 rows, and each row was labeled from "1" through to "12" in the first column.]

Hand-out Sheet: Example of Paired Passages (provided to study participants to familiarize and "train" them for their task)

Example #1: The following two passages form a "pair" because of a similar structure and wording. In both John is the key figure and in both he quotes the prophet Isaiah from the Old Testament regarding the voice crying in the wilderness. This is a very strong parallel.

> *Passage A:* This is the testimony given by John when the Jews sent priests and Levites from Jerusalem to ask him, "Who are you?" He confessed and did not deny it, but confessed, "I am not the Messiah." And they asked him, "What then? Are you Elijah?" He said, "I am not." "Are you the prophet?" He answered, "No." Then they said to him, "Who are you? Let us have an answer for those who sent us. What do you say about yourself?" He said, "I am the voice of one crying out in the wilderness, 'Make straight the way of the Lord,'" as the prophet Isaiah said.

> *Passage B:* In the fifteenth year of the reign of Emperor Tiberius, when Pontius Pilate was governor of Judea, and Herod was ruler of Galilee, and his brother Philip ruler of the region of Ituraea and Trachonitis, and Lysanias ruler of Abilene, during the high priesthood of Annas and Caiaphas, the word of God came to John son of Zechariah in the wilderness. He went into all the region around the Jordan, proclaiming a baptism of repentance for the forgiveness of sins, as it is written in the book of the words of the prophet Isaiah, "The voice of one crying out in the wilderness: 'Prepare the way of the Lord, make his paths straight.'"

Example #2: Here the theme and structure are quite different, but the distinct key word "bridegroom" is enough to suggest that the two passages form a parallel pair.

> *Passage A:* Jesus said to them, "You cannot make wedding guests fast while the bridegroom is with them, can you? The days will come when the bridegroom will be taken away from them, and then they will fast in those days."

> *Passage B:* He who has the bride is the bridegroom. The friend of the bridegroom, who stands and hears him, rejoices greatly at the bridegroom's voice. For this reason my joy has been fulfilled. He must increase, but I must decrease.

Example #3: The two following passages have parallel themes, structure and words. Each passage starts by describing a surprising visit by an angel (first paragraph), and then continues with instruction as to what name is to be given to the baby being announced (second paragraph).

Passage A, paragraph 1: Now at the time of the incense offering, the whole assembly of the people was praying outside. Then there appeared to him [Zechariah] an angel of the Lord, standing at the right side of the altar of incense. When Zechariah saw him, he was terrified; and fear overwhelmed him.

Passage A, paragraph 2: But the angel said to him, "Do not be afraid, Zechariah, for your prayer has been heard. Your wife Elizabeth will bear you a son, and you will name him John. You will have joy and gladness, and many will rejoice at his birth, for he will be great in the sight of the Lord."

Passage B, paragraph 1: In the sixth month the angel Gabriel was sent by God to a town in Galilee called Nazareth, to a virgin engaged to a man whose name was Joseph, of the house of David. The virgin's name was Mary. And he came to her and said, "Greetings, favored one! The Lord is with you." But she was much perplexed by his words and pondered what sort of greeting this might be.

Passage B, paragraph 2: The angel said to her, "Do not be afraid, Mary, for you have found favor with God. And now, you will conceive in your womb and bear a son, and you will name him Jesus. He will be great, and will be called the Son of the Most High, and the Lord God will give to him the throne of his ancestor David."

Example #4: The two following passages have parallel themes and structures as each starts with (1) a brief introduction to the setting (being alone), and then is followed by three main points: (2) Jesus is tempted to turn rock into bread/Jesus feeds 5,000; (3) Jesus is tempted with power/Jesus is acknowledged as God's Messiah; and (4) Jesus is tempted to have angels save him from death/Jesus' followers lose their lives to save them.

Passage A, paragraph 1: Jesus, full of the Holy Spirit, returned from the Jordan and was led by the Spirit in the wilderness, where for forty days he was tempted by the devil.

Passage A, paragraph 2: He ate nothing at all during those days, and when they were over, he was famished. The devil said to him, "If you are the Son of God, command this stone to become a loaf of bread." Jesus answered him, "It is written, 'One does not live by bread alone.'"

Passage A, paragraph 3: Then the devil led him up and showed him in an instant all the kingdoms of the world. And the devil said to him, "To you I will give their glory and all this authority; for it has been given over to me, and I give it to anyone I please. If you, then, will worship me, it will all be yours." Jesus answered him, "It is written, 'Worship the Lord your God, and serve only him.'"

Passage A, paragraph 4: Then the devil took him to Jerusalem, and placed him on the pinnacle of the temple, saying to him, "If you are the Son of God, throw yourself down from here, for it is written, 'He will command his angels concerning you, to protect you,' and 'On their hands they will bear you up, so that you will not dash your foot against a stone.'" Jesus answered him, "It is said, 'Do not put the Lord your God to the test.'"

Passage B, paragraph 1: [Jesus took his disciples] with him and withdrew privately to a city called Bethsaida. When the crowds found out about it, they followed him; and he welcomed them, and spoke to them about the kingdom of God, and healed those who needed to be cured.

Passage B, paragraph 2: The day was drawing to a close, and the twelve came to him and said, "Send the crowd away, so that they may go into the surrounding villages and countryside, to lodge and get provisions; for we are here in a deserted place." But he said to them, "You give them something to eat." They said, "We have no more than five loaves and two fish—unless we are to go and buy food for all these people." For there were about five thousand men. And he said to his disciples, "Make them sit down in groups of about fifty each." They did so and made them all sit down. And taking the five loaves and the two fish, he looked up to heaven, and blessed and broke them, and gave them to the disciples to set before the crowd. And all ate and were filled. What was left over was gathered up, twelve baskets of broken pieces.

Passage B, paragraph 3: Once when Jesus was praying alone, with only the disciples near him, he asked them, "Who do the crowds say that I am?" They answered, "John the Baptist; but others, Elijah; and still others, that one of the ancient prophets has arisen." He said to them, "But who do you say that I am?" Peter answered, "The Messiah of God." He sternly ordered and commanded them not to tell anyone, saying, "The Son of Man must undergo great suffering, and be rejected by the elders, chief priests, and scribes, and be killed, and on the third day be raised."

Passage B, paragraph 4: Then he said to them all, "If any want to become my followers, let them deny themselves and take up their cross daily and follow me. For those who want to save their life will lose it, and those who lose their life for my sake will save it. What does it profit them if they gain the whole world, but lose or forfeit themselves? Those who are ashamed of me and of my words, of them the Son of Man will be ashamed when he comes in his glory and the glory of the Father and of the holy angels. But truly I tell you, there are some standing here who will not taste death before they see the kingdom of God."

Appendix B

Usage of *Kurios* in Luke to Describe God and Jesus

Chapter seven examined all the passages in Luke where the word *kurios* refers to a person who is the "master" of an *oikos*. However, this same word *kurios* is translated as "Lord" when Luke uses it to refer to God (34 times) or Jesus (45 times). It turns out that there are some consistent themes that characterize what the word *kurios* refers to when it is used for Jesus and God. Moreover, these themes may have some overlap with the four key groupings of KOG passages described in chapter ten. Overall, the passages point to four modes that *oikos* managers who wish to emulate Jesus and God as *kurios* should attend to:

1. Being prepared and preparing others for KOG;
2. Learning and teaching KOG ways;
3. Implementing countercultural KOG ideas;
4. Facilitating and enjoying KOG outcomes.

References to Jesus as *Kurios*

Consider how these four modes are evident in the 45 mentions of Jesus as *kurios*:

1. Nine mentions describe people preparing the way for Jesus:
    i. With the spirit and power of Elijah he will go before him, to turn the hearts of parents to their children, and the disobedient to the wisdom of the righteous, *to make ready a people prepared for the Lord* (Luke 1:17);
    ii. And you, child, will be called the prophet of the Most High; for *you will go before the Lord to prepare his ways* (Luke 1:76);
    iii as it is written in the book of the words of the prophet Isaiah, "The voice of one crying out in the wilderness: '*Prepare the way of the Lord,* make his paths straight'" (Luke 3:4);
    iv. After this *the Lord appointed seventy others and sent them on ahead of him* in pairs to every town and place where he himself intended to go (Luke 10:1);
    v. He said to them, "The harvest is plentiful, but the laborers are few; therefore ask *the Lord of the harvest to send out laborers into his harvest*" (Luke 10:2);
    vi. If anyone asks you, "Why are you untying it?" just say this, "*The Lord needs it*" (Luke 19:31);
    vii. They said, "*The Lord needs it*" (Luke 19:34);

viii. They said, *"Lord, look, here are two swords."* He replied, "It is enough" (Luke 22:38);

   ix. When those who were around him saw what was coming, they asked, *"Lord, should we strike with the sword?"* (Luke 22:49).

2. Seven mentions describe Jesus as a teacher and counselor:
   i. She had a sister named Mary, who *sat at the Lord's feet and listened* to what he was saying. But Martha was distracted by her many tasks; so she came to him and asked, "Lord, do you not care that my sister has left me to do all the work by myself? Tell her then to help me." But the Lord answered her, "Martha, Martha, you are worried and distracted by many things" (Luke 10:39–41; three mentions);

   ii. He was praying in a certain place, and after he had finished, one of his disciples said to him, *"Lord, teach us to pray,* as John taught his disciples" (Luke 11:1);

   iii. Peter said, "Lord, are you telling this parable for us or for everyone?" (Luke 12:41);

   iv. Then *they asked him, "Where, Lord?"* He said to them, "Where the corpse is, there the vultures will gather" (Luke 17:37);

   v. And *the Lord said, "Listen* to what the unjust judge says" (Luke 18:6).

3. Twelve mentions describe how following Jesus means acting in countercultural ways:
   i. *Why do you call me "Lord, Lord," and do not do what I tell you?* (Luke 6:46; two mentions);

   ii. To another he said, *"Follow me."* But he said, "Lord, first let me [follow convention and] go and bury my father" (Luke 9:59);

   iii. Another said, *"I will follow you,* Lord; but let me first [follow convention and] say farewell to those at my home" (Luke 9:61);

   iv. Then *the Lord said* to him, "Now you Pharisees clean the outside of the cup and of the dish, but *inside you are full of greed and wickedness"* (Luke 11:39);

   v. And the Lord said, "Who then is *the faithful and prudent manager* whom his master will put in charge of his slaves, to give them their allowance of food at the proper time?" (Luke 12:42).

   vi. But the *Lord answered him and said, "You hypocrites!* Does not each of you on the sabbath untie his ox or his donkey from the manger, and lead it away to give it water?" (Luke 13:15);

   vii. Zacchaeus stood there and said to the Lord, *"Look, half of my possessions, Lord, I will give to the poor;* and if I have defrauded anyone of anything, I will pay back four times as much" (Luke 19:8; two mentions);

   viii. And he said to him, *"Lord, I am ready to go with you to prison and to death!"* (Luke 22:33);

   ix. The Lord turned and looked at Peter. Then Peter remembered the word of the Lord, how he had said to him, "Before the cock crows today, *you will deny me three times"* (Luke 22:61; two mentions);

4. The remaining 18 mentions describe Jesus as powerful, holy savior or benefactor.
   i. And why has this happened to me, that the mother of *my Lord* comes to me? (Luke 1:43);

   ii. to you is born this day in the city of David *a Savior, who is the Messiah, the Lord* (Luke 2:11);

   iii. But when Simon Peter saw it, he fell down at Jesus' knees, saying, *"Go away from me, Lord, for I am a sinful man!"* (Luke 5:8);

iv. Once, when he was in one of the cities, there was a man covered with leprosy. When he saw Jesus, he bowed with his face to the ground and begged him, *"Lord, if you choose, you can make me clean"* (Luke 5:12);

v. Then he said to them, "The Son of Man is *lord of the sabbath"* (Luke 6:5);

vi. And Jesus went with them, but when he was not far from the house, the centurion sent friends to say to him, *"Lord, do not trouble yourself, for I am not worthy* to have you come under my roof" (Luke 7:6);

vii. When *the Lord* saw her, he had compassion for her and said to her, "Do not weep" [Jesus *raises her son from the dead*] (Luke 7:13);

viii. and sent them to the Lord to ask, *"Are you the one who is to come,* or are we to wait for another?" (Luke 7:19);

ix. When his disciples James and John saw it, they said, *"Lord, do you want us to command fire to come down from heaven* and consume them?" (Luke 9:54);

x. The seventy returned with joy, saying, *"Lord, in your name even the demons submit to us!"* (Luke 10:17);

xi. Someone asked him, *"Lord, will only a few be saved?"* He said to them (Luke 13:23);

xii. The apostles said to the *Lord, "Increase our faith!"* (Luke 17:5);

xiii. *The Lord replied, "If you had faith the size of a mustard seed,* you could say to this mulberry tree, 'Be uprooted and planted in the sea,' and it would obey you" (Luke 17:6);

xiv. "What do you want me to do for you?" He said, *"Lord, let me see again"* (Luke 18:41);

xv. For David himself says in the book of Psalms, "The Lord said to my Lord, *'Sit at my right hand'"* (Luke 20:42; one mention);

xvi. *David thus calls him Lord;* "so how can he be his son?" (Luke 20:44);

xvii. but when they went in, they *did not find the [Lord's] body* (Luke 24:3);

xviii. They were saying, *"The Lord has risen indeed,* and he has appeared to Simon!" (Luke 24:34).

REFERENCES TO GOD AS *KURIOS*

Consider how these four modes referred earlier are also evident in the 34 mentions of God as *kurios*:

1. Ten mentions refer to God preparing the way for Jesus and his message:

i. Then there appeared to him an angel of the Lord, standing at the right side of the altar of incense [*God prepares the father of John*] (Luke 1:11);

ii. This is *what the Lord has done for me* when he looked favorably on me and took away the disgrace I have endured among my people [God prepares the mother of John] (Luke 1:25);

iii. And he came to her and said, "Greetings, favored one! The Lord is with you" [*God prepares the mother of Jesus*] (Luke 1:28);

iv. He will be great, and will be called the Son of the Most High, and *the Lord God will give to him the throne* of his ancestor David (Luke 1:32);

v. All who heard them pondered them and said, "What then will this child become?" For, indeed, *the hand of the Lord was with him* [God prepares John] (Luke 1:66);

vi. Blessed be the Lord God of Israel, for *he has looked favorably on his people* and redeemed them [God prepares Israel] (Luke 1:68);

vii. Then an angel of *the Lord stood before them*, and the glory of the Lord shone around them, and they were terrified [God prepares shepherds] (Luke 2:9; two mentions);

viii. When the angels had left them and gone into heaven, the shepherds said to one another, "Let us go now to Bethlehem and see this thing that has taken place, which *the Lord has made known to us*" (Luke 2:15);

ix. *It had been revealed to him* by the Holy Spirit that he would not see death before he had seen the Lord's Messiah [Simeon was prepared] (Luke 2:26).

2. Ten mentions refer to receiving God's law and instruction:
   i. Both of them were righteous before God, *living blamelessly according to all the commandments and regulations of the Lord* (Luke 1:6);

   ii. he was chosen by lot, *according to the custom of the priesthood*, to enter the sanctuary of the Lord and offer incense (Luke 1:9);

   iii. for he will be great in the sight of the Lord. *He must never* drink wine or strong drink; even before his birth he will be filled with the Holy Spirit (Luke 1:15);

   iv. When the time came for their purification *according to the law of Moses*, they brought him up to Jerusalem to present him to the Lord (Luke 2:22);

   v. (*as it is written in the law of the Lord*, "Every firstborn male shall be designated as holy to the Lord") (Luke 2:23; two mentions);

   vi. and they offered a sacrifice according to what is stated in *the law of the Lord*, "a pair of turtle-doves or two young pigeons" (Luke 2:24);

   vii. When they had finished everything required by *the law of the Lord*, they returned to Galilee, to their own town of Nazareth (Luke 2:39);

   viii. Jesus answered him, "It is said, '*Do not put the Lord your God to the test*'" (Luke 4:12);

   ix. He answered, "*You shall love the Lord your God with all your heart, and with all your soul, and with all your strength, and with all your mind; and your neighbor as yourself*" (Luke 10:27).

3. Nine mentions refer to responding to God (often with countercultural actions):
   i. He will *turn many of the people of Israel to the Lord their God* [away from their conventional ways] (Luke 1:16);

   ii. Then Mary said, "*Here am I, the servant of the Lord; let it be with me according to your word.*" [Mary accepts the countercultural news that she is pregnant with the Son of God]. Then the angel departed from her (Luke 1:38);

   iii. "And blessed is she who believed that there would be a fulfillment of what was spoken to her by the Lord." And Mary said, "*My soul magnifies the Lord*" [Mary's acceptance that she is pregnant]. (Luke 1:45 and 46; two mentions);

   iv. Jesus answered him, "It is written, '*Worship the Lord your God, and serve only him*' [rather than seek authority and glory on this earth]" (Luke 4:8);

   vi. At that same hour Jesus rejoiced in the Holy Spirit and said, "*I thank you, Father, Lord of heaven and earth, because you have hidden these things from the wise and the intelligent [according to the conventional ways of this world] and have revealed them to infants; yes, Father, for such was your gracious will*" (Luke 10:21);

   vi. See, your [conventional] house is left to you. And I tell you, you will not see me until the time comes when you say, "*Blessed is the one who comes in the name of the Lord*" (Luke 13:35);

   vii. saying, "*Blessed is the king* who comes in the name of the Lord! Peace in heaven, and glory in the highest heaven!" [conventional leaders did not like this response to Jesus' entry to Jerusalem] (Luke 19:38);

viii. For David himself says in the book of Psalms, "The Lord said to my Lord, '*Sit at my right hand*'" (Luke 20:42; one mention).

4. The remaining five mentions refer to God's benevolence to humankind:

   i. Her neighbors and relatives heard that *the Lord had shown his great mercy to her,* and they rejoiced with her (Luke 1:58);

   ii. The Spirit of the Lord is upon me, because *he has anointed me to bring good news* to the poor. He has sent me to proclaim release to the captives and recovery of sight to the blind, to let the oppressed go free, to proclaim the year of the Lord's favor (Luke 4:18–19);

   iii. One day, while he was teaching, Pharisees and teachers of the law were sitting near by (they had come from every village of Galilee and Judea and from Jerusalem); and *the power of the Lord was with him to heal* (Luke 5:17);

   iv. And the fact that *the dead are raised* Moses himself showed, in the story about the bush, where he speaks of the Lord as the God of Abraham, the God of Isaac, and the God of Jacob (Luke 20:37).

SUMMARY

As described in greater length in the leadership model presented in chapter sixteen, the implications for managers seeking to emulate the kind of *kurios* associated with Jesus and God include

1. being prepared and preparing others for signs of the KOG;
2. learning and teaching KOG principles;
3. implementing countercultural KOG ideas; and
4. facilitating and enjoying KOG outcomes.

NOTES

I INTRODUCTION

1. About 2 billion people, or one-third of the world's population, consider themselves to be Christian, and there seems to be considerable interest in what Jesus might have to say about management (Adherents, 2007). For example, Jesus is ranked third in Hart's (1992) list of most influential people in history, and is listed in Pollard's (1997) *100 Greatest Men*. The scriptures associated with Christianity also seem to be of some interest. It is estimated that at least 2.5 billion Bibles have been sold (Terego & Denim, 2006: 146), and the total number in print increases to up to 6 billion if all the free copies that have been distributed are included. In second place are the *Qu'ran* and the Quotations from Chairman Mao (*The Little Red Book*) each at about 800 million copies (Greise, 2010). By way of comparison, sales of the Harry Potter series have been estimated at over 500 million copies.

2. See Frey (1998), Golembiewski (1989), Herman (1997), Hershberger (1958), Jackall (1988), Jones (1997), Nash (1994), Naughton and Bausch (1994), Novak (1996), Pattison (1997), Pfeffer (1982), and Redekop, Ainlay, and Siemens (1995). *The Protestant Ethic and the Spirit of Capitalism* was first published in 1903 (Weber, 1958). Max Weber (1864–1920) is considered to be one of the principal architects of the modern social sciences, along with Karl Marx (1818–1883) and Emile Durkheim (1858–1917). In addition to being the father of organization theory, Weber's work has been rated as the most important in total and for Organizational Behavior in particular (Miner, 2003), and he continues to be recognized as one of the leading moral philosophers of management (Clegg, 1996). It is not surprising then that Weber continues to be among the most highly cited scholars in management journals, being mentioned in 15 percent of all articles published in two top journals (*Administrative Science Quarterly* and *Organization Studies*) between 1980 and 2002 (Lounsbury & Carberry, 2005: 508). In comparison, the most-cited *active* author between 1981 and 2002 (Kathleen Eisenhardt) in 30 leading management journals is cited 3,628 times in 26,209 articles (if these cites were distributed so that there was no more than one cite in each article, then Eisenhardt's work would be cited in 13.8 percent of these articles) (Podsakoff et al. 2008: 655, 682).

3. Weber (1958: 182). The secularized materialistic-individualistic ethic that underpins modern management is thoroughly engrained in "the modern economic order" and has an "irresistible force" that determines the lives of *everyone* born into it (i.e., "not only those directly concerned with economic acquisition"): "Perhaps it will so determine them until the last ton of fossilized coal is burnt" (181–182).

4. For example, Weber (1958) notes that the "individualistic" and "acquisitive manner of life" associated with the modern economic order has been so thoroughly secularized that "it no longer needs the support of any religious forces, and feels the attempts of religion to influence economic life [to be] an unjustified interference" (72; see also 83, 182, 240; cf. Dyck & Schroeder, 2005).

5. For example, a content analysis of the first ten decades of articles in the *Journal of Biblical Integration of Business* found that the dominant overarching theme among the

most-frequently cited biblical passage was "the contrast between the ways of God and the ways of the world" (Dyck & Starke, 2005). Similarly, as we will see in chapter ten, references to biblical ideas such as "the kingdom of God" in secular scholarly management journals are almost always countercultural to the dominant contemporary paradigm (see also Dyck, forthcoming).

6. The past decade has seen a "remarkable growth rate" for sales of books in the religious market generally (Elinsky, 2005: 11; in the United States self-proclaimed evangelical Christians account for over 40 percent of overall religious sales, Catholics 17 percent, and Christian/Protestants 14 percent), and in the growing number of books integrating faith and business issues in the popular press. Overall, sales in the Christian retail industry have grown from $3 billion in 1996 to $4 billion in 2002 and were expected to be about $9.5 billion in 2010, according to Hirdes, Woods, and Badzinski (2009). Similar interest is also evident within the academic community, where this millennium has seen the development of the "Management, Spirituality and Religion" interest group within the Academy of Management (the world's largest and most respected secular scholarly management association) and the launch of a number of related journals such as: *Journal of Religious Leadership* (started in 2002), *Journal of Management, Spirituality and Religion* (started in 2004), *Journal of Biblical Perspectives in Leadership* (started in 2006), *Journal of Religion and Business Ethics* (started in 2010), *Journal of Islamic Accounting and Business Research* (started in 2010). Finally, there is a host of excellent work that has been written at the intersection of faith and business, though none of it is as thoroughly grounded in a first-century understanding of management as presented in this book, including: Alford and Naughton (2001), Bakke (2005), Delbeq (2005), Dodd and Gotsis (2009), Miller (2007), Mitroff and Denton (1999), Sandelands (2010), van Duzer (2010), Volf (2001), Wood (1991), and Zigarelli (2002). For some interesting research looking at modern-day organizations as secular religions, see Ashforth and Vaidyanath (2002).

1   OVERVIEW OF THIS BOOK

1. These variations are interchangeable for present purposes.

2. Similarly, the word "management" can be traced back to the French word for "house" related to the English word "manor."

3. As will be elaborated in chapter five, modern commentators speculate that perhaps the rich man felt outsmarted by the manager, and grudgingly conceded that the manager had beat the rich man at his own "game." Or, perhaps Jesus praised the manager not for unilaterally scattering the rich man's wealth, but rather for being shrewd; Jesus would like it if everyone was shrewd for Godly purposes like this manager was shrewd for his self-serving purposes. However, if Jesus had wanted to make this point, surely he could have done so in a less awkward manner.

4. For example, this is unlike Bruce Barton's *The Man Nobody Knows* (1925), where Jesus is described as "the founder of modern business" (159), and which has been called the second most-read life of Jesus ever written in the United States, with two hundred and fifty thousand copies sold in 1925 and 1926 alone. The book even resulted in a silent movie of the same title (Elzey, 1978). This is also unlike Laurie Beth Jones's (1995) best seller *Jesus CEO*, which presents Jesus as a "'CEO' who took a disorganized 'staff' of twelve and built a thriving enterprise" (Jones, 1995: back cover).

2   A SHORT INTRODUCTION TO THE GOSPEL OF LUKE

1. Weber (1958: 182).

2. Actually, I had initially intended to focus my study on the material that is found in the so-called Q source, which predates and is consistent with the Gospels. I changed my

mind after talking to John Kloppenborg, perhaps the world's leading authority on Q, who listened to my project and encouraged me to study the Gospel of Luke instead. That was obviously excellent advice, and I am thankful for it.

3. Luke is commonly accepted to be the author of both Luke and Acts, making him the most prolific author in the New Testament (see Achtemeier, Green, & Thompson, 2001: 269). According to the "Analytical Greek New Testament" there are 19,482 words in the Gospel of Luke, and 18,451 words in Acts, which are the two longest books in the New Testament and together account for 27.5 percent of the entire New Testament (138,020 words in Greek; 180,552 words in English KJV) (Just, 2005). By way of comparison, altogether the 66 books of the Bible have 783,137 words (KJV), which is the equivalent to about 72 percent of the entire seven-book "Harry Potter" series (1,084,170 words). This book, *Management and the Gospel*, has about 150,000 words.

4. For example, Fitzmyer (1970, 1985) and Green (1997).

5. For example, no other New Testament writer "speaks out as emphatically as does Luke about the Christian disciple's use of material possessions wealth, and money" (Fitzmyer, 1970: 247). Luke is well-known for placing relatively high emphasis on issues related to economic and social justice. For research like that being described in this book it makes sense to choose the Gospel where the phenomenon under investigation is most "transparently observable" (Pettigrew, 1989).

6. The word *kurios* is applied to God or Jesus 75 percent of the time (for an analysis of these verses, see appendix B). Of the total of 240 mentions of *kurios* in all four Gospels, 94 (39 percent) are found in Luke, 78 in Matthew, 17 in Mark, and 51 in John.

7. This is not meant to be an exhaustive analysis of all words related to management in Luke or the other three Gospels. Rather, this is more of a first round of analysis using some of the most frequently mentioned words that have some face validity as being related to management. A similar word count using English words in the New Revised Standard Version (NRSV) translation yielded a similar result. Of the 90 mentions of the following words in all four gospels, 43 (48 percent) appeared in Luke: manage/r/ment, owner (of a house), steward, leader/s/ship, lord (did not count references to God/Jesus), and master (did not count references to God/Jesus). These analyses were performed using Accordance software, which was also used to do similar analyses in other parts of the book.

8. Of the remaining mentions of "*oikos/oikian*" in the other three Gospels, 36 appeared in Matthew, 31 in Mark, and 10 in John. Of the 133 total mentions of "house" in the NRSV translation of the four Gospels, 54 (41 percent) occur in Luke, 41 in Matthew, 29 in Mark, and 9 in John. The present study will follow the common practice of using the two terms *oikos* and *oikian* interchangeably (Trainor, 2001: 8).

9. In the first century these assets would belong to an *oikos*, generally not to its individual members.

10. Again, the frequencies for a rough and ready list of Greek words are similar, with Luke accounting for 50 of 107 (47 percent) of relevant variations of the following words in all four Gospels: *arguria/on/os,chruson, denarius, drachme, huparchonta, leptos, mamonas, mina, ousia, ploutou/ton/siois/sious, stater, talenton*.

11. See Bock (2006: 10–12); others suggest that as little as 35 percent of Luke's content is unique to Luke. Of the four subsections within Luke described later in this chapter, its third subsection (Luke 9:51–19:40, the so-called Journey Narrative) contains a relatively high proportion of material unique to Luke (49 percent), including 15 of its 17 parables (Bock, 2006: 23).

12. Bock (2006: 13); cf. Fitzmyer (1970: 14).

13. Bock (2006: 13).

14. Johnson (1991: 4).

15. Fitzmyer (1970: 15). All ancient historians had a motive, and Luke is no different in that his writing is concerned more with the signification of events than with their validation (Green, 1997: 3, 20). Other points in this discussion are found in Bock (2006: 6, 16), Bovon (2002: 3, 9), Fitzmyer (1970), and Green (1997: 7, 21).

16. Information and quotes in this paragraph are from Bovon (2002: 3, 4; emphasis in original).

17. As an explanation for readers who may find it odd that the four main sections of Luke do not correspond to the chapters and verses that are conventionally used to divide the Gospel into its smaller parts (e.g., why isn't Luke simply divided into four main chapters, possibly with subsections in each chapter?), note that these chapter and verse designations were not included in any of the original biblical texts—they were added in the Middle Ages.

18. See Bovon (2002: 2–3); Bock (2006: 20ff).

19. For example, Luke 1:5; 2:1.

20. Luke 2:11, 30.

21. John the Baptist quotes the Old Testament prophet Isaiah (Luke 3:6).

22. Note that Jesus' temptations are not unlike those facing contemporary managers, namely, for authority of all the kingdoms of the world (a counterfeit version of the "creation mandate" described in Genesis 1 to have dominion over the world), taking unnecessary/self-ish risks with the understanding that God will protect, and breaking natural laws to take care of one's personal needs (counters the "creation mandates" to nurture community, care for the environment, and seek meaningful work).

23. Jesus grew up in the small Galilean village of Nazareth (population of about two hundred), about three miles from its capital city Sepphoris (population of about eight thousand). Galilee is a province about a two-day walk north of Jerusalem. Jesus carried out most of his early ministry on the eastern side of Galilee (Capernaum, Sea of Galilee).

24. Buehler (1998: 26). Note that Luke also provides four parallel woes.

25. Of Luke's 97 mentions of the following Greek words, 71 appear in Luke 9:51–19:40 (73 percent): *oikonomia/os* (manager), *oiko/despote/s* (owner of house), *epitropos* (steward), *epistates* (chief, master), *kurios* (not God/Jesus), *mamonas* (wealth), *huparchonta* (possessions), *ousia* (property), *ploutou/ton/siois/sious* (rich), *argurion* (money), and *drachme, leptos, mina, denarius* (coinage). Similarly, of the 96 mentions of the following words in the NRSV translation of Luke, 72 appear in Luke 9:51–19:40 (75 percent): manage/r/ment, owner (of a house), steward, leader/s/ship, master (not God/Jesus), lord (not including God/Jesus), wealth/y, possess/ions, goods, property, rich/es, money, coin/s, pound/s, and denarius/i.

26. Fitzmyer (1970); cf. van Duzer (2010). Note that some are questioning this four-phase framework, arguing that it is more influenced by Greco-Roman ideas than by biblical ideas (McLaren, 2010; Spangenberg, 2007).

27. For more information on how these three are related to management theory and practice, see Dyck and Schroeder (2005).

28. Genesis 1:28b; note that to "have dominion" is clearly different than "to dominate." Note also that this mandate includes care for creation (Gen. 1:29–30).

29. For example, this is evident in how humankind is to "name" creation (Gen. 2:15,19–20a).

30. Genesis 1:27,28a; 2:18,20b–24.

31. "And the Lord commanded the man: 'You may freely eat of every tree of this garden; but of the tree of the knowledge of good and evil you shall not eat, for in the day that you eat of it you shall die'" (Gen. 2:16–17).

32. Genesis 3:15.

33. Genesis 3:17–19. Note that when the serpent and ground are said to be "cursed" (Gen. 3:14,17), it means "to be excluded from community" (Kessler & Deurloo, 2004: 54).

34. Genesis 3:16b.

35. Which can subdivided into the three parts as identified earlier (i.e., Jesus' ministry in Galilee, Jesus' journey to Jerusalem, and Jesus' death/resurrection/ascension in Jerusalem). Note also that others start the "Period of Jesus" as early as Luke 3:1 or 3:2 (Fitzmyer, 1970: 185).

3   MANAGERS, GOODS AND SERVICES PRODUCING ORGANIZATIONS, AND FIRST-CENTURY PALESTINE

1. Much of the historical background of first-century management found in this chapter is drawn from Dyck, Starke, and Weimer (2012), which provides a detailed analysis of whether Weber's (1958) description of the Protestant ethic is plausibly consistent with the biblical ethic understood in its first-century context.

2. Neyrey (2008a: xxiii). Drakopoulou Dodd and Gotsis (2009: 101) call this the "reading back" problem, a phenomenon that arises when the purported meaning of a text is influenced by the assumptions built into the contemporary lens that is used to interpret it (but when those contemporary assumptions are inconsistent with the assumptions held when the text was originally written). This "reading back" problem is called *eisegesis*, and stands in contrast with the more familiar term in biblical interpretation called *exegesis*, which refers to interpreting a text in its context or by drawing upon known views of the author.

3. Rapinchuk (2004: 98).

4. Manz (1999: 75).

5. Winston (1999: 37).

6. "Even to gesture with the left hand at Qumran carried the penalty of ten days' penance" (Wink, 1992: 176). The analysis in this section of the "turn the cheek," "give your undergarment," and "go the second mile" passages draws heavily from Wink (1992).

7. Wink (1992: 176, 177) states: "A backhand slap was the usual way of admonishing inferiors . . . [If a man] hits with a fist, he makes the other his equal, acknowledging him as a peer. But the point of the back of hand is to reinforce institutionalized inequality . . . [Thus 'turning the other' cheek is not unlike what] Gandhi taught, 'The first principle of nonviolent action is that of noncooperation with everything humiliating.'"

8. Ibid., 177.

9. For example, see Lantos (2002: 43) and Porter (1999: 29).

10. Wink (1992: 179).

11. For a third teaching along these same lines, consider the subsequent verse in Matthew 5:41, where Jesus tells readers to go a second mile if anyone forces them to go one mile. Here Jesus' listeners would have known that he was talking about the right of a Roman soldier to force civilians to carry the soldier's backpack for one mile, but not further. This was considered onerous and oppressive, as the backpacks were heavy (60–85 pounds, plus the weight of weapons). Imagine the soldier's confusion if *the civilian took charge* by deciding to carry the backpack a second mile. Is the civilian insulting the soldier's strength? Will the civilian file a complaint with Roman authorities that he carried the backpack for more than a mile? "Imagine the situation of a Roman infantryman pleading with a Jew to give back his pack! The humor of the scene may have escaped us, but it could scarcely have been lost on Jesus' hearers, who must have regaled at the prospect of thus discomfiting their oppressors" (ibid., 182).

12. One reason that we lack a comprehensive analysis of management in first-century Palestine is because the contemporary idea of "management" would have been foreign to its inhabitants. Even so, historians studying that era have called for contemporary scholars to use the lens of contemporary management theory and practice to examine what was going on in that era: "It is only with such a change in perspective that modern scholars can expect to be able to reconstruct the history of ancient business management. Historical discourse should not be reluctant to use the modern concepts and criteria to formulate the theoretical basis for the study of a range of activities that clearly fall outside the sphere of interest of ancient writers" (Aubert, 2001: 18–19; cf. Aubert, 1994).

13. Goldsmith (1984).

14. Ibid., 22; see also Svyantek (1999).

15. George (1968: 11). Osai et al. (2009) recognize Moses's father-in-law and advisor, Jethro, as the "patriarch of management" and ascribe to him many of the core ideas subsequently associated with Max Weber ("father of bureaucracy"), Henri Fayol ("father of modern management"), Frederick Taylor ("father of scientific management"), and Robert Owen ("father of personnel management").

16. Crossan (2007: 100).

17. It is interesting to note that the etymology of the word hierarchy points to its religious beginnings: *hiereus* = priest, and *hieros* = what is holy, and *arkhe* = rule, hence priestly or sacred rule (Hopfl, 2000: 315).

18. Malina and Rohrbaugh (2003: 391).

19. van Eck (2007: 913).

20. Judge (1960: 30).

21. Terms such as stewards, retainers, scribes, and accountants are relatively interchangeable for our purposes (see Dyck, Starke, & Weimer, 2012: 160).

22. For interested readers, Dyck, Starke, & Weimer (2012) provide more detailed discussions of the interplay between the various roles identified in figure 3.1.

23. Gotsis and Drakopoulou Dodd (2004), and Osiek and Balch (1997).

24. Elliott (1981: 173, 174).

25. Lambert (2009: 21).

26. See Finley (1973: 17–21), cited in Moxnes (1997: 20). "As is well known there is no term in Greek for what, in modern Western languages, is referred to as 'the family,' that is, the nuclear family of husband, wife and children" (Nagle, 2006: 15). The Latin word *familia* has a different meaning compared to the contemporary word family. In Columella (I,V,7) *res familiaris* means the *villa* as a property. Gardner and Wiedemann (1991: 3–4) provide four different meanings for *familia*: (1) property; (2) "a certain body of persons, defined either by a strict legal bond . . . or in a general sense of people joined by a looser relationship of kinship"; (3) slaves; and (4) "several persons who all descend by blood from a single remembered source." *Familia* therefore has the meaning of first-century "household" and not of a contemporary "family" (Destro & Pesce, 2003: 211–212).

27. "The family was a rich social concept that vertically included ancestors and horizontally included the extended family, even though not living together; unrelated persons such as slaves and freedpersons attached by legal bonds; and even the property and assets of the household" (Osiek & Balch, 1997: 216).

28. Balch (1981), Hanson (1989), Judge (1960), Osiek and Balch (1997: 216). Based on Nagle's (2006: 312) calculations, a typical complete *oikos* in an ideal state would have managed land about 12 hectares (30 acres) in size, and have been comprised of parents, children, and one or two slaves.

29. Judge (1960: 32); Drakopoulou Dodd and Gostsis (2009: 102).

30. Herzog (1994).

31. Nagle (2006).

32. And this would counteract the tendency to move even further from its first-century meaning evident when contemporary biblical translations increasingly translate *oikos* as "home." Perhaps the most appropriate way to translate *oikos* is as a "company," because a company literally refers to a place where people come together to eat (from the Latin word *companio*, which means "one who eats bread with you"; *cum* means "with"; and *panis* means "bread") (see Hopfl, 2000: 316). Early Christians practiced life in companies that differed significantly from conventional first-century *oikoi* (Stevens, 2006: 61).

33. Nagle (2006: 2).

34. The term *oikos* or *oikia* appears over 1,860 times in the LXX (i.e., the LXX basically refers to the Greek translation of the Old Testament) (Elliott, 1981: 182).

35. Of the 57 mentions of *oikoi* (*oikos, oiko, oikia*) in Luke, there are at least 25 distinct first-century households mentioned. Note that some of these *oikoi* are referred to more than once (e.g., Zechariah), and about half of the mentions refer to the *oikos* of David or Jacob or God.

36. In 39 of these 64 allusions to an *oikos*, a good or service being produced by the household is identified. The number would be higher if repeated mentions of the same household were recorded.

37. This is consistent with Aaron Kuecker's (2010) observation that Luke is stock full of references to people in their places of work. For example, the opening scene of Luke describes the Spirit talking to Zechariah as he performs his priestly duties at the temple in Jerusalem.

38. For more on this, see Dyck, Starke, & Weimer (2012).

39. Nagle, 2006.

40. Malina and Rohrbaugh (2003: 414; emphasis added here).

41. Such "expendables" could represent up to 15 percent of the population, and its members typically died within 5–7 years after joining: "As the elites squeezed the dwindling resources of their peasant base, they forced households to exile their children into the most degrading and lethal forms of poverty" (Herzog, 1994: 66).

42. Quotes in this paragraph are taken from Meeks (1989: 95, 116, 93; emphasis added here). The reference to strangers/foreigners is taken from Elliott (1981: 24).

43. Quotes in this paragraph taken from Elliott (1981: 188, 192, 194, 197; emphasis added here).

II Problem Recognition

1. This implies that first-century Judeo-Christian teachings about management are not consistent with those that Weber associated with what he called the Protestant ethic (Dyck, Starke, & Weimer, 2012). There could be a number of explanations for this apparent disconnect between the Judeo-Christian ethic of the first century and the Protestant ethic. First, the Protestant founders, no matter how sincere, simply misunderstood the biblical teachings. Perhaps they did not have access to adequate knowledge of first-century sociopolitical and economic norms, and thus were unable to properly interpret the biblical writings in their original context. Second, perhaps Weber got it wrong, and his rendition of the Protestant ethic does not accurately reflect the teachings of the Protestant founders. Indeed, Weber has been criticized on this basis. Third, perhaps the popularized and subsequently secularized understanding of the Protestant ethic transformed it in such a way as to be inconsistent with first-century Judeo-Christian writings. For example, by taking specific hallmarks of the Protestant ethic out of their larger context, it would skew and eventually change the larger understanding of Christianity. Or perhaps the explanation involves all three of these factors. While a further analysis of these factors may be valuable, that is not our present task, which is to analyze what the Gospel of Luke says about management, as interpreted through a first-century understanding of management.

2. Tucker (1987: 44); see also Moxnes (1988: 56, 62) and Oakman (1986).

3. Burrell (1999: 397); see also Morgan (1988).

4. Metzger (2007: 15).

5. For example, see Herzog (1994: 13) and Julicher (1910, original 1898, 1899).

4 A Three-Dimensional First-Century Lens for Understanding Management

1. This is consistent with the following observations from Goodrich (2010).

   As Aristotle [384–322 BCE] explains, "[A]ll people rich enough to be able to avoid personal trouble have a steward who takes this office.". . . But though absentee landownership during the fourth century BCE was perhaps a rare privilege even among the rich, by about the second century BCE it had become commonplace among the landed elite to entrust the responsibilities of business administration to various kinds of delegates (82).

Although [*oikonomos*] originally referred to a free proprietor of an estate, over time the title and the responsibilities of estate and business management came to be identified almost exclusively with slaves and freedmen. Administrators, therefore, were typically the subordinates of wealthy masters/patrons, although administrators themselves were normally located in positions of authority as well. Granted the responsibility of running an enterprise, private administrators were charged with making steady—though not excessive—profits for the proprietor and with directing a group of subordinate labourers to achieve that end. Administrators were often authorised to enter into contract negotiations with potential third contracting parties. Both to their slave staffs as well as to third parties, then, administrators acted as representatives of their principals and were entrusted with the right to act for them as such. Administrators, however, were generally not liable for their contracts. Rather, when formally authorised, the principal was normally held responsible for all commercial dealings, as long as the agent acted within the scope of his commission (116).

2. A Seneca put it: "He who entrusts the care of his patrimony to one who has been condemned for the bad management of his affairs will be considered a poor head of a household" (cited in Baergen, 2006: 33). Thus to accuse a manager of incompetence is more an accusation against the householder than against the manager. After awhile the term *oikonomia* became increasingly generic. It expanded from describing (1) the work of a householder (initial meaning), to (2) the work of a king, a lord, or a mere administrator (i.e., the work of managing was deemed the same, and was not differentiated based on the manager's position in the *oikos*), to (3) how the whole world was managed as a house, and to (4) how the human body or natural world were organized/managed (Richter, 2005: 7, 13). It was also used to describe the *oikonomia* of salvation.

3. Nagle (2006). Subsequent notable Roman writings about *oikonomia* are provided by Cato the Elder (second century BCE), Varro (first century BCE) and Columella (first century C.E.) (Aubert, 2001). These writings mostly extended Aristotle's views about management (especially as larger *oikoi* become more prevalent): "The most striking features of their descriptions are the stress they put on division of labour, and the existence of a rather sophisticated chain of command, from individual workers, skilled or not, to foremen, overseers, supervisors, administrators, and landowners" (8).

4. Readers familiar with the New Testament will note that these three components are also evident in the "Rules of How to Manage a Household"—often called *Haustafeln*—found in biblical writings such as Colossians 3:18–4:1; Ephesians 5:21–6:9; I Peter 2:13–3:7 (see Balch, 1981; Schroeder, 1959; Yoder, 1972: 164ff).

5. Aristotle (2007: Book 1, VII); "Again, the male is by nature superior, and the female inferior; and the one rules, and the other is ruled; this principle, of necessity, extends to all mankind" (Book 1, V).

6. Nagle (2006).

7. Neyrey and Stewart (2008a: 163).

8. Landry and May (2000: 299).

9. Aristotle (2007: Book 1, XII).

10. Honor was ascribed (especially via familial lineage) and could be acquired (through acts of benefaction). "Being born into an honorable family makes one honorable, since the family is the repository of the honor of past illustrious ancestors and their accumulated honor" (Malina & Neyrey, 1991a: 28). When people were described as "the child of so-and-so" it was to give an indication of how much honor that child has. The good name of a family signaled the amount of honor held by its members, and influenced which other households would deal with them. To disobey one's parent was to dishonor or shame him or her (33, 26).

11. Bowen (1978) cited on page 73 of Malina and Neyrey (1991b). They go on to say that our twenty-first-century understanding of "[i]ndividualism was and still is a way of being a person totally alien to the scenarios of the first-century Mediterranean world" (72).

12. Westermann (1955: 15). Note also that "[t]he Mishnah explains that a slave is a property, a thing" (Udoh, 2009: 316).

13. Aristotle (2007).

14. According to Nagle (2006: 105), "Aristotle does not press this argument very strongly" regarding whether slaves have the capacity to form moral concepts.

15. Aristotle (2007: Book 2).

16. Ibid., Book 1, VI; see also Nagle (2006: 133).

17. See pages 107 and 108 in Finley (1973). This general principle also helps to explain why clients entered into relationships with patrons, because patrons could protect clients "from dispossession, from the harsh laws of the debt, and on the whole from military service" (108).

18. Crespo (2008) based on Aristotle (2007: Book I, Part 8). The discussion in these paragraphs draws from Aristotle (2007), Crespo (2008), and Meikle (1994).

19. The ideas in this paragraph are drawn from Meikle (1994).

20. Aristotle (2007: Book 1, IX; emphasis added here).

21. Ibid., Book 1, X. Modern readers will note the irony that what we today call the "economy" seems less similar to Aristotle's idea of *oikonomia* (from which we get the word "economy"), and more akin to his description of unnatural *chrematistics*. That is, when moderns think about the economy they think almost exclusively about the management of financial wealth, and in particular how to maximize financial wealth. This modern preoccupation is more closely aligned with the idea of *chrematistics* than *oikonomia*, and is exactly what Aristotle warned against. In light of this, I think it would be very helpful if we would consistently add the adjective "financial," or perhaps the adjective "acquisitive," whenever we talk about the contemporary idea of economics, or related ideas such as "value creation." If we were to begin to talk about "*financial* economics" or "*financial* value creation" it would serve as a reminder that there are other forms of well-being beyond financial well-being that are being overlooked (perhaps unintentionally). For example, it might prompt people to think more about "*ecological* economics" or "*spiritual* value creation." This more holistic approach, which recognizes that there are multiple forms of well-being and multiple stakeholders, seems much more consistent with Aristotle's idea of *oikonomia*.

22. Quotes taken from Nagle (2006: 42).

23. Polanyi (1944: 53–54), as cited in Stahel (2006); see also Dierksmeier and Pirson (2009).

24. Dyck and Neubert (2010: 76). Dyck and Neubert go on to add that this idea of "self-interest with guile" is associated with Oliver Williamson's transaction cost theory, and opportunistic self-interest with agency theory, two of the leading schools of economic thought in management. These ideas are discussed again in chapter seventeen.

25. Dyck and Neubert (2010: 87). It also recognizes the inherent value of relationships.

26. Goodrich (2010: 95). Varro "advised the estate owner to seek from his investments both 'profit and pleasure,'" adding that profit was more important than pleasure. Cicero makes the same point, and Columella makes it even more strongly (Goodrich, 2010: 96).

27. Aristotle (2007: Book 1, chapter XI).

28. See Finley (1973) and Herzog (1994).

29. Balch (1981).

30. Malina and Rohrbaugh (2003: 400). Perhaps the ancients weren't that far off on their ideas about a zero-sum economy, given that the fossil fuel energy being used to drive the modern economy is essentially being taken from future generations (who will also have to pay for the clean-up associated with pollution being created today).

31. Thus, for many people: "Profit making and the acquisition of wealth were automatically assumed to be the result of extortion or fraud. The notion of an honest rich man was a first-century oxymoron" (Malina & Rohrbaugh, 2003: 400). Malina and Rohrbaugh quote St. Jerome (347–420), who is best-known for translating the Bible into Latin: 'Every rich person is a thief or the heir of a thief.'"

32. Scholars agree that (1) within-*oikos* relationships, and (2) between-*oikos* patron-client relationships represent "the two principal vertical relationships in society" (Ferguson, 2003: 67–68).

33. Ibid., 254. In first-century Palestine there was no such thing as a bank: if you needed to go into debt, the only source of financing was another person or *oikos*. The resulting patron-client relationship made the client subordinate to the patron, which was

something that Jesus wanted to rectify when he taught followers to forgive their debtors (Luke 11:4). Any time interest was charged, a patron-client relationship was established (cf. Green, 1995: 114–115).

34. Hanson and Oakman (1998: 70–71) and Moxnes (1988: 42). One thing that differentiates Rome from modern bureaucratic societies is that in Rome public figures, from emperors to municipal administrators, were not only *expected* to, but they were *supposed* to use their position to bestow benefits only on their "clients," rather than to bestow them impartially on nonclients (Moxnes, 1991: 245).

35. Bartchy (2008: 167).

36. Neyrey and Stewart (2008b: 85).

37. Neyrey (2008b: 88).

38. For example, see Destro and Pesce (2003) and Neyrey (2005). Marshall (2009) explains that this is the *sociohistorical* conceptualization of "patron-client" relationships. The strict legal definition of *patrocinium* (e.g., between a *patronus* and a *cliens*) is narrower and quite different.

39. For example, the main "benefit"—if that is the correct term—for most people living in the Roman Empire was the positive effect of so-called *pax Romana*. Because everyone was under the control of the center, there was less regional conflict and political upheaval.

40. Neyrey and Stewart (2008c: 47).

41. Hanson and Oakman (1998: 170).

42. "[I]t is clear from the way that Luke tells his story that the position of mediator or broker is of particular importance. Luke employs this role to give a picture of society in which the broker has an important function within the system of social stratification and social relations" (Moxnes, 1991: 254).

43. See Hanson and Oakman (1998: 73). Managers were not restricted to estate management, but were also evident in government, religious institutions, and the military (Herzog, 1994: 57). Because managers played the role of both client (to their patrons, whom they honored) and patron (to the people they managed), they had to act honorably and be trusted by both. This dual patron-client role is evident in many sectors of ancient society. Client-kings were both clients of the emperor and patrons to their subjects. The emperor was a client of the Roman gods and a patron of the entire empire. Jewish high priests were clients of both Jehovah and the emperor, and patrons to other Jews.

44. deSilva (1996: 93) and Kloppenborg (2008).

45. "The language of benefaction shifted in the period of Roman domination of the Greek-speaking world. Greeks attributed the title 'common benefactor' to the Roman emperors, and the meaning of the term benefactor appears to have gradually shifted to acknowledge the inferior/superior notions common to patronage" (Neyrey & Stewart, 2008c: 47).

46. Batten (2008: 51).

47. Landry and May (2000: 308).

48. Aristotle (2006, Book 9, VII). "Aristotle's *Nichomachean Ethics* describes two forms of benefaction in ancient Greece. The first is the noble individual who provides important benefits for the community as a whole, and the second is the one who exchanges goods and services on an individual level with others who are equals, or nearly so, status equal . . . A key attribute of the ideal benefactor, therefore, is her or his lack of self-interest" (Batten, 2004: 260–261).

49. Neyrey (2005: 481).

50. For more on alternative approaches to contemporary management thinking, see chapters sixteen–eighteen.

5   Interpreting Luke's Parable of the Shrewd Manager via a First-Century Lens

The core argument and many of the ideas in this chapter are drawn from Dyck, Starke, and Dueck (2006), who provide a more in-depth analysis of this parable.

1. While both this parable and the parable of the ten pounds (analyzed in the next chapter) refer to a master-slave (or master-servant) relationships, neither of these two parables refers to the other two dimensions of managing relationships within an *oikos* (i.e., husband-wife relations, parent-child relations).

2. Capon (2002: 302) and Herzog (1994: 233); see also Liefeld (1984: 986). Some of the difficulty in interpreting this parable is already evident in the variety of headings that have been used in different Bible translations for it. Most translations agree the central character in the passage is a "manager" (New Revised Standard Version, New International Version, Good News), also called a "steward" (New American Standard Bible, New Jerusalem Bible). However, there is little agreement about which adjective to use to describe the manager. Some translations refer to him as a shady figure, describing him as "dishonest" (NRSV, KJV) and "unrighteous" (NASB). Other translations emphasize his cleverness, describing him as "shrewd" (NIV, Good News) or "crafty" (NJB). For our present purposes he will be called a "shrewd" manager because this adjective seems appropriate when interpreting him from via a twenty-first- as well as a first-century lens (Dyck, Starke, & Dueck, 2006: 116).

3. Similar assumptions were also present in the first century: the agricultural manuals of Catto, Columella, and Varro also warned against self-serving actions of managers who use their access to *oikos* finances for their own purposes (Baergen, 2006: 33).

4. The value of the reduced debt was about 500 *denarii* for each client (one *denarius* is about the same as one day of wage labor).

5. Lockyer (1963).

6. Chewning, Eby, and Roels (1990: 97).

7. The Greek word *diaskorpizon* in Luke 16:1 is translated as "wasting" in three translations of the Bible (NIV, RSV, Good News), "being wasteful" in another (NJB), and as "squandering" in three others (KJV, NASB and NRSV).

8. Matthew 25:24,26 (see also Luke 1:51 and Acts 5:37). The parable of the prodigal son—who is said to waste his inheritance—is the only other place in the New Testament where translators have given the pejorative twist of "wasting" to the word *diaskorpizon* (Landry & May, 2000: 306). For readers who cannot quite bring themselves to accept that the word *diaskorpizon* is better translated as "scattering" in Luke 16:1, consider also that the word translated as "accused of" (*diaballo*) in that same verse hints at the fact that the manager may not have been squandering. The term *diaballo* is often translated as false accusation or slander, which also casts doubt on the meaning of what the manager was doing. This might suggest that the charges being brought against the manager are false. Or, it might simply indicate that the rich man was facing peer pressure from other rich people who had noted that the rich man's *oikos* was not being managed according to conventional acquisitive economic principles. These peers, perhaps jealous of the honor the rich man was enjoying thanks to his sustenance economic manager, would have had some motivation to slander the manager and thereby the larger *oikos*.

   Finally, even if *diaskorpizon* is translated as "squandering," then it results in two back-to-back parables with that word—the parable of the prodigal son (Luke 15:11–32) and what we might call the parable of the prodigal manager (Luke 16:1–13) (Landry & May, 2000: 307). In both parables the prodigal (i.e., wasteful) character is forgiven after they act in ways to restore their householder's honor (see later).

9. Lygre (2002: 23); see also Landry and May (2000: 298). If the master believed that his manager was "wasting" *oikos* resources, then why didn't the master *immediately* fire his manager? Perhaps the master wants to discover whether the manager is scattering the wealth in order to serve the manager's own financial self-interests, or to bring honor to the *oikos*.

10. As Landry and May (2000: 301) point out: "The manager's actions make his master appear to be generous, charitable, and law-abiding." In doing so, the manager also increases the likelihood that he will be welcomed into another *oikos* as a manager, in particular an *oikos* that does not want to participate in acquisitive economics.

11. Ibid., 308.

12. Ibid., 304.

13. We don't know whether or not the rich man rehires the manager in the end, though the pressures from peers not to rehire him would still be strong.

14. If the *manager* is the one who was dishonest, then a more common expression— such as *adikos oikonomos* (literally, an unjust manager)—could have been used (Dyck, Starke, & Dueck, 2006: 124–125). In any case, note that the manager's "dishonesty" differs qualitatively from the dishonesty exhibited by modern-day white-collar criminals: the manager in the parable did not feather his own nest by his scattering (Wright, 2000: 228; noting that this observation goes back at least as far as Bonaventure, 1221–74).

15. As will become apparent in the next chapter, this echoes a similar idea found in the parable of the ten pounds, namely, that how a manager responds to acquisitive economic temptations can be seen as a test to see how the manager will manage resources of ultimate worth.

16. A comprehensive analysis of the Greek words translated as "eternal" or "everlasting" (*aion-aionios*) concludes that these terms do not mean "endless." The idea that eternal means endless is not supported by its etymology, nor by definitions of lexicographers, nor by Greek writers before and at the time the Septuagint was made, nor by its general usage in the Old Testament, nor by the Jewish Greek writers in the first century, nor by how it is employed in the New Testament, nor by the Christian Fathers for the first three centuries after Christ. Augustine (c.e. 354–430) was the first known to argue that *aionios* signified endless (Hanson, 1875: 73, 76–77). Thus, a first-century understanding of the New Testament term "eternal life" (e.g., Luke 10:25, 18:18,30) emphasizes "the quality of the Blessed Life . . . the life of the gospel, spiritual life . . . It consists of knowing, loving and serving God. It is the Christian life, regardless of its duration" (43,55). Quoting E.H. Sears: "Not duration, but quality, is the chief thing involved in this word rendered 'eternal.' . . . The word *aion* and its derivatives, rendered 'eternal' and 'everlasting', described an economy complete in itself, and the duration must depend on the nature of the economy" (Hanson, 1875:60). Barclay (1964: 33–34) adds that the term *aionios* was in "Hellenistic Greek times the standing adjective to describe the Emperor's power. The royal power of Rome is a power which is to last forever" and notes that the term "eternal life" had three meanings in classical Greek: (1) a lifetime, (2) an age or a generation or an epoch, and (3) a very long space of time.

17. Note that this dispersing is purposeful and planned—not haphazard squandering—and different from handouts that create a dependency that may lead to a lack of motivation for recipients.

18. Quote here is found in Just (2003: 256; emphasis added here, quoting Cyril of Alexandra, Commentary on Luke, Homily 109).

19. Cited in Just (2003: 255–256; emphasis added here; though note that Chrysostom's rationale—"that in the future we may count on them"—could also be interpreted to be instrumental in nature, and thus not entirely inconsistent with a broad interpretation of conventional patron-client logic).

20. According to Augustine:

> [T]o our prayers we must add, by almsgiving and fasting, the wings of loving-kindness, so that they may fly more easily to God and reach him. For this the Christian mind can readily understand how far removed we should be from the fraudulent filching of other people's property; when it perceives *how similar it is to fraud when you don't give to the needy what you don't need yourself* (cited in Just, 2003: xxvi; emphasis added here: Augustine was commenting on Luke 6:37–38).

21. Senger (1970).

6   INTERPRETING LUKE'S PARABLE OF THE TEN POUNDS VIA A FIRST-CENTURY LENS

This chapter borrows heavily from Dyck, Starke, and Dueck (2009), which provides a more detailed analysis of the parable of the ten talents.

1. This is the only passage in the Gospel of Luke where the explicit purpose of money is to make money (Oakman, 2002), even though in first-century Palestine it was apparently not unusual for slaves to be given such managerial responsibilities (e.g., Fitzmyer, 1985: 1235; Goodrich, 2010; Green, 1997: 678).

2. The third slave describes the nobleman's business practices as exploitive, fraudulent, and unlawful (Green, 1997: 679–680). The idea of the master taking what he did not deposit "is drawn from banking, and is used here to describe a person who seeks a disproportionately high return from his investments" (Marshall, 1978: 707).

3. It has been noted that the master kills those who opposed his rule, but does not kill his slave (Green, 1997: 680)—perhaps this is because he owns the slave and does not want to reduce his own wealth.

4. Oakman (2002: 340). The five functions of money listed here are based on Oakman (2002), whose analysis builds on the work of economic historians. This is the only mention of the word "business" in the NRSV translation of Gospel of Luke.

5. Marshall (2000: 50).

6. Marshall (1978: 701).

7. For example, see Fitzmyer (1985: 1233) and Marshall (1978: 701). Whereas in the parable of the shrewd manager the word *kurios* is translated as "master" (as it is in most other occasions in Luke where it refers to someone other than Jesus or God), it is curious that in the parable of the ten pounds the same word *kurios* is translated as "Lord" (this happens only one other time in Luke—in Luke 13:8—whereas the other more than 70 times the word "Lord" is used it refers to God or Jesus [see appendix B]). An unintended consequence of this translation may be that modern readers are more likely to interpret the nobleman to represent God.

8. This is consistent with the third manager in Matthew's parable of the talents (Herzog, 1994: 153).

9. Some modern commentators (perhaps grudgingly) acknowledge such problems, but are quick to dismiss parts that don't fit well with a twenty-first-century interpretation by deeming them to be "secondary additions to the parable" and thus not relevant for its main message (e.g., Marshall, 1978: 701).

10. Herzog (1994: 165).

11. Archelaus was the ethnarch of Judea from 4 BCE to 6 C.E. (Fitzmyer, 1985: 1235; Green, 1997: 676; Marshall, 1978: 703).

12. Temin (2004: 14) and Myers (2001). However, Marshall (1978: 705) suggests that "1,000% profit . . . was quite possible under ancient conditions with enormous interest and commission rates."

13. Green (1997: 678). There was not yet any understanding of the modern idea of "growing an economy" (Osiek, 1991).

14. With regard to earning interest from a bank, recall in that time there were no "banks" as there are today. The reference literally means to place the money "on a (moneylenders') table" (compare Matt. 21:12; Mark 11:15; Luke 19:45; John 2:15). Recall also that charging interest was permissible only when Jews lent to non-Jews (e.g., Deut. 23:19–21) (Fitzmyer, 1985: 1237). At a more fundamental level, earning interest also seems to go against the Creation story, where God desires work to be inherently meaningful and for people to work as God worked. Does the desire to use money to make money reflect an attempt to avoid working by the sweat of our brow (Gen. 3:19)? In this light, perhaps it is no coincidence that the third manager had wrapped his pound inside in a *soudarion* (literally, "a cloth for perspiration"), which refers to a sweat cloth used for face or neck for protection from the sun (Fitzmyer, 1985: 1236; Marshall, 1978: 706). By using "money

to make money" the managers in the parable were likely increasing the amount of literal and metaphorical sweat on the brows of the relatively poor.

15. Eusebius was commenting on a variation of this parable from the (now lost) "Gospel of the Nazoreans" (Eusebius, *Theophania* on Matt. 25:14ff, cited in Schneemelcher, 1990: 149; cited in Malina & Rohrbaugh, 2003: 386). Eusebius was one of the more renowned Church Fathers who became a bishop of Caesarea in Palestine in 314. Eusebius also suggests that the threat uttered at the end of the parable of the talents may not have been directed at the third manager who hid the talent in the ground.

16. According to Just (2003: xxii), "The oldest commentary on Luke is a series written by Origen" [185–254], though elsewhere Just suggests Tertullian (160–220) may have written "the first Lukan commentary" (xvii).

17. Origen (1996). Origen also sees the good in the third manager when he likens him to one of the apostles (which he also does with the other managers; 218). However, in other writings Origen differs from the first-century interpretation described here, in that on one occasion he likens the pounds "to the grace of the Holy Spirit" (220), on another he seems to liken them to virtues (219), and in yet another he likens the nobleman to "Christ after the Ascension" (218).

18. See Rees (2002) and Dyck, Bruning, and Buckland (2003).

19. Richard Wilkinson and Kate Pickett (2009) analyze data across nations, and within the United States across states. Their measure of income inequality is based on calculating how much richer the richest 20 percent are compared to the poorest 20 percent in a society. For example, in the United States, which has among the highest income gaps in the so-called developed world, the richest 20 percent are on average 8.5 times richer than the poorest 20 percent. In contrast Japan, which has a relatively low income gap, the rich are on average 3.4 times richer than the poor. In the United States over 25 percent of the population has been diagnosed as having some sort of mental illness, whereas that rate is less than 10 percent in Japan.

7 PASSAGES ABOUT MANAGING RELATIONSHIPS *WITHIN* ORGANIZATIONS (*OIKONOMIA*)

1. Elliott (1991a: 102). See also Elliott (1991b: 212, 225) and other analyses on the *oikos* in Luke as reviewed in chapter three.

2. Note that Luke never actually uses the terms "husband" and "wife" to describe Mary and Joseph's relationship to one another.

3. Joanna is among several women who provide "resources" to Jesus. "Luke's terminology implies that these women do not merely 'provide,' but what they do is an act of 'service . . . Having service as their main task, many of the women in Luke-Acts exemplify in their lives the model of Jesus" (Moxnes, 1991: 263).

4. This includes 6 mentions of parent(s), 27 mentions of child(ren), 25 mentions of mother or daughter, 61 mentions of father, and 69 mentions of son. Note that 69 percent (130) of these 188 references are to "father" and "son," a reflection of the importance placed on male-centrism in the first century. However, only 48 percent (63) of the 130 mentions of "father" and "son" refer to typical fathers and sons living in first-century Palestine. Instead, 27 of the 130 mentions (21 percent) of the words "father" or "son" are related to *God* (11 refer to a son of God, 16 to God as the father). An additional 16 of the 130 (5 percent) references are to *ancestors* (5 refer to a son of Israel/David, 11 to David/ Abraham/ancestors as fathers). And in another 24 (18 percent) passages Jesus refers to himself as the Son of Man.

5. This includes all the passages in Luke that describe a verbal exchange or the dynamics of an ongoing relationship between parent(s) and their child(ren) in a first-century *oikos* setting. It does not include passages that mention both parent and child figures but where (1) the children are infants or even unborn (especially in the first four chapters of Luke); or (2) where the parent-child relationship is not described in any depth (e.g., several

passages describe the situation where a parent brings to Jesus' attention a child who is sick or dying so that Jesus may heal them).

6. Lest the reader surmise that these words foreshadowed a tumultuous teen-parent relationship, Luke goes on to say that Jesus returned to Nazareth and was obedient to Mary and Joseph, and that he grew in wisdom and in years, and in divine and human favor.

7. Most commentators note that many common social conventions are broken in this parable, and Park (2009) emphasizes how doing so serves to dismantle the traditional norms of *oikos*, and thus prepares the way for an alternative way of managing enterprise.

8. For an excellent discussion on the pedagogical importance of breaking down existing norms, perhaps especially for peasants who are oppressed by those norms, see the analysis and application of Paulo Freire in Herzog (1994: especially chapter 1).

9. That is, life in a new life-giving era of *oikoi*—see chapter five, note 16.

10. Neyrey (2008b: 88).

11. In this context the word "hate'" does not refer primarily to an affective quality, but rather it refers to a disavowal of one's primary allegiance to their kin. This is consistent with Jesus' other teachings that reinterpret the meaning *oikos* in a larger framework (Green, 1997: 565). Marshall (1978: 592) suggests "hate" in this context may mean "to love less." Destro and Pesce (2003: 221) note that "[t]he *logion* seems to imply not just the obligation of a clear separation, but also a radical condemnation of the normal relations within the *oikos*."

12. Note that the verses immediately following the three passages quoted here provide some hints regarding how this alternative *oikos* can be developed:

> Householders should take note of the larger trends happening around them, judge for themselves what is the right thing to do, and then act in countercultural ways (i.e., literally change their ways by 180 degrees, repent), lest they find themselves imprisoned by the status quo (Luke 12:54–13:5).

> Householders consider financial issues *before* they start a new building (root = *oikos*) project, lest their building contributes to the downfall of their *oikoi* (Luke 14:27–30).

> The son of man (inherently an *oikos* relationship) will suffer due to the dominant institutional structures and systems, and he will rise up on the third day (Luke 18:31–33).

13. For a more detailed analysis regarding the difference between adult children and their parents, see Destro and Pesce (2003).

14. The most notable possible exception is the shrewd manager in Luke 16.

15. Note that in each of these three cases the word "slave"(*doulos*) is translated in the NRSV as "servant," perhaps aware of the negative (and misleading) connotations of the word "slave" to twenty-first-century readers.

16. These five passages do not include other passages that we have already looked at, perhaps most notably the parable of the ten pounds.

17. Liddell and Scott (2000), Fitzmyer (1985: 1145).

18. Kimball (1993: 78).

19. Adolf Julicher (1910, original 1898, 1899) provides a foundational treatise arguing that Jesus' parables would not have been interpreted as allegories in their original form, nor should they be interpreted as allegories today. A more recent literature review of the various approaches to interpreting parables that have been utilized over the past century suggests that scholars still largely ignore the material world described in parables' social scripts. The notion that the language used in a parable "once lived as part of a social, political, economic system, which gave it birth and provided its resonance" has been given "cursory examination" at best and still usually remains "foreign to the enterprise of interpreting the parable" (Herzog, 1994: 13).

20. Though it is unclear why God "went to another country for a long time."

21. The Greek word for reject means to "reject as unworthy" (Liddell & Scott, 2000).

22. "[L]arge-scale viticulture was a costly and speculative enterprise...Textual evidence indicates that vineyard owners normally came from the population sector just below the class

of the civic and political elite (the upper class cavalry, soldiers, officers and administrators)" (van Eck, 2007: 917, 921).

23. "[T]he parable opens with a description of a familiar process, the takeover of peasant land and its subsequent conversion into a vineyard" (Herzog, 1994: 104). When these farmers lost their land they also lost their *oikos*. "Losing land meant losing one's Israelite identity which normally led to one becoming a day laborer or a beggar" (van Eck, 2007: 916).

24. Vineyards built on a largescale were "oriented towards exportation, rather than local consumption" (van Eck, 2007: 917). Archaeological and literary evidence shows that large estates were being increasingly created at that time. "Free smallholders farming with grain, olives and grapes aimed at local consumption were displaced by larger estates concentrating on monoculture dedicated to the production of export crops" (920).

25. Vineyards, being the most labor-intensive of agricultural activities at that time, had a severe effect on the structure and nature of labor: "It created and exploited a class of underemployed non-slave laborers, forced smallholders off their productive land to marginal land and drew on the labor inputs from underemployed non-slave labor and smallholders during certain key periods (e.g., cropping). Viticulture needed substantial capitalization, was uncertain and risky (a vineyard took 4–5 years to come into full production), and was usually associated with wealth and the wealthy" (ibid., 921).

26. Van Eck (2007) suggests that it has only been in the last 20 years or so that modern interpreters have recognized that the owner is not the hero of the story, but rather the villain, and that Jesus told the parable to warn other landowners (Kloppenborg, 2006: 131).

27. "[L]andowners despised hard labor, had neither the inclination nor the expertise to work their land and therefore turned to either slave-run estates or tenancies to skilled vinedressers. Given the nature of viticulture, it was the rule rather than the exception for an owner not to be present on his property (Kloppenborg 2006: 314–316)" (van Eck, 2007: 921). In situations like this "indebtedness was systemic and violence and conflict were the norm rather than the exception" (917).

28. "[T]he son's appearance made the tenants believe the landlord was dead, and—by killing the heir—they tried to appropriate the vineyard on the grounds of an existing law according to which the estate of an interstate proselyte could be appropriated by a claimant who was already occupying it (the law of adverse possession or *usucaptio*)" (van Eck, 2007: 913).

29. Herzog (1994: 113). Luke's emphasis on nonviolent civil disobedience will become evident in part five when we look at the passages that describe how to move away from conventional and toward alternative ways of managing.

30. "The elites of Galilee and Judea imitated their imperial overlords" in the way they became absentee landowners taking land from the poor (ibid., 104).

31. See also ibid., 113.

32. There are "many indications in the psalm that point in the direction of explaining the experiences of the individual in this psalm as that of a group of people" (Botha, 2003: 210; see also Kwon, 2009: 52).

33. "In the psalm [118], use of builders as a term refers to the nations. However, Luke applies the term to the builders of Israel, meaning the leaders of Israel" (Kwon, 2009: 52, 54).

34. Just as the Hebrew people were marginalized and without a homeland in Psalm 118, so also the tenants in Luke 20 can be seen as lacking their own land and thus likened to the rejected stone. Note again how this lack of land is associated with a lack of *oikos* or "homelessness" (*paroikos*): "Whereas *oikos* connotes associations and impressions of home, belongingness, and one's proper place, *paroikos* depicts the 'DP,' the displaced and dislocated person, the curious or suspicious-looking alien or stranger" (Elliott, 1981: 24; cf. 28).

35. Akin to the symbolic "individual" in Psalm 118, in Acts 4:11 Jesus is portrayed as a prototypical representative of socially marginalized people who exemplifies and ushers in the kingdom of God. Jesus' crucifixion symbolizes the extreme case of being socially marginalized in the Roman empire.

36. Niemelä (2011).
37. This is in contrast with the common understanding that views closure of an organization (and perhaps especially of a religious organization) as a failure that is to be avoided at all costs. Rather, it embraces the idea of cycles of life, and provides opportunities for new generations to create places of worship that are grounded in their contemporary settings. Research is also clear that having supportive parent congregations is helpful, though not necessary, for the establishment of new congregations. This somewhat provocative view requires more study, and may represent a unique way to think about Jubilatory practices. For more on this, see Dyck (1997, 2003), and Dyck and Starke (1999).
38. The brief literature review and findings presented here are from Scuderi (2010); see also Bivins (2005) and Ming (2005).

8 PASSAGES ABOUT MANAGING MONEY (*CHREMATISTICS*)

1. This is a paraphrase of Timothy Luke Johnson (1977: 13) who said: "Luke consistently speaks about possessions . . . [but] he does not speak about possessions consistently" (cited in Metzger, 2007).
2. Includes mentions of coin/s, *denarius, denarii,* pound/s, and silver (Luke does not mention gold or talents). Note also that, for the sake of reader-friendliness, the analysis in this chapter was done using the English NRSV translation of Luke. A rough and ready list of parallel keywords in Greek would include variations of: *arguria/on/os, denarius, drachme, leptos, mamonas, mina, ploutou/ton/siois/sious, ptochos, stater.*
3. Malina and Rohrbaugh (2003: 400); see also Green (1997: 267).
4. Malina and Rohrbaugh (2003: 410).
5. Aristotle (2007: Book 9).
6. This parable will be discussed more fully in chapter fourteen.
7. In particular, followers are called to leave behind their possessions and the traditional financial security (economic safety net) associated with their position in their conventional *oikos*, and to instead carry their metaphorical cross, knowing that this cross is countercultural and threatens the social order that is favored by the elite members of society.
8. Thus, this passage provides an explanation for the opening theme in Luke's passages about money: rich people are too distracted by their riches to be receptive to the kingdom. This echoes and reinforces an earlier passage that described how riches are like thorns that choke and prevent the maturation of seeds of the word of God (Luke 8:4–15). The problem is that people who focus on financial prosperity are not rich toward God.
9. This contrasts with some twenty-first-century interpretations of Jesus' teaching to "Seek first God's kingdom and God's and then things like food and clothing will be given to you as well," which tend to emphasize that if people seek the "kingdom of God" as their destination in the afterlife, then God will give them material wealth in this world.
10. Note again how this community nurturing statement "From everyone to whom much has been given, much will be required; and from the one to whom much has been entrusted, even more will be required" (Luke 12:48) stands in stark contrast to the more negative reinforcing cycle attributed to the acquisitive economic nobleman in the parable of the ten pounds: "[T]o all those who have, more will be given; but from those who have nothing, even what they have will be taken away" (Luke 19:26). Again, one cycle reduces the gap between the rich and the poor, and the second widens the gap. In short, managers are called to be responsible stewards, to treat employees well, and to act as servant leaders.
11. Note that salvation does not come from believing that someone (in this case Lazarus) has risen from the dead, but rather from sharing resources with the poor.
12. This is typically interpreted as suggesting that the man became sad because he was unwilling to sell everything. It could also be interpreted to suggest that the man was sad because, in an instant, he realized how futile his previous wealthy lifestyle had been.

13. Note that an "urban myth" suggests that the term "eye of a needle" "actually refers to a narrow gateway into Jerusalem that a relatively unencumbered camel could, in fact, squeeze through. A camel that was heavily laden with a rich man's goods, however, could not, and thus Jesus refers to our worldly possessions as excess baggage that we must be prepared to shed if we are to enter" (Gomes, 2001: 64). However, according to biblical scholars there is no historical evidence to support such an interpretation (e.g., Fitzmyer, 1985: 1204).

14. Which means that he had other "junior" tax collectors reporting to him.

15. Together worth about a day's wage for a day laborer (Green, 1997: 728).

16. Scholars debate whether Jesus considers it to be praiseworthy, or it is a travesty, that the poor widow donated "all she had to live on." On the one hand, it may be considered praiseworthy because she gives a greater proportion of her means than the extravagant rich people (Fitzmyer, 1985: 1230). Moreover, her having given "all she had to live on" seems to be consistent with earlier passages in Luke that call for Jesus' disciples to leave behind or sell *all* their possessions (e.g., the rich young ruler, Jesus' disciples), and is consistent with subsequent passages in Acts where followers *do* sell all their possessions (Acts 2:45).

    On the other hand, where it is inconsistent with earlier passages is regarding what happens to the proceeds from the sold possessions—earlier passages suggest the proceeds are to be given to the poor so that everyone has enough. However, in this case they are given to a temple treasury that is run by leaders whom Jesus has condemned; e.g., see the passage immediately prior to this one—Jesus criticizes the leaders of the temple and thus its treasury, believing that it is being managed by people who use it for unjust purposes (Green, 1997: 729). It has been noted Jesus does not suggest that the widow's actions are praiseworthy or exemplary. Rather, Jesus has come to champion structures and systems that save the poor from their poverty, not to celebrate practices that impoverish them further (728). In light of the overall propoor theme in Luke, it seems unlikely that Jesus is praising the actions of a widow who is going from poverty to destitution.

17. "And here is the very core of this issue and the emergence of Jesus' ethic; wealth should not be generated or accumulated at the expense of another. When an individual acquires and holds wealth to the detriment of another individual, those activities are unacceptable to God. Which is not to say that wealth, even very large measures of wealth, are not to be generated and accumulated by individuals, but only that this cannot be done to the detriment and deprivation of others" (Tyson, 2006: 173).

18. This is not to suggest that Jesus wants everyone to be at the same economic level. For example, Jesus does not lament that King Solomon was dressed in glory, nor does he call the chief tax collector Zacchaeus to forsake his position and sell *everything* that he owns. It seems that some economic diversity is appropriate, *so long as no one in society is impoverished*. A clear implication of this is to reverse the widening gaps between the rich and the poor within organizations, within nations, and between nations.

19. See especially Kasser (2003). A materialist-individualist lifestyle may contribute to lower satisfaction with life (Burroughs & Rindfleisch, 2002), poorer interpersonal relationships (Richins & Dawson, 1992), an increase in mental disorders (Cohen & Cohen, 1996), environmental degradation (McCarty & Shrum, 2001), and social injustice (Rees, 2002).

20. Tierney (2008). See also Dunn, Aknin, and Norton (2008).

9 PASSAGES ABOUT MANAGING RELATIONSHIPS *BETWEEN* ORGANIZATIONS

1. Neyrey (2005: 481).

2. Moxnes (1991: 264). Of all the passages in the New Testament that describe the preference for "true benefaction" versus Roman patronage: "Perhaps most clear in this regard is Luke 14:12–24. The introductory saying to the parable of the Great Supper makes

explicit that benefaction is in view. Those who are invited are invited precisely because of their inability to repay their patron. They have nothing to offer, and their very low status in society means that even any honor they attribute to the benefactor who is inviting them will not alter the honor status of the host" (Neyrey & Stewart, 2008c: 48).

3. "And you shall hallow the fiftieth year and you shall proclaim liberty throughout the land to all its inhabitants. It shall be a jubilee for you: you shall return, every one of you, to your property and every one of you to your family. That fiftieth year shall be a jubilee for you: you shall not sow, or reap the aftergrowth, or harvest the unpruned vines" (Lev. 25:10–11).

4. Bock (2006: 410).

5. Green (1997: 212).

6. However, it can tempting to interpret passages like these (and others, perhaps most notably those where Jesus heals people) as suggesting that Jesus represents "a new-and-improved" patron, a patron whose indebted clients need not fear that they will be oppressed. For example, some scholars suggest that the ancient patronage model can be applied to the biblical story insofar as "God is the patron, Christ is the broker, and human beings are the clients" (Downs, 2009: 130). "In adopting (even re-adopting) the role of divine Patron and thus guaranteeing to meet those physical needs that many children were or would be unable to meet themselves, Jesus seems to be suggesting that God was hereby rendering those [earthly] patron-client relationships, which formed the very basis of the political-economy, redundant for His children" (Tryon, 2006: 183). While there may be some merit in viewing God as divine patron, this seems appropriate only if the meaning of patron-client relationships is totally transformed/reinvented; there is a danger that using it as an analogy will inadvertently lead to cooptation into conventional view. In any case, others have argued that "Luke presents Jesus primarily in terms prevalent in Hellenistic Jewish culture (reciprocity and friendship), secondarily as a benefactor, and not as a patron" (Marshall, 2009: 331).

7. See Danker (1982: 501–502). The three passages we look at here are ones that Danker refers to on more than ten pages in his analysis.

8. Even though the centurion is accustomed to commanding clients, he is clear that he has no intention of making Jesus into client (Malina & Rohrbaugh, 2003: 390). Recall that we have already taken a look at this passage in our earlier discussion about master-slave relations. By calling Jesus "Lord" the centurion seems to give Jesus the opportunity to be a "patron" while he accepts the role of the "client" (Moxnes, 1991: 253).

9. Danker (1982: 406).

10. Moxnes (1991: 253); see also Danker (1982).

11. "There is, then, a break with the patron-client relationship at its most crucial point; a service performed or a favor done shall *not* be transformed into status and honor" (Moxnes, 1991: 261). As will be discussed in greater detail in chapter fourteen, the Luke 10 passage can be seen as describing peacemaking between Jesus' followers (Jews) and the Samaritans in the villages into which Jesus sends the 70 followers. Samaritan and Jewish relations were strained at best (e.g., several verses earlier in Luke 9:54 two of Jesus' disciples ask if they should command fire to consume a Samaritan village). In Luke 10 Jesus creates a situation where these Samaritan "enemies" essentially become the hosts of his followers, a variation of Ford's (1984) idea that "My Enemy is my Guest."

12. Note that the English word for "leader" appears only nine times in Luke, and this is the only passage in Luke where it refers to Jesus' disciples. This is also the only time where it is translated from the Greek word *hegoumenos*, which means "to lead, consider, count, regard" or "to go before, to lead the way" (Liddell & Scott, 2000). In the other eight passages the "leaders" referred to either leaders within Judaism (Luke 8:41; 8:49; 13:14; 14:1) and/or to other civic leaders involved in Jesus' crucifixion (Luke 19:47; 23:13, 35; 24:20). In each of these passages the Greek word for leader is *archon* (or *archisunagogu*), which also appears three additional other times in Luke where it is translated as "ruler" (Luke 11:15; 18:18) and as "magistrate" (Luke 12:58). Of all these other leaders, the only

one who is described in favorable terms is the religious leader Jairus, who showed humility (Jairus fell at Jesus' feet, and begged Jesus to come to his *oikos*, where his 12-year-old daughter was dying—Jesus raised the daughter—Luke 8:40–56).

13. "The question [in this passage] is not how to obtain greatness, but how the great should behave. It is possible, therefore, to read Luke at this point as accepting structures of leadership, but emphasizing a transformation of their role and their status. The greatest and the leaders will have no different status from the young and those who serve at table, that is, they will have no special no power or special honor" (Moxnes 1991: 260–261).

14. "Luke presents a radical transformation of the patronage system as a model for social relations within the Christian community" (Moxnes, 1991: 267).

15. Much of the content supporting this paragraph is taken from Dyck (2012a). For an excellent review of sustainable agriculture programming in Africa, see Pretty, Toulmin, and William (2011).

IV   New Way of Seeing

1. "Jesus thus calls on people to live as he lives, in contradistinction to the agonistic, competitive form of life marked by conventional notions of house and status typical of the larger Roman world. Behaviors that grow out of service in the kingdom of God take a different turn: Love your enemies. Do good to those who hate you. Extend hospitality to those who cannot reciprocate . . . Within the Third Gospel, the chief competitor for this focus stems from Money—not so much money itself, but the rule of Money, manifest in the drive for social praise and, so, in forms of life designed to keep those with power and privilege segregated from those of low status, the least, the lost, and the left-out" (Green, 1997: 24).

2. "In the New Testament period, neither religion nor economics had a separate institutional existence and neither was conceived of as a system on its own, with a special theory of practice and a distinctive mode of organization. Both were inextricably intertwined with the kinship [e.g., *oikos*] and political systems [e.g., patron-client relations]" (Malina & Rohrbaugh, 2003: 397).

10   The Kingdom of God is Enacted and Manifest in Organizational Settings

Many of the ideas in this chapter are drawn from and build upon Dyck and Sawatzky (2010).

1. "Voluntary commitment to a community distinct from the total society provides resources for practical moral reasoning of a kind which are by definition unthinkable where that option is not offered and where the only way to be an individual is to rebel" (Yoder, 1984: 25).

2. "The 'Kingdom of God/Heaven' is a subject of major importance in the Bible for two primary reasons: its frequency in the first three canonical (synoptic) gospels of the NT, and the conviction that it stands at the very center of the message of the historical Jesus. Its meaning, which is derived from a world of oriental monarchs and monarchies that is very different from modern Western democracies, has been interpreted in various ways. Historically it has been associated with the future state of the resurrected, immortal blessed; the Church; monastic contemplation; mystical ecstasy; pious religious experience; the progressively redeemed society inspired by love; the future transformation of this world; apocalyptic hope for the next world; and an open-ended symbol possible of many interpretations" (Duling, 1992: 49).

3. This is evident in a series of article I've written with colleagues (e.g., Dyck & Schroeder, 2005; Dyck & Weber, 2006; Dyck, Starke, & Dueck, 2009) as well other writings in

secular journals, which suggest biblical KOG teachings challenge the emphasis in contemporary management on materialism (Gomes, 2001: 64; Roels, 1997: 113; Rossouw, 1994: 559) and individualism (Johnson, 1957: 74, 75; Selznick, 1992: 479; Pava, 2002: 49; Campbell, 2008: 431). Even Weber (1958) himself suggested that the particular Reformational "Protestant ethic" that he described may be inconsistent with the biblical record interpreted in its historical context. As explained in Dyck and Sawatzky (2010), a review of references to "kingdom of God" in over 25 leading management journals, over 20 books on the general topic of "Christian management" (most were popular press books), and other publications with a primary focus on the "kingdom of God" (these latter sources provided the foundation for the analysis that follows; none of them had a sustained emphasis on management) found that there is a persistent view that (1) the KOG is relevant for management theory and practice; (2) the message of the biblical KOG is generally at odds with conventional (materialist-individualist) management theory and practice; and (3) there has been no attempt to develop a comprehensive and historically grounded understanding of the managerial implications of biblical KOG teachings interpreted via a first-century lens.

4. Though, as our analysis has shown, Luke has more references to *oikos* than to the "kingdom of God." The idea of a KOG serves as a foundational concept in each of the three Abrahamic religions: Judaism, Christianity, and Islam.

5. "The key question is whether Jesus saw the kingdom as a future apocalyptic event or as a present mysterious reality. A majority of contemporary scholars hold a primarily or exclusively 'present' view, emphasizing those traditions in the Synoptics (Matt 12:28 = Luke 11:20; Luke 17:20–21) and Thomas (*Gos. Thom.* 3, 113) which speak of a present kingdom, understood in either or both of the compatible senses of a mysterious presence pervading reality or as a power presently active in the world. A few hold a wholly or primarily future understanding, and the remainder maintain a 'both/and' understanding. For those holding a partially or wholly future view, an important question is whether Jesus saw the future kingdom as coming in a dramatically objective and visible manner" (Borg, 1992: 811).

6. This points to what theologians refer to as an eschatological understanding of the KOG. Some biblical texts give the impression that the KOG is yet-to-come, while others suggest that the KOG is already at hand. Interpretations that focus only on its future coming and its other-worldly realm reduce the KOG to a "skyhook Second Coming" (McLaren, 2004: 267) that will save humankind by removing people from the earth and all their material problems (Sawatzky, 2006). Rather, a more accurate and balanced interpretation of the biblical text suggests that in Jesus the "eschatological order [had come] in advance of the eschatological event" (Ladd, 1974: 188); the full consummation of the KOG for humankind is still coming. Indeed, it is precisely knowing that the KOG is assured that gives Jesus' followers the power to manifest it on earth. From this perspective the phrase the KOG is at hand means "God's new benevolent society is already among us" (McLaren, 2010: 138).

7. Ever since Julius Caesar had been divinized by the Roman Senate subsequent Roman emperors proclaimed themselves to be "sons of God" and their empires became "kingdoms of God" (Reed, 2007).

8. The Greek word *basileia* relates most closely to the notion of a royal administration; a reign. Thus "kingdom of God" does not refer primarily to a territory that comes under God's governance, but rather to the fact of God's rule, God's royal reign (Kraybill, 1978: 25). To enter the KOG, then, is not to exist in a new place, but rather to experience the kingly rule of God, or in more contemporary terms, to experience the particular management style favored (and modeled) by God.

9. Note that the KOG also extends beyond human relationships.

10. Recall that in first-century Palestine people who were sick and demon-possessed would not have had a place in a conventional *oikos*; when Jesus heals them they can again become full members of society. Whereas twenty-first-century readers tend to interpret healing passages as Jesus curing someone from a physical disease, people in the first century

would have been much more likely to see Jesus as restoring people into community. As Malina and Rohrbaugh (2003: 368–369) explain, anthropologists differentiate between "disease" (a *physical* malady) and "illness" (a *socially* constructed phenomenon, which results in a lack of social position). For an example of "illnesses," consider Leviticus 21:17-20, which describes the attributes of people who are not permitted to approach the altar: "For no one who has a blemish shall draw near, one who is blind or lame, or one who has a mutilated face or a limb too long, or one who has a broken foot or a broken hand, or a hunchback, or a dwarf, or a man with a blemish in his eyes or an itching disease or scabs or crushed testicles." The New Testament describes not so much the healing of "diseases" (i.e., physical ailments) as the healing of illnesses (e.g., allowing people with blemishes to draw near to God). See also Pilch (1991: 199) who notes: "[I]n the first-century Mediterranean world, the political dimensions [i.e., 'political actions performed for the purpose of restoring correct order to society'] of Jesus' healing activity would be self-evident to all witnesses, friendly and hostile alike."

11. As will become even more apparent in Group #4 passages, this sharing of bread and wine among believers is not only enacting the KOG, but it can also be seen as an outcome of the KOG. Put differently, when followers share meals with each other, it also predisposes them to share meals with others who do not have an *oikos* to belong to. As Elliott (1991a: 103, 104) demonstrates: "Put briefly, food codes embody and replicate social codes . . . [For Luke meals represent] symbols of life shaped by the principles and values of the kingdom of God." Thus eating together as an open-to-all fictive *oikos* is a powerful symbol of the KOG.

12. In the one passage where Jesus does not explicitly *address* the social elite, he talks to people on the way to Jerusalem *about* an elite group of past leaders (Abraham, Isaac, and Jacob) (Luke 13:28–30).

13. Note that the emphasis on *oikos* is least apparent in (1) Luke 17:20–21, which simply alludes to it by saying the KOG is evident in the relationships "among" Jesus' listeners, and (2) in Luke 23:50–56 where Joseph of Arimathea places Jesus' dead body in a tomb (his final "home" so to speak).

14. See Marshall (1978: 655).

15. Moreover, this has some similarities to a parallel argument in Aristotle. For Aristotle, the *polis* (city) was where the fullest expressions of human flourishing and happiness (*eudaimonia*) could take place, and the *oikos* was expected to enshrine and inculcate the *polis*'s values. *Oikoi* were considered "good" if they "reflected the character of, and were productive of, the character of the *polis*" (Nagle, 2006: 9).

16. Even though Luke's prologue states that he pays particular attention to the sequential order in which he presents his account (Luke 1:3), and even though biblical scholars encourage readers to attend to the order in which Luke places events ("[t]he sequence itself provides the larger meaning," Johnson [1991: 4]), it may nevertheless seem surprising to find the evidence of the four KOG themes in this central passage.

17. This is true even for interpretations that appropriate these parables toward countercultural purposes. For example, the "weediness" of mustard is not mentioned in the *Mustard Seed Conspiracy* (Sine, 1981).

18. God's kingdom is characterized by a new world order that embraces the marginalized in the salvific work of God. Such an understanding of the KOG is consistent with and provides the lens through which to interpret the laws of the Hebrew Scriptures (Green, 1997: 603).

19. See work by H. Riesenfeld and A. Wikgren described in Marshall (1978: 655).

20. Becoming a member of such an alternative form of *oikos* may also require selling all that you own and distributing the money to the poor (Luke 18:22–24) as you leave your conventional *oikos* (Luke 9:62; 18:29).

21. All the quotes in this paragraph are taken from Hamel (2009), mostly from page 94. Gary Hamel is one of the most-cited management scholars in the literature. Other scholars who call for the development of nonconventional management theory and practice include Dyck et al. (2011), Ghoshal (2005), and Giacalone (2004).

11 Salvation is Facilitated when People are Saved *from* Oppressive Structures and Systems, and are Saved *for* Work in Liberating Organizational Structures and Systems

1. See review in Kalberg (2001). Recent research in world religions indicates that the religious beliefs that have the greatest effect on economic growth are those related to an afterlife or lack thereof (McCleary, 2007: 71; Barro & McCleary, 2003; see also Graafland, Kapstein, & van der Duijn Schouten, 2007; Albertson, 2009). Note also that the early Christian literature made not infrequent "use of *oikonomia* for the divine plan of salvation." For example, early church leaders like Ignatius [35–108] talk about the "the economy relation to the new man Jesus," and "Origen [185–254] likewise uses *oikonomia* for the earlier ordering of salvation and the new covenant arrangement transferred to Christians" (cited in Reumann, 1959: 282, 283; though the meaning of *oikonomia* was drawn from rhetoric rather than from economics). "The word *oikonomia* originally came from the political-economic domain, and was taken over by Christian writers and given a new meaning, but remained connected with the political and economic until present time, so that today it has two qualitatively different meanings" (Richter, 2005: 2; my translation).
2. Dyck and Wiebe (2012).
3. Alvesson and Willmott (1992), Barker (1993), Maslow (1954), and Lincoln et al. (2002).
4. For example, Hamel (2009) essentially describes hallmarks of Management 2.0 that can "save" people from the shortcomings of Management 1.0.
5. "The concept of salvation is central to Christianity. From a historical perspective, the experience of Jesus as savior is the basis from which the Christian movement sprang . . . *Yet despite this centrality and importance, the Church has never formulated a conciliar definition of salvation nor provided a universally accepted conception*" (Haight, 1994: 225; emphasis added). Even so, there are several simple definitions that would probably get widespread support. For example, one detailed examination of the New Testament concludes that salvation can be summarized as "Jesus makes God present in a saving way" (229, citing Schillebeeckx, 1980: 463). Insofar as God's presence is related to a lack of suffering, this New Testament understanding of salvation is consistent with Weber's general idea that salvation is evident when God liberates humankind from suffering. Another definition suggests that salvation refers to how "[t]hrough Jesus, repentant humankind can enjoy a restored right relationship with God" (Dyck & Wiebe, 2012; drawing from McCleary, 2007: 57). A third definition is evident in what has become the most popular verse in the Bible: "For God so loved the world that he gave his only Son, so that everyone who believes in him may not perish but may have eternal life. Indeed, God did not send the Son into the world to condemn the world, but in order that the world might be saved through him" (John 3:16–17; considered most popular verse in Bible according to sites such as http://www.biblegateway.com/blog/2009/05/the-100-most-read-bible-verses-at-biblegatewaycom/ and http://www.topverses.com/).
6. M. Douglas Meeks (1989: 36) argues that "*oikos* also suggests itself as a soteriological/ praxis key, that is, a way of speaking about access to the source of life, God's righteousness. It encompasses the questions of inclusion in the household as well as solidarity with those who are excluded from the household, both of which are primary signs of liberation . . . Finally, *oikos* is an ecclesiological key for speaking of the church as the 'household of God,' existing for the sake of God's liberation of the *polis* and *kosmos* through God's liberation of the poor, the oppressed, the sinners and the dying."
7. This is consistent with the rest of the New Testament, where the understanding of "salvation includes a practical concern here and now for needy people (Rom 12:8; 1 Cor 13:3; Heb 13:16; 1 John 3:17; Jas 1:27; 2:14–17)" (O'Collins, 1992: 911). Similarly, even in John 3:16, which is often interpreted as having a primary emphasis on the future eternal

life, it is clear from the grammar of the verse that its emphasis "has largely to do with the present/immediate circumstances of the 'world." "The *traditional* stance on and *kerygma* of these words [in John 3:16] seem to enunciate the futuristic and eternal aspect of *eternal life* (which would support the 'evangelistic' thrust). But, however, while the futuristic and eternal should and cannot be denied, the *life* referred to here, and as it is indicated by the grammar, has largely to do with the present/immediate circumstances of the 'world'" (Botha & Rousseau, 2005: 1153). Similarly, when it comes to questions of the Second Coming, there is some agreement among leading biblical scholars that New Testament writers were not anticipating the "end of the world" in terms of destroying the space-time universe, but rather they were anticipating "the end of the world as we know it" (McLaren, 2010: 197). Thus, "eternal life" refers to "the new way of KOG living" associated with Jesus' teachings. For more on the meaning of eternal life, see chapter five, note 16.

8. Powell (1992) also makes this observation. For more on the relationship between healing and social restoration, see chapter ten, note 10.

9. Reed (2007) and Neyrey (2005). It is true that there was a decrease in warfare within the Roman Empire thanks to the presence of the Roman army and its systems of control and domination (including the operation of patron-client relations, which served the interests of the elite). But for the subjugated peoples this lack of active warfare was often experienced as institutionalized oppression rather than as living in peace.

10. For more on this, see Dyck and Wiebe (2012). Note that the Gospel of Luke never indicates that it is Jesus' death itself that achieves salvation from sin (Ehrman, 2008: 166), though other Gospels do talk of how Jesus came "to give his life a ransom for many" (Matt., 20:28; Mark 10:45; see also 1. Tim. 2:6; Rom. 3:25; and Heb. 2:17). The emphasis on Jesus' death as an act of "atonement" or as a "ransom" for the sins of humankind was increasingly emphasized in the writings of theologians who came centuries later. Post-Constantine and into the middle ages era there was a transition from salvation coming via Jesus as (subversive) role model, to salvation coming via Jesus as sacrifice. Athanasius (293–373) serves somewhat as a transition figure. He is well-known for saying that "He [Jesus] was humanized that we might be deified" (Haight, 1994: 236). However, rather than focus on how Jesus accomplishes this by being a *role model* for humankind (as in the pre-Constantine era), "in Athanasius Jesus also saves by revealing and by undergoing sacrificial death" (ibid.). The theme of Jesus' death having redemptive qualities is evident in Gregory of Nyssa (335–after 394), who "developed a mythic subtext to Jesus' passion and death: Jesus was innocent bait for Satan's lust for dominion, and, by destroying Jesus unjustly, Satan lost any justification for his hold on humankind" (ibid.). Augustine of Hippo (354–430) builds on this idea, referring to Jesus' death as a redemption—a payment of ransom—and a sacrifice. Several centuries later, Anselm (1033–1109) develops this further via his theory of satisfaction: "Jesus took our place, he died in our stead" (237).

11. For example, drawing on Pauline writings, Irenaeus (?–202) argues that Jesus offers salvation via becoming a sort of new-and-improved Adam who serves as an example to show how humankind was intended to live: "Jesus repeats the role of Adam; the incarnate Word [i.e., Jesus] takes up and reenacts the entire pattern of human existence but this time 'gets it right.' He thus sets things back in their original created order" (ibid., 236). For early church leaders like Irenaeus, salvation came by way of Jesus' incarnation (e.g., by imitating Jesus his followers can also overcome corruption and death), not by way of Jesus' crucifixion (although his crucifixion was an important part of what it meant to live as the second Adam). Origen (185–254) has a similar emphasis on Jesus as a role model. Origen essentially described Jesus as serving as sort of a "replica" of God who helped people to better understand what God was like and thus helped lead humankind back to God: "Jesus is savior by revealing God and being an exemplar of human existence" (ibid.).

12. John Howard Yoder (1972: 97) underscores this social emphasis noting that "the cross" that Jesus' followers are called to "take up" does not refer to internal things like "an

inward wrestling of the sensitive soul with self and sin." Instead, in Luke the cross of salvation reflects "the social character of Jesus' cross . . . the price of his social nonconformity . . . it is the social reality of representing to an unwilling world the Order to come."

13. For example, an inscription found in Ephesus dating to 48 C.E. calls Julius Caesar "god manifest and common savior of human life" (Fitzmyer, 1970: 204). *Soter* also had a background in the Hebrew Scriptures, where it is used to describe God and God's agents who deliver people from oppression (ibid.). Note also that the literal meaning of the name "Jesus" is savior, going back to the Hebrew words *Yascha* and *Yeshua*.

14. For example, "Israel's restoration from international shame to a position of honour" has been identified the dominant theme of Psalm 118 (Botha, 2003: 195), which is referred to 24 times in the New Testament (11 quotations, 13 allusions) making it "the most frequently quoted Old Testament chapter in the New Testament [tied with Exodus 20, which contains the Ten Commandments]"(Kwon, 2009: 50).

15. For more on these dual meanings, see Powell (1992).

16. There is one important exception to this pattern, and that is the story of Zacchaeus, which will be discussed more fully later in this chapter, where Jesus says: "Today salvation has come to this *oikos*." This is the only time Jesus himself uses the noun form, and also the only time he refers to salvation coming to an identifiable group of people (*oikos*).

17. The use of Greek words to highlight a Greek understanding of salvation is also evident the only time Luke refers to God as *despotes* (a Greek term for "master of the house") when Simeon says: "Master [*despotes*] . . . my eyes have seen your salvation, which you have prepared for *all peoples, a light of revelation* to the *Gentiles* and for glory to your people *Israel*" (see Luke 2:25–32). The relative emphasis in this passage is on a Greek understanding of salvation, as "a light of revelation to the Gentiles"—clearly consistent with a Greek view of salvation—rather than as a redemption from enemies (though it is also noteworthy that this "light of revelation" is also important for Israel).

18. This linkage with physical healing is consistent with the Greek verb for "save," meaning "to save from death, keep alive, preserve" (Liddell & Scott, 2000). Sometimes in Luke "to be saved" is translated as "to be made well." For example, the NRSV translates the exact same Greek phrase as: (1) "Your faith has saved you" in Luke 7:50 (prostitute) and 18:42 (blind man), but as (2) "Your faith has made you well" in Luke 8:48 (bleeding woman) and 17:19 (leper).

19. Indeed, given that there were other people doing similar sorts of healing in Jesus' time (e.g., Luke 9:49), the point of these passages is not so much that Jesus has some unique ability to heal people, but rather on the fact that: (1) the healing allowed the persons being saved to become full community members, and (2) Jesus healed people with "no strings attached" (e.g., contrary to the acquisitive economic and patron-client norms of first century, none of the healed were asked to become "clients" of Jesus or to make financial payment to him). This interpretation is entirely consistent with the emphasis on welcoming the marginalized into community that is evident throughout Luke.

20. The first of two exceptions to this active role for the individual being saved is when Jesus raises Jairus's 12-year-old daughter, in which case it is the father Jairus who fell at the feet of Jesus and asked him to heal his daughter (Luke 8:42). The other exception is when Jesus heals a Gerasene man, the only Gentile in these passages, in which case the man simply met Jesus (Luke 8:27). Lest Luke's reader be unaware of the social practices among Gerasenes with regards to the man's status as an outcast vis-à-vis his community, the beginning of this passage explicitly states that the man "did not live in a *house* [*oikos*]" but in the tombs" (verse 27), and that after the man is healed he is explicitly restored to community: "Go to your home [*oikos*], and declare how much God has done for you" (verse 39).

21. Note that there may be some overlap in the kinds of soils described in this parable, and the four groupings of KOG passages described in the previous chapter: (i) the trampled path may be associated with "crowds" to whom the KOG is proclaimed; (ii) the rocky

ground may be associated with potential "disciples" who fail to adequately become grounded in KOG teachings; (iii) the thorny ground may be associated with potential "followers" whose attempts to enact the KOG are overwhelmed by the acquisitive economic temptations around them; and (iv) the good soil may be associated with KOG outcomes.

22. It is important to note that the reference to the cross in this passage should not be read as a metaphorical allusion to the cross that Jesus will bear. Scholars agree that, unlike other writings, the Gospel of Luke does not link salvation to Jesus' death on the cross. This passage may be as close as we get, but even here it is interesting that if verse 23 was intended to foreshadow Jesus' own death on the cross, certainly a writer as skilled as Luke would have then later in his Gospel referred to Jesus explicitly carrying his own cross, yet Luke does not do this (Fitzmyer, 1970: 785).

23. Green (1997: 373). See also Marshall (1978: 373).

24. They may fail to act because they feel some sense of entitlement as a group, or because of their earlier understanding about salvation.

25. Genesis 2:8; cf. Genesis 13:10 for garden of God (Fitzmyer, 1985: 1510–1511).

26. The word "paradise" is a reference to "God's garden," which is "an eschatological image of new creation" (Green, 1997: 823). Moreover, the fact that Jesus says that this will happen that very day "signifies that the era of salvation has become a reality" (Marshall, 1978: 873). Note again how the saved *from/for* language fits into the four-phase "salvation history" often said to represent overall story-line in the Bible (described in chapter two): people are saved from the *Fall*, and are saved for the *KOG*.

27. This adds further meaning to the verse we looked at earlier: "If any want to become my followers, let them deny themselves and take up their cross daily and follow me. For those who want to *save* their life will lose it, and those who lose their life for my sake will *save* it" (Luke 9:23–24). John Howard Yoder (1972) noted that this is the only point at which Jesus calls others to follow his example: "Only at one point, only on one subject—but then consistently, universally—is Jesus our example: in his cross." Yoder goes on to emphasize the countercultural socioeconomic nature to what it means for Jesus' followers to take up their cross (Luke 9:23; 14:27). The believer's cross does not refer to "any and every kind of suffering, sickness, or tension, the bearing of which is demanded. The believer's cross must be, like his [*sic*] Lord's, the price of social nonconformity" (96–97).

28. Zacchaeus is sort of like a "district manager" who has other toll collectors that work for him as subordinates (Green, 1997: 668).

29. Even though Zacchaeus has a "thoroughly Jewish name" (Marshall, 1978: 696; cf. Fitzmyer, 1985: 1221), as a tax collector he and others like him would have been despised by almost everyone in the first-century Greco-Roman world (Green, 1997: 669).

30. For Jews in general Jesus lodging "in such a person's" *oikos* was "tantamount to sharing in his sin" (Marshall, 1978: 697).

31. This is consistent with such regulations as found in the Pentateuch (e.g., Ex 32:37: "four sheep for a [stolen] sheep") (Fitzmyer, 1985: 1225). Note also that Zacchaeus is not using his wealth as a patron who wishes to gain clients. Rather, his almsgiving is consistent with the classic idea of benefaction in so far as he gives resources to others without expecting reciprocation (Green, 1997: 672).

32. It is striking how Zacchaeus, "even though he has become one of the 'lost sheep in the house of Israel'" (Marshall, 1978: 698), seems to understand better than Jewish leaders what it means to manifest membership in the *oikos* of Abraham. Because his economic practices show a kinship to Abraham, Zacchaeus is not the lost outsider he was thought to be (Green, 1997: 672).

33. An allusion to Ezekiel 34:16: "I shall seek out what was lost and shall turn back what was going astray" (Fitzmyer, 1985: 1226).

34. Luke 7:50, 8:48, 17:19, 18:42.

35. More precisely, whereas this may be unexpected for twenty-first-century readers, it may not have been surprising for first-century listeners. They would have been more attuned

than twenty-first-century readers to the two salvific dimensions (i.e., to be saved from and saved for), and thus may have noticed the patterns evident in tables 11.1 and 11.2 much more readily than modern readers do.

36. Note that the original verbs in Luke 19:8 could also be translated to be read in the present tense: "I give away half of what I own to the poor. If I extorted anything from anyone, I pay it back fourfold" (Fitzmyer, 1985: 1218). In either case, Zacchaeus "is presented in this case as an exemplary rich person who has understood something of Jesus' ministry and message and concern for the poor and the cheated" (1222).

37. This is consistent with other "outsiders" in Luke who model what it means to manage their *oikos* in ways that are consistent with the kingdom of God. This includes, for example, the Roman centurion of whom Jesus says: "I tell you, not even in Israel have I found such faith" (Luke 7:9), and the Good Samaritan, of whom Jesus said, "Go and do likewise" (Luke 10:37). To become members of Jesus' *oikos* is to "hear the word of God and do it" (Luke 8:21).

38. The remaining chapters will focus more on how to implement these new *oikos* structures and systems, and what they look like.

39. For example, in *Acts* people are saved when they come into contact with KOG-inspired structures and systems (e.g., Acts 2:44–47).

40. More recent examples using a similar nonviolent approach to challenge oppressive structures and systems include Mahatma Gandhi and Martin Luther King, Jr. A longer discussion of emancipation, and its historical association with salvation and its current similarities and differences, can be found in Dyck and Wiebe (2012).

12   THE HOLY SPIRIT IS KEY TO SALVIFIC KINGDOM OF GOD MANAGEMENT

1. Marcic (2000: 629).
2. Lambert (2009: 43).
3. Weber (1958: 113–114, 128, 130, 145) associated the "inward "view with Luther and the "outward" view with Calvin.
4. Van Duzer et al. (2007: 115, see also 112; emphasis added here). They go on to say: "While we would emphatically deny that the Christian scriptures support the conclusion that good ethics always translates into profitable business decisions, empirical evidence suggests that it often does so" (115). Pheng (1999: 126) points to the importance of the Holy Spirit more specifically in an *oikos* setting, and describes how early Christians left a wide variety of diverse *oikoi* and became members of a KOG *oikos*, where they would: "walk and live with the Holy Spirit controlling their lives . . . living together. The attributes of living a Spirit-controlled life are equally applicable in today's households and organisations as they were in the past." Vasconcelos (2010: 609) suggests that the Holy Spirit is involved in revealing the shortcomings of current social structures and systems, including at the ecological, political, and organizational levels of analysis.
5. For example, Dyck and Schroeder (2005), and Hamel (2009).
6. Ferraro, Pfeffer, and Sutton (2005: 14).
7. See Godbout and Caillé (1998: 15). As Juergen Habermas (1991: 79) notes: "[I]ntuitions which had long been articulated in religious language can neither be rejected nor simply retrieved rationally" (cited in Harrington, 2007: 46–47). To be clear, at the same time, the theological turn need not accept sacred scriptures normatively: "Post-metaphysical thinking should be open to learning from religion and at the same remain agnostic" (Habermas, 2005: cited in Harrington, 2007: 54).
8. Weber (1958: 182). To begin to understand how the theological turn has implications at the most fundamental level, simply note its implications for everyday actions and relationships: for Levinas, God "looks at me in the face of the Other"; for Derrida, God "humbly hopes for my works of love and justice"; and for Chrétien, God "calls to me in the voice

and touch of the Other" (Simmons, 2008: 920). This results in concepts and ideas that transcend and are inconceivable from a secular perspective.

"For Marion, God is the absolutely self-given pure gift of love. This gift is not presented with the expectation of payback (i.e., according to an economic logic), but instead is an-economic. It is pure givenness (*donation*) without return. Henry claims that according to Christianity all humans exist in the condition of being 'sons' of God according to the 'truth of life.' This status requires a radical rupture of the power-relations that obtain according to the objectifying tendencies constitutive of the 'truth of the world.' In pure life, as sons, all beings are constituted in their relation to God/Life as such and not according to their socio-economic, gendered, raced, sexed, identity. <u>This is not to say that these identity markers are not radically important, but merely that in relation to God, our relations to others are bathed in the light of other-service and not self-interest</u>. Similarly, Lacoste proposes a 'kenotic treatment of the question of man' in which the self is established precisely in its being dispossessed *from itself*. This dispossession is a fundamental challenge to all egoism and arrogance. Overcoming these self-interested dispositions is hard work and Lacoste contends that our task is to live towards the <u>'kingdom of heaven'</u> in which the relation of self, God, and others is able to come into absolute harmony" (Simmons, 2008: 919; italics in original, underlining added here).

9. Quotes in this paragraph taken from Weber (1958: 181, 182; emphasis added here).
10. Turner (2003: 146).
11. Hur (2001: 41–42). "The MT [Old Testament] has 389 references to *rûah*, which have been generally classified in the following way: 125 referring to wind; 48 to breath; 97 to anthropological spirit; 21 to an evil spirit; 98 to the Spirit of the Lord/God" (38–39).
12. Turner (2003: 148, summarizing Menzies, 1991). The Spirit is the author of: (a) revelatory visions and dreams, (b) revelatory words or instruction or guidance, (c) revelatory discernment or divine wisdom, (d) invasive praise, and (e) charismatic preaching, witness, and teaching. However, the Jewish tradition did not understand the Spirit "as a gift a person needs to receive in order to *experience* salvation, nor as the source of spiritual/ethical renewal, nor as the power of miraculous activities in the physical realm (such as healings)."
13. Strecker (2002: 120). In short, the modern view often assumes that inspiration comes from within an individual, whereas the ancient view suggests that it comes from outside.
14. The fruit of the Spirit includes "love, joy, peace, patience, kindness, generosity, faithfulness, gentleness, and self-control" (Gal. 5:22–23) and with regard to gifts: "To one is given through the Spirit the utterance of wisdom, and to another the utterance of knowledge according to the same Spirit, to another faith by the same Spirit, to another gifts of healing by the one Spirit, to another the working of miracles, to another prophecy, to another the discernment of spirits, to another various kinds of tongues, to another the interpretation of tongues. All these are activated by one and the same Spirit, who allots to each one individually just as the Spirit chooses" (1 Cor. 12:8–11).
15. Actually the full term "Holy Spirit" only appears 13 times; the total of 17 here includes 3 mentions to "Spirit" where it is clear that the Holy Spirit is being referred to (e.g., see Luke 2:27; Luke 4:1,14), and 1 mention to a passage from Isaiah where the Holy Spirit is inferred (Luke 4:18). The full term "Holy Spirit" has 5 mentions in Matthew, 4 in Mark, and 3 in John. More generally, compared to Luke's 36 total references to *pneumatos*, Matthew has 19 references, Mark 24 references, and John 23 references.
16. Two are mentions where death is described as "giving up one's spirit" (Luke 8:55; 23:46), two are references to the risen Christ appearing as a "ghost" (Luke 24:37, 39), and the rest refer to someone's inner vitality (Luke 1:17; 1:47; 1:80).
17. Vengeance is ill-suited to the period of salvation being inaugurated at this point (Fitzmyer, 1970: 533).
18. The "fire" could be as reference to purification, or simply an allusion to the fact that when the Holy Spirit comes in Acts in comes in the form of fire (Acts 2:3–4).

19. The term "Holy Spirit" appears a total of 89 times in all of the New Testament, of which 54 (61 percent) are in Luke's two volumes. Luke's second volume, Acts, was not originally entitled "Acts *of the Apostles*"—the part in italics was added by others later.

20. Kuecker (2008: 214–215; emphasis in original). Perhaps the most striking difference between Luke's community (alternative *oikos*) and most human social groups is that Luke portrays a community whose boundaries have been commandeered by the Holy Spirit, a figure who appears in the narrative as one determined to disregard (conventional) social barriers in order to create a singular transethnic people for God. This is true both when viewed against Luke's portrayals of other social groups in the text—both Israelite and non-Israelite groups—but also against basic data from social groups across contemporary cultures. The Spirit, for Luke, creates the possibility of loving the "other" and incorporating even the threatening "other" (while allowing the "other" to retain a large measure of ethnic particularity) in a way that simply does not occur very often in contemporary intergroup and especially interethnic situations (220).

21. As has been oft-noted, people who believe that they can save themselves by their own willpower are deluding themselves, and thereby unintentionally empower that from which they wish to be saved (Foster, 1978: 4). Foster describes at some length how spiritual disciplines can help people to escape the materialist-individualist paradigm that stifles the human spirit: "Superficiality is the curse of our age. The doctrine of instant satisfaction is a primary spiritual problem. The desperate need today is not for a greater number of intelligent people, or gifted people, but for deep people" (1). For more on how the four corporate spiritual disciplines can be applied to management, see Dyck and Wong (2010).

22. Luke 12:10 says: "And everyone who speaks a word against the Son of Man will be forgiven [*aphethesetai*, to free, to forgive]; but whoever blasphemes [i.e., whoever consciously rejects the saving power and grace God provides for humankind; Marshall, 1978: 517] against the Holy Spirit will not be forgiven [*aphethesetai*]." "The image being used in *aphesis* is derived from an economic and social background in antiquity, either from the remission of debts or punishment or release from captivity or imprisonment" (Fitzmyer, 1970: 223). This verse suggests that people cannot be freed (forgiven: *aphesis*) from oppressive structures and systems if they consistently reject the Spirit and thereby the saving power and grace that God provides humankind. "The unforgivable sin is not to be understood merely as the rejection of Christian preaching or the gospel, but the persistence in consummate and obdurate opposition to the influence of the Spirit . . . a mentality which obstinately sets the mind against the Spirit of God, and as long as that obstinate mindset perdures, God's forgiveness cannot be accorded to such a person" (Fitzmyer, 1985: 964).

23. Strecker (2002: 128).

24. "You faithless and perverse generation, how much longer must I be with you and bear with you?" (Luke 9:41).

25. "The image is drawn from the ancient records of cities or kingdoms, which listed the citizens who belonged to them" (Fitzmyer, 1985: 863).

26. Consistent with this argument, research among a sample of self-professing Christian managers shows that there is a positive relationship between managers who: (1) emphasize spiritual virtues (e.g., prayer, striving to integrate faith in the workplace, consider God to be their ultimate Boss at work), (2) hold nonconventional values (e.g., less materialistic and less individualistic), and (3) adopt countercultural management practices (Dyck & Weber, 2006).

27. For example, see Agle and Van Buren (1999), Lecourt and Puachant (2011), and Sherman and Smith (1984). For a longer review of this literature, see Dyck (forthcoming).

28. Hopefully this exploratory analysis will encourage others to delve into these issues more deeply. For example, this might include an examination of the work of the Holy Spirit in Acts interpreted through a management lens. Or it might include using a managerial interpretive lens to look at other key themes, such as prayer, the way, prophets, prayer, grace, mercy, and so on.

V   Institutional Change

The research in this section has benefitted from comments by Laurence Broadhurst (whose contribution in developing the chiasm presented here was invaluable), Dan Epp-Tiessen, John Kloppenborg, Gordon Zerbe, and David Schroeder (who first alerted me to the chiastic form of Luke's Journey Narrative). I also thank Ian Brown, Katelyn Cove, Buffy Cowtan, and Glenn Sawatzky for their research assistance and contributions.

13   A Four-Phase Process Model Embedded in Luke's Journey Narrative

1. Other scholars have also noted that this section of Luke has a focus on how to implement Jesus' teachings in everyday life. For example, Gill (1970) highlights how Luke uses this section to convey teachings on discipleship, Resseguie (1982: 47) suggests that the purpose of the entire Journey Narrative is to highlight the contrasts between two "diametrically opposed ways of thinking," and Flender (1967) argues that in this section Luke exemplifies the relation between the Christian message and the world, and shows how the disciples, through Jesus, became bound into a community over the course of the journey.

2. "The problem of an unmitigating dissonance of form from content in the central section (9:51–19:44) of Luke's Gospel has become one of the central problems in Lukan studies. Both the silence concerning any developing journey to Jerusalem and the seemingly chaotic scramble of teaching units that bear no relation to a journey motif continue to baffle scholars" (Moessner, 1983: 575–76).

3. Recall that biblical scholars often encourage readers to attend to the order in which Luke places events (e.g., Johnson, 1991: 4).

4. For example, Bailey (2003), Goulder (1964b), Talbert (1974), Farrell (1986), Kariamadam (1987), and Baarlink (1992).

5. Or, ABCB'A' if there is a midpoint. For more on chiasms, see Ernesti (1962, original 1795), Lanham (1991), or Anderson (2000).

6. Klassen-Wiebe (2001: 93).

7. See Welch (1981).

8. Lissner (2007: 72ff); Marrou (1964: 151).

9. The technical term for this written form that lacks punctuation and where wordsarenotseparatedfromoneanother is called *scriptio continua*. As a result "passages had to be studied very attentively. They were not only read aloud but also learnt by heart, recited in a sing-song manner, syllable by syllable. Little wonder that readers of that time were very alive to the configuration of a text [such as evident in chiastic structure]" (Stock, 1984: 25).

10. Sometimes the paired twin-passages essentially duplicate one another, and other times they mirror each other (i.e., invert left and right). Put differently, sometimes the paired passages say the same thing (e.g., Jesus is traveling on a road), and sometimes they present opposite sides of the same coin (e.g., Jesus is beginning, versus completing, his trip to Jerusalem).

11. The four-phase model depicted in figure 13.1 is never referred to *explicitly* in the Gospel of Luke. Nowhere does Jesus say: "Here is a four-phase process model of community discernment and learning." However, this is not as troublesome or unusual as it may first appear. For example, Socrates also never explicitly spells out the steps of his highly influential dialogical model. Rather, just as the four-step Socratic method is implicit in the texts describing *how* he taught that were written after he had died by his followers (e.g., Plato and Xenophon), so also might there be a four-phase model embedded in how the Lukan text unfolds. Moreover, that the model would be embedded in a journey narrative is entirely consistent with the pattern of Hellenistic literature in that day, where "the story

of the travelling teacher or wonder-worker was a favourite theme," and "[t]he imagery of life as a journey or as a road was often accompanied by motifs of ethical choice" (Baban, 2006: 81, 41). This tradition goes back to Greek classics; e.g., in Homer's writings "journeying together brings 'unity in thinking'" (40) and, "as illustrated by Plato, one of the recurring Hellenistic stories is that of a young person . . . [who] journeys alone or with company . . . needing to question others or himself on what is the truly good direction in life" (40, 41).

12. The three "keywords" associated with the first phase—rebuke, disciple, two—are consistent with this theme. As described more fully in appendix A, these "keywords" are terms that recur in phase 1 passages, but are rarely found in other Journey Narrative passages.

13. This sensitization to a problem can come from a variety of sources, including spiritual nudgings and Jesus' example and teachings.

14. The three "keywords" for the second phase—find, give, parable—support the idea that the second phase deals with ways to respond to the issues raised in the first phase.

15. These themes are consistent with the keywords for phase 3—to hear and to see/receive sight. Many of the passages that describe Jesus healing people are found in the phase 3.

16. McLaren (2010: 244, emphasis added here).

17. These themes are consistent with the keywords for phase 4—law/yer, rich/poor, place/position.

18. Note how this four-phase interpretation has some overlap with other commentators who also draw attention to the fourfold nature of this passage. In particular, Green (1997: 534) suggests that the passage turns on its "four statements of desire [which] dramatize the conflict at work throughout the Lukan narrative and are key to our appreciation of the role of this brief scene within the larger Gospel": (1) Herod wants to kill Jesus (Luke 13:31); (2) Jesus continues his actions to help those who have been social outcasts (Luke 3:32–33); (3) Jesus wants to be seen as a mother hen who "gathers her brood under her wings" (Luke 13:34a); and (4) the people of Jerusalem do not want to be led by Jesus and his ideas (Luke 13:34b–35).

19. In one sense Jesus heading to Jerusalem is consistent with the Pharisees' advice to "get away from here" because Jerusalem is in Judea, which is outside of Herod's jurisdiction in Galilee. While this may seem to solve the immediate problem (i.e., Herod wanting to kill Jesus), Jesus is also reinforcing that he is doing this "my way." And it is equally clear that Jesus' is an act of civil disobedience vis-à-vis Herod's desire to kill Jesus.

20. Fox would be understood in the first century as an "unflattering term" (Fitzmyer, 1985: 1029) meaning relatively "insignificant" and of "low cunning" (Marshall, 1978: 571).

21. Note that Jesus' reply may also provide implicit support for the four-phase change model embedded in the Journey Narrative. In particular, Jesus twice refers to the three-day pattern where he will be doing his work (today, tomorrow, and the next day). Perhaps each *day* Jesus refers to—i.e., each 24-hour cycle encompassing morning, noon, evening, and night—corresponds symbolically with each four-phase *cycle* in the change model (i.e., problem recognition, action response, changed way of seeing, and institutional change). If so, then the first three "days" Jesus refers to might allude to the first three cycles through the model that come prior to this midpoint in the chiasm, and the second three "days" would allude to the three cycles in the second half of the chiasm. This interpretation helps to make sense of a puzzling double reference to three days, and is entirely consistent with Luke's self-described attention to the order in which he presents his material.

22. An interesting exception is Taylor (1986: 201), who notes how striking it is that Jesus chose to see himself as a hen, rather than take other images from the Old Testament like a mighty eagle or a proud lion. Taylor adds that, upon further reflection, it seems entirely appropriate for Jesus to liken himself to a female hen, given his penchant for up-turning the social customs of the day, his ideas about servant leadership, and his sayings such as "the last shall be first." Jesus paints a picture where he "is a mother hen, who stands between the chicks and those who mean to do them harm. She has no fangs, no claws, no rippling muscles. All she has is her willingness to shield her babies with her own body. If the fox wants them, he will have to kill her first." Beavis (2003:14) adds that in Jewish

tradition "the hen can symbolize divine love and care, fertility, atonement, concern for the poor, and perhaps even the eternity of the human soul."

23. That is, they are in charge of some of the organizational structures and systems, the institutions and the practices, that shaped life in Palestine (Green, 1997: 539).

24. Fitzmyer (1985: 1037) and Marshall (1978: 577).

25. "There are therefore many indications in the psalm that point in the direction of explaining the experiences of the individual in this psalm as that of a group of people" (Botha, 2003: 210; see also Kwon, 2009: 52). For more information, see chapter seven and the interpretation the parable of the wicked tenants/oppressive landlord.

26. For more elaboration on these ideas, see Yoder (1972) on revolutionary subordination.

27. See Argyris (1990) and Nielsen (2001). Other similar four-phase organizational learning models have been developed by Crossan, Lane, and White (1999) and Nonaka (1994) (see also Dyck & Broadhurst, 2008).

14 LUKE'S THREE "FORWARD" CYCLES THROUGH THE FOUR-PHASE PROCESS MODEL

1. The disciples' question alludes to a passage in the Old Testament, where the prophet Elijah calls down fire from heaven to consume 50 people representing the Samaritan king Ahaziah (2. Kings 1:9-12).

2. Note that the passage does not explicitly mention that Jesus sends his followers to *Samaritan* villages, but this seems to be a reasonable inference from the context of the passage (e.g., Luke 9:52–54; 10:30–37). Support is also evident in the allusion to the Old Testament text from 2. Kings 1:9–12 where fire comes down from heaven twice to consume representatives of the Smaritan king Ahazia (verses 10 and 12), which is analogous to two parallel references in Luke: (1) Luke 9:51 refers to fire falling from heaven, and (2) Luke 10:18 refers to Satan falling from heaven "like a flash of lightning."

   Note also that an argument could be made that the followers are offering their services to *oikoi* in the villages to help during a busy harvest season (Luke 10:2), perhaps recognizing that the poor would be the first ones to suffer if there was a lack of food due to lack of laborers during the harvest. Jesus instructs his followers to ask the master in charge of the harvest if they can help with the harvest, aware that as relatively vulnerable foreign migrant workers they might be like sheep among wolves (Luke 10:3).

   Finally, although this passage is often interpreted as Jesus sending out missionaries to convert other people, perhaps it is his own followers that Jesus wants to be converted. After all, it is the disciples whom he has rebuked for their bad attitudes toward the Samaritans. Consistent with this, in the very first verse where it says that Jesus "appoints" the 70, the Greek word for "appoints" could also be translated as Jesus wanting his followers to see more clearly something that has been hidden (Klassen-Weibe, 2001: 288), a translation that seems especially plausible in light of Luke 10:21 (as we shall see). Taken together, it seems entirely possible that Jesus is sending out his followers, at least in part, so that they can deal with their bad attitudes toward rivals like the Samaritans.

3. Apparently one lesson learned from the earlier (Luke 9:1–6) mission is evident in the updated instructions Jesus gives to the 70 (Luke 10:6), when he tells them to ensure that the *oikos* they stay in while visiting the villages has a member who is a "child of peace" (i.e., someone who, like Jesus' followers, is open to listening to and learning from others). Note also that of the 13 mentions of the word "peace" in all of Luke, 3 (23 percent) appear in this passage, more than any other single passage. One of these mentions is where Jesus instructs his followers to say "Peace to this *oikos*" (note the parallelism in Jesus' statement "Today salvation has come to this *oikos*" in Luke 19:9).

4. Jesus also challenges conventional norms about the role of women more generally, who would not normally be listening to a teacher as Mary was.

5. Jesus can't be working for both because: "Every kingdom divided against itself becomes a desert, and house falls on house" (Luke 11:17).

6. The Greek word *makorios* is usually translated as "blessed"; in the Greek world this adjective referred to a person's "inner happiness" (Fitzmyer, 1970: 632).

7. See Green (1997: esp. 460–470).

8. Marshall (1978).

9. Green (1997: 480).

10. Jesus goes on to tell his listeners not to fear even conventional leaders who have the authority to "kill the body"—nor to worry about how they will defend themselves when brought "before the synagogues, the rulers, and the authorities"—because the Holy Spirit will reveal to them what they "ought to say" (Luke 12:4,11,12). To freely live a "good life" people cannot consciously and persistently reject the saving power and grace that God provides for humankind (Marshall, 1978: 517; Fitzmyer, 1970: 223; 1985: 964). For more on this passage, see chapter twelve, note 22.

11. Some relevant passages are found in Numbers 27:1–11; 36:7–9; Deuteronomy 21:16–17. Because these passages do not apply to every kind of imaginable situation, the kind of request the man makes is not unusual. Addressing Jesus as a "teacher" acknowledges Jesus' authority to make such a decision. Jesus' response echoes language from Exodus 2:14 (repeated in Acts 7:27)—"Who made you a ruler and a judge over us?"—thereby drawing attention to dysfunctional things that can happen when people act as judges and rulers (Fitzmyer, 1985: 968–69; Green, 1997: 488; Marshall, 1978: 522).

12. "'Greed' can denote the hunger for advanced social standing as well as the insatiable desire for wealth, though in Luke's world these two images are inextricably related" (Green, 1997: 488–89).

13. This label of "fool" is sometimes used in Hebrew Scriptures to describe people who go against God; applying it to the rich man in this case is consistent with an understanding of "greed" that recognizes it "as a form of idolatry" (Green, 1997: 491).

14. Bill Gates (2007) quotes a letter from his mother when he explains why he and his wife Melinda became so involved in helping the world's poor: *"From those to whom much is given, much is expected."*

15. Quote from Hartman (1992: 583); see also Fitzmyer (1985: 996–97).

16. The example described here is from Plowman et al. 2007. Other examples include a description of the four-phase process of how the rower-pump was developed and became the institutionalized norm for agricultural irrigation in Bangladesh (Dyck et al. 2000), and how the microfinancing movement spread in Bolivia (Dyck, 2002).

15 LUKE'S THREE "REVERSE" CYCLES THROUGH THE FOUR-PHASE PROCESS MODEL

1. Institutionalized customs surrounding meals and food were of great importance in the first century, and in this passage Jesus challenges the norms of both Jews and Greco-Romans (Green, 1997: 542; Elliott, 1991a).

2. Just as people with dropsy are filled with fluid but desire more to drink, so also money-lovers loaded with money crave more of it—both to their own demise. The Pharisees are called lovers of money elsewhere in Luke (11:37–44; 16:14). It is unclear why this man with dropsy would have been at the meal, because he was clearly a marginalized person and would have also been too unclean to sit with Pharisees (Green, 1997: 546, 547).

3. This list is notable because its members were on the margins of society, and unable to reciprocate in kind.

4. "The behaviors Jesus demands would collapse the distance between rich and poor, insider and outsider; reverting to anthropological models of economic exchange, such relations would be characterized by 'generalized reciprocity'—that is, by the giving of gifts, the extension of hospitality, without expectation of return" (Green, 1997: 553).

5. Some might argue that this story is not so much a call for what people should actually do, but more an allusion to God and the eschatological banquet. However, such a reading is problematic because it suggests that God did not initially invite the marginalized (ibid., 556).

6. Five yoke of oxen would be needed for a farm of one hundred acres or more, substantially larger than the three–six acres required per adult at the time (ibid., 560).

7. Ibid., 550.

8. This may have been a tower for a vineyard, a city wall, or perhaps some more elaborate structure (ibid., 566).

9. Ibid., 570. The term "sinners" is often used to describe people of low social status, without particular regard to whether they are especially guilty of having wronged God. For example, note people of higher status are seldom called sinners, even though they are strongly criticized by Jesus for misunderstanding Scripture and misleading people (though see Luke 6:34; 24:7).

10. At the end of each of the first two parables in this phase Jesus describes the great joy that is prompted in heaven when a sinner repents (Luke 15:7,10). It is not entirely clear, however, who the "sinner" is and what the "repentance" was. It seems odd to think that the lost sheep or the lost coin would be seen as "sinners" who "repented," unless one argues that they are the ones who changed their "mind or purpose" (which is the meaning of the word "repentance" or *metanoeo*: Liddell & Scott, 2000). In this light there may be an irony in Jesus' teachings, namely that although the conventional usage of the term "sinner" refers to the outcasts, the "real" sinners are the people who create and perpetuate social structures and systems that create outcasts in the first place. Thus, in this light Jesus can be interpreted to be saying that rejoicing is prompted in heaven when the "real" sinners (e.g., leaders who by their actions and religious rules about purity exclude marginalized people from community) change their minds, and begin to find and implement ways to restore these "lost" marginalized people to society. This interpretation is not inconsistent with Luke's other mentions of repentance (Luke 11:32; 13:3,5; 16:30).

11. This passage has been described more fully in chapter seven, and the passage about Lazarus is discussed more fully in chapter eight.

12. See, e.g., Exodus 4:6, Numbers 5:2–3, and Deuteronomy 24:8 (Fitzmyer, 1970: 574).

13. Green (1997: 647).

14. Though, as the passage tells us, only God is good.

15. See ibid., 663.

16. See chapter eleven for more on Zacchaeus, and chapter six for more and the parable of the ten pounds.

17. For more on *pax Romana*, see chapter eleven.

18. For more on how the dominant theme in Psalm 118 is on the redemption of social outcasts, see chapters seven and thirteen.

19. For example, see Oliver (1992), Lawrence and Suddaby (2006), Hensmans (2003), and Heugens and Lander (2009). The example described in this paragraph is drawn from Summers and Dyck (2011).

VI IMPLICATIONS FOR TWENTY-FIRST-CENTURY MANAGEMENT THEORY AND PRACTICE

1. See Weber (1958: 47).

2. Note that the exemplars are not and need not be drawn from managers who claim to be followers of Jesus. Just as Luke's Roman centurion had "such faith" that Jesus had not seen in all of Israel, just as Jesus told his listeners to follow the example of the Good Samaritan, and just as salvation came to the house of a chief tax collector (Zacchaeus) who had not been in good standing among the religious community, so also KOG management is by no means the exclusive domain of followers of Jesus. Nor should we expect it to be, given the popular alignment between conventional management theory

and the Protestant ethic and its conventional Catholic variation (Weber, 1958; Novak, 1982).

3. Readers interested in a more comprehensive analysis that contrasts and compares conventional management theory with an alternative approach may be interested in a book I coauthored with Mitch Neubert called *Management: Current Practices and New Directions* from which some of the material in part six has been adapted. Note that the alternative approach to management in the Dyck and Neubert (2010) book is not based on a religious or faith perspective. Rather, the book examines management theory and practice from two parallel moral-points-of-view. "Mainstream management" is based on a materialistic-individualistic moral-point-of-view that places emphasis on *maximizing* productivity and profits for shareholders. "Multistream management" is based on a moral-point-of-view that suggests management is all about *balancing* multiple forms of well-being (e.g., financial, social, ecological, spiritual, physical) for multiple stakeholders (owners, employees, customers, suppliers, competitors, neighbors, future generations). As it turns out, the moral-point-of-view undergirding the Multistream approach has important similarities with the moral-point-of-view found in Luke.

16 Managing Relationships *within* Organizations: Organizational Structure, Motivation, and Leadership

1. This is an adapted and somewhat simplified interpretation of Weber's ideas. A more detailed description of these four fundamentals and their theological implication, as well as theoretical and empirical support for the Mainstream versus Multistream approaches to the four fundamentals, can be found in Dyck and Schroeder (2005), Dyck and Weber (2006), and Dyck and Neubert (2010).

2. This case draws heavily from Dyck and Neubert (2010), which draws from Semler (2004, 1989) and Vogl (2004).

3. Semler (1989: 77).

4. Semler (2004: 12).

5. Ibid., 92.

6. Maslow's (1954) work has been called a "classic of classics" and has been considered in the top ten of "the most influential management books of the 20th century" (Bedeian & Wren, 2001), and one of the most important (Miner, 2003).

7. Miner (2003), Mitchell and Daniels (2003).

8. Maybe one reason Jesus instructs his followers to pray for their "daily bread" is to remind those who can afford to store bread for much longer periods of time that they, too, have physiological needs whose being met should not be taken for granted.

9. See Despain and Converse (2003: 20, 142–143, 169; emphases in these quotes have been added here).

10. These two dimensions are drawn from some of the most important and influential leadership theories and research in the scholarly literature (Miner, 2003; Yukl, 2006).

11. Avery and Ryan (2002), Grover and Walker (2003). Perhaps the most well-known variations of this model are associated with Hersey and Blanchard (1977).

12. This is evident in the parable of the fig tree, where a landowner asks his gardener to chop down a fig tree that hasn't borne fruit for three years. Rather than obey the landowner, the gardener asks for permission to tend the fig tree for one more year, to dig around it and provide manure (Luke 13:6–7). Similarly, other subordinates who are better than their masters at enacting KOG ways include the shrewd manager and the third manager in the parable of the ten pounds.

13. See also chapter nine, note 12. Based on Luke, the hallmark of KOG leadership is regarding the views of others, serving others, and refusing to lord it over others.

14. And, from the perspective of Maslow's hierarchy of needs theory, impoverished people will be motivated to meet their physiological needs, so meeting their needs for love or

esteem is not likely to improve productivity. Consider how this way of thinking may be evident in "sweat shops" in low-income countries.

15. "one who stands near, or by, a suppliant" (Liddell & Scott, 2000).

16. The only other occasion where this term is found is in Luke 17:13, when ten lepers call out to Jesus as "master" to have mercy on them (Klassen-Wiebe, 2001: 164).

17. The aforementioned passages where the disciples call Jesus "master" (*epistates*) could be added in this category.

18. The example described in this chapter is drawn from Nielsen (1998), which also describes how Greenleaf used the four-step method to reduce discrimination facing African Americans at AT&T. Greenleaf based his approach on the example of John Woolman, a cloth merchant and ethics activist in Philadelphia in the colonial era who "developed and used friendly, disentangling dialogue with merchants and farmers to address the issues of slavery, peacemaking with Indians and the British, farmer-banker relations, trading practices with Indians, and child labour" (ibid., 127).Woolman observed that this method "in different Places and Ages hath different Names . . . It is deep, and inward, confined to no Forms of Religion, nor excluded from any" (cited in ibid., 144).

    Technically, rather than see the four steps of the friendly disentangling method as directly analogous to the four phases of the process model embedded in Luke's Journey Narrative, it may be more accurate to see the steps as the "transitionary" activities that link one phase to the next, as follows:

    1. the first part of the friendly disentangling model (i.e., to look for the source of current problematic behavior within the biased organizational norms rather than blaming individuals) bridges ideas from phase 4 and phase 1;

    2. the second part (approach those involved in a friendly manner) bridges phase 1 and phase 2;

    3. the third part (get input from the people involved regarding possible solutions that are consistent with a frame of reference that transcends a conventional perspective) bridges phase 2 and phase 3;

    4. and the fourth part (support those who are willing to implement nontraditional behaviors/governing values) bridges phases 3 and phase 4.

19. This realization is not inconsistent with Luke, insofar as the individuals presented in the first phase of Luke's cycles are often depicted as "stock characters" who represent society-at-large and its institutional problems.

20. Note that there is no language like "rebuke" in Greenleaf's account. Thus Greenleaf's approach may be more deliberately "friendly" than the approach described in Luke, or perhaps the Lukan use of the word "rebuke" would have been perceived less harshly in the first century than its translated word is today.

17   Managing Money: Economics, Finance, and Accounting

1. For a fuller analysis of these two passages, see chapters five and eleven, respectively.

2. Barney and Hesterly (1999: 112 and 118).

3. For example, compared to students who were taught nonconventional economic theory, students exposed to only conventional economic theory are more likely to act in their own narrow financial self-interests (e.g., they are less likely to return "lost" money to its rightful owner, and less likely to point out an undercharge on a purchase) (Frank, Gilovich, & Regan, 1993; 1996). Similarly, management students tend to become more individualistic and materialistic during their programs of studies (Ferraro, Pfeffer, & Sutton, 2005; Krishnan, 2003).

4. For more on this research and general topic, see Dyck et al. (2011).

5. It is often claimed that it is "natural" for people to maximize their own material interests, and that it is naïve (or perhaps even irresponsible) to develop theories based on ideas that counteract this innate feature of the human condition. However, there is ample evidence

to suggest that people living in high-income countries have been *socialized* to accept a materialistic-individualistic moral-point-of-view, and to suggest that this is not innate to humankind. Indeed, research on ancient economies and on modern hunting-gathering societies suggests that sustenance economics is natural, and that it is innate to the human condition to: share resources in community (e.g., because it would be impossible for one person to eat a gazelle before the meat would rot), work only until they meet their basic subsistence needs (which is about six hours a day, on average, even for hunting-gathering societies that live in harsh environments—why collect more berries if you already have enough?), and minimize their belongings (e.g., no one wanted to carry two or three spears from one place to the next if one spear would suffice). Thus, if we look through the lens of the history of humankind, then the present fascination in "self-interest with guile" economics in so-called developed economies seems to be an aberration of normal human activity (e.g., Sahlins, 1972).

6. This example is taken almost verbatim from Dyck and Neubert (2010), drawn from Batstone (2003) and others.

7. Batstone (2003: 133).

8. Malden Mills was in bankruptcy between 2001 and 2003. Feuerstein left the company's board in 2004 (he still owned about 5 percent of the company). By 2006 its annual revenue was around $160 million, including $25 million from the US military for high-tech clothing. However, heavy debts forced the firm to declare bankruptcy again. It sold its assets to Chrysalis Capital Partners where the company reemerged as Polartec LLC in 2007.

9. Though, as has often been noted, commentators who invoke the imagery of the invisible hand often forget that Adam Smith describes at considerable length the "virtuous arm" that the hand is attached to (Dyck & Neubert, 2010: 14). Smith's argument that everyone should be free to pursue their individual interests must take into account the contextual virtues described in his book *The Theory of Moral Sentiments* (1982 [1759]).

10. Rees (2002).

11. An important exception is for about ten months in 2008/2009, when the percentage went below 20 percent (Madigan, 2011).

12. Consider the "game" played by "derivatives" dealers, who bet on others' *expectations* of prices of currencies, shares, and bonds in the future (e.g., three months to five years). The nominal value of contracts in over-the-counter derivatives in 2010 was approaching $600 trillion (McKenzie, 2010). Already by 1995 speculative investment accounted for 95 percent of all transactions, whereas as recently as 1970 trade and long-term investment accounted for 90 percent of transactions (Wilson, 2005; see also Martin & Schumann, 1997: 52; Soros, 1998: 141–146). Taken together, *objective* economic relationships are increasingly less significant in the flurry of money being traded around the world. What has become more important is the *expectation* of what others will do. The shortcomings of this kind of trading are well-known, but potential solutions to address them have not been well received. For example, already in the 1970s Nobel Prizewinner James Tobin recognized the difficulties associated with the deregulated flow of capital, which prompted him to suggest governments implement 1 percent tax on all foreign currency exchanges. This would encourage more stable financial decisions related to real production and changes in the market, rather based on the whims of financial traders. However this idea, though recognized as theoretically brilliant, goes against the dominant ideology of the free movement of capital (Martin & Schumann, 1997: 83). For a longer discussion on the shortcomings of conventional globalization and what alternative globalization might look like, see Dyck, Bruning, and Buckland (2003).

There are some changes that signal a slight shift away from acquisitive economics toward sustenance economics. For example, there has been an increase in the number of people making investment decisions based on criteria that go beyond financial performance. In the United States about one out of ten dollars under professional management are invested using some sort of criteria of social and environmental responsibility. This is called socially responsible investing (SRI), which has been overall doubling about every 5 years, with SRI mutual funds doubling every 2.5 years (Dyck & Neubert, 2010: 81).

13. These axioms are taken from Keown et al. (1998: 11–23), who suggest that they are little more that statements of common sense. For a further discussion of a countercultural approach to these axioms, and others, see Dyck (2012b).

14. Jones and Netter (2008).

15. Studies like Miller and Sardois (2011) also turn conventional agency theory on its head by arguing that, instead of assuming that managers will opportunistically exploit a firm to serve their own financial self-interests, there are cases where managers may forgo their own interests and their owner's perceived self-interests, choosing instead to serve the long-term interests of all stakeholders (including the owners). They provide a specific example where a manager deliberately reduces organizational profits. When he was CEO of Renault in the 1950s, Pierre Lefaucheux noted that the firm was likely "to make too much profit" and concluded that "it will be necessary to reduce profits by 2 billion francs per year . . . [and] discussed the possibilities of lowering profits by cutting prices, higher salaries, providing better incentives to dealers, and finding other expenditures to improve the business" (8).

16. Unless otherwise specified, the quotes in this section are drawn from Yunus (1996; emphasis added here).

17. At the time Yunus started, the membership of women in banks in Bangladesh was only 1 percent. In the beginning Yunus was aiming for 50 percent women, aware that women are more likely than men to make decisions that improve the long-term conditions in their community. This policy to provide loans to women prompted a negative reaction from some sectors of that Muslim society. According to Yunus, "[T]he first opposition came from the husbands, who thought we were insulting them. The second were the *mullahs*, who started preaching that [for women to be] taking money from the Grameen Bank was against religion and that they should leave it to their husbands." Some even accused the bank of being Christian missionaries, forgetting that women had been businesspeople in Islamic history, including the Prophet's first wife. The radical Left accused Grameen Bank of being part of an American conspiracy that was bringing capitalism to poor people, and the people on the Right thought the bank was organizing people to make them into a communist threat (quoted in Tharoor, 2006).

18. According to Yunus, each branch is a self-standing entity, made up of community borrowers and local staff, where relationships are based on trust: "There is no attempt on anyone's part to outsmart anyone" (quoted in ibid.).

19. See Dyck and Neubert (2010) and Yunus, Moingeon, and Lehmann-Ortega (2010).

20. This discussion around accounting draws heavily from Christie et al. (2004). Thanks also to Janet Morrill for her feedback on this section and table 17.1.

21. For example, Kieso et al. (2002).

22. Roberts and Jones (2009). From a KOG-management perspective, the boundaries of the firm should be relatively porous, especially with regard to creating room for the marginalized. From this holistic view, the organization is seen as an essential means for nurturing the larger community. Just as for Aristotle the *oikos* should reflect the character of the larger ideal *polis*, so also in Luke the *oikos* is seen as enacting the character of the larger KOG. Such an enlarged understanding of the entity makes its managers more likely to see beyond conventional organizational issues and, e.g., to consider the well-being of larger ecological environment, of the unemployed, and of where to redistribute financial wealth.

23. Monetization can also lead to commodification. Money has a tendency to reduce qualities into quantities. It has the effect of flattening the world of things and stripping them of their color, taste, and texture. Akin to how the Romans used money to the disadvantage of the poor in first-century Palestine, it has been argued that *monetariza-tion* was instrumental to the objectives of colonialization and that it encouraged the appropriation of wealth by the colonials and the genocide of Canada's First Nations (Neu, 2000).

24. The use of nonfinancial performance measures is becoming increasingly prevalent (Upton, 2001), with development of alternate performance reporting in the areas of sustainability and corporate social responsibility, and in research that is consistent with the idea of "radical accounting" and the triple-bottom-line (e.g., see Kaplan & Norton, 1992; Mitchell et al. 2012).

25. Ample anecdotal evidence testifies to the shortcomings of a conventional approach where employees are driven to make decisions that maximize their short-term bonuses to the detriment of the long-term health of the entity (and the larger community). The KOG approach recovers aspects of the concept of voyage accounting (akin to "journey" accounting?), accounting for actual work projects and "moments of truth" along with routine business events (Ramo, 2002).

26. Gold (2010: 52–53). A second institutional structure associated with the Focolare is its now 33 permanent "model towns" around the world, founded on a principle of daily lives of mutual love. These model towns provide a countercultural alternative to the dominant norms in social, economic, and religious spheres. But unlike previous attempts to build utopian egalitarian societies (e.g., kibbutz), these towns have more porous boundaries evident in the fact that they: (1) do not see themselves closed off from the rest of society; (2) have frequent turnover in the majority of their inhabitants; and (3) compete in global markets.

27. Gold (2010: 39).

28. See Golin and Parolin (2006).

29. The first Focolare members wanted to solve the major problems facing people in Trent, and more generally sought to bring mutual respect and solidarity to all members of the human family (Gold, 2010: 71, 40). Because of the great physical devastation and human need during the war, many people were questioning and blaming God for allowing such atrocities to occur. However everything changed after Chiara Lubich, the founder of the Focolare, had the insight that God was "present everywhere"—even in the middle of suffering (65). Jesus suffered, and Jesus can be experienced by ministering to people who are suffering.

For each person who has been touched in some way be the Focolare spirituality and lifestyle, the initial step is similar to Chiara's—as a response to the discovery of God's love, to move beyond comfortable or familiar horizons [e.g., their previous understanding of *oikos*] in order to turn with love to neighbors in need. They often face all over the world what war-torn Trent continues to represent—not only war and violence but also poverty, injustice, and discord of every kind, in families and between people of different religions and cultures. They work to bring love, to build unity (Uelmen, 2005: 54–55).

30. "Then came the night of 13 May 1944. That was the night when Chiara and her family saw their home destroyed from the hillside where they had gone for safety. That was the night when Chiara took the decision, through her tears, to leave here family, who had decided to quit the city, and go back down to stay with her companions . . . As well as having left her family, Chiara was now homeless. She needed somewhere to stay, and was offered a little flat adjoining the Capuchin church . . . It had two rooms and became known to the girls as 'the little house,' with its connotation of the little house in Loreto ['reputed to be the house of the Holy Family of Nazareth . . . transported from the Holy Land by angels' (Gallagher, 1997: 12)]" (Gallagher, 1997: 35–36).

31. These actions were inspired by what had happened in the early church, described in Acts 4:32–35 (Gold, 2010: 68). According to Chiara, such sharing of possessions characterized the early church and in time helped to liberate people from "long-standing situations of institutional injustice" (taken from Robertson, 1993: 77; cited in Gold, 2010: 69).

32. Gold (2010: 65).

33. Cited in ibid., 66. God was a benevolent God, and signs of benefaction were evident in the sharing of resources.

34. Gallagher (1997: 41). "When the war ended, people of the [Focolare] community traveled to other cities for work or study and carried with them their newly discovered lifestyle. Focolare houses were opened first in other cities in Italy, then throughout Europe,

and, starting in the late 1950s and into the 1960s, in North and South America, Asia, and Africa" (Uelmen, 3005: 56).

35. In other words, the Focolare's understanding of the Gospel went far beyond a narrow understanding of spiritual edification.

36. Gold (2010: 69–67).

37. Ibid., 84–85.

38. This discussion draws from ibid., 88–92.

39. For more on this, see ibid., 161, 165.

40. Drawn from ibid., 127–128; see also 121ff.)

41. This includes new ways of seeing the purpose of business, and new ways of seeing its employees, customers, and competitors (ibid., 130–31).

42. Ibid., 137. EOC firms also support no-layoff policies.

43. Whereas implementing EOC principles can lead to increased costs and thus decreased profits, they can also foster the development of unusually resilient networks of relationships both within and outside of the business that are reliable even during times of crisis (ibid., 59).

44. Insofar as EOC firms are owned by members, decisions are not driven by remote anonymous shareholders who demand quarterly increases in profits, share price or dividends (ibid., 156). This also tends to invert the so-called agency problem: in EOC firms managers and owners who have firsthand or face-to-face knowledge of the needs of their employees and other stakeholders are more likely to act on these interests, rather than merely in their own financial self-interests.

45. Ibid., 136–137.

46. See ibid., 147, 149. The term "externalities" refers to the "invisible" costs and benefits borne by the rest of society that are not reflected in the prices organizations pay for inputs or get paid for their outputs. For example, when a consumer purchases gasoline to drive their car, the conventional price of gas does not fully reflect the financial and nonfinancial "costs" borne by others (e.g., health costs associated with pollution, costs associated with climate change, reduced fossil fuels for future generations, and so on).

47. Ibid., 141, 144.

48. Quoted in ibid., 145.

18   Managing Relationships between Organizations: Marketing, Supply Chain, and Strategy

1. Galen Lehman tells of seeing such a sign in Kidron, Ohio.

2. This quote is from Kent (1986: 153) who is one of the many critics of these four P's, which were first developed by McCarthy (1960). Note also that some of the ideas described here under KOG marketing are consistent with view of contemporary scholars in marketing, including that: (a) the "product" includes the relationships and connections formed among organizations and people in the creation, distribution, and usage of the product; (b) "place" can go beyond seeing an organization "as a sole and self-sustaining operator in a competitive world but as a company that operates with loyal networks of partners"; and (c) promotion can involve cocreating products with outsiders (see Kotler, Kartajay, & Setiawan, 2010: 33, xii, 10, respectively). Note also that this draws from material in Dyck (2012b).

3. While it may seem crass to do so, consider the KOG to be a product that is being "marketed" in the Gospel of Luke. From the analysis in chapter ten, it is clear that this *product* is one that is designed to meet the needs of the larger community, rather than simply the needs or wants of a narrowly defined consumer. In terms of *price*, although the KOG demands giving up the perceived financial security associated with conventional *oikos*, it is clear that the KOG is "free" and cannot be purchased with financial

means. With regard to *place*, in Luke the KOG may be seen as competing with the kingdom of the (oppressive) Roman Empire, but there is little evidence that KOG is fostering competition among different religions (e.g., Jesus was born and died a Jew, Jesus spoke highly of the faith of the centurion, Jesus called listeners to follow the example of the Samaritan). And in terms of *promotion*, while the KOG may be communicated via one-to-one relationships, it is striking the passages that proclaim core KOG ideas are always addressed to crowds, and that the visible signs of the KOG are enacted by groups of people in *oikos* settings.

4. For more information on Shared Farming, see Dyck (1994a and b).

5. Larson and Halldorsson (2004).

6. In terms of a first-century understanding, where it was a fixed sum economy, a powerful *oikos* continued to increase its profits thanks to smaller *oikoi* becoming poorer. In modern terms where the earth's resources are considered a fixed sum, it means that using more resources to feed the profits of one business results in fewer resources for others.

7. The information for this description is drawn from Anderson (1998), Dean (2007), Dyck and Neubert (2010), Haque (2011), and Hawken, Lovins, and Lovins (1999).

8. From Dean (2007).

9. Bedeian and Wren (2001), Miner (2003), and Porter (1980).

10. The study goes on to describe what happened after these companies were purchased by larger corporations who followed a more conventional approach, where contracts were negotiated up front. An unintended consequence of this transition was that fashion became more of a mere product or commodity, with less time and less emphasis placed on ensuring its aesthetic beauty. For example, a supplier was less likely to make the costly changes required for unexpected characteristics of fabrics and to ensure that the cloth would "hang" the right way. The price of the clothes was lower, but to the trained eye the quality and artistic beauty had been compromised. And, the sense of interorganizational neighborliness and trust had been lost (Uzzi, 1997).

11. Similarly, pioneering organizations in the microfinancing movement are eager to share best practices with other banks and nonprofit organizations who wish to provide credit to microentrepreneurs.

12. A conventional approach argues that competitiveness is good for society because it motivates people and organizations to do their best, encourages continuous improvement, promotes efficiency, and reduces the opportunity for consumers to be taken advantage of. However, even proponents of competitiveness admit that it can go awry, most notably when people cheat in order to win (e.g., think of Worldcom or Enron). A "win at all costs" form of competitiveness can bring out the worst in humankind when people are willing to injure themselves (e.g., think of performance enhancing drugs) or others (e.g., tearing down an opponent) in order to improve their chances of winning.

    From a KOG-management perspective competitiveness, even at its best, simply does warrant having a central role in organization theory. Rather than assume that the desire to compete brings out the best in humankind, why not assume that the desire to share, or to live sustainably on the planet, or to eradicate poverty, or to ensure that everyone is treated with dignity is more likely to truly bring out the best in people? What if organizational strategies and practices were designed toward these ends, instead of designed to out-compete an "opposition"? (a very similar point is made in Dyck & Neubert, 2010: 275).

13. This example is described in Chewning, Eby, and Roels (1990).

14. All these relationships happened spontaneously without direct government intervention or regulation. Initially these initiatives had acquisitive economic motivations, but over time sustenance economic motivators became more dominant, though they have nevertheless still yielded financial benefits. This example is taken from Hawken (1993: 62–63; see also description in Dyck & Neubert, 2010: 277).

Final Thoughts

1. For other research that explicitly develops an understanding of "radical" management consistent with a theology of management, see Dyck and Schroeder (2005), Dyck and Weber (2006), and Dyck, Starke, and Dueck (2009); see also Bell and Dyck (2012).

2. All quotes in this paragraph and the next are taken from the *Merriam-Webster's Student Dictionary* (http://www.wordcentral.com/cgi-bin/student?radical).

3. Note that others have argued that documents about Jesus that are even more radical in terms of their rootage (e.g., they were written even earlier than the Gospel of Luke) are also more radical in terms of being countercultural (e.g., Gowler, 2007; Oakman, 1991, 2004). In any case, the radical approach developed from Luke is consistent with Charles Perrow's (1985: 282; emphasis added here) call to describe what management theory and practice would like if it were based on the life and teachings of "the Man from Galilee and his *radical* social doctrine."

4. For a paper where this point is developed more fully, namely, that a Protestant ethic approach to management is not consistent with how Jesus' teaching were likely understood in the first-century approach, see Dyck, Starke, and Weimer (2012).

5. Luke's radical institutional structures are precisely the sort being called for by leading contemporary business scholars and social movements like "Occupy Wall Street" (which is all over the media as these words are being written). The analysis provided in this book, then, seems particularly timely and relevant. I tip my hat to the committee of scholars at SSHRC who had the foresight to recognize this and prioritize this research by awarding a grant already in 2006.

6. I still remember the counsel of a business scholar, early on in this process, who advised me not to place my countercultural interpretation of the parable of the ten pounds so early in the book, explaining that it would cause some readers to close the book and read no further (and she thought there were enough other good ideas in the book that it merited reading). Perhaps she was right. Perhaps the message of this book is so countercultural that many readers deeply steeped in and committed to conventional interpretations of the biblical readings will simply refuse to read this book, essentially dismissing it as heresy. I have no doubt that my colleague was correct in her analysis, and yet I felt compelled to keep my countercultural interpretation up front. Why? Partly because of the response of a second colleague, a scholar in biblical studies. He told me that at first he did not accept my countercultural interpretation of the parable of the ten pounds. However, after reading through the rest of my manuscript he became convinced by the overwhelming consistency in the whole of the Gospel of Luke. So I realize that this book may be troubling for many, and that I may be considered a heretic by some, but nevertheless I did not want to water down Luke's message to make it more palatable for readers unwilling to be open to an interpretation based on a first-century understanding of management.

7. This may seem difficult to imagine for those of who have been socialized to believe that acquisitive economics and competitiveness are natural human conditions. However, these norms are relatively recent in the history of humankind. For example, as described in chapter seventeen, note 5, a spirit of cooperation and community seems to be entirely natural in hunting gathering societies where success is almost never measured by maximizing production or by storing up wealth.

8. In today's dictionaries *spiritual* is defined as "not bodily or material," and *material* is defined as "physical rather than spiritual" (*Merriam-Webster's Student Dictionary*). The holistic view of the first century is ancient history. This, coupled with the lingering suspicions raised by sentiments like Marx's popularized "Religion is the opiate of the masses" have conspired to make it difficult for a radical connection between spirituality and the material world of management.

9. "In fact, it [the capitalist system] no longer needs the support of any religious forces, and feels the attempts of religion to influence economic life, in so far as it can be felt at all, to be as much unjustified interference as its regulation by the State" (Weber, 1958: 72).

10. Ibid., 181–182; see also Dyck and Schroeder (2005).

11. Weber (1958: 182).
12. Ibid., 277–278.
13. "It was not for nothing that the first [pre-Constantine] Christians were attacked in the Roman Empire as dangerous anarchists, as agents subverting Roman order. They had conscientious objections against military service, against the administration, and against the emperor . . . We have to recognize that [the post-Constantine relationship between the church and the imperial power] perverted the first expressions of the incarnation of Christ in the church . . . Our only reproach against the [post-Constantine] church leaders and theologians is that they set about justifying and legitimating the powers by trying to show that there is no contradiction, particularly between wealth and Jesus Christ, using the (undeniable) strand in the Old Testament that treats riches as a tangible proof of divine blessing. The worm was in the fruit . . . Now from the fourth century onward, belonging to Christianity became the main trend. The words and teachings of priests and bishops were blindly accepted . . . Christianity became what one might call the structural ideology of the particular [Roman] society. It ceased to be an explosive ferment calling everything into question in the name of the truth that is in Jesus Christ, in the name of the incarnation . . . It serves as a framework and mold for individuals as well as for institutions. It has structural force because the empire did indeed need to gain its second wind and it found it here. But by this very fact Christianity suffers a radical change of character. Its prophetic proclamation, welcomed at first among the religions of escape, changes into a religion that give cohesion to society. We thus arrive at an astounding situation that has lasted some fifteen centuries and is only just beginning to be questioned" (Ellul, 1986: 13–14, 30–31, 33, 36, 39, 40, 41).
14. For more on this, see Dyck and Schroeder (2005).
15. Dyck and Wiebe (2012).
16. For example, recall that Augustine (C.E. 354–430) was one of the first to argue that the term "eternal life" meant "endless" or everlasting life, whereas in the first century it would have referred to a life of "knowing, loving and serving God" and living according to the KOG (see chapter five, note 16).
17. Kennedy (1999).
18. See Langton (1984) and Perrow (1985).
19. The content in this paragraph is drawn from an excellent study by Gotsis and Drakopoulou-Dodd (2004).
20. The contrast between Weber and Paul described here draws heavily from Muthiah (2010).
21. Ibid.
22. Weber (1947: 358–359).
23. Consistent with this, research shows that, at least among religious organizations, religious beliefs do influence management practices and organizational structures and systems. In short, people can and do implement the values that they believe in (Dyck et al. 2005).

Appendix A: Analysis of the Chiasm in Luke's Journey Narrative

1. Breck (1994), Blomberg (1989), Clark (1975), Dewey (1973, 1980), Lund (1992) and Welch (1981).
2. For example, see Baarlink (1992), Farrell (1986), Goulder (1964b), Kariamadam (1987), and Talbert (1974).
3. The five researchers had in total identified 180 different possible breakpoints within the Journey Narrative (on average, each researcher identified 36 breakpoints). Of the 180 total, over 60 percent (N =110) coincided with the 25 breakpoints that were used in the chiasm described in this study (on average, each breakpoint had been identified by 4.4 of the 5 researchers). In addition, closer inspection showed that several of the paired passages could meaningfully be subdivided into subcomponents within themselves, thus

creating another 24 "subbreakpoints" (this included an additional 37 of the 180 breakpoints that had originally been identified). (Note that these subbreakpoints occur *within* parallel passages. They cannot not considered to be an independent "full" breakpoint because, due to the nature of the overall chiastic structure, doing so would essentially "flip" their order and make them go "out of step" vis-á-vis their "twinned" passage.) Thus, in the end only 33 of the originally identified 180 breakpoints (18 percent) were not incorporated in the complete chiasm.

4. For example, it is assumed that Luke would have received a classical training, which would have included Homer's epic 24-chapter poem the *Iliad*, which is said to have been written in a variation of chiastic form called *hysteron proteron* (Whitman, 1958). The biblical book of *James* has also been argued to contain a chiasm with 12 paired passages (i.e., a total of 24 passages) (Welch, 1981, cited in Lissner, 2007).

5. These data and analyses, not reported here, also looked at whether similar content is found elsewhere in the Journey Narrative (or the overall Gospel). By way of quick summary, of all the different words in the Journey Narrative, 32 keywords were chosen that seemed especially important for pointing the reader to which passages formed chiastic pairs (e.g., three keywords were important for identifying the first chiastic pair, three different keywords for identifying the second chiastic pair, and so on). Each of these 32 keywords could be found in *both* halves of their focal pair, but they were virtually never shared within both halves of any of the other chiastic pairs.

6. We found that the longer the passages, the more difficult the pairing task seemed to be. For example, the six shortest pairs (by total word count) were sorted correctly over 55 percent of the time, whereas the six longest pairs were sorted correctly only 38 percent of the time.

7. Recall also the comments from scholars like Johnson (1991: 4) that in Luke "[t]he sequence itself provides the larger meaning."

8. Note that commonly used words that receive at least 20 mentions in the Journey Narrative account for almost 60 percent of the total word count, so that the use of less frequently used words is more striking than their simple numerical frequency would suggest.

9. The first phase is not unlike the first stage of the four-part Socratic method that will be described at the end of this chapter: "The interlocutor [e.g., the person with whom Socrates was discussing something] asserts a thesis, *p*, which Socrates considers false and targets for refutation" (Vlastos, 1994: 11). For the case of Socrates, he used this method to refute theses such as the following: (1) in matters of justice, people should not follow "the many" (but rather follow "the man who knows best"); (2) people should never return evil for evil; (3) the just person will not harm their enemies; (4) the piety of an action is not determined by whether it is god-loved (but rather pious action is god-loved because it is pious); (5) a just person does not rule for his or her own benefit (but rather for the benefit of their subjects); and (6) "it is better to suffer wrong than to commit it and to suffer deserved punishment than to escape it" (taken from 11–12).

10. This emphasis on "dialogue" is not inconsistent with the emphasis on dialogue in Socrates's four-step dialogical method. Of the 420 verses in the Journey Narrative, there are about 100 mentions of dialogue attributed to someone other than Jesus (i.e., there are 100 occasions where quotation marks are used to attribute a statement to someone other than Jesus, which averages out to 0.24 dialogues per verse, or about one dialogue for every four verses). About half the verses in the Journey Narrative (201) contain material that is unique to Luke, and the other half (219 verses) contains material that parallels/overlaps with at least one of the other Gospels. In the verses that are unique to Luke, there are about 72 occasions where there is dialogue attributed to someone other than Jesus (e.g., someone asks Jesus a question, Jesus tells a parable where he attributes a quote to one of its characters); this averages out to 0.36 dialogues per verse. In the verses that are shared with the other Gospels, there are only about 28 occasions where there is a dialogue attributed to someone else; this averages out to 0.13 dialogues per verse. (Note also that on about 6 occasions Luke's material does not contain a quote that is found in the parallel passage described in one of the other Gospels;

adding these six verses would increase the average to 0.15 dialogues per verse in the parallel material). Overall then, about every fourth verse in the Journey Narrative has a quote attributed to someone other than Jesus, and quotes are 2.5 times more likely to be found in material that is unique to Luke (versus content that overlaps with Mark and/or Matthew).

When comparing the total number of dialogues per phase, phase 1 has the highest frequency at 0.33 dialogues per verse, phases 2 and 4 each have an average of about 0.25 dialogues per verse, and phase 3 has 0.15 dialogues per verse. This suggests that there is a particular emphasis on dialogues in the first phase.

A more nuanced understanding of the nature of these dialogues can be obtained by examining who the dialogue partners are. Are these dialogues with Jesus (N=32), or among others (N=68)? The overall average ratio of "Dialogue directed to Jesus" / "Other dialogue" is 0.47 (=32/68). However, this ratio is quite different among the four phases. For phase 1 the ratio drops to 0.19, suggesting that the four-phase model often starts with dialogue among others. The ratios are closer to the overall average in phases 2 (0.33) and 3 (0.5), suggesting that these stages place greater emphasis on dialogues with Jesus than the first phase. The ratio jumps to 0.71 in phase 4, suggesting that dialogues in that phase place greater relative emphasis on dialogues with Jesus (in this phase, talking with the leaders). (Note that these counts comparing different Gospels are based on analysis using Aland, 1982.)

11. Note that this phase represents a qualitative departure from the second step in the four-step Socratic method. Rather than follow the Socratic method and try to *argumentatively* demonstrate a point, passages in phase 3 have an *experiential* learning focus. This points to the importance of trying different things, and then learning from them. Put somewhat differently, whereas the Socratic model may emphasize emancipation from wrong-headed ethical principles, the Lukan model seeks liberation via *enacting* and thus learning new principles (see Raelin, 2008: 534–535).

12. Note that this attention to social structures and systems is not evident in Socrates's dialogic method, discussed at the end of this appendix.

13. "Just then a lawyer stood up to test Jesus" (end of first cycle, Luke 10:25); "While [Jesus] was speaking a Pharisee invited him to dine with him" (second cycle, Luke 11:37); "Now [Jesus] was teaching in one of the synagogues [where the leader became indignant]" (third cycle, Luke 13:10); "On one occasion when Jesus was going to the house of a leader of the Pharisees" (Luke 14:1, fourth cycle); "The Pharisees, who were lovers of money, heard all this, and they ridiculed [Jesus]. So [Jesus] said to them" (fifth cycle, Luke 16:14); "And a certain ruler asked [Jesus]" (sixth cycle, Luke 18:18).

14. Walker (2006).

15. Of course, there are other ways to divide Acts. This discussion is based on Goulder (1964a: 76ff).

16. This is implied in cycle 2 (Acts 6:1–9:43), but is explicit in the other three cycles.

17. Moreover, note that Goulder (1964a) suggests that the fourth cycle can itself also be divided into an additional four mini-cycles.

18. See Oster (2010) for a study that draws on four-phase organizational learning models (Crossan, Lane, & White, 1999; Nonaka, 1994) to interpret this passage. Also, note similarities between this cycle in Acts and the "Samaritan cycle" described at the beginning of the Journey Narrative (see chapter thirteen).

19. Elliott (1991a: 106) notes that this passage makes an explicit connection between "common and unclean" as it applies to both animals/food and to persons.

20. This is not to suggest that the Lukan four-phase model is identical to the Socratic model—in fact, there are significant differences. Rather, the goal in this section is simply to suggest that it is plausible that Luke and his educated readers would have been familiar with the idea of there being a methodical process to discover virtue. As should be expected, there are significant differences between the Socratic method and the four-phase model consistent with Jesus' teachings because of the epistemological (questions about "how we know") differences between them (Hattersley, 2009: 1). One fundamental

difference is that Socrates placed much greater emphasis on abstract debate, whereas Jesus placed relatively greater emphasis on grounded experience:

"Jesus was concerned not with *knowing* the good but with *being* good. Thus where Socrates ends Jesus begins . . . Thus when Socrates made us *know* the Absolute Good, Jesus showed *the way* to indentification [*sic*] with it . . . The ideal Socrates, as set forth by Plato, is the creation of the philosopher-king, *endowed* with all knowledge, virtue, wisdom and love of truth. The ideal Jesus is the creation of the saint, who would win salvation through love and service, and help others *do the same*" (Davar, 1972: 414–415; emphasis added here).

21. Vlastos (1994: 7).

22. Note that people in first-century Palestine may not have recognized the Socratic method as the four-step process model we describe here, which builds on scholars who have stylized Socrates's framework into a four (or three or five) step model (especially Vlastos, 1994, and Bolten, 2001).

23. Quotes in the description of the Socrates's four-step method are drawn from Vlastos (1994: 7, 17, 10; see also Bolten, 2001, and Nielsen, 1993).

24. Sandnes (1993: 22) describes the "extensive use of Socrates tradition in antiquity . . . Socrates was one of the best-known figures of Greek history. He is praised everywhere, as Lucian of Samosata (c. 120–180 CE) puts it (Somnium 13), and the early church is no exception, although there are some critical words against him." Hattersley (2009: 56) posits that: "While it seems unlikely—though not impossible—that Jesus quoted Socrates, it's certain that Paul, John, and the author of Thomas were aware of Socrates' teachings."

25. Quotes in this section are taken from Sandnes (1993: 21).

References

Achtemeier, P. J., J. B. Green, & M. M. Thompson. 2001. *Introduction to the New Testament: Its literature and theology*. Grand Rapids, MN: Wm. Eerdmans Publishing Company.

Adherents. 2007. *Major religions of the world ranked by number of adherents*. http://www.adherents.com/Religions_By_Adherents.html#Christianity (first accessed September 21, 2010).

Agle, B. R. & H. J. Van Buren. 1999. God and Mammon: The modern relationship. *Business Ethics Quarterly*, 9(4): 563–582.

Aland, K. 1982. *Synopsis of the four gospels*. New York, NY: American Bible Society.

Albertson, T. 2009. *The gods of business: The intersection of faith and the marketplace*. Los Angeles, CA: Trinity Alumni Press.

Alford, H. & M. Naughton. 2001. *Managing as if faith mattered*. South Bend, IN: Notre Dame Press.

Alvesson, M., & H. Willmott. 1992. On the idea of emancipation in management and organization studies. *Academy of Management Review*, 17(3): 432–464.

Anderson, R. C. 1998. *Mid-course correction: Toward a sustainable enterprise: The Interface model*. Atlanta, GA: Peregrinzilla Press.

Anderson, R. D. 2000. *Glossary of Greek rhetorical terms connected to methods of argumentation, figures and tropes from Anaximenes to Quintilian*. Leuven, Belgium: Peeters.

Argyris, C. 1990. *Overcoming organizational defenses: Facilitating organizational learning*. Boston, MA: Allyn & Bacon.

Aristotle. 2006. *Nicomachean ethics*. (Translated by W. D. Ross.) http://ebooks.adelaide.edu.au/a/aristotle/nicomachean/. Adelaide, Australia: University of Adelaide Library, eBooks@Adelaide.

———. 2007. *Politics*. (Translated by Benjamin Jowett.) http://ebooks.adelaide.edu.au/a/aristotle/a8po/. Adelaide, Australia: University of Adelaide Library, eBooks@Adelaide.

Ashforth, B. E. & D. Vaidyanath. 2002. Work organizations as secular religions. *Journal of Management Inquiry*, 11(4): 359–370.

Aubert, J. 1994. *Business managers in ancient Rome: A social and economic study of Institores, 200 B.C.–A.D. 250*. Leiden, The Netherlands: EJ Brill.

———. 2001. The fourth factor: Managing non-agricultural production in the Roman world. In D. J. Mattingly & J. Salmon (eds.), *Economies beyond agriculture in the classical world*: 90–111. London: Routledge.

Avery, G. C. & J. Ryan. 2002. Applying situational leadership in Australia. *Journal of Management Development*, 21(4): 242–262.

Baarlink, H. 1992. Die zyklische Struktur von Lukas 9.43b–19.28. *New Testament Studies*, 38: 481–506.

Baban, O. 2006. *On the road encounters in Luke-Acts: Hellenistic mimesis and Luke's theology of the way*. Milton Keynes, UK: Paternoster Press.

Baergen, R. A. 2006. Servant, manager of slave: Reading the Parable of the Rich Man and his Steward (Luke 16.1–8a) through the lens of ancient slavery. *Studies in Religion*, 35: 25–38.

Bailey, K. 2003. *Poet & peasant and through peasant eyes* (combined edition). Grand Rapids, MI: William B. Eerdmans Publishing Company.

Bakke, D. W. 2005. *Joy at work: A revolutionary approach to fun on the job.* Seattle, Washington: PVG.

Balch, D. L. 1981. Let wives be submissive: The domestic code in I Peter. In J. Crenshaw and R. Tannehill (eds.), *Society of Biblical Literature Monograph Series:* Number 26. Ann Arbor, MI: Scholars Press.

Barclay, W. 1964. *New Testament words.* Louisville, KY: The Westminster Press.

Barker, J. R. 1993. Tightening the iron cage: Concertive control in self-managing teams. *Administrative Science Quarterly,* 38: 408–437.

Barney, J. B. & W. Hesterly. 1999. Organizational economics: Understanding the relationship between organizations and economic analysis. In S. R. Clegg and C. Hardy (eds.), *Studying organization: Theory and method:* 109–141. London: Sage.

Barro, R. I. & R. M. McCleary. 2003. Religion and economic growth. *American Sociological Review,* 68: 760–781.

Bartchy, S. S. 2008. Who should be called "father"? Paul of Tarsus between the Jesus tradition and Patri Potestas. In J. H. Neyrey and E. C. Stewart (eds.), *The social world of the New Testament: Insights and models:* 165–180. Peabody, MA: Hendrickson Publishers.

Barton, B. 1925. *The man nobody knows: A discovery of the real Jesus.* Indianapolis, IN: Bobbs-Merrill Company.

Batstone, D. 2003. *Saving the corporate soul & (who knows?) maybe your own.* San Francisco, CA: Jossey-Bass.

Batten, A. 2004. God in the Letter of James: Patron or benefactor? *New Testament Studies,* 50(2): 257–272.

Beavis, M. A. 2003. "I like the bird": Luke 13:34, avian metaphors and feminist theology. *Feminist Theology,* 12(1): 119–128.

Bedeian, A. G. & D. A. Wren. 2001. Most influential management books of the 20th century. *Organizational Dynamics,* 29(3): 221–225.

Bell, G. G. & B. Dyck. 2012. Conventional Resource-Based Theory and its radical alternative: A less materialist-individualist approach to strategy. *Journal of Business Ethics,* 99(1): 121–130.

Bivins, D. C. 2005. A study of the correlation between servant leadership and ministry satisfaction in church leaders in Alaska. *Dissertation Abstracts International,* 66(3): 941.

Blomberg, C. 1989. Structure of 2 Corinthians 1–7. *Crisswell Theological Review,* 4(1): 3–20.

Bock, D. L. 2006. *Luke Volume 1: 1:1–9:50.* Grand Rapids, MI: Baker Academic.

Bolten, H. 2001. Managers develop moral accountability: The impact of Socratic dialogue. *Reason in Practice,* 1: 21–34.

Borg, M. J. 1992. The teaching of Jesus Christ. In D. N. Freedman (ed.), *The Anchor Bible Dictionary,* (3): 804–12. New York: Doubleday.

Botha, J. E. and P. A. Rousseau. 2005. For God did not so love the whole world—only Israel! John 3:16 revisited. *HTS Teologiese Studies/Theological Studies,* 61(4): 1149–1168.

Botha, P. J. 2003. Psalm 118 and social values in Ancient Israel. *Old Testament Essays,* 16(2): 192–215.

Bovon, F. 2002. *Luke 1: A commentary of the Gospel of Luke 1:1–9:50.* Minneapolis, MN: Fortress Press.

Bowen, M. 1978. *Family therapy and clinical practice.* New York, NY: Jason Aronsons.

Breck, J. 1994. *The shape of biblical language: Chiasmus in the scriptures and beyond.* Crestwood, NY: St. Vladimir's Seminary Press.

Buehler, R. C. 1998. *Building on the rock: Practical advice from Jesus!* Victoria, Canada: Trafford Publishing.

Burrell, G. 1999. Normal science, paradigms, metaphors, discourses and genealogies of analysis. In S. R. Clegg and C. Hardy (eds.), *Studying organization: Theory and method:* 388–404. London: SAGE.

Burroughs, J. E. & A. Rindfleisch. 2002. Materialism and well-being: A conflicting values perspective. *Journal of Consumer Research,* 29: 348–370.

Campbell, R. A. 2008. Leadership succession in early Islam: Exploring the nature and role of historical precedents. *The Leadership Quarterly,* 19: 426–438.

Capon, R. F. 2002. *Kingdom, grace, judgment: Paradox, outrage, and vindication in the parables of Jesus.* Grand Rapids, MI: William B. Eerdmans Publishing Company.

Chewning, R. C., J. W. Eby, & S. J. Roels. 1990. *Business through the eyes of faith.* San Francisco, CA: Harper.

Christie, N., B. Dyck, J. Morrill, & R. Stewart. 2004. *Escaping the materialistic-individualistic iron cage: A Weberian agenda for alternative radical accounting.* Paper presented at the APIRA conference, Singapore.

Clark, D. J. 1975. Criteria for identifying chiasms. *Linguistica Biblica,* 35: 63–72.

Clegg, S. 1996. The moral philosophy of management: Book review. *Academy of Management Review,* 21: 867–871.

Cohen, P. & J. Cohen. 1996. *Life values and adolescent mental health.* Mahway, NJ: Erlbaum.

Crespo, R. F. 2008. *On Aristotle and economics.* Working Paper, IAE Business School DT 11, Austral University, Buenos Aires province, Argentina.

Crossan, J. D. 2007. *God and empire: Jesus against Rome, then and now.* New York, NY: HarperOne.

Crossan, M., H. Lane, & R. White. 1999. An organizational learning framework: From intuition to institution. *Academy of Management Review,* 24: 522–537.

Danker, F. W. 1982. *Benefactor: Epigraphic study of a Graeco-Roman and New Testament semantic field.* St. Louis, MO: Clayton Publishing, Inc.

Davar, F. C. 1972. *Socrates and Christ.* Ahmedabad, India: Gujarat University Publication.

Dean, C. 2007. Executive on a mission: Saving the planet. *New York Times,* May 22.

Delbeq, A. L. 2005. Spiritually-informed management theory: Overlaying the experience of teaching managers. *Journal of Management Inquiry,* 14(3): 242–246.

deSilva, D. A. 1996. Exchanging favor for wrath: Apostasy in Hebrews and patron-client relationships. *Journal of Biblical Literature,* 115(1): 91–116.

Despain, J. & J. B. Converse. 2003. *. . . And dignity for all: Unlocking the greatness of value-based leadership.* Upper Saddle River, NJ: Prentice-Hall/Financial Times.

Destro, A. & M. Pesce. 2003. Father and householder in the Jesus movement: The perspective of the Gospel of Luke. *Biblical Interpretation,* 11(2): 211–238.

Dewey, J. 1973. The literary structure of the Controversy Stories in Mark 2:1–3:6. *Journal of Biblical Literature,* 92(3): 394–401.

Dewey, J. 1980. *Markan public debate: Literary technique, concentric structure, and theology in Mark 2:1–3:6.* Chico, CA: Scholars Press.

Dierksmeier, C. & M. Pirson. 2009. *Oikonomia* versus *chrematistike*: Learning from Aristotle about the future orientation of business management. *Journal of Business Ethics,* 88: 417–439.

Dodd, S. D. & G. Gotsis. 2009. "Enterprise values" in the New Testament and antecedent works. *Entrepreneurship and Innovation,* 10(2): 101–110.

Downs, D. J. 2009. Is God Paul's patron? In B. W. Longenecker & K. D. Liebengood (eds.), *Engaging economics*: 129–156. Grand Rapids, MI: William B. Eerdmans Publishing Company.

Duling, D. C. 1992. Kingdom of God, kingdom of heaven. In D. N. Freedman (ed.), *The Anchor Bible Dictionary,* (4): 49–69. New York: Doubleday.

Dunn, E. W., L. B. Aknin, & M. I. Norton. 2008. Spending money on others promotes happiness. *Science,* 319 (5870): 1687–1688.

Dyck, B. 1994a. Build in sustainable development, and they will come: A vegetable field of dreams. *Journal of Organizational Change Management,* 7 (4): 47–63.

———. 1994b. From airy-fairy ideals to concrete realities: The case of shared farming. *Leadership Quarterly,* 5: 227–246.

———. 1997. Exploring organizational family trees: A multi-generational approach for studying organizational births. *Journal of Management Inquiry,* 6: 223–234.

———. 2002. Organizational learning, microfinance, and replication: The case of MEDA in Bolivia. *Journal of Developmental Entrepreneurship,* 7(4): 361–382.

———. 2003. Exploring congregational clans: Playing the "Mennonite Game" in Winnipeg. *Journal of Mennonite Studies,* 21: 137–155.

———. 2012a. *A radical resource-based view of small-scale farms in low-income countries: An exploratory study.* Paper presented at the Hickson Research Days, I.H. Asper School of Business, University of Manitoba, Winnipeg, Canada.

———. 2012b. What happens when students are taught two different approaches to management, the first consistent with mainstream management theory, the second consistent with Catholic Social Thought. In M. Naughton (ed.), *Proceedings of the International Conference on Catholic Social Thought and Management Education:* 62–66.

———. Forthcoming. God on management: Religion, the "theological turn," and organization and management theory and practice. *Research in the Sociology of Organizations.*

Dyck, B. & L. Broadhurst. 2008. Applying four-phase organization learning theory to the Gospel of Luke: An interdisciplinary study. In G. T. Solomon (ed.), *Proceedings of the Academy of Management.* (CD) ISSN: 1543–8643.

Dyck, B., E. Bruning, & J. Buckland. 2003. A critical view of conventional globalization: Making an argument for a new paradigm for the new millennium. In D. Wicks (ed.), *Proceedings of the Administrative Sciences Association of Canada, International Business Division,* Halifax, N.S, Canada.

Dyck, B., J. Buckland, H. Harder, & D. Wiens. 2000. Community development as organizational learning: The importance of agent-participant reciprocity. *Canadian Journal of Development Studies,* 21: 605–620.

Dyck, B. & M. Neubert. 2010. *Management: Current practices and new directions.* Boston, MA: Cengage/Houghton Mifflin.

Dyck, B. & G. Sawatzky. 2010. *Does the kingdom of God support contemporary management theory, or call for alternatives?* Paper presented at the annual meeting of the Academy of Management, Montreal, CA.

Dyck, B. & D. Schroeder. 2005. Management, theology and moral points of view: Towards an alternative to the conventional materialist-individualist ideal-type of management. *Journal of Management Studies,* 42(4): 705–735.

Dyck, B. & F. Starke. 1999. The formation of breakaway organizations: Observations and a process model. *Administrative Science Quarterly,* 44(4): 792–822.

———. 2005. Looking back and looking ahead: A review of the most frequently cited biblical texts in the first decade of *The JBIB. Journal of Biblical Integration in Business,* Fall: 134–153.

Dyck, B., F. Starke, & C. Dueck. 2006. Just what was Jesus saying?: Two interpretations of the parable of the shrewd manager. *Journal of Biblical Integration in Business,* Fall: 111–140.

———. 2009. Management, prophets and self-fulfilling prophecies. *Journal of Management Inquiry,* 18(3): 184–196.

Dyck, B., F. Starke, H. Harder, & T. Hecht. 2005. Do the structures of religious organizations reflect their statements-of-faith? An exploratory study. *Review of Religious Research,* 47(1): 51–69.

Dyck, B., F. Starke, & J. Weimer. 2012. Toward understanding management in first century Palestine. *Journal of Management History,* 18(2): 137–165.

Dyck, B., K. Walker, F. Starke, & K. Uggersley. 2011. Addressing concerns raised by critics of business schools by teaching multiple approaches to management. *Business and Society Review,* 116 (1): 1–27.

Dyck, B. & J. M. Weber. 2006. Conventional and radical moral agents: An exploratory look at Weber's moral-points-of-view and virtues. *Organization Studies,* 27(3): 429–450.

Dyck, B. & E. Wiebe. 2012. Salvation, theology and organizational practices across the centuries. *Organization,* 19(3): 52–77.

Dyck, B. & K. Wong. 2010. Corporate spiritual disciplines and the quest for organizational virtue. *Journal of Management, Spirituality and Religion,* 7(1): 7–29.

Ehrman, B. D. 2008. *The New Testament: A historical introduction to the early Christian writings.* New York: Oxford University Press.

Elinsky, R. 2005. Religious publishing for the red state consumers and beyond. *Publishing Research Quarterly,* 21(4): 11–29.

Elliott, J. H. 1981. *A home for the homeless: A sociological exegesis of 1 Peter, its situation and strategy.* Philadelphia: Fortress Press.

———. 1991a. Household and meals vs. temple purity replication patterns in Luke-Acts. *Biblical Theology Bulletin: A Journal of Bible and Theology,* 21: 102–108.

———. 1991b. Temple versus household in Luke-Acts: A contrast in social institutions. In J. H. Neyrey (ed.), *The social world of Luke-Acts: Models for interpretation:* 211–240. Peabody, MA: Hendrickson Publishers.

Ellul, J. 1986. *The subversion of Christianity.* (Translated by G. W. Bromiley.) Grand Rapids, MI: William B. Eerdmans Publishing Company.

Elzey, W. 1978. Jesus the salesman: A reassessment of "The man nobody knows." *Journal of the American Academy of Religion,* 46 (2): 151–177.

Ernesti, J. C. G. 1962 (1795). *Lexicon Technologiae Graecorum Rhetoricae.* Hildesheim, Germany: Georg Olms.

Farrell, H. K. 1986. The structure and theology of Luke's Central Section. *Trinity Journal,* 7: 33–54.

Ferguson, E. 2003. *Backgrounds of early Christianity* (2nd ed.). Grand Rapids, MI: William B. Eerdmans Publishing Company.

Ferraro, F., J. Pfeffer, & R. I. Sutton. 2005. Economic language and assumptions: How theories can become self-fulfilling. *Academy of Management Review,* 30(1): 8–24.

Finley, M. 1973. *The ancient economy.* Berkeley and Los Angeles, CA: University of California Press.

Fitzmyer, J. A. 1970. *The Gospel according to Luke 1–IX (The Anchor Bible, vol. 28).* New York, NY: Doubleday.

———. 1985. *The Gospel according to Luke X–XXIV (The Anchor Bible, vol. 28a).* New York, NY: Doubleday.

Flender, H. 1967. *St. Luke, theologian of redemptive history.* London: SPCK.

Ford, J. M. 1984. *The enemy is my guest: Jesus and violence in Luke.* Maryknoll, NT: Orbis Books.

Foster, R. J. 1978. *Celebration of discipline: The path to spiritual growth.* San Francisco, CA: Harper & Row.

Frank, R. H., T. D. Gilovich, & D. T. Regan. 1993. Does studying economics inhibit cooperation? *The Journal of Economic Perspectives,* 7 (2): 159–171.

———. 1996. Do economists make bad citizens? *The Journal of Economic Perspectives,* 10(1): 187–192.

Frey, D. E. 1998. Individualist economic values and self-interest: The problem in the Puritan Ethic. *Journal of Business Ethics,* 17: 1573–1580.

Funk, R. W., Scott, B. B., & J. R. Butts. 1988. *The parables of Jesus: Red letter edition.* Sonoma, CA: Polebridge.

Gallagher, J. 1997. *A woman's work: Chiara Lubich.* Hyde Parke, NY: New City Press.

Gardner, F. & T. Wiedemann. 1991. *The Roman household: A sourcebook.* London: Routledge.

Gates, B. 2007. *Remarks of Bill Gates: Harvard commencement.* http://www.news.harvard.edu/gazette/2007/06.14/99-gates.html (September 24).

George, C. R. 1968. *The history of management thought.* Englewood Cliffs, NJ: Prentice-Hall, Inc.

Ghoshal, S. 2005. Bad management theories are destroying good management practices. *Academy of Management Learning & Education,* 4(1): 75–91.

Giacalone, R. A. 2004. A transcendent business education for the 21st century. *Academy of Management Learning & Education,* 3(4): 415–420.

Gill, D. 1970. Observations on the Lukan Travel Narrative and some related passages. *Harvard Theological Review,* 63: 199–221.

Godbout, J. T., with A. Caillé. 1998. *The world of the gift.* (Translated by D. Winkler.) Montreal, Canada: McGill-Queens University Press.

Gold, L. 2010. *New financial horizons: The emergence of an economy of communion.* Hyde Park, NY: New City Press.

Goldsmith, R. W. 1984. An estimate of the size and structure of the national product of the early Roman empire. *Review of Income and Wealth*, 30(3): 263–288.

Golembiewski, R. T. 1989. *Men, management, and morality: Toward a new organizational ethic.* New York, NY: McGraw-Hill Book Company.

Golin, E. & G. Parolin. 2006. RainbowScore®; A strategic approach for multi-dimensional value. In J. Jonker and M. de Witte (eds.), *Management models for corporate social responsibility*: 28–36. Heidelberg, German: Springer.

Gomes, P. J. 2001. Is success a sin? *Harvard Business Review*, 82: 63–69.

Goodrich, J. K. 2010. *Paul, the oikonomos of God: Paul's apostolic metaphor in 1 Corinthians and its Graeco-Roman context.* Doctoral dissertation, Durham University, Durham.

Gotsis, G. N. & S. Drakopoulou-Dodd. 2004. Economic ideas in the Epistle of James. *History of Economic Ideas*, 12(1): 7–35.

Goulder, M. D. 1964a. *Type and history in Acts.* London: SPCK.

———. 1964b. The chiastic structure of the Lucan Journey. In F. L. Cross (ed.), *Studia Evangelica: Papers Presented to the Second International Congress on New Testament Studies Held at Christ Church, Oxford, 1961*: 195–202. Berlin, Germany: Akademie.

Gowler, D. G. 2007. *What are they saying about the historical Jesus?* Mahwah, NJ: Paulist Press.

Graafland, J., M. Kapstein, & C. M. van der Duijn Schouten. 2007. Conceptions of God, normative convictions, and socially responsible business conduct: An explorative study among executives. *Business and Society*, 46(3): 331–369.

Green, J. B. 1995. *The theology of the Gospel of Luke: New Testament theology.* Cambridge, UK: University of Cambridge Press.

———.1997. *The Gospel of Luke (The New International Commentary on the New Testament).* Grand Rapids, MI: William B. Eerdmans Publishing Company.

Greenleaf, R. K. 1977. *Servant leadership: A journey in the nature of legitimate power and greatness.* New York, NY: Paulist Press.

Greise, N. L. 2010. *The Bible vs. Mao: A "best guess" of the top 25 bestselling books of all time.* http://publishingperspectives.com/2010/09/top-25-bestselling-books-of-all-time/ (accessed May 2012).

Grover, R. A. & H. F. Walker. 2003. Changing from production to quality: Application of the situational leadership transtheoretical change models. *The Quality Management Journal*, 10(3): 8–25.

Habermas, J. 1991. Transcendence from within, Transcendence in this world. In E. Mendietta (ed.), *Religion and rationality: Essays on reason, God, and modernity*: 67–94. Cambridge, UK: Polity Press.

———. 2005. *Zwischen Naturalismus und Religion: Philosophische Aufsätze.* Frankfurt a/M: Suhrkamp.

Haight, R. 1994. Jesus and salvation: An essay in interpretation. *Theological Studies*, 55: 225–251.

Hamel, G. 2009. Moon shots for management. *Harvard Business Review*, 90 (February): 91–98.

Hanson, J. W. 1875. *The Greek word* aion-aionios *translated everlasting-eternal in the Holy Bible, shown to denote limited duration.* Chicago, IL: Northwestern Universalist Publishing House.

Hanson, K. C. 1989. The Herodians and Mediterranean kinship part 1: Genealogy and descent. *Biblical Theology Bulletin: A Journal of Bible and Theology*, 19: 75–84.

Hanson, K. C. & D. E. Oakman. 1998. *Palestine in the time of Jesus: Social structures and social conflicts.* Minneapolis, MN: Fortress Press.

Haque, U. 2011. *The new capitalist manifesto: Building a disruptively better business.* Boston, MA: Harvard Business Review Press.

Harrington, A. 2007. Habermas's theological turn? *Journal for the Theory of Social Behaviour*, 37(1): 45–61.

Hart, M. H. 1992. *The 100: A ranking of the most influential persons in history, revised and updated for the nineties.* New York, NY: Carol Publishing Group/Citadel Press.

Hartman, L. 1992. Baptism. In D. N. Freedman (ed.), *The Anchor Bible Dictionary* (1): 583–594. New York: Doubleday.

Hattersley, M. E. 2009. *Socrates and Jesus: The argument that shaped western civilization*. New York, NY: Algora Publishing.

Hawken, P. 1993. *The ecology of commerce: A declaration of sustainability*. New York, NY: HarperBusiness.

Hawken, P., A. Lovins, & L. H. Lovins. 1999. *Natural capitalism: Creating the next industrial revolution*. Boston: Little, Brown and Company.

Hensmans, M. 2003. Social movement organizations: A metaphor for strategic actors in institutional fields. *Organization Studies*, 24: 355–381.

Herman, S. W. 1997. *Durable goods: A covenantal ethic for management and employees*. Notre Dame, IN: University of Notre Dame Press.

Hersey, P. & K. H. Blanchard. 1977. *Management of organizational behavior*. Englewood Cliffs, NJ: Prentice-Hall.

Heugens, P. & M. W. Lander. 2009. Structure! Agency! A meta-analysis of institutional theories of organization. *Academy of Management Journal*, 52(1): 61–85.

Hershberger, G. F. 1958. *The way of the cross in human relations*. Scottdale, PA: Herald Press.

Herzog II, W. R. 1994. *Parables as subversive speech: Jesus as pedagogue of the oppressed*. Louisville, KY: Westminster/John Knox Press.

Hirdes, W., R. Woods, & D. M. Badzinski. 2009. A content analysis of Jesus merchandise. *Journal of Media & Religion*, 8: 141–159.

Hopfl, H. M. 2000. Ordered passions: Commitment and hierarchy in the organizational ideas of the Jesuit founders. *Management Learning*, 31(3): 313–329.

Hur, J. 2001. *A dynamic reading of the Holy Spirit in Luke-Acts*. Sheffield, UK: Sheffield Academic Press.

Jackall, R. 1988. *Moral mazes: The world of corporate managers*. Oxford, UK: Oxford University Press.

Johnson, H. L. 1957. Can the businessman apply Christianity? *Harvard Business Review*, 38: 63–76.

Johnson, T. L. 1977. *The literary function of possessions in Luke-Acts*. SBL Dissertation Series 39; Missoula, MT: Scholars Press.

———. 1991. *The Gospel of Luke*. Collegeville, MN: Liturgical Press.

Jones, H. B. Jr. 1997. The Protestant ethic: Weber's model and the empirical literature. *Human Relations*, 50: 757–778.

Jones, L. B. 1995. *Jesus CEO: Using ancient wisdom for visionary leadership*. New York, NY: Hyperion Press.

Jones, S. L. & J. M. Netter. 2008. Efficient capital markets. In D. R. Henderson (ed.), *The Concise Encyclopedia of Economics*. Library of Economics and Liberty. http://www.econlib.org/library/Enc/EfficientCapitalMarkets.html (first accessed May 2012).

Judge, E. A. 1960. *The social pattern of Christian groups in the first century*. London: Tyndale Press.

Julicher, A. 1910. *Die Gleichnisreden Jesu*. Tubingen, J.C. Mohr.

Just, A. A. 2003. *Luke (ancient Christian commentary on Scripture)*. Downers Grove, IL: InterVarsity Press.

Just, F. 2005. *New Testament statistics*. http://catholic-resources.org/Bible/NT-Statistics-Greek.htm (accessed May 2012).

Kalberg, S. 2001. Should the "dynamic autonomy" of ideas matter to sociologists?: Max Weber on the origin of other-worldly salvation religions and the constitution of groups in American society today. *Journal of Classical Sociology*, 1(3): 291–327.

Kaplan, R. S. & D. P. Norton. 1992. The Balanced Scorecard: Measures that drive performance. *Harvard Business Review*, 73 (January–February): 71–79.

Kariamadam, P. 1987. The composition and meaning of the Lukan Travel Narrative. *Bible Bhashyam*, 13: 179–198.

Kasser, T. 2003. *The high price of materialism*. Cambridge, MA: Bradford Book, MIT Press.

Kennedy, M. H. 1999. Fayol's principles and the Rule of St Benedict: Is there anything new under the sun? *Journal of Management History,* 5(5): 269–276.

Kent, R. S. 1986. Faith in four Ps: An alternative. *Journal of Marketing Management,* 2(2): 145–154.

Keown, A., W. Petty, D. Scott, & J. Martin. 1998. *Foundations of finance: The logic and practice of financial management* (2nd ed). Englewood Cliffs, NJ: Prentice-Hall, Inc.

Kessler, M. & K. Deurloo. 2004. *A commentary on Genesis: The book of beginnings.* Mahwah, NJ: Paulist Press.

Kieso, D. W., J. J. Weygandt, T. D. Warfield, V. B. Irvine, W. H. Silvester, N. M. Young, & I. M. Wiecek. 2002. *Intermediate accounting.* Etobicoke, ON: John Wiley and Sons.

Kimball, C. A., III. 1993. Jesus' exposition of scripture in Luke 20:9–19: An inquiry in light of Jewish hermeneutics. *Bulletin for Biblical Research,* 3: 77–92.

Klassen-Wiebe, S. A. 2001. *Called to mission: A narrative-critical study of the character and mission of the disciples in the Gospel of Luke.* Doctoral dissertation, Union Theological Seminary and Presbyterian School of Christian Education, Richmond, Virginia.

Kloppenborg, J. S. 2006. Associations in the ancient world. In A. J. Levine, D. C. Allison Jr., & J. D. Crossan (eds.), *The historical Jesus in context*: 232–338. Princeton, NJ: Princeton University Press.

———. 2008. The growth and impact of agricultural tenancy in Jewish Palestine (III BCE–1 CE). *Journal of the Economic and Social History of the Orient,* 51: 31–66.

Kotler, P., H. Kartajay, & I. Setiawan. 2010. *Marketing 3.0: From products to customers to the human spirit.* John Wiley and Sons.

Kraybill, D. B. 1978. *The upside-down kingdom.* Scottdale, PA: Herald Press.

Krishnan, V. R. 2003. Do business schools change students' values along desirable lines? A longitudinal study. In A. F. Libertella and S. M. Natale (eds.), *Business education and training: A value-laden process,* vol 8: 26–39. Lanham, MD: University Press of America.

Kuecker, A. J. 2008. *The spirit and the "other": Social identity, ethnicity and intergroup reconciliation in Luke-Acts.* Doctoral dissertation, University of St. Andrews, Scotland.

Kuecker, A. 2010. Luke and work. In J. Pennington, S. McDonough, & W. Messenger (eds.), *Theology of Work Project.* http://www.theologyofwork.org/ (accessed May 2012).

Kwon, H. J. 2009. Psalm 118 (117 LXX) in Luke-Acts: Application of a "New Exodus Motif." *Verbum et Ecclesia,* 30(2): 50–55.

Lambert, L. III. 2009. *Spirituality Inc.: Religion in the American workplace.* New York, NY: New York University Press.

Landry, D. & B. May. 2000. Honor restored: New light on the parable of the prudent steward (Luke 16: 1–8a). *Journal of Biblical Literature,* 119(2): 287–310.

Langton, J. 1984. The ecological theory of bureaucracy: The case of Josiah Wedgwood and the British pottery industry. *Administrative Science Quarterly,* 29(3): 330–354.

Lanham, R. A. 1991. *A handlist of rhetorical terms* (2nd ed.). Berkeley, CA: University of California Press.

Lantos, G. P. 2002. How Christian education can help overcome the failure of secular ethics education. *Journal of Biblical Integration in Business,* 8(1): 19–52.

Larson, P. D. & A. Halldorsson. 2004. Logistics versus supply chain management: An international survey. *International Journal of Logistics: Research and Applications,* 7(1): 17–31.

Lawrence, T. B. & R. Suddaby. 2006. Institutions and institutional work. In S. R. Clegg, C. Hardy, T. B. Lawrence, & W. R. Nord (eds.), *The SAGE handbook of organization studies* (2nd ed.): 215–254. London: SAGE Publications.

Lecourt, V. & T. C. Pauchant. (2011). Ignatian spirituality and management: A study of Ignatian executives. *Journal of International Business Ethics,* 4(1): 18–27.

Liddell, H. G. & R. Scott. 2000. *An intermediate Greek-English lexicon* (7th ed.). Oxford, UK: Clarendon Press.

Liefeld, W. L. 1984. Luke. In F. E. Gaebelein (ed.), *The expositor's Bible commentary*: 797–1059. Grand Rapids, MI: Zondervan.

Lincoln, N. D., C. Travers, P. Ackers, & A. Wilkinson. 2002. The meaning of empowerment: The interdisciplinary etymology of a new management concept. *International Journal of Management Reviews,* 4(3): 271–290.

Lissner, P. A. 2007. *Chi-thinking: Chiasmus and cognition*. Doctoral dissertation, University of Maryland, Maryland.

Lockyer, H. L. 1963. *All the parables of the Bible*. Grand Rapids, MI: Zondervan Publishing House.

Longenecker, R. N. 2000. Luke's parables of the Kingdom. In R. N. Longenecker (ed.), *The challenge of Jesus' parables*: 125–147. Grand Rapids, MI: William B. Eerdman's Publishing Company.

Lounsbury, M. & E. J. Carberry. 2005. From king to court jester?: Weber's fall from grace in organizational theory. *Organization Studies*, 26(4): 501–525.

Lund, N. W. 1992 (1942). *Chiasmus in the New Testament: A study of the form and function of chiastic structures*. Peabody, MA: Hendrickson Publishers.

Lygre, J. G. 2002. Of what charges? (Luke 16:1–2). *Biblical Theology Bulleting: A Journal of Bible and Theology*, 32: 21–28.

Madigan, K. 2011. Like the phoenix, U.S. finance profits soar. *Wall Street Journal* (March 25).

Malina, B. J. & R. Rohrbaugh. 2003. *Social-science commentary on the synoptic Gospels*. Minneapolis, MN: Fortress Press.

Malina, B. J. & J. H. Neyrey. 1991a. Honor and shame in Luke-Acts: Pivotal values of the Mediterrannean world. In J. H. Neyrey (ed.), *The social world of Luke-Acts: Models for interpretation*: 25–65. Peabody, MA: Hendrickson Publishers.

———. 1991b. First century personality: Dyadic, not individual. In J. H. Neyrey (ed.), *The social world of Luke-Acts: Models for interpretation*: 67–96. Peabody, MA: Hendrickson Publishers.

Manz, C. C. 1999. *The leadership wisdom of Jesus: Practical lessons for today*. San Francisco, CA: Berret-Koehler.

Marcic, D. 2000. God, faith and management education. *Journal of Management Education*, 44(5): 628–649.

Marrou, H. I. 1964. *A history of education in antiquity*. (Translated by G. Lamb.) New York, NY: New American Library.

Marshall, I. H. 1978. *The Gospel of Luke (The New International Greek Testament Commentary)*. Grand Rapids, MI: William B. Eerdmans Publishing Company.

Marshall, J. 2009. *Jesus, patrons, and benefactors: Roman Palestine and the Gospel of Luke*. Tuebingen, Germany: Mohr Siebeck.

Marshall, R. 2000. *God@work: Discovering the anointing for business*. Shippensburg, PA: Destiny Image Publishers.

Martin, H.-P. & H. Schumann. 1997. *The global trap: Globalization and the assault on democracy and prosperity*. (Translated by P. Camiller.) Montreal: Black Rose Books.

Maslow, A. 1954. *Motivation and personality*. New York, NY: Harper.

McCarthy, E. J. 1960. *Basic marketing*. Illinois, R.D. Irwin.

McCarty, J. A. & L. J. Shrum. 2001. The influence of individualism, collectivism, and locus of control on environmental beliefs and behavior. *Journal of Public Policy and Marketing*, 20(1): 93–104.

McCleary, R. M. 2007. Salvation, damnation, and economic incentives. *Journal of Contemporary Religion*, 22(1): 49–74.

McKenzie, D. 2010. *Derivatives 2010*. London, UK: TheCityUK Research Centre.

McLaren, B. D. 2004. *A generous orthodoxy*. Grand Rapids, MI: Zondervan.

———. 2010. *A new kind of Christianity: Ten questions that are transforming the faith*. New York, NY: HarperOne.

Meeks, M. D. 1989. *God the economist*. Minneapolis, MN: Fortress Press.

Meikle, S. 1994. Aristotle on money. *Phronesis*, 39(1): 26–44.

Menzies, R. P. 1991. *The development of early Christian pneumatology with special reference to Luke-Acts*. Sheffield: SAP.

Metzger, J. A. 2007. *Consumption and wealth in Luke's Travel Narrative*. Leiden, The Netherlands: Koninklijke Brill BV.

Miller, D. & C. Sardois. 2011. Angel agents: Agency theory reconsidered. *Journal of Management Perspectives*, 25(2): 6–13.

Miller, D. W. 2007. *God at work: The history and promise of the faith at work movement.* Oxford, UK: Oxford University Press.

Miner, J. J. 2003. The rated importance, scientific validity, and practical usefulness of organizational behavior theories: A quantitative review. *Academy of Learning and Education,* 2(3): 250–268.

Ming, H. S. 2005. Servant leadership and its effect on the church organization. *Dissertation Abstracts International,* 66(3), 1032A.

Mitchell, M., A. Curtis, & P. Davidson 2012. Can triple bottom line reporting become a cyle for "double loop" learning and radical change? *Accounting, Auditing & Accountablity Journal,* 25(6): 1048–1068.

Mitchell, T. R. & D. Daniels. 2003. Motivation. In W. C. Borman, D. R. Ilgen, & R. J. Klimoski (eds.), *Handbook of psychology: Industrial and organizational psychology:* 225–254. Hoboken, NJ: John Wiley & Sons Inc.

Mitroff, I. & E. I. Denton. 1999. *A spiritual audit of corporate America: A hard look at spirituality, religion, and values in the workplace.* San Francisco, CA: Jossey-Bass.

Moessner, D. P. 1983. Luke 9:1–50: Luke's preview of the journey of the prophet like Moses of Deuteronomy. *Journal of Biblical Literature,* 102(4): 575–605.

Morgan, G. 1988. *Images of organization.* London: Sage.

Moxnes, H. 1988. *The economy of the kingdom: Social conflict and economic relations in Luke's gospel.* Philadelphia, PA: Fortress Press.

Moxnes, H. 1991. Patron-client relations and the new community in Luke-Acts. In J. H. Neyrey (ed.), *The social world of Luke-Acts: Models for interpretation:* 241–268. Peabody, MA: Hendrickson Publishers, Inc.

———. 1997. *Constructing early Christian families: Family as social reality and metaphor.* London: Routledge.

Muthiah, R. 2010. Charismatic leadership in the church: What the Apostle Paul has to say to Max Weber. *Journal of Religious Leadership,* 9(2): 7–26.

Myers, C. 2001. *The biblical vision of sabbath economics.* Washington, DC: Tell the Word.

Nagle, B. D. 2006. *The household as the foundation of Aristotle's Polis.* Cambridge, UK: Cambridge University Press.

Nash, L. L. 1994. *Believers in business.* Nashville, TN: Thomas Nelson Publishers.

Naughton, M. J. & T. A. Bausch. 1994. The integrity of a Catholic management education. *California Management Review,* 38(4): 119–140.

Neu, D. 2000. Accounting and accountability relations: Colonization, genocide and Canada's First Nations. *Accounting, Auditing and Accountability Journal,* 13: 268–288.

Neyrey, J. H. 2005. God, benefactor and patron: The major cultural model for interpreting the deity in Greco-Roman antiquity. *Journal for the Study of the New Testament,* 27(4): 465–492.

———. 2008a. Preface. In J. H. Neyrey & E. C. Stewart (eds.), *The social world of the New Testament:* xxi–xxiv. Peabody, MA: Hendrickson Publishers.

———. 2008b. Loss of wealth, loss of family, loss of honor: The cultural context of the original makarisms in Q. In J. H. Neyrey & E. C. Stewart (eds.), *The social world of the New Testament: Insights and models:* 87–102. Peabody, MA: Hendrickson Publishers.

Neyrey, J. H. & E. C. Stewart. 2008a. Gender. In J. H. Neyrey & E. C. Stewart (eds.), *The Social World of the New Testament: Insights and models:* 163–164. Peabody, MA: Hendrickson Publishers.

———. 2008b. Honor and shame. In J. H. Neyrey & E. C. Stewart (eds.), *The Social World of the New Testament: Insights and models:* 85–86. Peabody, MA: Hendrickson Publishers.

———. 2008c. The patron-client institution. In J. H. Neyrey & E. C. Stewart (eds.), *The social world of the New Testament: Insights and models:* 47–48. Peabody, MA: Hendrickson Publishers.

Nielsen, R. P. 1993. Woolman's "I am We" triple-loop action-learning: Origin and application in organization ethics. *Journal of Applied Behavioral Science,* 29 (1): 117–138.

———. 1998. Quaker foundations for Greenleaf's servant-leadership and "friendly disentangling" method. In L. C. Spears (ed.), *Insights on leadership:* 126–144. New York, NY: John Wiley & Sons.

————. 2001. Can ethical character be stimulated and enabled? An action-learning approach to teaching and learning organization ethics. *Business Ethics Quarterly*, 8 (3): 581–604.

Niemelä, K. 2011. Female clergy as agents of religious change? *Religions*, 2: 358–371.

Nonaka, I. 1994. A dynamic theory of organizational knowledge creation. *Organization Science*, 5: 14–37.

Novak, M. 1982. *The spirit of democratic capitalism*. New York, NY: Touchstone.

————. 1996. *Business as a calling: Work and the examined life*. New York, NY: The Free Press.

Oakman, D. E. 1986. *Jesus and the economic questions of his day*. Lewiston, NY: The Edwin Mellen Press.

————. 1991. The country-side in Luke-Acts. In J. H. Neyrey (ed.), *The social-world of Luke-Acts: Models for interpretation*: 151–179. Peabody, MA: Hendrickson.

————. 2002. Money in the moral universe of the New Testament. In W. Stegemann, B. J. Malina, & G. Theissen (eds.), *The social setting of Jesus and the gospels*: 335–348. Minneapolis, MN: Fortress Press.

————. 2004. The radical Jesus: You cannot serve God and Mammon. *Biblical Theology Bulletin: A Journal of Bible and Theology*, 34(1): 122–129.

O'Collins, G. G. 1992. Salvation. In D. N. Freedman (ed.), *The Anchor Bible Dictionary*, (5): 907–914. New York: Doubleday.

Oliver, C. 1992. The antecedents of deinstitutionalization. *Organization Studies*, 13(4), 563–588.

Origen. 1996. *Homilies on Luke, Fragments on Luke*. (Translated by J. T. Lienhard.). Washington, DC: The Catholic University of America Press.

Osai, O. J., L. U. M. Eleanya, J. M. Orukwowu, & N. V. C. Okene. 2009. Jethro as the patriarch of administration and management: An analysis of his works. *Journal of Social Science*, 18(3): 157–162.

Osiek, C. 1991. Jesus and money, or did Jesus live in a capitalist society? *Chicago Studies*, 30(1): 17–28.

Osiek, C. & D. L. Balch. 1997. *Families in the New Testament world: Households and house churches*. Louisville, KY: Westminster John Knox Press.

Oster, G. 2010. Innovation and the early Christian church. *Journal of Biblical Integration in Business*, 12: 27–38.

Park, R. 2009. Revisiting the parable of the prodigal son for decolonization: Luke's reconfiguration of *oikos* in 15:11–32. *Biblical Interpretation*, 17: 507–520.

Pattison, S. 1997. *The faith of the managers: When management becomes religion*. London: Cassell.

Pava, M. L. 2002. The path of moral growth. *Journal of Business Ethics*, 38: 43–54.

Perrow, C. 1985. Comment on Langton's "Ecological Theory of Bureaucracy." *Administrative Science Quarterly*, 30: 278–283.

Pettigrew, A. 1989. *Longitudinal field research on change: Theory and practice*. Unpublished manuscript, Centre for Corporate Strategy and Change, University of Warwick.

Pfeffer, J. 1982. *Organizations and organization theory*. Marshfield, MA: Pitman Publishing Inc.

Pheng, L. S. 1999. Toward managerial efficacy: Back to 2,000 year-old guiding principles. *The Learning Organization*, 6(3): 121–131.

Pilch, J. J. 1991. Sickness and healing in Luke-Acts. In J. H. Neyrey (ed.), *The social world of Luke-Acts: Models for interpretation*: 181–209. Peabody, MA: Hendrickson Publishers.

Plowman, D. A., L. T. Baker, T. E. Beck, M. Kulkarni, S. T. Solansky, & D. V. Travis. 2007. Radical change accidentally: The emergence and amplification of small change. *Academy of Management Journal*, 50(3): 515–543.

Podsakoff, P. M., S. B. MacKenzie, N. P. Podsakoff, & D. G. Bachrach. 2008. Scholarly influence in the field of management: A bibliometric analysis of the determinants of university and author impact in the management literature in the past quarter century. *Journal of Management*, 34(4): 641–720.

Polanyi, L. 1944. *The great transformation: The political and economic origins of our time*. Boston, MA: Beacon Press.

Pollard, M. 1997. *100 greatest men.* Danbury, CT: Grolier Educational.

Porter, B. E. 1999. Another Christian perspective on accounting. *Journal of Biblical Integration in Business*, 5(1): 28–31.

Porter, M. E. 1980. *Competitive strategy.* New York, NY: The Free Press.

Powell, M. A. 1992. Salvation in Luke-Acts. *Word & World*, 12(1): 5–12.

Pretty, J., C. Toulmin, & S. William. 2011. Sustainable intensification in African agriculture. *International Journal of Agricultural Sustainability*, 1: 5–24.

Raelin, J. A. 2008. Emancipatory discourse and liberation. *Management Learning*, 39(5): 519–540.

Ramo, H. 2002. Doing things right and doing the right things: Time and timing in projects. *International Journal of Project Management*, 20: 569–574.

Rapinchuk, M. 2004. The Galilee and Jesus in recent research. *Currents in Biblical Research*, 2: 197–222.

Redekop, C., S. C. Ainlay, & R. Siemens. 1995. *Mennonite entrepreneurs.* Baltimore, MD: The John Hopkins University Press.

Reed, J. L. 2007. *The HarperCollins visual guide to the New Testament: What archeology reveals about the first Christians.* New York, NY: Harper Collins.

Rees, W. E. 2002. Globalization and sustainability: Conflict or convergence? *Bulletin of Science, Technology and Society*, 22(4): 249–268.

Resseguie, J. 1982. Point of view in the Central Section of Luke (9:51–19:44). *Journal of the Evangelical Theological Society*, 25(1): 41–47.

Reumann, J. 1959. Oikonomia = "covenant": Terms for *Heilsgeschichte* in early Christian usage. *Novum Testamentum*, 3(4): 282–292.

Richins, M. L. & S. Dawson. 1992. A consumer values orientation for materialism and its measurement: Scale development and validation. *Journal of Consumer Research*, 19: 303–316.

Richter, G. 2005. Oikonomia*: Der Gebrauch des Wortes* Oikonomia *im Neuen Testament, bei den Kirchenvaetern und in der theologishen Literature bis ins 20. Jahrhundert.* Berlin, Germany: Walter de Gruyter GmbH & Co.

Roberts, J. & M. Jones. 2009. Accounting for self interest in the credit crisis. *Accounting, Organizations and Society*, 34: 856–867.

Robertson, E. 1993. *Catching fire.* Guilford: IPS.

Roels, S. J. 1997. The business ethics of evangelicals. *Business Ethics Quarterly*, 7(2): 109–122.

Rossouw, G. J. 1994. Business ethics: Where have all the Christians gone? *Journal of Business Ethics*, 13: 557–570.

Sahlins, M. 1972. *Stone age economics.* Chicago: Aldine-Athertone, Inc.

Sandelands, L. E. 2010. *God and mammon.* Lanham, MD: University Press of America.

Sandnes, K. O. 1993. Paul and Socrates: The aim of Paul's Areopagus speech. *Journal for the Study of the New Testament*, 50: 13–26.

Sawatzky, G. 2006. *The natural roots of God's kingdom.* Unpublished manuscript, Canadian Mennonite University, Winnipeg, CA.

Schillebeeckx, E. 1980. *Christ: The experience of Jesus as Lord.* (Translated by J. Bowden.) New York, NY: Seabury.

Schneemelcher, W., ed. 1990. New Testament Apocrypha (revised ed.). (Translated by R. McL. Wilson.) Louisville, KY: Westminster/John Knox Press.

Schroeder, D. 1959. *Die Haustafeln des Neuen Testaments: Ihre Herkunft und ihr theologischer Sinn.* Unpublished doctoral dissertation, University of Hamburg, Germany.

Scuderi, N. F. 2010. *Servant leadership and transformational leadership in church organizations.* Doctoral dissertation, George Washington University, Washington DC.

Selznick, P. 1992. *The moral commonwealth: Social theory and the promise of community.* Berkeley, CA: University of California Press.

Semler, R. 1989. Managing without managers. *Harvard Business Review*, 70 (September/October): 76–84.

———. 2004. *The seven-day weekend: Changing the way work works.* New York, NY: Penguin/Portfolio.

Senger, J. 1970. The religious manager. *Academy of Management Journal*, 13: 179–188.

Sherman, J. D. & H. L. Smith. 1984. The influence of organizational structure on intrinsic versus extrinsic motivation. *Academy of Management Journal*, 27(4): 877–885.

Simmons, J. A. 2008. God in recent French phenomenology. *Philosophy Compass* 3(5): 910–932.

Sine, T. 1981. *The mustard seed conspiracy*. Waco, TX: Word Books.

Smith, A. 1982. *The theory of moral sentiments*. Indianapolis, IN: Liberty Press.

Soros, G. 1998. *The crisis of global capitalism*. New York, NY: Public Affairs.

Spangenberg, I. J. J. 2007. Can a major religion change? Reading Genesis 1–3 in the twenty-first century. *Verbum et Ecclesia*, 28(1): 259–279.

Stahel, A. W. 2006. Complexity, *oikonomia* and political economy. *Ecological Complexity*, 3(4): 369–381.

Stevens, R. P. 2006. *Doing God's business: Meaning and motivation for the marketplace*. Grand Rapids, MI: William B. Eerdmans Publishing Company.

Stock A. 1984. Chiastic awareness and education in antiquity. *Biblical Theology Bulletin: A Journal of Bible and Theology*, 14: 23–27.

Strecker, C. 2002. Jesus and the demoniacs. In W. Stegemann, B. J. Malina, & G. Theissen (eds.), *The social setting of Jesus and the gospels*: 117–133. Minneapolis, MI: Fortress Press.

Summers, D. B. & B. Dyck. 2011. A process model of social intrapreneurship within a for-profit company: First Community Bank. In G. T. Lumpkin & J. A. Kats (eds.), *Advances in entrepreneurship, firm emergence and growth*: 141–177. Bingley, UK: Emerald Group Publishing.

Svyantek, D. J. 1999. "Make haste slowly": Augustus Caesar transforms the Roman world. *Journal of Management History*, 5(6): 292–306.

Talbert, C. H. 1974. *Literary patterns, theological themes, and the genre of Luke-Acts*. Missoula, MT: Scholars Press.

Taylor, B. B. 1986. As a hen gathers her brood. *The Christian Century*, February 25: 201.

Temin, P. 2004. *A market economy in the early Roman Empire*. www.stanford.edu/group/sshi/Papers/classics/temin.pdf (December 22, 2004).

Terego, A. & S. Denim. 2006. *Riddikulus*! Consumer reflections on the Harry Potter phenomenon. In S. Brown (ed.), *Consuming books: The marketing and consumption of literature*: 146–159. London: Routledge Taylor & Francis Group.

Tharoor, I. 2006. Paving the way out of poverty: Bangladeshi economist Muhammad Yunus was awarded the 2006 Nobel Peace Prize not for giving to the poor, but for helping them to help themselves. *Time*. http://www.time.com/time/world/article/0,8599,1546100,00.html (posted October 13, found May 23, 2012).

Tierney, J. 2008. *Yes, money can buy happiness*... http://tierneylab.blogs.nytimes.com/2008/03/20/yes-money-can-buy-happiness/ (March 24).

Trainor, M. F. 2001. *The quest for home: The household in Mark's community*. Collegeville, Minnesota: The Liturgical Press.

Tryon, D. B. 2006. *Accounting for anxiety: An analysis of an early first-century material ethic from Matt 6:19-34*. Thesis, Master of Theology, University of Stellenbosch, South Africa.

Tucker, G. 1987. *The faith-work connection*. Toronto, Canada: Anglican Book Centre.

Turner, M. 2003. The work of the Holy Spirit in Luke-Acts. *Word & World*, 23(2): 146–153.

Tyson, J. B. 2006. *Marcion and Luke-Acts: A defining struggle*. Columbia, SC: University of South Carolina.

Udoh, F. E. 2009. The tale of the unrighteous slave (Luke 16:1–8 [13]). *Journal of Biblical Literature*, 128(2): 311–336.

Uelmen, A. 2005. Chiara Lubich: A life for unity. *LOGOS: A Journal of Catholic Thought and Culture*, 8(1): 52–64.

Upton, W. S. 2001. *Business and financial reporting: Challenges from the new economy*. Stanford, CT: Financial Accounting Standards Board.

Uzzi, B. 1997. Social structure and competition in interfirm networks. *Administrative Science Quarterly*, 42(1): 35–68.

Van Duzer, J. 2010. *Why business matters to God (and what still needs to be fixed)*. Downer Grove, IL: InterVarsity Press.

Van Duzer, J., R. S. Franz, G. L. Karns, K. L. Wong, & D. Daniels. 2007. It's not your business: A Christian reflection on stewardship and business. *Journal of Management, Spirituality & Religion*, 4(1): 99–122.

van Eck, E. 2007. The tenants in the vineyard (GThom 65/Mark 12:1–12): A realistic and social-scientific reading. *HTS Teologiese Studies/Theological Studies*, 63(3): 909–936.

Vasconcelos, A. F. 2010. Spiritual development in organizations: A religious-based approach. *Journal of Business Ethics*, 93: 607–622.

Vlastos, G. 1994. Socratic studies. In *The Socratic elenchus: Method is all*: 1–38. Cambridge: Cambridge University Press.

Vogl, A. J. 2004. The anti-CEO. *Across the Board*, May/June, 30–36.

Volf, M. 2001. *Work in the Spirit: Toward a theology of work*. Eugene, OR: Wipf and Stock.

Walker, P. 2006. *In the steps of Jesus: An illustrated guide to the places of the Holy Land*. Grand Rapids, MI: Zondervan.

Weber, M. 1922/1947. Charismatic authority. (Translated by T. Parsons and A. M. Henderson.) In T. Parsons (ed.), *The theory of social and economic organization*: 358–363. New York, NY: The Free Press.

———. 1958 (orig. 1904–1905). *The Protestant ethic and the spirit of capitalism*. (Translated by T. Parsons.) New York, NY: Scribner's.

Welch, J. W. 1981. *Chiasmus in antiquity: Structures, analyses, exegesis*. Hildesheim: Gerstenberg.

Westermann, W. L. 1955. *The slave system of Greek and Roman antiquity*. Philadelphia, PA: American Philosophical Society.

Whitman, C.H. 1958. *Homer and the Homeric tradition*. Cambridge, MA: Harvard University Press.

Wilkinson, R. & K. Pickett. 2009. *The spirit level: Why equality is better for everyone*. London, England: Penguin Books.

Wilson, D. J. 2005. The growth syndrome: Economic destitution. *Future Times*, 4: 3–5.

Wink, W. 1992. *Engaging the powers: Discernment and resistance in a world of domination*. Minneapolis, MI: Augsburg Fortress.

Winston, B. W. 1999. *Be a manager for God's sake*. Virginia Beach, VA: Regent University School of Business Press.

Wood, J. 1999. *Christians at work: Not business as usual*. Scottsdale, PA: Herald/Pandora Press.

Wright, S. I. 2000. Parables on poverty and riches. In R. N. Longenecker (ed.), *The challenge of Jesus' parables*: 217–239. Grand Rapids, MI: William B. Eerdman's Publishing Company.

Yoder, J. H. 1972. *The politics of Jesus*. Grand Rapids, MI: William B. Eerdmans Publishing Company.

———. 1984. *The priestly kingdom: Social ethics as gospel*. Notre Dame, IN: University of Notre Dame Press.

Yukl, G. 2006. *Leadership in organizations* (6th ed.). Upper Saddle River, NJ: Pearson Education, Inc.

Yunus, M. 1996. *Fighting poverty from the bottom up*. http://www.grameen-info.org/index.php?option=com_content&task=view&id=338&Itemid=375 (found May 25, 2012).

Yunus, M., B. Moingeon, & L. Lehmann-Ortega. 2010. Building social business models: Lessons from the Grameen experience. *Long Range Planning*, 43: 308–325.

Zigarelli, M. A. 2002. *Ordinary people, extraordinary leaders: A landmark study of Christians in business and ministry: How they lead, where they stumble, what helps them succeed*. Gainesville, FL: Synergy Publishers.

INDEX OF SCRIPTURE PASSAGES

SUBJECT INDEX

Made in the USA
Middletown, DE
04 September 2015